P9-CKH-483

MANAGEMENT LAUREATES:

A Collection of Autobiographical Essays

VOLUME 3

Editor: ARTHUR G. BEDEIAN
Ralph and Kacoo Olinde Distinguished Professor,
College of Business Administration, Louisiana State University

MANAGEMENT LAUREATES:

A Collection of Autobiographical Essays

by

LYMAN W. PORTER
EDWARD H. SCHEIN
WILLIAM H. STARBUCK
GEORGE A. STEINER
GEORGE STRAUSS
ERIC L. TRIST
STANLEY C. VANCE
VICTOR H. VROOM
KARL E. WEICK
WILLIAM FOOTE WHYTE
JAMES C. WORTHY

JAI PRESS INC.

Greenwich, Connecticut *London, England*

Library of Congress Cataloging-in-Publication Data
(Revised for vol. 3)

Management laureates.

Includes bibliographical references.
1. Executives--United States--Biography. 2. Executives--Canada--Biography. 3. Industrial management--United States. 4. Industrial management--Canada. 5. Master of business administration degree--United States. 6. Master of business administration degree--Canada. I. Ansoff, H. Igor. II. Bedian, Arthur G.
HC102.5.A2M32 1992 658.4′092′273 [B] 92-34213
ISBN 1-55938-469-7 (v. 1)
ISBN 1-55938-471-9 (v. 3)

55 Old Post Road, No. 2
Greenwich, Connecticut 06836

JAI PRESS LTD.
The Courtyard
28 High Street
Hampton Hill
Middlesex TW12 1PD
England

ISBN: 1-55938-471-9

Library of Congress Catalog Card Number: 92-34213

Manufactured in the United States of America

CONTENTS

PREFACE

For many years, I have contemplated compiling a volume such as this, containing the autobiographies of the management discipline's most distinguished laureates. The impetus to do so was reinforced when, in preparing my Academy of Management presidential address, I re-read Theophile S. Krawiec's *The Psychologists* (1972-1978). Phil argues, and I agree, that "one way to learn about and understand psychology is to study psychologists as they reveal themselves in writing about their lives" (1972, p. vi). Moreover, I would make the same argument for management and its leading thinkers, since I share the belief that you cannot fully understand an individual's work without knowing a great deal about the person behind that work.

Unfortunately, the available management literature provides little insight into the personal and intellectual lives—the frustrations as well as the triumphs—of the individuals in the management discipline. Although such understanding could be conveyed in many forms, perhaps the most intimate and fascinating of these for gaining behind-the-scenes insights is the autobiography. Thus, as self-exemplifying exercises, the autobiographies in this volume, as in the two companion volumes, offer the reader not only a glimpse of the subjective determinants and personal experiences of the management discipline's most distinguished laureates, but also a deeper understanding of what management is and what it is becoming. Those who have contributed to this undertaking are all distinguished by their successes, comprising a sample of the highest achievers in the management discipline. They are widely diversified in background and involvement in various areas of management, and their experiences are indelibly marked by societal and intellectual trends that span the entire twentieth century. To borrow a term from Robert K. Merton (cited in Riley, 1988, p. 25), the management laureates included in this undertaking are "influentials." Their lives have had and continue to have significant consequences for both management and society.

The difficulty and trepidations of preparing a verbal portrait of one's life should not be underestimated. Any sincere attempt to portray an unencapsulated personal and intellectual history is risky. It requires that one stand naked in front of oneself in a state of self-communion. Such immersion in the self, with its inevitable introspection, retrospection, and interpretation, may well lead to conflict with others, as well as result in internal dissensions. Moreover, the honest reconsideration of one's own motivations and thoughts may not only influence the rest of one's career, but also impart a sense of premature semi-closure. In this sense, preparing an autobiography is an adventure.

Editorial intervention has been purposefully kept at a minimum. Although all contributions open with a photograph and conclude with a complete bibliography of the author's published works, no rigid model was specified. Thus, the various accounts reflect a diversity of approaches, interests, and experiences. Contributors were free to choose not only their manner of presentation, but also the aspects of their lives they wished to emphasize. Some have offered rounded autobiographies, while other have emphasized intellectual and scholarly achievements. Many are laced with "confessions" of one sort or another, and virtually all reflect on the many people who have influenced their lives and their work.

It is an accepted psychological fact that such personalized accounts do not proceed as mechanical reproduction, but tend toward creation (Misch, 1951, p. 11), suffering from what Lindzey (1974) has labeled an "astigmatism imposed by personal needs and too little perspective" (p. ix). For this reason, autobiographies should not be regarded as objective narratives. The lack of objectivity is offset, however, by certain advantages. In methodological terms, autobiographers are the "ultimate participants in a dual participant-observer role," having privileged (if not monopolistic) access to their own inner thoughts (Merton, 1988, p. 18). By providing insights that are direct and not secondhand, the autobiographer is better qualified than anyone else to describe his or her private feelings. Autobiographies, therefore, should be regarded not as objective narratives, but as a means for evaluating an individual's self-definition (Sjoberg & Kuhn, 1989, p. 312), documenting inner thoughts that are unobtainable from other sources.

Autobiographers, however, are not without some measure of control over errors in recollection and observation. By using historical documents and other external facts, one can transform the remebered past into what Merton (1988) has termed a "series of hypotheses to be checked" (pp. 18-19). Empirical contemplation of reality, therefore, can afford at least some protection from excessive tendentiousness. The incentive to minimize such bias is high, of course, since narrators who exaggerate their positions or engage in shallow attempts at self-justification risk damaging their professional credibility.

It is an historical truism that the past is invariably interpreted in terms of the present (Sjoberg & Kuhn, 1989). A review of the narratives in this volume, supplemented by correspondence and conversations with the authors, indicates that the narrators are no exception to this historical axiom. Each invariably interprets his reminiscences in light of what has occurred since. For virtually all, writing an autobiography has been an emotionally moving experience, leading to self-revelation as each author recalled facts and feelings, actions and reactions, the incidents that prompted him, the persons he met, and the transactions in which he was involved. Several contributors have divulged that this self-revelation has enabled, if not forced, them to perceived their lives as a single whole. As a consequence, each of this latter group has benefitted by growing in ways that others could not do for them (Misch, 1951).

Further review of the following narratives highlights a second historical truism (Riley, 1988). Though the management laureates included in these volumes are indeed "influentials," they were likewise *influenced by* the social, cultural, and environmental changes to which they were exposed. Collectively, the narratives clearly show how management thinkers living at a particular point in history have been influenced by existing social policies, practices, and structures; and how these influences have, in turn, affected their thinking. The narratives, as a group, also show that the experiences, interests, accomplishments, and failures of the various contributors were in no small way a function of the historical moment at which they entered the management discipline (Merton, 1988). For instance, those entering the discipline shortly after World War II were in an appreciably different historical context than their predecessors. As several of the contributors suggest, their common wartime experiences greatly influenced the intellectual evolution of management thinking by introducing new theoretical concepts and redirecting scientific attention to new research domains.

The relevance of historical context underscores a final point. As Phil Krawiec, for one, is found of observing, "autobiographies are an introduction to the past of our discipline" (personal interview, January 28, 1990). Contemporary as they now seem, the autobiographies in this volume are also a contribution to the history of management. Even today, readers can sense in these accounts the attitudes of earlier generations and their interpretations of changing social policies, practices, and structures. Tacitly and explicitly, the narratives also tell of dominant research philosophies and the importance of reference groups and reference individuals, the significant others who helped shape the character of contemporary management thought and inquiry.

In perusing these narratives, one might ask why only North Americans, and exclusively males at that, are included as contributors to the present volumes? Historically, the professional study of management has been predominantly American. With the spread of management training on six continents, this condition is quickly changing. Likewise, the entry over the last two decades of numerous female scholars who are now notably influencing management thought is a welcomed phenomenon. Consequently, it is hoped that any future volumes will not only be truly international, but also include distinguished female contributors. Thus, the absence of international and female contributors should not be interpreted to suggest that the editor is xenophobic or sexist, but rather to reflect an absence of appropriate candidates either belonging to the cohorts from which autobiographers were selected or who had not already prepared autobiographical memoirs.

Special thanks goes to the contributors. It is hoped that each will find some satisfaction in the immortality that the present undertaking provides. All have hereby gained a medium of access that will allow them, decades after they are gone, to speak to those management scholars who will be heirs to their intellectual legacy.

Arthur G. Bedeian
July 1991

REFERENCES

Krawiec, T.S. (1972-1978). *The psychologists* (Vols. 1-2). New York: Oxford University Press. (Vol. 2): Brandon, VT: Clinical Psychology Press.

Lindzey, G. (Ed.). (1974). *A history of psychology in autobiography* (Vol. 6). Englewood Cliffs, NJ: Prentice-Hall.

Merton, R.K. (1988). Some thoughts on the concept of sociological autobiography. In M.W. Riley (Ed.), *Sociological lives* (pp. 17-21). Newbury Park, CA: Sage.

Misch, G. (1951). *A history of autobiography in antiquity* (Vol. 1). Cambridge, MA: Harvard University Press.

Riley, M.W. (Ed.). (1988). Notes on the influence of sociological lives. *Sociological lives* (pp. 23-40). Newbury Park, CA: Sage.

Sjoberg, G., & Kuhn, K. (1989). Autobiography and organizations: Theoretical and methodological issues. *Journal of Applied Behavioral Science, 24*, 309-326.

If I have seen farther, it is by
standing on the shoulders of giants.

—Sir Issac Newton

Lyman W. Porter

An Unmanaged Pursuit of Management

LYMAN W. PORTER

Throughout my life I've always had trouble deciding what I *really* wanted to do when I grow up. I still do. As far back as high school, or even before, I always envied my friends who seemed to know exactly what they were going to do in their life's work when they "grew up": One of them (Lou Doyle) very early wanted to be a doctor (and he is), one (Joan Samson) wanted to be a teacher (and she has been for most of her adult life), one (Kelley Carr) wanted to be a dentist (and still is), one (Bob Ryder) wanted to be an engineer (and has always been one since graduation from college), and so on. Alas, I was never blessed with any certainty about what I wanted to be—partly because I was interested in many different things but a master of absolutely none, and partly because I simply hated to make a choice and close out other alternatives. Hence, as the title of this story indicates, my life has been composed largely of a series or string of unplanned, unanticipated, and—frequently—extremely fortuitous events. Consequently, writing about it is an exercise in retrospective sense making in the truest sense of that concept.

As I describe the various meanderings of my life in the pages that follow, I think that several themes will emerge. (Even if they don't, I've decided to make the data conform to what I think are those themes!) First and foremost is the fact that I am a product of a middle-class, *middle-west upbringing*. Even though all of my professional years have been spent in California, my roots and basic character formation were anchored in my first eighteen years growing up in a college town in Indiana. Secondly, since I've always felt I was never endowed with any particularly strong talents in specific areas of endeavors—whatever overall talents I possess have, unfortunately, been spread rather thinly over several areas—I have had to make up for this fact by sheer dogged *persistence*: Persistence in the pursuit of certain short-term goals or objectives that I've set for myself from time to time. (Perhaps this explains one of my later deep interests, namely, motivation—"what energizes, directs, and [especially] sustains behavior." For certain, it also explains my firm belief that performance is a function of ability *times motivation*.) Even though I've tended to have this stubborn streak of persistence, I've also had, as contradictory as it sounds, an *urge to maximize variety* in my life. This in turn has sometimes led to a desire for change for the sake of change. So, I guess I would have to say that this desire for variety, which has led to a certain restlessness at some periods, is a third theme that pops up at various places in this account. A fourth thread, as I look back on the past five or so decades, has been a constant *association with education*. Despite the best efforts of my parents, this association was never really planned or anticipated, but it has been with me since the age of five. Why it has turned out that I have been a sort of perpetual student and have had my life so intertwined with the educational process is something of a mystery to me, but a fact nevertheless. Another constant has been a strong sense of *enjoyment of working with others*. Although at any given point in time I can be as independent and lone-wolfish as the next person, my natural tendency is to want to work together with colleagues on some collective task. I know that I think better when I am actively engaged in intellectual give-and-take with others rather than isolating myself for any extended period. Furthermore, and most important for me, I find it just a lot more fun to strive to accomplish something that represents a team or collaborative achievement. The final theme that has dominated my life over the years has been *luck*—sheer, unadulterated good luck. I won't elaborate on that motif here, but I will identify in various later places in this treatise those occurrences of luck that have contributed tremendously to my life and my professional career.

So much for a prologue. Now, on to what happened and, hopefully, if I can muster a modest degree of insight, why. As I look back, my life so far seems to have been divided—like Caesar's Gaul—into three parts: the "formative years," the "Berkeley years," and the "Irvine years."

THE FORMATIVE YEARS

As I have indicated, my early life was dominated by the fact that I was born and grew up in a small-to-medium size college town in the heart of the middle-west. That town was West Lafayette, Indiana, "on the banks of the Wabash." I was the last of three boys to be born to my parents. (As my next older brother was some eleven years older than me, I later as a teenager remarked to my father that I "must have been something of an after-thought"; in his usual candid manner he replied: "You were.")

My early childhood years in the 1930s in West Lafayette consisted of the typical midwest boyhood activities, mostly involving some kind of sports-type activity or games with other neighborhood friends after school and on weekends. Come rain or shine, we were outdoor playing ball. The major event of my early childhood was spending half a year in London with my parents in the latter half of 1938, less than 12 months before World War II started. I was eight at the time, just old enough to realize the significance of the various historical landmarks we visited throughout Great Britain and, for a month, on the Continent. That total experience of being abroad and living and traveling in a quite different environment than the U.S. middle west had a profound influence on me. Ever since, I have been a confirmed "internationalist," and an avid travel enthusiast.

By the time I had reached high school my four prominent interests were girls, sports, journalism, and schoolwork—in that order. Although my athletic talents were modest at best, my proudest moments in high school were earning "letters" in football and track. (In the case of the latter sport, I ran the 440-yard dash and was lead-off on the mile relay team. It seemed that before each race I was always complaining to the coach that I had some minor ailment—twisted ankle, swollen toe, cold, and so on—because he wrote in my graduation-year yearbook: "Porter, if you ever told me you were totally healthy before a race, I would have been really worried!") My journalistic interests had been kindled by my father, who was a college professor in biology. These interests led to working my way up to be the editor of my school paper in my senior year in high school. They also led to a then-hobby that probably no one else in the entire country had: since 10 or so I had acquired a collection of one or more different newspapers from each of the cities we had visited on vacations or other trips. Since my parents liked to travel, that meant that I had acquired a large stack of papers from around the United States by the time I had graduated from high school. (To illustrate the extent of the traveling we did as a family when I was growing up and my own travel in my first several years in college, by the time I was 21 I had visited every one of the then-48 states.) My academic studies in high school had progressed rather well, such that I was eager to go on to college when I graduated in 1948.

Given my strong interests in journalism at the time, and also given that I did not want to live at home while I was going to college (too confining), I chose Northwestern University even though most of my high school friends were electing to stay in West Lafayette and attend Purdue. My choice of Northwestern (NU, as it was referred to by students) turned out to be a great decision on my part, looking back in retrospect. It was the right distance from home, the education I received was first-rate, and I made a lot of good friends during my four years in Evanston. Although my initial reason for deciding to go to NU was because of its highly-rated Medill School of Journalism, I decided in my second year of college that I didn't really want to have to write every day for a living. (How ironic, as it has turned out, since my ultimate career involved writing almost every day for a living.) I switched to psychology at the beginning of my junior year, but not before the two years of being in the journalism school with its intensive writing exercises—and even more intensive feedback on that writing—had considerably improved and sharpened my composition skills. (This had not been achieved without a certain amount of pain, since my weekly required papers in J-school often came back with a great amount of blood [red ink] all over them.)

By my senior year at Northwestern I was reluctantly having to face up to what I was going to do when I graduated. ("Gee, I don't know," was my typical response when asked the question by my friends.) Early in that year, my chief undergraduate mentor in psychology—and the very model of what a professor should be—Benton J. Underwood, called me aside and said he wanted to talk to me about applying for graduate school in psychology. Until that moment, I had not really thought about the possibility of entering graduate school and becoming a professor myself, even though that was my father's own occupation. Underwood told me in no uncertain terms that I should only apply to certain schools (his personal list of the best psychology programs at that time) and not others. Thus, I applied to Yale, Stanford, Wisconsin, and Indiana, and was accepted by all four (no doubt because of Underwood's very helpful letters of recommendation). Even as far back as those days I had always had a desire to spend some time in California, so I was strongly motivated toward attending Stanford. However, I heard from Yale first and, since the acceptance was coupled with the most generous of the financial support packages, I decided to go there. Again, it turned out to be a wise choice, but I am sure that I would have been happy at any of the other three schools, too. Also, during my senior year at NU, I took a psychology honors class from Carl Duncan and for my class project conducted a verbal learning experiment. Out of this project, and with great assistance from Duncan, came a coauthored publication—"Negative Transfer in Verbal Learning"—that was subsequently accepted for publication in the *Journal of Applied Psychology*. This was my first-ever publication, and to say that it had a positive motivating effect on my desire to become, if possible, a scholar, would be a considerable understatement. (My concurrent thought: "Well, at least I have one publication—but, will there ever be a second one?")

In the fall of 1952, I arrived in New Haven. My first challenge was not, however, my first-year, Ph.D.-level classes in psychology. Rather, it was the necessity of passing "reading exams" in two foreign languages, a (then) Yale Graduate School requirement to be met no later than the end of the first year. Fortunately, I had taken enough German at Northwestern to pass that exam without too much difficulty; French, however, was another matter, but by a lot of cramming during the summer preceding my entry I was able to squeeze a pass out of the exam taken early in my first semester. What a relief, since I had visions of spending my whole first year at Yale bogged down in a miasma of French language courses while I was struggling to get started on my psychology graduate studies. At any rate, I escaped that fate and was able to concentrate on matters at hand relating to psychology.

I had gone to Yale on my (and the Yale Psychology Department's) assumption that I would be concentrating in the area of experimental psychology. But, just as in my undergraduate years, my interests began to shift once again. While I found my courses and my research assistantship work for Fred Sheffield and Neal Miller to be both interesting and intellectually stimulating and challenging, I came to the conclusion that if I continued to pursue that subfield of psychology—experimental psychology—I would end up spending too much of my time in laboratories, frequently isolated from the "real world" of other people. Regrettably for me, I did not come to this conclusion until near the end of the third of my (eventual) four years at Yale. What to do? I was too far along to shift totally my subfield within the Yale program, so I ended up doing a "human learning" experiment involving the administration of an adversive stimulus—a very mild, tingling electric shock administered to the wrist—to study its effect on recall of verbal materials. This study was designed with the great assistance and encouragement of Fred Sheffield, to whom I have always been grateful for his help in this regard. Meanwhile I had been serving as a research assistant in the animal learning laboratories of the widely-renowned psychologist Neal Miller; from him (through both the assistantship and his courses that I took) I learned the fundamentals of the scientific method in a way that has stood me in good stead ever since. Nevertheless, I still faced the issue, in my fourth year at Yale, of my gradually changing interests and what to do about them. I turned to one of Yale's most famous psychologists of that or any other time, Carl Hovland, and asked him for his advice since he was highly familiar with experimental psychology but more oriented toward social and industrial psychology. I told him of my possible interest in—but total lack of knowledge of—the latter field, so he suggested a reading course with an adjunct professor (Paul Burnham). Thus somewhat tentatively launched in what basically would be my future field of professional endeavor, I proceeded to read a series of basic texts in industrial psychology throughout that final year at Yale. It was not exactly an in-depth introduction to the field, but it at least got me started.

As an aside, and to demonstrate what I said at the beginning of this autobiographical piece about my inability to decide what I really wanted to do "when I grow up," I had in my first year at Yale flirted with the possibility of transferring from the psychology program to either the Harvard MBA program, about which I had learned from a friend, or to the Yale Law School. Although I seriously considered both possibilities, especially the one closest at hand (Yale Law School), I never took the ultimate step of applying. To this day, I think that I could have been just as happy in my professional life if I had in fact carried through with either possibility (on the rather vain assumption that I would have been accepted). I have no regrets about passing up these "could-have-beens," but likewise never have I subsequently devalued them as once-viable options.

As I approached the latter part of my last year at Yale in the spring of 1956, I was again faced with the somewhat fearsome problem of what I was going to do after I graduated, a problem similar to the one I had faced four years previously when I was preparing to finish up at Northwestern. The only difference was that this time it merely involved the question of "what was I going to do for a living." With the end, so to speak, rapidly approaching, I was the beneficial recipient of one of the many lucky breaks I have received over the years: A highly desirable job possibility appeared almost out of thin air around March of that year. Edwin Ghiselli, one of the country's premier industrial psychologists, and at that time also chairman of the psychology department at UC-Berkeley, wrote to Hovland saying that Berkeley had a faculty opening in the area of "industrial-social psychology" and, furthermore, they wanted someone who was "broadly-trained in psychology in general, and not someone who was narrowly trained only in industrial psychology." Since I more than fit the latter part of that job specification and to a degree fit the first part, Hovland wrote back and suggested me as a possibility for the position. Within a few weeks I was being interviewed by Ghiselli who was on the East coast on other business, and a few weeks after that received a telegram that would forever change the course of my life. It said: "Department votes unanimously to offer you position as Instructor in industrial-social psychology at salary of $4,296. Congratulations. Please reply within a week." It took me about five seconds to decide on my response, but I coolly waited several days before sending my affirmative answer. At least, for a couple of years I would not have to worry about how I would obtain a paycheck, and I was going to a part of the country—California—that had always had an attraction for me. Little did I know, of course, that I would still be in California some 35 years later. There was only one small problem: I would be teaching courses and doing research in an area in I which I myself had never had a formal course!

THE BERKELEY YEARS

Before arriving at Berkeley in August 1956, I had spent the summer working for Bell Laboratories in New Jersey and New York City on a project involving interviews of managerial and technical personnel regarding sources of job satisfaction and dissatisfaction. This project had been arranged through Hovland, who at that time was a high-level consultant to AT&T. It turned out to be an excellent experience for me both with respect to honing my interviewing skills but also for getting me acclimated to "real" organizational situations. It was a perfect transition phase between the conclusion of my Yale years and the beginning of my Berkeley years.

I finished the Bell Labs project early in August and headed west. On the way I stopped in West Lafayette to buy a new car which I used to drive to California. Since this was before the days of the Interstate system of highways, it took me five days, during which time the only persons I spoke with were waitresses in diners and motel clerks. I was glad to see Berkeley, but was Berkeley equally glad to see me? As it turned out, I felt quickly accepted by my new colleagues on the faculty in the psychology department and forthwith turned my attention to preparing my first set of lecture notes for the first course I ever taught anywhere, "Industrial-Social Psychology." Since, as noted, I had never *taken* a course in this area, I had no available notes of my own. What to do? I consulted with my other chief colleague in addition to Ed Ghiselli in the industrial psychology area, namely, Mason Haire. Since he was the only person on the faculty who had previously taught the course, he seemed like the logical source of good notes. Unfortunately, Mason told me that he lectured only from a very sparse set of notes, since that was his preferred style. Mason was excellent with this highly extemporaneous approach, but I knew that that would never do for me, at least in the first few years. Although Haire had no available set of notes from which I could begin to build my own, he directed me to a senior psychology major, Jeff Keppel, who had been a student in his (Haire's) most recent class on this topic and whom Haire knew had taken comprehensive notes. Luckily for me, Keppel had indeed taken detailed notes which proved to be extremely useful as I struggled in my preparation for my first few classes. (Jeff and I became good friends; the following year he went on to graduate school, subsequently going on to a distinguished career as an experimental psychologist and expert in verbal learning and serving as a long-time faculty member at—Berkeley.) With the help of Jeff's notes and my own reading of as many books in the area as possible over the summer and that fall, I was able to keep about one lecture ahead of where the students were in their reading. Two good things happened as a result of teaching that first class: one, I survived the course and even received decent student evaluations of my frosh-like teaching; and, two, I met a student, Andy Moreland, with whom I became a good friend and through whom I was later (the next summer) to meet the girl who was to become my wife—Meredith Moeller. (For the record, Andy went on to medical school and for the past several decades has been an anesthesiologist in Santa Cruz.)

Almost my total first year existence at Berkeley was taken up with preparing for my teaching assignments—for obvious reasons. My need to feel at least acceptably prepared for each class, in the context of my relative lack of familiarity with the field, meant that little time was left over to think about research let alone actually to *carry out* a research project. Once again, fortune smiled on me in the form of that prince of colleagues, Ed Ghiselli. Toward the latter half of my first Berkeley year Ed dropped around my office and said that he had some data that he had collected recently that he hadn't yet had a chance to analyze or write up. Would I be interested, he asked, in looking at the raw data and see if there was anything there, and, if so, to do an initial draft of a coauthored manuscript? It was Ed's gentle way of offering to help get me started on doing scholarly work in the industrial-social psychology field. Of course, I accepted his offer with alacrity and soon I had analyzed the data and prepared a first draft of a manuscript that became my first publication in my newly-adopted field: "The Self-perceptions of Top and Middle Management Personnel" (1958). (By that time, I already had five previous journal publications from my undergraduate and graduate work, but all of them were related to issues in experimental psychology.) That article with Ghiselli helped shape my early interests in focusing in on *management* and managers as the object of my research efforts. I knew that my lack of formal training in industrial psychology and related areas such as labor relations would probably preclude me from ever gaining any sort of high-level expertise with respect to rank-and-file workers, especially those in unionized work situations; hence, my decision to concentrate most of my attention on management and managers. The right decision for me, as I look back with hindsight.

My early years at Berkeley progressed well largely because of the help and encouragement I received from Ghiselli and Haire. They became close, personal friends and served, in effect, as my mentors. If I have achieved any subsequent scholarly success in fields related to industrial psychology, it is directly attributable to the tremendous influence these two had on me at the beginning of my career. They literally "taught" me the field, helped me formulate my views of issues in the field, introduced me to major figures in the field, and provided guidance that could not be equaled anywhere. No junior faculty member could ever be as fortunate as to have two senior colleagues of the caliber of Ed Ghiselli and Mason Haire.

As my first year at Berkeley drew to a close, I was well into several incipient and small-scale research projects on which I hoped to make progress in the next few months, especially before I had to start teaching again in the second session of summer school in 1957. That particular summer teaching period turned out to be fateful for me because my former student and now friend, Andy Moreland, introduced me to a particular group of girls that were in the Berkeley environs that summer. One of them, the most attractive (of course), was the one that turned out to be the love of my life and (about 10 months later) my wife, the aforementioned Meredith Moeller. Fortunately, she had not been around to attract me, and distract me, during my prior first year, because otherwise I never would have been able to prepare my first-time lectures, read voraciously in my field to catch-up, and try to launch some research efforts. There would not have been enough time. (Others could probably do all of those things simultaneously and still have time for a lively social life, but I'm not that agile.) Since, however, the chain of events that led to matrimony started after my first year, I was better able to juggle the diverse set of activities that occupied my second year at Berkeley. Meredith, first as fiance and later as newly-married wife, was *very* understanding—as she has continued to be for the 33-plus years since then.

Because of the fact that I had arrived in the psychology department at Berkeley as both the newest member of the faculty and also the youngest (at 26), I had one great advantage: no one really expected anything from me for a while. Consequently, whenever I did something of modest note, such as making a half-way cogent argument in a faculty meeting or getting an article accepted for publication, everyone was pleasantly surprised. Unfortunately, however, one can only be the newest and youngest for a very short period of time. (I remember with dismay when an even younger faculty member was hired during my second year.) This meant that if I wanted to have the opportunity to stay at Berkeley it would be wise to keep up an aggressive program of research. This was what I wanted to do, and intended to do, anyway, so it was no particular burden. (To be frank, during my Instructor and Assistant Professor years at UCB I never thought much about "tenure." My view was that I was going to do what I was going to do, and if that was enough, then "fine." If not, "so be it." It would hurt my pride, no doubt; but I figured, perhaps somewhat cavalierly, that there were plenty of other places to work, even if not with the prestige of Berkeley, and I believed that I could be happy professionally in any number of institutions. As things turned out, I never actually had to test that belief.) The one disadvantage of being the "newest kid on the block" was that the several Ph.D. students that were already working on their degrees in industrial psychology in the department were not exactly, and automatically, desirous of working with me. They were very friendly, but they correctly sensed that I could contribute relatively little to their knowledge of the field. In fact, when I arrived in 1956, all of the doctoral students obviously were way ahead of me in this regard. Given this situation, I turned to working with a couple of new, entering students after I had been there for a couple of years. Fortunately, they were not as aware of my relative newness to the field (nor to the faculty). Thus, due to our reciprocal naïveté, as it were, I was able to begin my first intensive work with doctoral students, a challenge and pleasure that I have enjoyed ever since.

Following my first article in the "organizational" (industrial psychology) field with Ghiselli, I had proceeded over the next couple of years to write several articles[1] that utilized the extensive data set that had been collected originally by Ghiselli for other purposes relating to the development of his Self Description Inventory. My interests were in understanding the structure of organizations, particularly the management sector, and how that structure was related to the types of individuals who were most likely to be found in the different component parts of an organization. This in turn led me to thinking about how job attitudes might vary throughout the typical organizational structure and the possible implications of those patterns of attitudes. Due to the fortuitous circumstances of the fact that the Ford Foundation had taken an interest in business education and issues relating to it, I was able, in 1959, to obtain a Ford Foundation Faculty Research Fellowship. This provided a relief from teaching responsibilities for the 1959-60 academic year and furthermore allowed me to employ a graduate research assistant (RA), since the department of psychology did not have the resources to provide such funds to junior faculty. With these funds, I hired my first RA, Mildred Henry (now the president of a small college in the San Francisco Bay Area). With Millie's willing and tireless help, I was able to develop a need satisfaction instrument based on (but not testing) Maslow's need hierarchy theory. Concurrently, and with the help of contacts provided by Mason Haire, I was able to persuade the American Management Association (AMA) to help sponsor an extensive study of the job attitudes, including need satisfactions, of a large nationwide sample of managers and executives. This was another piece of good luck, because this one single, but very large, data collection effort provided the bases for a set of six future articles, all published over a several year period in the *Journal of Applied Psychology*, as well as a summary monograph—*Organizational Patterns of Managerial Job Attitudes* (1964). In the later stages of this particular project, I was greatly assisted by another graduate student RA, I. R. (Bob) Andrews. Meanwhile, also during this period, I worked on several other smaller-scale projects relating to work group characteristics and behavior with several other graduate students including Tom Lodahl (later to be the Editor of *Administrative Science Quarterly*). Tom (who was really Mason Haire's student but whose dissertation I directed during Haire's sabbatical leave) and I had a lot of fun working together designing and implementing a research study that was carried out on small work teams at the United Airlines maintenance base in South San Francisco just prior to the introduction of jet engines on commercial aircraft (which goes to show how old Tom is, if not myself).

One student who entered Berkeley's Ph.D. program in industrial psychology in the late 1950s (1959, to be exact), but who only stayed one year before transferring to Indiana University, was one Larry L. Cummings. Through a combination of totally inadvertent circumstances, Larry and I had little contact with each other during his "Berkeley year"—we were both total "unknowns" at that time—and only got to be very close and personal friends around the time he was finishing his doctoral work at I.U. The following year (1960) at Berkeley, however, another new Ph.D. student entered the industrial psych program. This person I also did not get to know during his first semester or so, but from that time on we formed an intense partnership—in the best sense of that word—that persisted for many years after he received his degree in 1964. That "student" was Edward E. Lawler, III. By the beginning of Ed's second year in the program we found that we had strong common interests in a number of intriguing intellectual issues in our field. Furthermore, we also found that we had a number of other common nonwork interests, particularly sports (I'll never forget, for example, watching Loyola of Chicago win the 1963 NCAA basketball championship game on TV in Ed's recreation room in his home) and bridge, among others. We first published together in 1963 in an article, on "Perceptions Regarding Management Compensation," and two years later our third coauthored paper was one that was published in the *Psychological Bulletin*—it had been a joyous moment when we two relative rookies received the acceptance letter for that article from the editor—"Properties of Organizational Structure in Relation to Job Attitudes and Job Behavior" (1965). That literature review article gained a certain amount of subsequent visibility and was an important early career boost for both of us.

It was during Ed's last year or so at Berkeley that we began to formulate our ideas regarding the variables that act together to determine motivation and job performance. Our initial thinking was mightily influenced by the publication of Victor Vroom's classic book, *Work and Motivation*, in the spring of 1964, because we immediately saw that Vic's explication of an expectancy theory approach had great applicability to our own data and ideas. We proceeded to spend much of the summer of 1964 in many discussions about how we might extend the theory in ways that made sense to us and about which we had collected previous data that could be analyzed from that perspective. Thus was born the so-called Porter-Lawler model of motivation. It took us another two years or so to develop the model fully and to test with our data set some of the relationships between and among its variables, but the end result was our jointly authored book, *Managerial Attitudes and Performance* (1968). Our two names have been linked ever since, though Ed, of course, has gone on to establish a highly prominent and visible position in our field—quite independent of our early joint collaborations—through his numerous and extremely valuable contributions. Regrettably, I don't have the space to go on in more detail about Ed's many abilities and attributes, but I will mention one that stands out for me, and one that has a certain relevance to our motivational model: Ed Lawler, far and away, is better at converting effort into outstanding performance than anyone I have ever met in my entire life.

At this point I need to backtrack to note one other major project on which I worked during my Berkeley years (in the period between 1956 and 1967). In 1960, primarily through Mason Haire's initiative, the threesome of Haire, Ghiselli, and Porter submitted a research proposal to the Ford Foundation to undertake a cross-national study of managerial job attitudes. The proposal was funded, and we proceeded to carry out the study in 1961 and 1962. Data were collected *in situ* in various countries by ourselves singly or jointly and with the help of several other colleagues around the world, most notably Frank Heller (who, at that time, was working in Chile for an agency of the United Nations). Not the least of the benefits of this project was the fact that each of the three principal investigators got to live abroad for a period during that time. In my case, my wife and I decided to spend a six-month period in Copenhagen, where I could concentrate on data collection activities in Scandinavia and Germany. With our then-two-year-old daughter, we lived in a penthouse suite atop a modern apartment building on the outskirts of Copenhagen that was rented for the grand sum of $108 a month. We never had it so good, before or since. The experience provided a chance to learn about another culture as well as to participate in an active way in our research project. As luck (again) would have it, on one of my data forays to Germany, I happened to arrive in Berlin two days after the East German government began the construction of "the wall" in August 1961. Watching the wall actually being built brick by brick and block by city block has made for an unforgettable experience. (The fact that it suddenly started to come down on November 9, 1989, exactly on my wife's birthday, added a coincidental conclusion to my personal Berlin Wall saga begun some 28 years earlier.) By the finish of our data gathering efforts we had obtained extensive questionnaire responses from more than 2,000 managers from 14 countries in Europe, Asia, and South America. Our findings were published in a book titled *Managerial Thinking: An International Study* (1966). While some of our data analyses could be considered somewhat primitive by today's standards, many of our findings and conclusions have in fact held up rather well for these past 25 or so years. A number of other large-scale cross-national studies of managerial attitudes have been conducted since the publication of our book, of course, but we took a small amount of pride in being one of the earliest group of researchers to carry out this type of study in our field. Besides, we had a lot of enjoyment in just doing the study and working on it together.

Before closing out the account of my years at Berkeley, a few other facets that were especially memorable for me during that 11-year period might be worth noting. One was my rejection for membership in (then) Division 14—the Division of Industrial Psychology—of the American Psychological Association. (Division 14 later was renamed the Division of Industrial-Organizational Psychology and even later came to be called by its current name, the Society of Industrial-Organizational Psychology.) I had applied for membership in 1959, but had received a polite—but firm—note from the Membership Committee saying that my application had been denied because there was insufficient evidence that I was committed to this particular field (despite the fact that I had already had two articles published in the field, three more in press, and had been recommended by two senior members of the Division, Ghiselli, and Tom Harrell of Stanford). I did get "admitted" two years later, and I must say that I permitted myself a small measure of self satisfaction when I later was elected president of the Division in 1975, sixteen years and some 40 journal articles and two books after having been turned down for not demonstrating that I really was actively involved in this field. (This trail of events might help to explain some of my interest in studying motivated behavior.)

A second experience, of a different type, was serving during the early 1960s, as the "Faculty Representative" to the student government. My confidence in my effectiveness in this role was somewhat shaken by the eruption of the Free Speech Movement in the fall of 1964, and the subsequent arrest of several hundred students for invading Sproul Hall and effectively closing down the university for several days. Aside from that "minor incident" that affected the Berkeley campus for the next 10 years or so, I found the experience of being in the faculty representative role to be fascinating and even enjoyable at times. It cemented my belief that university service is an integral part of any faculty member's basic set of responsibilities.

Still another, and clearly more consistently enjoyable, vignette from those years was the series of touch football games in which I participated on Sunday afternoons every few weeks each fall. For the record, some of the other players included Stan Nealey (now at the Battelle Institute in Seattle), Ray Miles (now professor and former dean of the business school at Berkeley), and Ed Lawler. We were all young and vigorous, but I was a 5-10 pygmy among those 6-3-or-so tall giants. I made up for lack of height with what I considered blazing speed, but Ray always used to say of me: "He's small but slow." (I think he was kidding, but maybe he wasn't.)

Last but by far not least among events of my Berkeley years: our two children, Anne and Bill, were born there at the end of the 50s and early in the 60s. As young children, they made sure that their father did not lose track of what the real meaning of life is all about.

THE IRVINE YEARS

In the Fall of 1965 I had received an invitation from Don Taylor, then chair of the Department of Industrial Administration at Yale, to spend the 1966-67 academic year as a visiting professor at Yale in that department. Although this represented a very appealing proposition for a number of reasons, especially because Ed Lawler was now at Yale as a junior faculty member, it was not an easy decision for me. This primarily was because I was heavily into a number of research activities at Berkeley and also because I was enjoying working with the then current set of graduate students, including Karlene Roberts and (from the School of Business) Ed Miller, and Vance Mitchell. Nevertheless, the opportunity to go to Yale for a year was too attractive to turn down and, in addition, it would provide Ed and me a setting where we could work together in close proximity (down the hall, so to speak) to finish up our manuscript on *Managerial Attitudes and Performance*. So, together with my family (including, by now, two young children ages seven and four), I made plans to spend from September 1966 to June 1967 in New Haven.

In the Spring of 1966, however, as we were making travel preparations, my friend Scott Myers, then employed as an industrial psychologist on the staff of Texas Instruments, invited me to spend the intervening summer months between Berkeley and Yale in Dallas at TI. I accepted his invitation, and the resulting three-month working interlude turned out to be especially informative and interesting. Most of my time was spent interviewing a number of TI managers and executives regarding various facets of their jobs and their views about managing, as well as having the opportunity to observe firsthand a number of TI's advanced (for those days) human resource practices.

The year at Yale was all that I had hoped it would be. Ed and I completed our book manuscript work as well as wrapping up several research papers on which we had been working. One of the major delights of the year was getting to know one Richard Hackman, who had only recently arrived to join the Industrial Administration faculty. (The department, incidentally, chose that year to change its name to "Administrative Sciences," and it was to become the forerunner of today's School of Organization and Management.) Among other activities that year, Richard and I formulated and conducted a research study of "expectancy theory predictions of work effectiveness," and this experience showed me what a superlative scholar Yale had hired when they had recruited this brand-new Ph.D. psychologist from the University of Illinois. Also around Yale that year was another young faculty member who became a good friend, namely, Tim Hall. Furthermore, Chris Argyris had become department chairman and this allowed me to get to know someone whom I had admired from afar for his pioneering work in our field but whom I had only met one time previously. All in all, as might be imagined, it was an exceptionally stimulating year, and it had a major positive impact on my subsequent career.

One other event, however, happened that year that had even greater impact: I made a fateful decision to leave Berkeley and go to a two-year old university, UC-Irvine. It would take too long here to go into all of the details regarding the reasoning behind my decision. Many people, including my wife, were perplexed by this decision. Suffice to say, it was agonizing. I was just being promoted (during the 1966-67 year) to full professor at Berkeley and had greatly enjoyed my work and all of the friends we had made in the psychology department and elsewhere around the campus. Thus, there were absolutely no "push" reasons. The "pull" reasons were several but not all fully explainable—even to myself. Probably the biggest factor was simply a sort of inexplicable feeling on my part that it was time to (in the words of John Gardner) "repot" myself. I had been at Berkeley for eleven years (counting the visiting year at Yale) and had achieved far more than I ever expected or even had hoped for. But, I was restless, and this brand new campus with its infant Graduate School of Administration (GSA), held a sort of "frontier allure" for me. I had been thinking for several years that a business/management school, whether at

Berkeley or elsewhere, might be a better home, as it were, for my interests. "Management" as an area of study and object of research seemed more central to a business school than to a psychology department. But, if a change to a management school, why Irvine? (My good friend, Jack Miner, had said to me shortly after my move: "I can't understand why you would go there—it's like buying a 'pig in a poke'"; several years later, after he had visited me at Irvine, he recanted: "I see now why you moved to UCI.") There were three specific reasons: Richard Snyder, GSA's first dean, had done an effective job of recruiting me; second, helping to build a new campus of the University of California (the umbrella institution which I knew would insure high quality) was a challenge that I found hard to pass up; and, third, the southern California costal area around Newport Beach (which is contiguous with Irvine) had always impressed me as an especially attractive place to live—and, I can now attest, it definitely is. Nevertheless, despite these reasons that I gave to myself (and to Meredith), the decision to leave Berkeley—which I made around March 1967 during my year at Yale—was absolutely wrenching. Perhaps because it was so wrenching, I have never made another "permanent" move.

Just after the six-day Arab-Israel war had finished in mid-June 1967, we departed New Haven by car for the Irvine campus to drop off a large number of books and files I had taken with me to Yale the previous September. We then would proceed back up to Berkeley to sell our house before returning to the Irvine area to look for housing. I mention this small detail of dropping off a set of books at my new campus office on a few-days-visit to Irvine before returning for good because of one particular incident that occurred at that time. I had asked the dean's secretary if she could get someone to help me carry up a number of boxes of books from my car. She said "Sure, here's one of our master's degree students, and he will be glad to help you." It was John Van Maanen. I don't think either John or I realized that early July day in 1967 that we would eventually be working together so closely during the next four or five years.

The transition from Berkeley to UCI went fairly smoothly that first year for me, though it was not very easy on my family (since we had no relatives or close friends in the region when we moved to the Newport Beach/Irvine area). I was kept busy in my new role as Associate Dean of the GSA (later renamed the Graduate School of Management) as well as adjusting to my new surroundings and making all sorts of new acquaintances. By the end of the 1967-68 year I had my feet more-or-less on the ground and was able to start focusing more intensively on resuming my research activities which had been interrupted, for all intents and purposes, by the move. One problem, though, was that GSA did not yet have a Ph.D. program in place. Since I was used to working closely with doctoral students, this seemed like a fairly serious obstacle. Indeed, I was concerned enough to ask Jim March, the founding dean of the School of Social Sciences at Irvine, what he thought I should do. Jim, in his usual incisive manner, said: "Well, just go out and create them." It was then that I decided to work with what seemed to be the most appropriate second year master's student available, Van Maanen, even though at that time he did not appear to be terribly interested in my particular field of interest relating to behavior in organizations. John turned out, of course, to be quite helpful, and we found we did have some common interests. The following year GSA started a Ph.D. program and John was one of the first two admitted. (As a footnote, and to be true to the record, I actually had argued in a faculty meeting *against* his admission, not because he wasn't intellectually qualified, which he obviously was, but because I was concerned that he didn't have sufficiently defined interests and was in danger of becoming too much of a dilettante. So much for my skills in selection of talent!)

Since I've already mentioned John Van Maanen, this is as good a place as any to talk about the remarkable string of doctoral students that I have been privileged to be associated with as major advisor during my years in GSA (GSM) at Irvine. In recounting these names, the reader will again see evidence of my recurring good luck. First, as noted, was Van Maanen. John was unlike any of the other students I have had before or since, but he was someone who would put his own unique stamp on the field. His doctoral dissertation study of the Seattle Police Force training program was an especially insightful piece of work, in my opinion, and my main contributions were simply to encourage him to do it and to try to be as supportive as possible. Following Van Maanen (who graduated in 1972), my next doctoral student at Irvine, Rick Steers, was as different (from John) as two people can be. Whereas John tended toward the impulsive with a devil-may-care attitude toward life, Rick was careful, planful, and serious—but no less talented. Just a different style. Rick and I have collaborated on several articles during and since his doctoral years and, as I write, the 5th edition of our edited text on motivation, *Motivation and Work Behavior*, has just been published. Concurrently with Rick's period in the Ph.D. program there was another Rick, Rick Mowday, who became my third Ph.D. "product." The two Ricks became fast friends and, of course, still are as colleagues on the faculty at the University of Oregon. Rick Mowday early on showed a great deal of promise, and my chief task, as I saw it, was simply to try to help develop his potential. Rick M, as well as Rick Steers, was at Irvine at the time that intense development was going on with respect to a research program I had started several years earlier dealing with organizational commitment. The three of us worked on several sets of data we had jointly collected (along with several other students, including Bill Crampon and Paul Boulian, and my great good friend and professional colleague [then] at Sears Roebuck & Co., Frank J. Smith). Ultimately, Rick M., Rick S., and I published a book on our research on commitment, *Employee-Organization Linkages: The Psychology of Commitment, Absenteeism and Turnover* (1982). The book was preceded in 1979 by an article,

"The Measurement of Organizational Commitment," which has apparently been heavily cited over the years.

Van Maanen—Steers—Mowday. Not a bad way to start an OB Ph.D. program from scratch at a university less than ten years old. Just luck, however; sheer luck. But other good OB doctoral students also came to Irvine in the 1970s. There is not enough space to list and talk about each one, but among others Eugene Stone certainly deserves mention. Gene, as would not surprise those who know him well, went through our program rapidly. He was always steadily focused, always applying himself to the task at hand, and always thinking about how to collect data to attack an interesting research problem. Together, and with great initiative on Gene's part, we published several articles dealing with job characteristics and their relationships to job attitudes. Gene Stone was (and still is) one of the best "scientists" I have had the pleasure to work with. (My long ago mentor at Yale, Neal Miller, would have been thrilled to have a student with Gene's drive and understanding of the scientific process.)

In the late 1970s and early 1980s the continuing succession of Ph.D. students with whom I worked included Bob Allen, Hal Angle, Dan Dalton, and David Krackhardt. The former two and I wrote what is still one of my own favorite pieces, a chapter titled "The Politics of Upward Influence in Organizations" (1981). Bob and I, along with my then-colleague Patty Renwick and two other graduate students, Dan Madison and Tom Mayes, had previously published articles utilizing an interesting set of data that we had collected dealing with perceptions of organizational politics in the managerial ranks of a sample of electronic companies. This empirical research in turn stimulated the Porter-Allen-Angle *ROB* conceptual chapter that put forth a number of testable propositions regarding upward (political-type) influence in organizations. The second author of that chapter, Bob Allen, has always been an astute observer of management both before and since he was a doctoral student, and the third author, Hal Angle, was a simply outstanding doctoral student and a person who is one of the three best psychologists qua psychologists that I have encountered as students over the years. (The other two are Gene Stone and Mordechai Eran [a former Ph.D. student at Berkeley who was then on leave as a high ranking officer in the personnel section of the Israeli Defense Forces].) Dan Dalton, though not my advisee, and I worked together on several articles dealing with turnover, and it was plain to see even then that Dan was headed for a productive scholarly career. David Krackhardt was a principal advisee of mine, and the two of us worked intensively on issues relating to organizational commitment and turnover. For his dissertation, David employed his (even then) expert knowledge of network analysis in studying what happens to those who remain when colleagues leave intact work groups. At the risk of overusing the word "brilliant," David certainly fit that label. Finally, in the late 1980s at Irvine I had the good fortune to work with someone who is sure to make his mark on issues dealing with international aspects of behavior in work organizations: Stewart Black. Stewart was like Gene Stone in that he was highly focused and was able to move through the doctoral program at rapid speed, and he is like Ed Lawler in that he knows how to get things done. His student colleague, Hal Gregersen, who graduated a year after Stewart at the end of the 1980s, is also someone who has the potential to be a major contributor to the OB field.

Even though much of my energy and efforts at UC-Irvine has been invested—with an abundance of pleasurable returns—in working with doctoral students, I have also found some time to work on behalf of the institution itself. For the first five years I was at Irvine I served as Associate Dean of GSM, and then for the following eleven years I was Dean (1972-1983). This stint as Dean was a very rewarding period for me in a personal sense—even though it was an extremely difficult time for the campus, for our school of management, and for me because of constantly tight budget and resource constraints (the Reagan and Brown years).

One direct benefit of my deaning experience that I had not anticipated was the opportunity to become involved in the American Assembly of Collegiate Schools of Business (AACSB) by serving several terms on its Board of Directors. This experience provided me with an overview of university-level management education on the national scene that I never would have been able to obtain as the dean of a single school. The experience also led, at least indirectly, to the opportunity of a lifetime: to be able to have a major role in the first comprehensive, nationwide study of management education that had been carried out in the United States in 25 years. This project, which was codirected with my good friend, Larry McKibbin of the University of Oklahoma, culminated with the publication of our report, *Management Education and Development* (1988). The reason that the chance to take part in this study was such an involving experience for me was because I had spent a good portion of the preceding 15 or so years thinking about management education and how to improve it, and here was an opportunity to visit over sixty different universities and more than fifty companies and discuss with faculty members, deans, and business executives what was right and what was wrong about the way we were carrying out management education in our country. No project I had ever done before, nor am ever likely to do in the future, was so intensely involving for such a continuous period (two and a half years).

My time deaning, working with doctoral students, and serving on AACSB committees were not my only sets of activities during the years since arriving at Irvine in 1967. As mentioned earlier, I had joined Division 14 of APA as far back as the beginning of the 60s and had become deeply involved in that organization. In 1975, after serving on its Executive Committee for several years, I was elected President, a proud moment for me. An equally proud moment was 14 years later when the (now) Society of Industrial-Organizational

Psychology presented me with the "Distinguished Scientific Contributions Award." (The fact that the presentation at the Annual Meeting held in New Orleans in 1989 was made by my former student, Gene Stone, added greatly to the occasion.)

The other professional organization with which I have been heavily involved over the years has been the Academy of Management. I had joined the national Academy in 1966 and had chosen to become as active as possible, since it was my belief that this was going to be the primary scholarly organization for those of us in the broad fields of management and organizational behavior, and I wanted to be where the intellectual and scholarly action was. (Little did I realize back in the mid-60s what a relatively mammoth organization the Academy would become.) In 1971 I was appointed the first Chairman of the Organizational Behavior Division of the Academy and subsequently elected Academy President in 1973. For someone who has been long associated with this organization, it was therefore a distinct and unforgettable honor to be selected with Herbert Simon as the first recipients of the Academy's "Scholarly Contributions to Management Award" (now called the "Richard D. Irwin Award") in 1983. (I can still remember as clearly as if it were yesterday when Art Bedeian called to tell me that I was to receive the Award. To say I was shocked would be to put it mildly; I wasn't even aware that the Academy had recently instituted the award.)

There have been still other activities that have engaged my attention and efforts over the years in relation to professional and educational interests. There is not enough space to go into all of them, but I will (again for the record) briefly mention the following: service on several committees of the American Psychological Association (including a task force involved in an unsuccessful attempt to reorganize that organization); service as an accreditor for the regional university accrediting association (the Western Association of Schools and Colleges); member of the Graduate Management Admission Council's (recent) Commission on "Graduate Management Education"; current (as I write) member of AACSB's Accreditation Task Force charged with re-writing AACSB's total set of accreditation standards; consultant to several publishing companies (starting with Goodyear which merged into Scott, Foresman which merged into, now, HarperCollins); and, capitalizing on my fantasized—but totally unrealized—athletic talents, current service as UC-Irvine's Faculty Athletic Representative to the NCAA.

As these last few pages probably demonstrate, and as I emphasized at the beginning as one of the themes characterizing my life and career to date, I seem to have a strong need to maximize variety in my life. Regardless of what has, or, more likely, hasn't been accomplished, this melange of activities has made for a great trip —an unmanaged trip that has largely been devoted to trying to understand what organized activity and its management is all about. For one who likes to travel, this trip certainly has been exhilarating.

PUBLICATIONS

1953

With C.P. Duncan. Negative transfer in verbal learning. *Journal of Experimental Psychology, 46*, 61-64.

1955

With C.J. Bailey. Relevant cues in drive discrimination in cats. *Journal of Comparative and Physiological Psychology, 48*, 180-182.

1957

The effect of 'right' in a modified Thorndikian situation. *American Journal of Psychology, 70*, 219-226.

With N.E. Miller. Training under two drives, alternately present, vs. training under a single drive. *Journal of Experimental Psychology, 54*, 1-7.

Effect of shock-cessation as an incidental reward in verbal learning. *American Journal of Psychology, 70*, 421-426.

With E.E. Ghiselli. The self-perceptions of top and middle management personnel. *Personnel Psychology, 10*, 397-406.

1958

Differential self-perceptions of management personnel and line workers. *Journal of Applied Psychology, 42*, 105-108.

1959

With P.H. Mussen. Personal motivations and self-conceptions associated with effectiveness and ineffectiveness in emergent groups. *Journal of Abnormal and Social Psychology, 59*, 23-27.

With R.A. Kaufman, & K.L. Hakmiller. The effects of top and middle management sets on the Ghiselli self-description inventory. *Journal of Applied Psychology, 43*, 149-153.

Self-perceptions of first-level supervisors compared with upper-management personnel and with operative line workers. *Journal of Applied Psychology, 43*, 183-186.

With R.A. Kaufman. Relationships between a top-middle management self-description scale and behavior in a group situation. *Journal of Applied Psychology, 43*, 345-348.

1960

With E.E. Ghiselli. A self-description scale measuring sociometric popularity among manual workers. *Personnel Psychology, 13*, 141-146.

1961

With T.M. Lodahl. Psychometric score patterns, social characteristics, and productivity of small industrial work groups. *Journal of Applied Psychology, 45*, 73-79.

A study of perceived need satisfactions in bottom and middle management jobs. *Journal of Applied Psychology, 45*, 1-10.

Perceived trait requirements in bottom and middle management jobs. *Journal of Applied Psychology, 45*, 232-236.

With W.M. Wiest & E.E. Ghiselli. Relationships between individual proficiency and team performance and team efficiency. *Journal of Applied Psychology, 45*, 435-440.

1962

Job attitudes in management: I. Perceived deficiencies in need fulfillment as a function of job level. *Journal of Applied Psychology, 46*, 373-384.

1963

Job attitudes in management: II. Perceived importance of needs as a function of job level. *Journal of Applied Psychology, 47*, 141-148.

Job attitudes in management: III. Perceived deficiencies in need fulfillment as a function of line vs. staff type of job. *Journal of Applied Psychology, 47*, 267-275.

With M. Haire & E.E. Ghiselli. Cultural patterns in the role of the manager. *Industrial Relations, 2*, 95-117.

With E.E. Lawler. Perceptions regarding management compensation. *Industrial Relations, 2*, 41-49.

Where is the organization man? *Harvard Business Review, 41*(6), 53-61.

With M. Haire & E.E. Ghiselli. Psychological research on pay: An overview. *Industrial Relations, 3*, 3-8.

Job attitudes in management: IV. Perceived deficiencies in need fulfillment as a function of size of company. *Journal of Applied Psychology, 47*, 386-397.

1964

With E.E. Lawler. The effects of "tall" vs. "flat" organization structures on managerial job satisfaction. *Personnel Psychology, 17*, 135-148.

With M.M. Henry. Job attitudes in management: V. Perceptions of the importance of certain personality traits as a function of job level. *Journal of Applied Psychology, 48*, 31-36.

With M.M. Henry. Job attitudes in management: VI. Perceptions of the importance of certain personality traits as a function of line vs. staff type of job. *Journal of Applied Psychology, 48*, 305-309.

Organizational Patterns of Managerial Job Attitudes. New York: American Foundation for Management Research.

1965

Organizational profile of the dissatisfied manager. *Personnal Administration, 28*(2), 6-11.

With E.E. Lawler. Properties of organizational structure in relation to job attitudes and job behavior. *Psychological Bulletin, 64*, 23-51.

With J. Siegel. Relationship of tall and flat organization structures to the satisfactions of foreign managers. *Personnel Psychology, 18*, 379-392.

1966

With M. Haire & E.E. Ghiselli. *Managerial thinking: An international study.* New York: Wiley.

Personnel management. *Annual Review of Psychology, 17*, 395-422.

With E.E. Lawler. Predicting managers' pay and their satisfaction with their pay. *Personnel Psychology, 19*, 363-373.

With F.A. Heller. Perceptions of managerial needs and skills in two national samples. *Occupational Psychology, 40*, 1-13.

With R.E. Miles & J.A. Craft. Leadership attitudes among public health officials. *American Journal of Public Health, 56*, 1990-2005.

With R.E. Miles. Leadership training: Back to the classroom? *Personnel, 43*(4), 27-35.

1967

With V.F. Mitchell. Comparative study of need satisfactions in military and business hierarchies. *Journal of Applied Psychology, 51*, 139-144.

With E.E. Lawler. Antecedent attitudes of effective managerial performance. *Organizational Behavior and Human Performance, 2*, 122-142.

With E.E. Lawler. The effect of performance on job satisfaction. *Industrial Relations, 7*, 20-28.

With V.F. Mitchell. Comparative managerial role perceptions in military and business hierarchies. *Journal of Applied Psychology, 51*, 449-452.

1968

With E.E. Lawler. *Managerial attitudes and performance*. New York: Irwin.

With E.E. Lawler. What job attitudes tell about motivation. *Harvard Business Review, 46*(1), 118-126.

With D.I. Slobin & S.H. Miller. Forms of address and social relations in a business organization. *Journal of Personality and Social Psychology, 8*, 289-293.

With H. Sutton. A study of the grapevine in a governmental organization. *Personnel Psychology, 21*, 223-230.

With E.E. Lawler & A. Tenenbaum. Managers' attitudes toward interaction episodes. *Journal of Applied Psychology, 52*, 432-439.

With J.R. Hackman. Expectancy theory predictions of work effectiveness. *Organizational Behavior and Human Performance, 3*, 417-426.

1969

Effects of task factors on job attitudes and behavior. (A Symposium) I. Introduction. *Personnel Psychology, 22*, 415-418.

1970

With J. Van Maanen. Task accomplishment and the management of time. In B.M. Bass, R. Cooper, & J.A. Haas (Eds.), *Managing for task accomplishment* (pp. 180-192). Lexington, MA: D.C. Heath and Co.

1973

Turning work into nonwork: The rewarding environment. In M.D. Dunnette (Ed.), *Work and Nonwork in the year 2001* (pp. 113-133). Monterey, CA: Brooks-Cole.

With R.M. Steers. Organizational, work, and personal factors in employee turnover and absenteeism. *Psychological Bulletin, 80*, 151-176.

1974

With R.E. Miles. Motivation and management. In J.W. McGuire (Ed.), *Contemporary management: Issues and miewpoints* (pp. 545-570). Englewood Cliffs, NJ: Prentice-Hall.

With R.M. Steers. The role of task-goal attributes in employee performance. *Psychological Bulletin, 81*, 434-452.

Motivation theory as it relates to professional updating. In *Proceedings of the XVII International Congress of Applied Psychology* (pp. 205-216). Brussels, Belgium: Editest.

Communication: Structure and process. In H.R. Fromkin & J.J. Sherwood (Eds.), *Integrating the organization* (pp. 216-246). New York: Macmillan.

With R.T. Mowday & R. Dubin. Unit performance, situational factors, and employee attitudes in spatially separated work units. *Organizational Behavior and Human Performance, 12*, 231-248.

With R.M. Steers, R.T. Mowday, & P.V. Boulian. Organizational commitment, job satisfaction and turnover among psychiatric technicians. *Journal of Applied Psychology, 59*, 603-609.

With K.H. Roberts, C.A. O'Reilly, & G.E. Bretton. Organizational theory and organizational communication: A communication failure? *Human Relations, 27*, 501-524.

With R. Dubin, E.F. Stone, & J.E. Champoux. Implications of differential job perceptions. *Industrial Relations, 13*, 265-273.

1975

With E.E. Lawler & J.R. Hackman. *Behavior in organizations*. New York: McGraw-Hill.

With K.H. Roberts. Communication in organizations. In M.D. Dunnette (Ed.), *Handbook of industrial and organizational psychology* (pp. 1553-1589). Chicago: Rand-McNally.

With E.F. Stone. Job characteristics and job attitudes: A Multivariate study. *Journal of Applied Psychology, 60*, 57-64.

1976

With W.J. Crampon & F.J. Smith. Organizational commitment and managerial turnover: A longitudinal study. *Organizational Behavior and Human Performance, 15*, 87-98.

With R. Dubin & J.E. Champoux. Central life interests and organizational commitment of blue-collar workers. *Administrative Science Quarterly, 20*, 411-421.

Leadership symposium: Introduction. *Organizational Dynamics, 4*, 2-5.

1977

With K.H. Roberts. (Eds.). *Communication in organizations*. New York: Penguin.

With E.F. Stone & R.T. Mowday. Higher order need strengths as moderators of the job scope-job satisfaction relationship. *Journal of Applied Psychology, 62*(4), 466-471.

With F.J. Smith. What do executives really think about their organizations? *Organizational Dynamics* (Autumn), 68-80.

1978

With R.T. Mowday & E.F. Stone. Employee characteristics as predictors of turnover among female clerical employees in two organizations. *Journal of Vocational Behavior, 12.*

With E.F. Stone. On the use of incumbent-supplied job-characteristics data. *Perceptual and Motor Skills, 46*, 751-758.

1979

With R.T. Mowday & R.M. Steers. The measurement of organizational commitment. *Journal of Vocational Behavior, 14*, 224-247.

With R.T. Mowday & E.F. Stone. The interaction of personality and job scope in predicting turnover. *Journal of Vocational Behavior, 15*, 78-89.

1980

With D.L. Madison, R.W. Allen, P.A. Renwick & B.T. Mayes. Organizational politics: An exploration of managers' perceptions. *Human Relations, 33*(2), 79-100.

With R.W. Allen, D.L. Madison, P.A. Renwick, & B.T. Mayes. Organizational politics: Tactics and characteristics of its actors. *California Management Review, 22*(1), 77-83.

With D.R. Dalton, G.J. Fielding, M.J. Spendolini, & W.D. Todor. Structure and performance: A critical review. *Academy of Management Review, 5*(1), 49-84.

With H.L. Angle. Manager-organization linkages: The impact of changing work environments. In K.D. Duncan, M.M. Gruneberg, & D. Wallis (Eds.), *Changes in working life* (pp. 269-293). London: Wiley.

1981

With R.W. Allen & H.L. Angle. The politics of upward influence in organizations. In L.L. Cummings & B.M. Staw (Eds.), *Research in organizational behavior* (Vol. 3, pp. 108-149). Greenwich, CT: JAI Press.

With D.M. Krackhardt, J. McKenna, & R.M. Steers. Supervisory behavior and employee turnover: A field experiment. *Academy of Management Journal, 24*(2), 249-259.

With D.R. Dalton & D.M. Krackhardt. Functional turnover: An empirical assessment. *Journal of Applied Psychology, 66*(6), 716-721.

1982

With R.T. Mowday & R.M. Steers. *Employee-organization linkages: The psychology of commitment, absenteeism and turnover.* New York: Academic Press.

With J.L. Perry. Factors affecting the context for motivation in public organizations. *Academy of Management Review, 7*(1), 89-98.

1983

With J.R. Hackman & E.E. Lawler III. (Eds.). *Perspectives on behavior in organizations* (2nd ed.). New York: McGraw-Hill.

With R.W. Allen. *Organizational influence processes.* Scott, Foresman.

With D.R. Dalton & D.M. Krackhardt. First appearances are deceiving: The impact of teller turnover in banking. *Journal of Bank Research, 14*, 184-192.

1985

With D.M. Krackhardt. When friends leave: A structural analysis of the relationship between turnover and stayers' attitudes. *Administrative Science Quarterly, 30*, 242-261.

With W.B. Stevenson & J.L. Pearce. The concept of 'coalition' in organization theory and research. *Academy of Management Review, 10*, 256-268.

1986

With D.M. Krackhardt. The snowball effect: Turnover embedded in communication networks. *Journal of Applied Psychology, 71*, 50-55.

With J.L. Pearce & W.B. Stevenson. Coalitions in the organizational context. In R.J. Lewicki, B.H. Sheppard, & M.H. Bazerman (Eds.), *Research on Negotiation in Organizations* (Vol. 1, pp. 97-115). Greenwich, CT: JAI Press.

With J.L. Pearce. Employee responses to formal appraisal feedback. *Journal of Applied Psychology, 71*, 211-218.

1987

With F.M. Jablin, L.L. Putnan, & K.A. Roberts. (Eds.). *Handbook of organizational communication.* Beverly Hills, CA: Sage.

1988

With L.E. McKibbin. *Management education and development: Drift or thrust into the 21st century?* New York: McGraw-Hill.

1991

With R.M. Steers. *Motivation and work behavior* (5th ed.). New York: McGraw-Hill.

With J.S. Black. Managerial behaviors and job performance: A successful manager in Los Angeles may not succed in Hong Kong. *Journal of International Business Studies, 22*, 99-113.

NOTE

1. "Differential Self-perceptions of Management Personnel and Line Workers" (1958); "The Effects of Top and Middle Management Sets on the Ghiselli Self-description Inventory" (1959); "Self-perceptions of First-level Supervisors Compared with Upper-management Personnel and With Operative Line Workers" (1959); "Relationships Between a Top-middle Management Self-description Scale and Behavior in a Group Situation" (1959); "A Self-description Scale Measuring Sociometric Popularity Among Workers" (1960).

The Academic As Artist: Personal and Professional Roots

EDGAR H. SCHEIN

This essay will be divided into two parts. In the first part, I want to explore the connection between my academic work and my background. In the second part, I speculate a bit more about the nature of creativity and how it plays itself out in a career.

BACKGROUND

I come from a mixed ethnic background. My father was a Hungarian living in the part of Slovakia that later merged into Czechoslovakia and was a Czech citizen. His family had moved from Germany several generations earlier. His father was a small town banker, but my father's interests went toward science. He was educated at Heidelberg University and later obtained a Ph.D. at the University of Zurich in experimental physics.

My mother was the only daughter of a German civil engineer who was working in Saxony. She too was interested in physics and ended up at the University of Zurich where they met, fell in love and got married in 1927. I was born there in 1928 and spent six years in Zurich while my father finished his degree and had a Dozentship at the university.

In those days the Swiss did not offer jobs to foreigners so in 1933 my father was faced with pursuing his academic career elsewhere, with the best choices being either China or the Soviet Union because those two countries were building their science establishment and offering excellent jobs to young academics. He chose to run an institute in Odessa where we spent from 1934 to 1936. The Stalin purges were beginning at that time and my parents became aware that even foreigners were no longer secure. They decided to leave the Soviet Union and relocate for the time being in Czechoslovakia where I attended a year of formal school. My base language was German, but I had learned Russian on the playground and became fairly proficient in Czech as well.

My father had tendencies toward what Kurt Lewin later identified as the "self-hating Jew." He had married a Lutheran and became essentially agnostic, denying his own Jewishness. He always saw it as a handicap and, in later years, even advised me to change my name to something less obviously Jewish. He did not go so far as many of his colleagues of those times who converted to Catholicism, but he felt very unsafe as a Jew.

As Hitler became more of a menace in Europe, my father realized he would have to leave and sought his fortune in the United States where he obtained a fellowship to the University of Chicago and started his career all over again in his mid-thirties. He became a full professor within 10 years and always talked about the "essence" of the United States being that everyone had to start at the bottom, but there was no constraint on moving up the ladder if one had talent. He felt very grateful to the University of Chicago and his mentors for allowing him the opportunity to show what he could do, and reminded me often of this aspect of America.

In early 1938 my mother and I left Prague to wait in Zurich for six months while my father made arrangements, including the obtaining of loans from his one older brother who was a successful businessman in Bolivia. He too had emigrated in the mid-1930s. We arrived in the United States in 1938 and settled in Hyde Park, the neighborhood in which the University of Chicago was located. Since I knew no English, I was put back two grades in school for a semester, but I learned the language fairly rapidly so caught up with my age group soon enough.

The thing I remember most about my socialization into the U.S. culture was the importance of good physical coordination that made it possible to participate in schoolyard sports. I happened to be pretty good with my hands so could learn to play baseball. All of the people who became real friends were originally acquaintances made during these ball games at recesses. I noticed that other immigrant kids with less coordination were physically and socially isolated in a way that I never had to endure.

Public school in Hyde Park was fun and profitable. Hyde Park High had a good reputation, some excellent teachers, and a strong record for getting their graduates into good colleges. I had high grades and entered the University of Chicago in 1945 at the tail end of the Hutchins experiment in general education. This meant four courses per year for two years followed by a degree called Bachelor of Philosophy (Ph.B.). The idea was that one would then go straight into a graduate school, but most of the other schools were not buying this concept so doing a more traditional "major" still seemed necessary.

I did not know what field I wanted to pursue so decided to take some more general education and try my hand at my father's field of physics. This was an especially good time to take the elementary course because it was taught by Enrico Fermi himself and the lectures were truly inspiring. The trouble was I could never do the problems so by mid-semester I was actually flunking the course, leading to my first experience in major negotiation. The drop date for the course had passed so I was facing the unacceptable situation of disgracing the family name by having an F in physics on my record. I made the instructor feel so sorry for me that he found a way to bend the rules to let me drop the course. My foray into physics ended quietly and decisively.

During this third year of college I also tried a psychology course which was taught by Carl Rogers and was, at that time, promulgating the Rogerian therapeutic approach very heavily. I still remember how my classmates and I caricatured the nondirective approach by mirroring responses back to each other ad nauseum, thinking at the time that this was surely the silliest thing we had ever encountered. However, psychology interested me, and it gave me the illusion that I was making a decisive break with my father's profession, something I felt I needed to do. It was only later that I realized that by becoming a professor I was mostly not breaking away at all. But at least psychology was different from physics.

I should mention that the excitement of academia became obvious to me even then because I was growing up in the midst of the group of physicists who were smashing the atom and creating nuclear fission. My father was a cosmic ray physicist who never participated in the atom bomb work and was strongly against it, but he knew the whole group who later went to Los Alamos, and I was able to see first hand the brilliance of theoretical physicists (a fact that Anne Roe later documented in her study of eminent scientists, *The Making of a Scientist* [Dodd, Mead, 1953]).

A vivid memory from a few years later will illustrate the point. I wrote a 300 page doctoral dissertation which was a history of the concept of imitation and the report of a fairly complex experiment showing a generalization gradient from a situation in which army inductees first learned to imitate one person in a problemsolving situation and then were tested to see whether or not they would continue to imitate on three tasks of decreasing similarity. They did learn to imitate and the response did generalize as a function of the similarity of tasks.

My father was very proud of the dissertation so he insisted on leaving it on the coffee table whenever we had a party. At one of these parties Enrico Fermi picked it up and started to leaf through it for about 10 minutes. At the end of that time he called me aside and asked a series of questions that were deeper and more consequential than any I had ever been asked about the thesis. This was a clear case in point of what Anne Roe later reported, that the theoretical physicists seemed to be intellectually the deepest and broadest of her sample of eminent scientists.

Social Psychology and Graduate School

I decided during my junior year at Chicago that social psychology was "it," only to discover that there was very little depth in that area in Chicago. So I transferred to Stanford and crammed an entire major into four quarters by taking every single psychology course they offered. The people who influenced me most at that time were Ernest Hilgard and Paul Farnsworth. To this day I consider my courses in learning theory to be one of the core foundations of my knowledge of psychology. My current work on organizational culture is still heavily influenced by learning theory.

The other major influence on me came from Harry Helson who was visiting Stanford in 1948-49. He had just finished his work on adaptation level theory and was interested in testing the ideas in the social realm with such things as judgments of weight, following the classic demonstrations of social influence that had been published by Muzafer Sherif. For my master's thesis at Stanford I did an experiment in which the subjects stuck one hand into a closed box, lifted weights and then judged their degree of "heaviness." Confederates were used to "anchor" the scales, and we were able to show that in this social realm Helson's predictions about the effects of anchors would hold up very well. In other words, what was judged heavy or light depended more on what the confederates said than on the absolute weights. This was an exciting time, but again, I had used up the resources in my environment so needed to go elsewhere for my Ph.D.

The two best choices in 1949 were Michigan and Harvard. I was admitted to both, agonized over where to go and chose Harvard in the end because the Department of Social Relations had just been formed. This would give me access to a broader faculty. To be able to take courses with Harry Murray, Gordon Allport, Sam Stouffer, Clyde and Florence Kluckhohn, Jerry Bruner, Dick Solomon, Pitirim Sorokin, Freed Bales, and Talcott Parsons was an opportunity not to be missed, and I never regretted taking it. In fact, I feel that this interdisciplinary program has been one of the most powerful forces shaping my subsequent view of the field of organizational psychology. I became deeply rooted in social psychology, but through fellow graduate students and faculty, I also developed a deep appreciation of clinical psychology, sociology and anthropology which is showing up in my work today more and more.

Opportunistic Military Service

In the early fifties there was still a possibility of being drafted, so during my second year in graduate school I joined the Army Clinical Psychology

Program. This gave me officer status and pay while completing my Ph.D., and guaranteed that my three "payback" years in the regular army would be professionally relevant. I was also required both by Harvard and the army program to do a one-year clinical internship, a requirement I fulfilled at the Walter Reed Army Institute of Research. My thesis data were gathered in the army where I could insert my experiment into the regular induction testing process, thus guaranteeing an ample supply of subjects who showed up on time and were suitably "naive."

Finishing Graduate School and the First MIT Connection

During my year back at Harvard for dissertation writing (1952) I took several seminars at MIT, especially one given by Alex Bavelas where I was first exposed to Hal Leavitt's research on communication networks, and Bavelas's research on one-way, two-way communication. I found these to be absolutely fascinating and creative experiments, and I found Bavelas to be one of the most stimulating people I had ever met. This fact is important in that it predisposed me toward MIT while still in graduate school.

I took two important messages from graduate school. From Gordon Allport I learned how important it is to put things into historical context and how crucial it is to be able to write. Allport put it very simply—"If you can't write it, you don't know it." My other thesis adviser was Richard Solomon who instilled in me a deep respect for good experimentation, and a desire to look for interesting problems—where results would affect both theory and practice. Solomon at the time was trying to devise an experiment to determine whether dogs only felt shame (e.g., when forced to defecate in a forbidden area), or whether they could feel guilt. That is, would they show signs of fear, and so forth only if they knew their misdemeanor had been observed (shame) or would they show it even in private (guilt). There was no evidence of guilt in spite of heroic efforts by Solomon to instill a Freudian conscience in dogs.

The Walter Reed Years

The next major life event was to be assigned to the Neuropsychiatry Division of the Walter Reed Institute of Research, a multidisciplinary research unit under the direction of David Rioch. Rioch was a psychiatrist who had been heavily influenced by Harry Stack Sullivan and was an active proponent of the interpersonal theory of psychiatry. His own work with schizophrenics was highly creative and he was a champion of interdisciplinary work, so he was building the group on a very broad base.

Opportunistic Creativity—Research on POWs

As I look back on my career, it seems, on the one hand, that I had incredible luck in being at the right place at the right time, but, on the other hand, I also wonder whether I had already learned to seize the moment, to turn an opportunity into a creative output. Doing my dissertation research with Army inductees was perhaps an obvious first instance. A more relevant example is a set of events that occurred while at Walter Reed.

I was busy in 1953 formulating a program of leadership experiments built on the Bavelas-Leavitt model. In the midst of this I received a telegram to report to Travis Airforce Base within 48 hours for an overseas assignment to be explained once I was en route. I found out that the United States had just signed an armistice agreement with the North Korean and Chinese Communists, and there was to be a major exchange of prisoners of war.

The military had learned from "Operation Little Switch," the exchange of sick and wounded prisoners nine months earlier, that many of them had "collaborated with the enemy," signed false confessions of germ warfare, and in other ways behaved in ways that suggested they had been "brainwashed." This term was introduced by the journalist Edward Hunter as an adaptation of the Chinese communist concept that all prisoners and members of the society had to "cleanse their minds" of bourgeois middle class concepts and adopt communist concepts. There was ample evidence that the Chinese had, during their long march, developed indoctrination, confession induction, and "thought reform" to a high degree, and were applying these methods to all prisoners under their control.

The military did not know what kind of emotional and mental shape the repatriates would be in, so it was not safe to fly them directly home. Instead, they would be put on ships for a sixteen day ocean voyage during which teams of psychologists, psychiatrists, and social workers would diagnose and treat them. To accomplish this task for 3,000 or so repatriates required the use of all available professionals from all three services. We were all flown directly to Tokyo and then on to Inchon, South Korea to board a boat home.

As luck would have it, my boat was delayed for three weeks in Inchon so I had nothing to do. I watched truck loads of repatriates come into the center and noticed that they also had very little to do. So I set up a cubicle and started to grab people off the line at random and do a detailed interview concerning their POW experience. I experienced this as a spontaneous decision at the time, but, in retrospect, it fitted perfectly my concerns with imitation and social influence. Only here was a natural experiment to be studied and understood.

The spontaneous response to this opportunity was, of course, based on building up a readiness to understand these events and to interview people about emotional traumas they had suffered. I remember vividly advice that Rioch had given all of us that if one is trying to elicit information in an area that may be socially or emotionally sensitive, DO NOT ASK ABOUT IT. Instead, rely on a chronology, on a natural history of events and let the sensitive stuff come out in its own way. So I asked people to tell me in as much detail as they cared to about the circumstances of their capture and then what happened. In other words I encouraged them to tell their story in their own way, and found that this elicited enormous amounts of very personal information without ever threatening anyone. The degree to which repatriates confessed to behaviors that might have been judged as reprehensible, if one did not know the conditions in the prison camps, also suggested that they were not biasing their stories just to make themselves look good. Rather I got the impression that they were relieved to be able to tell someone what actually had happened.

It was not difficult to put these stories into a social psychological paradigm. The control of communication into the camps, the manipulation of interpersonal forces, the removal of leaders, and so forth, made it quite obvious how people had come to lose their judgment and make confessions, inform on their buddies, march in peace parades, and so on, without having to rely on the effects of physical torture, drugs, hypnosis, Pavlovian conditioning, or other esoteric techniques. In fact, it became quite plain to me that the Chinese genius was to use interpersonal forces as the primary influence technique with the threat of physical force being more in the background. I mention this because I needed my psychological background in order to make sense out of the mass of data that the POW stories revealed, and I later became a spokesperson for this more common sense way of looking at the Korean prisoner of war episode.

During the trip home I continued to interview repatriates so I had quite a sizeable data base to build on. In addition my colleagues and I gave tests and questionnaires to repatriates in order to enlarge our sample and to determine what some of the correlates were of being an extreme resister or collaborator. We were able to get from the military files the judgment of the military as to who had "resisted to a heroic degree" and who had "collaborated to a degree to warrant possible courtmartial," roughly 5 to 10 percent at each end of the distribution.

Our psychometric and background research revealed, by the way, that one could not predict collaboration. Rather, the profiles of both extreme groups resembled each other, and differed from the large middle group. We came to believe that most of the POWs tried to survive by laying low, adapting as best they could, and remaining passive. In contrast the group who felt they needed to do something very active, who needed to take a stand, tended to end up either in the resister or collaborator group. We could not find variables that would distinguish between those extreme groups ("A Prisoner of War Syndrome," 1956; "Distinguishing Characteristics," 1957).

Much of the next several years was taken up with analyzing data, writing the narrative account of the POW experience, sharing data and insights with others in the group such as Robert Lifton, a psychiatrist who became very active in research on "thought reform," and planning follow-up studies to explore further what I came to call "coercive persuasion." The essence of this idea is that if you can physically constrain someone to remain in a setting over which you have milieu control, it is not too hard to persuade them. What made brainwashing so powerful was the combination of physical coercion with sophisticated interpersonal persuasion techniques.

Lesson 1 from the Academic Marketplace

By mid-1954 I had distilled my data down to a reasonably well analyzed story and written it up as a 50-page paper. I sent it to the various social psychology journals and was told that the paper was too long and did not fit some of the ground rules for empirical research. My "method" was twenty intensive detailed interviews and several hundred short interviews plus cross-checks with other investigators who had talked to POWs. My confidence in the data rested most on the internal consistency of the stories and the degree to which they were replicated in other accounts.

After many months of frustration I asked Rioch what might be done and he suggested sending it to the journal *Psychiatry* which was known for occasionally carrying longer articles. To my joy they took the piece and it was published in 1956. Incidentally I had also published my thesis experiment in the *Journal of Abnormal and Social Psychology* (1954). I had received maybe a dozen reprint requests for my experiment; the requests for the POW story soon hit the hundreds. I got calls to give talks about the POWs, was asked to lecture in training programs, learned that books of readings wanted to reprint the piece including the prestigious Swanson, Newcomb, and Hartley *Readings in Social Psychology*. My colleagues at meetings complimented me on the clarity of the story, and my professional name became increasingly associated with what the POW experience taught us about group and interpersonal dynamics.

As I think back on this, it became clear to me that if one has something interesting to communicate in an area that people do not know about, they will appreciate it even if it does not fit our traditional research paradigms. It also taught me how important it is to find a publication outlet and how constricted the psychology profession was (and perhaps still is) when it comes to rules for publication in the so-called "refereed journals."

The Early MIT Years

My remaining two years (1955-56) at Walter Reed were spent on various projects, including a carefully designed experiment on the effects of sleep deprivation (I was still totally committed to the experimental paradigm) and thinking about how to continue research on the repatriates (1957). I met my wife at Walter Reed and we were married there in July 1956. This also marked the end of my military service, so Mary and I set out for Cambridge and MIT that same July.

How did I get to MIT? Luck or creative opportunism? In the year prior to my departure from Walter Reed I did the usual academic job searching and turned up an excellent offer at Cornell in social psychology. Out of the blue I also received a letter from Douglas McGregor offering me a job at MIT in the newly formed Graduate School of Management. I knew of McGregor from readings, and I had attended the fascinating seminar with Bavelas (he was still at MIT) so I became quite interested in the offer. I was curious how they had gotten my name and learned that Gordon Allport and McGregor were good friends and that Allport had suggested me upon learning that MIT wanted to build its management program on a disciplinary base, and, of course, social psychology would be one of the core disciplines.

I sensed that the decision between these two choices would be fateful and probably irreversible. If I turned down a traditional kind of department such as Cornell had, I would forever be cutting myself off from the mainstream of social psychology. MIT offered a chance to be creative, to help build a new department, and, of course, it was in Cambridge which I had come to love. I also wonder in retrospect how much I was influenced by the lessons mentioned above. Maybe I was better at "applied" or "clinical" work. Maybe my love of experiments was not that deep. Maybe I was responding to the market pull of what my readers were really interested in. This latter factor played a role in that I could have a part-time appointment in the Center for International Studies at MIT where I could continue research on coercive persuasion with government funds that were available for such research. In any case, I decided on MIT and have never regretted it. I feel that my career has evolved and broadened while the profession of social psychology has stagnated and narrowed.

Learning to Teach

Just as David Rioch influenced by example, so did Doug McGregor. I have often recounted the conversation I had with him soon after arrival at MIT about what to put in my basic course on social psychology for management students. Bavelas had taught this course before and I asked McGregor (Bavelas was away) for guidance. Doug said quite bluntly that it did not make any difference, that what was needed was my approach, and that I should figure out for myself what and how to teach. This message correlated with what Dean Edward Pennell Brooks had told me about the Sloan School. He didn't care what we did so long as it was a new approach, and so long as it was clearly different from the "school up the river." Innovation was the watchword of the day. The implicit message was that each of us had to stand on our own feet and develop our own style.

My wife reminds me occasionally that this kind of mandate was not easy to implement when we reminisce about the endless evenings during my first year as I was relearning social psychology, processing what was relevant to my own sense of management, overdesigning lectures, agonizing over my own insecurity in being in a first job in a professional school environment. I fell back on basic psychology and was quite academic in my approach, and was not shaken loose from this until two other sets of experiences intervened—attendance at a Bethel Human Relations workshop and feedback from Sloan Fellows.

I have never known whether McGregor sensed I was too stiff in my approach or whether it was simply a general strategy for all new assistant professors, but he "suggested" in 1957 that I should attend a T-group in Bethel and learn what that was all about. It was an incredibly potent experience for me that forever changed my view of my field. For the first time I had a chance to look at what really went on in groups and to work with colleagues who were more interested in the clinical reality of group behavior than in formal research such as what Freed Bales and others were working on in a laboratory setting. I became very involved with the National Training Labs, took their internship in 1958, and began to run T-groups in the various management programs that NTL offered. I found these totally absorbing and began, through these groups, to learn something about managers and management.

At about the same time McGregor asked me to co-teach with him the middle executive course for Sloan Fellows. During my class sessions and in the postmortems afterward I first began to learn what I was doing right and wrong in teaching. Masters level students tend to take what you give them, but if the Sloan Fellows did not like what they were being taught, they reacted immediately and forced a change in content or style. I had to learn to cull my material, to package it differently, to be more provocative and applied, to interact more openly with students, to share my values and feelings, and generally loosen up. I learned gradually that managers (and maybe everyone) learns partly through identification with the teacher, and that I had to be more open and "present" not merely a conduit for "knowledge."

McGregor also introduced me to consulting which made available another whole universe of data that I had not previously paid much heed. By being able to talk to managers about real problems, and to sense the consequences of intervening in an organization where real careers were involved, I got the sense that what really matters in organizations is often not reflected in the choice of research variables that our formal research projects often make. Furthermore, I learned from consulting experiences that real organizations are neither rational nor fair, so that many of our academic models of organizational life are in fact quite utopian. These ruminations raised the real question of whether what the research process often treated as "error variance" or "deviant cases" was, in fact, where the truth of the matter was to be found.

The reality that I was experiencing was captured much better by the sociologists, especially those of the Chicago school. My exposure to the Hawthorne studies as interpreted by George Homans, my direct contact with Erving Goffman, my reading of William F. Whyte's *Streetcorner Society* (University of Chicago Press, 1943), Donald Roy's "Banana Time" (*Human Organizations*, 1959-60), and other sociological classics from the worker strata seemed much more relevant than the formal management literature. The only management book that seemed to really have it right was Melville Dalton's *Men Who Manage* (Wiley, 1959), a book that is sadly missing from most contemporary reading lists.

But utopia was in the air, and, in 1960, McGregor came out with his classic *Human Side of Enterprise* (McGraw-Hill, 1960) and "Theory Y." What has always struck me about this intellectual tour de force was that McGregor knew very well what he was saying, but that the world still has not really understood it. He wanted people to pay attention to the consequences of their own assumptions about human nature. His observations of effective managers had revealed that those who had an optimistic view of human nature, who were able to trust others, could choose a leadership style that genuinely fit the task at hand. On the other hand, those managers who were cynical about people, who did not trust them, could only manage by carefully manipulating incentives, rewards, and controls. The Theory X manager, in other words, is less flexible and less able to involve others when that is appropriate.

What the world seemed to hear is a gigantic argument for participative management. So every manager or professor who had his or her doubts about participative management said that there was no evidence for Theory Y. They would usually trot out several examples of autocrats they knew who were quite effective as managers. Of course McGregor had never said that Theory Y always leads to participation, and he was the first to show examples of how Theory Y managers could and would behave autocratically when that was appropriate. But that part of his message was never heard, and to this day I get into debates about Theory X and Y on the basis of whether or not one should be autocratic or democratic. The real lesson gets lost—one should be aware of one's assumptions and their consequences. But back to my story.

Developing a Research Agenda

The Sloan School's message on research was very similar to the message on teaching—"You figure it out." I had brought with me a contract to continue POW research so I started with a major follow-up study of repatriates in the United States and a study of civilians who had been incarcerated and coercively persuaded to make dramatic confessions in mainland China prisons. Two years of this research produced my first book *Coercive Persuasion* (1961). I also continued some network type leadership research but soon found that it was neither very interesting to me, nor produced easily publishable results. My "tenure track" research early on, therefore, was mostly on coercive persuasion and had virtually nothing to do with management.

I did try to figure out how I could apply my knowledge to the management situation and, once again, luck or creative opportunism produced results. In the late 1950s a number of books appeared indicting American companies for indoctrinating their new managers and, thereby, undermining their creative capacity. Companies were cloning themselves and writers such as William H. Whyte (*The Organization Man* [Simon & Schuster, 1956]) did not like it.

I was aware that at Sands Point, New York, IBM managers were being trained to think like IBMers by some very powerful techniques and that at Crotonville, New York, General Electric had a big center labelled without apology the "GE Indoctrination Center." For example, here is how Sands Point worked. A manager would send a subordinate for three weeks of training. In addition to a few outside lectures the trainee would be given cases to analyze. The case presentations were then scored by IBM instructors for how closely they matched the IBM solution, as revealed by the instructor. Grades on successive cases were accumulated and the total program grade for each participant was sent back to the person who sponsored him. If one wanted to design an indoctrination program one could not do much better than this.

I also knew from the IBM Sloan Fellows in my class that sales training was like bootcamp with two weeks of round-the-clock classes, activities, and even group events such as songs. I still have a copy of the IBM songbook, and I find it ironic that when we now see Japanese or Korean companies engaged in these group events we envy them instead of remembering that we used to do all that stuff and gave it up for presumably good reasons.

In any case, out of these observations grew my research agenda. I would formally study the process by which companies indoctrinated their managers. Once again I could not get away from the influence issue—imitation, coercive persuasion, and now indoctrination. In my first publication along these lines I extrapolated from my POW studies and tried to show how the techniques used in prisons were very similar to the techniques used in companies, where the golden handcuffs, or the threat of job loss effectively created the coercion part of the coercive persuasion paradigm (1961).

What was particularly exciting at that time was the discovery that different methods of indoctrination throughout history and across a wide variety of organizations bore incredible similarity to each other. I developed a course on persuasion and attitude change that drew on the POW material, the book *The Nun's Story*, and various other literary materials that showed common themes. For example, the ability to "resist" was shown in the POW case to be very much a function of having an audience. The presence of that audience would make it unthinkable for the prisoner to do something that would violate the values shared with the audience. I was thrilled to learn when reading Charles Henry Lea's history of the Spanish Inquisition that heretics who were burned at the stake sometimes recanted and sometimes did not, and that the key determinant was the physical presence or absence of other members of the heretical sect. No one apparently confessed if it meant disgracing oneself in front of one's group.

The generality of many of the findings led to a zany thought for a comparative study which, unfortunately never got done. Phil Slater and I wondered how much fun it would be to compare the GE indoctrination center, Sing Sing prison, and the Maryknoll missionary order school for future missionaries, three institutions that were located only a few miles apart in Ossining, New York.

That study never materialized, but I did want to gather some respectable data on how alumni of our school would be indoctrinated into the various companies that they would enter. I had developed a pretty good attitude survey and showed that students, faculty, and businessmen had quite different attitudes, thus making it possible to track student attitudes toward the business point of view (1967). By following panels of alumni into their organizational careers and measuring their attitudes at various points in time it should be possible to document indoctrination and its effects.

Three panels were made up in the early 1960s and each person was thoroughly interviewed and tested during the final semester in school. One year later the attitude surveys were given to the peers and supervisor of each panellist as well as to him, and a follow-up interview was conducted to determine career events and socialization processes encountered.

The results were disappointing. People's attitudes moved all over the map and there was very little patterning in terms of the attitudes of the peers and supervisors. On the other hand I learned a great deal about early career socialization and, in the opportunistic spirit that seemed increasingly to characterize my intellectual development, wrote some articles on organizational socialization for a more applied audience (1963, 1964).

I revisited my panel five years later and found similarly diverse results so put that study aside until 1973 when I decided to reinterview all of the panelists. They each came to MIT and spent two to four hours giving me a detailed career history with reasons for each major change that they made. It was in these interviews that a major new concept emerged, one that was polarly opposite to my interests in indoctrination, but one that forced itself upon me by the data. I "discovered" in the 44 panelist stories the concept of "career anchor," the self-image built around self-perceived competencies, motives, and values that was learned through successive job experiences and that came to guide and constrain career choices and career aspirations (hence the metaphor of "anchor"). The whole research stream led to an analysis of how careers evolved and how difficult it was to match individual and organizational needs, leading to my book *Career Dynamics* (1978).

It was also very evident in these interviews that the panelists benefitted a great deal from their career self-analysis and that their self-image was strong but implicit. By making it more explicit, they clarified for themselves much of what they had done and why they had done it. These observations led me to structure future work on career anchors more in terms of a developmental tool rather than a selection concept. I found myself suddenly wanting to help people in their struggle with organizations in that I could see from my consulting experience how people's careers were mismanaged because of stereotypes that organizations had of what people wanted. At the same time people did not know how to express their wants in such a way that they could negotiate more appropriate career moves for themselves.

Parts of the original research instrument lent themselves very well to a classroom exercise, so I converted the research interview and some of the questionnaire items into a self-diagnostic instrument which, after several years of testing in workshops, was published as *Career Anchors: Discovering Your Real Values* and is now in its second edition (1985, 1990).

I thought that in these efforts I was on a new track but, in reality, I was responding to the same two issues: (1) how to understand more fully the relationship between the individual and the organization, and (2) how to make the most of the data that revealed themselves in my empirical efforts. The creative opportunism here was clear in that I had never set out to develop a training instrument, yet the feedback from students and employees who tried it was so overwhelmingly positive, that I could not resist exploiting what I had unwittingly stumbled into.

On the research front I continue to be interested in the longitudinal study and plan to reinterview my panel once again when they are 20 to 25 years into their careers. I have completed about 15 of these follow-ups with the major issue being "are career anchors stable or do they evolve and change through the course of a career?" So far the evidence is on the side of stability which should not be surprising if we think about the stability of the self-image in general.

Organizational Psychology, Organization Development and Process Consultation

My years at Bethel and my acquaintance with Richard Beckhard, Lee Bradford, and others in the NTL movement increasingly focused my attention on organizational phenomena during the 1960s. My basic research was on career development and socialization, but my consulting and my clinical experience was increasingly on organizational matters. In 1964 Roger

Holloway, a creative editor from Prentice-Hall, proposed that I write a short textbook on organizational psychology to be part of the new series of paperbacks they were publishing on psychology.

I resisted the idea of a textbook because I did not want to be obligated to cover the whole field but Holloway convinced me that I could just write 100 or so pages of what I thought was important. I agreed and found, to my surprise, that I could think integratively about these issues and write such a book (1965). Following Hal Leavitt's *Annual Review of Psychology* article on this topic, Bernie Bass and I wrote the first two textbooks with the title *Organizational Psychology*, and, thereby, contributed to the formation and evolution of this field. The second and third editions (1970, 1980) were increasingly difficult to write because the field expanded so rapidly, and the prospect of a fourth edition is in limbo because I am not sure I know any longer how to encompass what organizational psychology has become.

In the meantime, my interest in consulting developed and my close friendship with Warren Bennis and Dick Beckhard led to the concept of the paperback series on Organization Development. We saw that paperback series were increasingly displacing big textbooks, and we knew that the field of OD was very fragmented so the idea arose of letting some of its major practitioners speak for themselves in short volumes. Addison-Wesley bought the idea and we were launched on an enterprise that continues under Beckhard's and my editorship to this day, having produced more than 20 volumes thus far.

My own first volume titled *Process Consultation* was an effort to compensate for something that I had observed in McGregor's career. I had heard him tell many wonderful stories about his adventures as a consultant and his philosophy, but none of this was ever written down. I resolved that if I ever had consulting experiences I would attempt to document what I did and what I learned. I did not at the time realize the connection between (1) my emerging philosophy of low-key inquiry and helping clients to solve their own problems with (2) my initial exposure to psychology via the concepts of Carl Rogers. But there are, of course, strong connections and these were reinforced by the training philosophy learned in NTL. Groups responded much better to facilitative remarks than to directions and interpretations. My consulting style thus grew directly out of my group training style, and was reinforced by my experiences with clients. They clearly seemed to like it better if I helped them to think things out rather than to make recommendations to them.

Though *Process Consultation* was written to explain myself to my colleagues, I discovered that the book was really very useful to managers because they often had to function as process consultants to their bosses, subordinates, and peers. I found myself doing many workshops on this topic and increasingly using the philosophy underlying process consultation as a way of teaching managers. In 1987 I decided to revise and update the book, only to find that I had enough new things to say that it has now turned into a two volume enterprise (1987, 1988).

Focus on Culture and Organizations

My focus on culture reflected an evolution of the career and socialization research. I had been so pre-occupied with process that I had not really paid much attention to content. What exactly did new members of organizations have to learn when they were socialized? And what difference did culture make to management?

Mason Haire and others had done creative research on variations in management across cultures and I had opportunities in the 1960's to do overseas teaching and consulting, so I became increasingly conscious of culture as a variable. Several events focused me increasingly on this area in the late 1970s: (1) teaching at INSEAD in Fontainebleau; (2) an opportunity to lecture to and consult with a Swiss company; (3) a trip around the world during which I did lectures and workshops in Hawaii, Australia, Singapore, and Europe; and (4) a sabbatical semester at the management institute in Geneva (then called CEI).

The faculty at the CEI were very interested in research on culture and asked me to prepare several presentations for the faculty research seminar. These presentations forced me to focus and led to a long paper on culture that eventually became the outline for my book. As I look back on this, I am again reminded that often my writing started with outlining lectures and later expanding them into papers and eventually books. I am conscious of deliberately agreeing to give presentations, knowing that these will force me to focus on and think through a given area.

I saw in the culture book an opportunity to integrate a great deal of my thinking, and to write a book that would be academically complete in the sense of pulling together what knowledge we had about this topic. I did not abandon my need to be relevant to the practitioner, but I saw a real opportunity to make a contribution to the academic field and, therefore, put a great deal of effort into thinking this area out very carefully. In the second edition, which was published in 1992, I was able to focus the argument specifically on organizational subcultures because I realized that the real dilemmas that organizations face derive from subcultural conflicts. At the same time, subcultural diversity is one of the main sources of innovation and adaptive change.

Interpersonal Dynamics

This theme has been with me throughout the years and was reflected in some of my most favorite writing. During the mid-1960s Warren Bennis and I found ourselves constantly stimulating each other around the issue of what really goes on between people and in groups. We found with our colleague Dave Berlew and our student Fritz Steele that we shared an interest in trying to teach this material through vivid, non-academic, literary material. This led to a hypothetical project of what would a reading list look like if each of us threw in our favorite articles.

This reading list, developed over the course of a year, looked so exciting that we decided we might try to publish these articles in a book of readings, supplemented with a series of analytical essays that each of us would prepare on some aspect of interpersonal dynamics. It turned out that publishers were interested, so our little project became a book which went through four editions and still, in retrospect, represents some of the most fun and interesting material that we had ever dealt with (*Interpersonal Dynamics* [Dorsey, 1973]; *Essays in Interpersonal Dynamics* [1979]). Not only was it creative and fun to find interesting articles but the team effort of sharing our insights with each other and later with John Van Maanen has left nothing but nostalgic memories of how much fun academic teamwork can be.

THEMES AND QUESTIONS: HOW DOES IT ALL FIT TOGETHER?

Several things strike me as I review the events of the past, and each bears some comment. First, I have a refugee mentality. Second, I am to some degree an intellectual opportunist. Third, I have a core conflict around autonomy vs. dependence. Each of these can be retrospectively "explained" by my early background, but I am also aware that unknown amounts of retrospective falsification occur in that process. In any case, let me spin out a few fantasies about what might be going on and begin to relate all this to the theme of the academic as artist.

There is an obvious concern in all of my work about the tension between dependence and autonomy, the power of the organization to impose itself on the individual vs. the power of the individual to protect him or herself and remain "free." I remember being intrigued from the beginning of graduate school with the Sherif and Asch studies showing how the group could influence the individual. This led directly to my masters and doctoral research on social influence and imitation, and continued with the studies of brainwashing and corporate socialization. I can only speculate that this "obsession" with social influence must be related to having had to make several transitions into new cultures, in two cases under stressful conditions.

But I felt basically successful in my adaptations to the new cultures I entered so was also very aware that it is possible for the individual not only to remain free, but to be creative in his adaptation. In fact, the contrast between my ability to adapt and the degree to which I saw others who had emigrated struggle, gave me some confidence in my own adaptive skills. I think I always felt that I could turn whatever situation arose into something useful, hence a developing self-image of a creative opportunist. Having had to learn how to get along in several new cultures sharpened my listening and observational skills. I had to figure out not only what was going on and to learn the local language, but also how to maintain my autonomy in situations that were very potent and overwhelming. When I later listened to stories from career occupants about their ability to maintain their self-image in the face of corporate socialization pressures, it was easy for me to relate to their dilemmas.

I can see how my interest in the research on career anchors and my evolving consulting and teaching styles reflect these same issues. Being a process consultant and a teacher who prefers experiential project oriented courses always permitted me to be influential without totally committing myself to the organization, the class, or the social situation. It is the marginality that one learns as a refugee turned into conceptual work that illuminates certain aspects of the tension between organizations and individuals.

Creative opportunism is perhaps the inevitable result when one tries to work out the tension described above in a way that utilizes talents. The organizational and interpersonal world is full of interesting problems to be analyzed and described and clarified, and the dependence/independence tension is endemic to all human relationships, so it is not difficult to study whatever happens to be at hand, but to study it with a certain frame of mind and a certain bias that reflects my underlying tensions.

The refugee mentality also comes into play in the passion for clarity. Though I am quite tolerant of ambiguity, I find that my passion is to understand and to clarify. I am always seeking theoretical simplifications that make sense, that explain a phenomenon, that make it clear to a student or reader. And this passion for clarification has proved to be functional in that I have discovered a talent in this arena. The most consistent feedback I get on my writing is that I am somehow able to make things clear.

With this passion to make things clear goes a related passion to make them clear to the layman. For reasons that I do not entirely understand, I have never been interested in theory for theory's sake. I find I always want to go down on the abstraction ladder and use examples, metaphors, or other simplifications to make theoretical points. In other words, parsimony is very important to me, but high level of abstraction is not. I believe that the interpersonal world (and underworld) is basically simple if we can decipher its basic logic. I have always loved the work of Everett Hughes and Erving Goffman because of their ability to simplify and clarify extremely complex phenomena.

The Academic as Artist

I want to close this autobiography with some thoughts on the metaphor of the artist. As I think about graduate training and the models of the professoriat that I see reflected in many of my colleagues, I get a sense of discouragement and unreality. There is something very limiting and depressing in the traditional model of science with its emphasis on precision, operational definitions, the hypothetico-deductive method, quantification, statistical manipulation, and deadly dry reporting (of generally only positive results).

When I think of work that has really influenced me, it is rarely work that has been done in that tradition. When I think of work of my own that seems to have influenced others, I reach the same conclusion—the traditional mode is not where one makes impact. On the other hand, I have always been very excited by seeing a phenomenon in a new context. For sociologists to see fundamental interpersonal relationships in an economic exchange model and a dramaturgical model is incredibly exciting because it lays out complex phenomena in terms of a simple understandable metaphor, and, thereby, reveals an immediately appreciable underlying structure that provides instant insight. This is the model of science that turns me on, and it is a model that is much better described by what artists do.

What made my research on brainwashing interesting to people is that I did not rely on abstract esoteric explanations, but showed how relatively understandable social processes could produce a milieu that would be extremely coercive in its effect. What happened in the POW camps and Chinese mainland prisons was not so different from what we know about social processes that occur in families, schools, prisons, and corporations.

The ability to represent something that is meaningful to others, that carries a message, is partly an artistic skill. We tend to overestimate the intuitive and creative side of artistry and to forget how much else goes into this. A good artist is not a creative dabbler. A good artist must have knowledge, skill, vision, and something to say. He or she must know about the human eye, color, the chemistry of paint and the qualities of other materials. Artists must have the skills of drawing, the eye-hand coordination necessary to manipulating whatever materials are being used, and the ability to judge their own work in order to know when to stop. And, finally, the good artist must have a message, a vision, something to say, some point he or she is trying to make or some phenomenon he or she is trying to make visible to others.

Artists have to go to school, have to train, have to develop. They do not spring upon the scene in a sudden creative burst. Artists are forever solving the problems of how to render something, how to express their inner vision in such a way that others get the appropriate response. Artists learn from each other and influence each other. The problems they wrestle with are sometimes solved by others and the solutions are incorporated into their own work. In the end, the quality of their work is judged by the degree to which it survives and communicates something important to the audience.

I find this an appealing model for the behavioral scientist working with human systems. Human personalities, groups, and organizations are infinitely complex, and our only hope of understanding them lies in our ability to find the right simplifications that will make essential phenomena clear and understandable. Our readers must have the shock of recognition when they read our work, and they must be able to see what we have described in other contexts. This goal cannot be achieved by the hypothetico-deductive method. That model is perhaps appropriate at a later stage in some sciences in the context of verification. I feel we are still in the context of discovery where good observation and good rendering of what we have observed is crucial. And it is entirely possible that in the human sciences the hypothetico-deductive method with tight operational definitions and precise quantification of variables will never be possible or desirable.

I see "artistry" in my own work at several levels. My insights into phenomena came unexpectedly and often at times when I was not thinking about that phenomenon at all. It was therefore always wise for me to juggle several intellectual domains at the same time instead of working on one thing until it was finished. I see in my writing the same kinds of "problems" of how to render something that artists talk about. I have creative bursts when everything seems to click and a paper or part of a chapter just flows in an uninterrupted way. I am very concerned about how my work comes across to others, but what I find I am most proud of is when I have had a theoretical insight and have been able to articulate it in a way that satisfies me even if no one else likes it or gets anything out of it.

What is ultimately exciting about the field of organizational psychology/sociology is that it does provide a context for discovery, that one can get students and clients to share in that excitement because the phenomena are complex and multifaceted, but not entirely out of reach. If we can improve our observational skills and learn to render what we see and hear in intelligible terms we will not only help ourselves but others as well. That seems to make it all worthwhile.

POSTSCRIPT

Some Thoughts on Intellectual Continuity

In tackling the task of writing some autobiographical notes, I am struck most by the fact that we retrospectively falsify. What now strikes me about my life and career are those things that make my current life meaningful and consistent, that justify my current image of myself. An essay like this one can then be either an exercise in exploring my own perceptions of how I got here, or can attempt to go beyond this by locating some data that are free of my perceptual distortions. I happened upon two pieces of such data recently and have decided, thereupon, to attempt to be a bit more objective about myself. Both of these were written while in Graduate School in 1950-51. I have included them unedited.

On Creativity

The fundamental fact of all biological functioning is that of seeking. In the lower animal forms this takes the form of seeking food, a mate, safety, and so on, and all creative energy that was available to the animal was spent in such purely biological pursuits. Man, however, has through civilization achieved a state where the pursuit of biological necessities expends far less energy or time which has freed much of his energy for other things. This energy has as its basic character a seeking expressive quality... it must find something, it can not simply be run off in random activity. Such seeking naturally leads to striving for understanding of the world about us. Primitive man, when he first obtained some leisure no doubt turned his energy to simple reflection, and such reflection made possible questioning of the world about him, its functions and purposes. Man, through reflection, began to see himself in relation to his environment, to see himself somewhat objectively, to see what he was doing: seeking food, shelter, and a mate. This very reflection made it possible for him to evaluate such activities and to entertain the possibilities of other ways of fulfilling the same functions. It was possible to think of obtaining food by some method different from that empirically worked out under the pressure of necessity. New methods in the process of being worked out alone and with others thus served as a channel for the creative energy which leisure had released, and such new ways when they showed themselves to be more effective than older ways were adopted and routinized and institutionalized. The further the process of institutionalization proceeded, however, the more life became routinized and simplified, again freeing creative energies for reflection and further seeking. Such processes made it possible for man to see his system of institutions in some kind of perspective and gave him the power to analyze and evaluate them in the same way as earlier methods of solving his simple problems of living had been attacked.

The second piece was untitled.

What do you think... is life indeed pointless, what are social functions and rituals but ways to routinize and conventionalize us to the point where our creativity is completely stifled. What is the outlet for creative forces... we must seek abortive solutions such as dabbling in art or literature without being given the time or opportunity to develop our talents in any of these fields. Our daily work routine eats up all our extra energy and leaves us with an unfulfilled desire to create something, to express ourselves, to leave our mark on this world in some way other than as a member of a complete bureaucratic system of organization in which our product is lost in the stream of the whole. What chance is there for us to find some form for our creativity, some test of our talents, some response to our efforts? Who is there to encourage, praise, teach? We must plod on, our own worst critics, trying desperately to find some human contact to whom our work means something other than a ritual form. We do not merely want the recognition that we have created something if it communicates nothing. The fact of creation without its actual acceptance is nothing but the conventionalized crumb thrown out by the bureaucratic system to the masses who need some solace or consolation to make up for their prostitution of their individualities to the group's will. Who wants merely such crumbs or such pats on the head for feeble efforts to find himself in the social labyrinth? Who is satisfied with communicating nothing more than form, no content or meaning? Who is willing to give up the struggle to achieve some kind of closeness with others when the barrier of routinization and standardization ever widens the gap between humans? Who is willing to be merely a position in a system, a role, a status, a function? The greatest danger of all lies in the fact that we may forget or lose awareness of what we are trying to communicate. Not merely our actions

> but our reactions come under the pressure of convention and ritual and all that is left of our creative urge and need for expression is the motivational force, the power, the need, the urge, the energy without any content to serve as its vehicle. We may struggle to express but there is nothing to express, there is nothing to communicate to another. Yet we know that there must be, if the urge is so strong, but that the content has been obscured, perpective has been lost, and we no longer know what to say or how to say it. We have lost the connections between feelings and the ways to express these feelings; our words and gestures are empty forms devoid of personal content, carriers only of rituals and rules. We turn to other forms, but we do not know whether we are making contact with another. For we have lost the power of recognizing meaning just as we have lost the power to communicate meaning. We struggle mutually to establish contact, but we talk past each other. Our aims are the same but we have lost the power to implement them, and perhaps out of this grows the bitter consequence that we do not even recognize our aims to be the same. And then the effort to understand another may itself be lost and with it the chance to make the contact that we long for so desperately. The system steps in once again to make the personal impersonal and to restrict human ties to organizational lines. What has happened to sympathy ...the willingness to assume that another has something to communicate, the power to create something that is good and useful and personal. Something that will enable [us] to make contact with him as he really is rather than the shell which is his position in the system. Where is the patience necessary to understanding another? Why have we become so asymmetrical... we try to communicate and want patience and sympathy from another, but we have not enough ourselves to permit another to express himself. Thus we go about mutually defeating the very purposes which we are trying so hard to implement.

AND NOW WHAT?

The phenomenon that will most influence organizations of the future is unarguably information technology. But the implementation of this technology has proven to be problematic in almost every case studied. I believe this is primarily due to the fact that the culture of this occupation, its basic assumptions about information and human organizations, are to some degree incompatible with the assumptions of management. I want to turn my interest in culture to this problem by examining such an occupational subculture and assessing its consequences globally and within the United States.

PUBLICATIONS

1954

The effect of reward on adult imitative behavior. *Journal of Abnormal and Social Psychology, 49*, 389-395.
The effect of reward on adult imitative behavior. *Journal of Abnormal and Social Psychology, 49*, 389-395.

[Review of *The Making of a Scientist*]. *Bulletin of Atomic Scientists, 10,* 297-298.

1955

With S.W. White, & W.F. Hill. The organization of communication in small problem solving groups. Abstract. *American Psychologist, 10,* 357.

1956

With H. Strassman, & M. Thaler. A prisoner of war syndrome: Apathy as a reaction to severe stress. *American Journal of Psychiatry, 112*, 998-1003.

The Chinese indoctrination program for prisoners of war: A study of attempted brainwashing. *Psychiatry, 19*, 149-172.

Some observations on Chinese methods of handling prisoners of war. *Public Opinion Quarterly, 20,* 321-327.

1957

The effect of sleep deprivation on the sending and receiving of complex instructions. *Journal of Applied Psychology, 41,* 247-252.

With W.F. Hill, H.L. Williams, & A. Lubin. Distinguishing characteristics of collaborators and resisters among American prisoners of war. *Journal of Abnormal and Social Psychology, 55*, 197-201.

With J.E. Donaghy. Spontaneous organization of communication in four-man problem solving groups. Abstract. *American Psychologist, 12,* 371.

With R.A. Bauer. (Eds.). Brainwashing. *Journal of Social Issues, 13,* No. 3.

Social disorganization, belief change, and collaboration with the enemy. Paper read at meetings of the American Association of Public Opinion Research, Washington, DC.

1958

With M.T. Singer. Projective test responses of prisoners of war following repatriation. *Psychiatry, 21,* 375-385.

1959

With E.J. Murray, K.T. Erikson, W.F. Hill, & M. Cohen. The effects of sleep deprivation on social behavior. *Journal of Social Psychology, 49,* 229-236.

Brainwashing. *Encyclopedia Brittanica.*

Brainwashing and totalitarianization in modern society. *World Politics, 11,* 430-441.

1960

Interpersonal communication, group solidarity, and social influence. *Sociometry, 23,* 148-161.

1961

Management development as a process of influence. *Industrial Management Review* (*MIT*), 2, 59-77.

Brainwashing. *The Yearbook of World Affairs, 1961.* London: Steven & Sons.

With I. Schneier & C.H. Barker. *Coercive persuasion.* New York: W.W. Norton.

1962

With M.T. Singer. Follow-up intelligence test data on prisoners repatriated from North Korea. *Psychological Reports, 11,* 193-194.

With J.S. Ott. The legitimacy of organizational influence. *American Journal of Sociology, 67,* 682-689.

With I.R. Weschler. *Issues in training* (NTL Selected Reading Series No. 5). Washington, DC: National Education Association.

Statement: To set straight the Korean POW episode. *Harvard Business Review, 40,* 94-95.

Man against man: Brainwashing. *Corrective Psychiatry, 8,* 90-97.

1963

Forces which undermine management development. *California Management Review, 5*(4), 23-34.

1964

With W.G. Bennis, D.E. Berlew, & F.I. Steele. *Interpersonal dynamics: Essays and readings on human interaction.* Homewood, IL: Dorsey Press.

Training in industry: Education or indoctrination. *Industrial Medicine & Surgery, 33.*

How to break in the college graduate. *Harvard Business Review, 42*, 68-76.

1965

With W.G. Bennis. *Personal and organizational change through group methods: The laboratory approach.* New York: Wiley.

Organizational psychology. Englewood Cliffs, NJ: Prentice-Hall.

With W.W. McKelvey, D.R. Peters, & J.M. Thomas. Career orientations and perceptions of rewarded activity in a research organization. *Administrative Science Quarterly, 9,* 333-349.

1966

With G.L. Lippitt. Supervisory attitudes toward the legitimacy of influencing subordinates. *Journal of Applied Behavioral Science, 2,* 199-209.

The problem of moral education for the business manager. *Industrial Management Review, 8,* 3-14.

1967

Attitude change during management education: A study of organizational influences on student attitudes. *Administrative Science Quarterly, 11*, 601-628.

The wall of misunderstanding on the first job. *Journal of College Placement, 27,* 48-56.

With D.T. Hall. The student image of the teacher. *Journal of Applied Behavioral Science, 3,* 305-337.

1968

Organizational socialization and the profession of management. *Industrial Management Review, 9*, 1-15.

The first job dilemma. *Psychology Today* (March), pp. 22-37.

With W. Bennis, F.I. Steele, & D.E. Berlew. *Interpersonal dynamics: Essays and readings on human interaction* (2nd ed.). Homewood, IL: The Dorsey Press.

1969

The problem of moral education for the business manager. In C. Faust & J. Feingold (Eds.), *Approaches to education for character: Strategies for change in higher education.* New York: Columbia University Press.

Process consultation: Its role in organization development. Reading, MA: Addison-Wesley.

1970

The role innovator and his education. *Technology Review, 73,* 3-7.

The reluctant professor: Implications for university management. *Industrial Management Review, 12,* 35-49.

Organizational psychology (2nd ed.). Englewood Cliffs, NJ: Prentice-Hall.

1971

Occupational socialization in the professions: The case of role innovation. *Journal of Psychiatric Research, 8*, 521-530.

The individual, the organization, and the career: A conceptual scheme. *Journal of Applied Behavioral Science, 7*, 401-426.

1972

Professional education: Some new directions. New York: McGraw Hill.

The general manager: A profile. *Proceedings of the Eastern Academy of Management.*

With L. Bailyn. Where are they now, and how are they doing? *Technology Review, 74,* 3-11.

1973

With M.S. Polvnick & F.I. Steele. Expanding professional design education workshops in the applied behavioral sciences. *Journal of Higher Education, 44,* 380-387.

Organizational psychology: Problems and prospects for the future. *Training and Development Journal, 27,* 43-49.

With W.G. Bennis, D.E. Berlew, & F.I. Steele. *Interpersonal dynamics: Essays and readings on human interaction* (3rd ed.). Homewood, IL: Dorsey Press.

1974

Behavioral sciences for management. In J.W. McGuire (Ed.), *Contemporary management: Issues and viewpoints.* Englewood Cliffs, NJ: Prentice-Hall.

1975

The Hawthorne group studies revisited: A defense of Theory Y. In E.L. Cass & F.G. Zimmer (Eds.), *Man and work in society.* New York: Van Nostrand.

In defense of Theory Y. *Organizational Dynamics* (Summer), 17-30.

How career anchors hold executives to their career paths. *Personnel, 52*, 11-24.

Career development: Theoretical and practical issues for organizations. In *Career Planning and Development.* (Management Development Series No. 12). Geneva: International Labour Office.

Changing role of personnel manager. *Journal of the College and University Personnel Association, 26*, 14-19.

1976

With L. Bailyn. Life/career considerations as indicators of quality of employment. In A.D. Biderman & T.F. Drury (Eds.), *Measuring work quality for social reporting.* Beverly Hills, CA: Sage.

1977

Career anchors and career paths: A panel study of management school graduates. In J. Van Maanen (Ed.), *Organizational careers: Some new perspectives.* New York: Wiley.

With J. Van Maanen. Career development. In J.R. Hackman & J.L. Suttle (Eds.), *Improving life at work.* Santa Monica, CA: Goodyear.

With J. Van Maanen & L. Bailyn. The shape of things to come: A new look at organizational careers. In J.R. Hackman, E.E. Lawler, & L.W. Porter (Eds.), *Perspectives on behavior in organizations.* New York: McGraw-Hill.

Increasing organizational effectiveness through better human resources planning and development. *Sloan Management Review, 19,* 1-20.

1978

The role of the consultant: content expert or process facilitator? *Personnel and Guidance Journal* (February), 339-343.

Career dynamics: Matching individual and organizational needs. Reading, MA: Addison-Wesley.

What makes an organization attractive as a place to work in the 1980's. Invited address to the Polytechnic Association of Norway (Oslo), September 26.

1979

With J. Van Maanen. Toward a theory of organizational socialization. In B.M. Staw (Ed.), *Research in Organizational Behavior* (Vol. I). Greenwich, CT: JAI Press.

With W.G. Bennis, J. Van Maanen, & F.I. Steele. *Essays in interpersonal dynamics.* Homewood, IL: Dorsey.

1980

Organizational psychology (3rd ed.). Englewood Cliffs, NJ: Prentice-Hall.

Career theory and research: Some issues for the future. In C.B. Derr, (Ed.), *Work, family, and the career*. New York: Praeger.

Developing your career–Know your career anchors and develop your options. Working Paper No. 1148-80, M.I.T. Sloan School of Management.

1981

Improving face-to-face relationships. *Sloan Management Review, 22,* 43-52.

Does Japanese management style have a message for American managers? *Sloan Management Review, 23,* 55-68.

1983

The role of the founder in creating organizational culture. *Organization Dynamics,* (Summer), 13-28.

Career development: Key issues for organizations. In B. Taylor & G. Lippitt (Eds.), *Management development and training handbook* (2nd ed.). London: McGraw-Hill.

1984

Coming to a new awareness of organizational culture. *Sloan Management Review, 25,* 3-16.

Culture an environmental context for careers. *Journal of occupational behavior, 5,* 71-81.

1985

Organizational culture: Skill, defense mechanism, or addiction? In F.R. Brush & J.B. Overmier (Eds.), *Affect, conditioning, and cognition: Essays on the determination of behavior*. Hillsdale, NJ: Lawrence Erlbaum.

Organizational culture, and leadership. San Francisco, CA: Jossey-Bass.

Career anchors: Discovering your real values. San Diego, CA: University Associates.

How culture forms, develops, and changes. In R.H. Kilmann et al. (Eds.), *Gaining control of the corporate culture.* San Francisco, CA: Jossey-Bass.

Deep culture. In J.C. Glidewell (Ed.) *Corporate Cultures.* Alexandria, VA: American Society for Training Directors.

1986

A critical look at current career development theory and research. In D.T. Hall et al. (Eds.), *Career development in organizations.* San Francisco, CA: Jossey-Bass.

Are you corporate cultured? *Personnel Journal, 65,* 82-96.

What you need to know about organizational culture. *Training and Development Journal* (January), 30-33.

International human resource management: New directions, perpetual issues, and missing themes. *Human Resource Management, 25,* 169-176.

How leaders embed and transmit culture. *Armed Forces Comptroller, 31,* 6-12.

1987

Leadership as managed culture change. *Executive Excellence* (February), 2-4.

Individual and careers. In J.W. Lorsch (Ed.), *Handbook of organizational behavior.* Englewood Cliffs, NJ: Prentice-Hall.

Process consultation, Vol. 2: Lessons for managers and consultants. Reading, MA: Addison-Wesley.

The clinical perspective in fieldwork. Newbury Park, CA: Sage.

[Editor]. *The art of managing human resources.* New York: Oxford University Press.

1988

Process consultation: Vol. 1. Its role in organization development (rev. ed.). Reading, MA: Addison-Wesley.

Speaking of careers: The future of career development. *The career forum* (Spring), 2-3.

1989

A social psychologist discovers Chicago sociology. *Academy of Management Review*, 14, pp. 103-104.

Reassessing the "divine rights" of managers. *Sloan Management Review, 30*(2), 63-68.

Organizational culture: What it is and how to change it. In P. Evans, Y. Doz, & A. Laurent (Eds.), *Human resource management in international firms.* London: Macmillan.

[Conversation with E.H. Schein]. *Organizational Dynamics,* pp. 60-76.

1990

Organizational culture. *American Psychologist, 45*, 109-119.

Career anchors (rev. ed.). San Diego, CA: University Associates.

A general philosophy of helping: Process consultation. *Sloan Management Review, 31*(3), 57-64.

Organization development and the study of organizational culture. *Academy of Management Newsletter* (Summer), 3-5.

Back to the future: Recapturing the OD vision. In F. Massarik (Ed.), *Advances in organization development* (Vol. 1). Norwood, NJ: Ablex.

Innovative cultures and adaptive organizations. *Sri Lank Journal of Development Administration, 7*(2), 9-39.

1991

The role of process consultation in the creation and implementation of strategy. *Consulting Psychology Bulletin* (Winter/Spring), 16-18.

1992

Career anchors and job/role planning: The links between career planning and career development. In D.H. Montross & C.J. Schinkman (Eds.), *Career development*. Springfield, IL: Charles C. Thomas.

The role of the CEO in the management of change: The case of information technology. In T.A. Kochan & M. Useem (Eds.), *Transforming organizations* (pp. 80-95). New York: Oxford University Press.

Organizational culture and leadership (2nd ed.). San Francisco, CA: Jossey-Bass.

1993

How can organizations learn faster? The challenge of entering the green room. *Sloan Management Review, 34* (Winter), 85-92.

William H. Starbuck

"Watch Where You Step!" Or Indiana Starbuck Amid The Perils of Academe (Rated PG)

WILLIAM H. STARBUCK

Look, this is not a factual account of what happened. Although my memories seem vivid, no troublesome documents curtail my imagination. I have never kept a diary, or even old letters, and many facts of my life are buried in dumps throughout America and Europe. For that matter, there may never have been objective facts about the important events in my life. You can be sure other people did not see events as I did, and would not remember events as I do.

Research says that no one remembers events accurately: Our brains involuntarily change our memories to make events seem likely and logical, and remembered details are often fictional. So people probably did not speak the exact words I recall. I include such details, nevertheless, because they are what I remember and they add realism. Joe Cox, a dear friend of my youth, always added coloration to stories. When I asked him why, he explained: "People pay less attention when I tell stories just as they happened."

What follows contains no intentional lies, and it certainly does not portray me as I wish I were. Some of my mistakes have caused serious harm. I easily embroil myself in arguments about matters that do not matter and questions that have no answers. Perhaps for the same reason, I am fanatical about details and waste hours perfecting trivia. I insist on wearing an extremely accurate watch, yet I am chronically late, mainly because I always do one more unnecessary thing before I start what I should be doing. I postponed getting a crew cut until it was going out of style, and I have postponed changing it for 25 years. I will be a fashion leader when crew cuts come back into style.

I work sporadically. Sometimes weeks or months pass without my doing much that one could call serious work. Sometimes I spend weeks writing frantically for sixteen or eighteen hours a day, and I concentrate so completely that I do not even hear those who speak to me. Thinking our children ought to have a kitten, I began to raise and show cats. Deciding to relearn computer programming, I became a software developer. I take risks, both personally and monetarily. People who know me always look shocked when I declare that my motto is "Moderation in all things." I am anything but moderate. So I have to explain that one does not need a motto if one already behaves as one should; one needs a motto only to remind one of one's deficiencies.

It is intimidating to be one of those people who write autobiographies. Although it is nice to think someone might want to read about me, I resist the thought that I am old enough to look back on my life. Inside my head, I am still 25 or 30, and I am still debating what to be when I grow up. Sadly, those illusions tarnish when I go jogging and hear my wheezes and see almost everyone breeze past me.

I have tried to write in a way that symbolizes life's texture, although real life was many times more complex than this abstraction. I do not extract morals very explicitly. Humor mixes with tragedy, good luck with bad, pleasure with pain, cynicism with idealism. Excerpts are revealing, sad, funny, typical, strange, and educational. One sees variations in academic culture and practices across universities. Many people find bits of my life interesting because I faced issues they face, or expect to, or hope not to.

Self, career, family, organization, and society tangle together. To abstract myself or my career from context would violate my scientific standards. Still, interactions of person with environment are both fascinating and confusing. Several times I have written original ideas and discovered later that other scholars wrote similar ideas around the same times. Although many issues and events seem peculiar to a time and place, similar ones occur at many times in many places.

My collaborators will probably claim I am stubborn and independent-minded, but I often respond to others' initiatives. Responsiveness has injected more variety into my life than I would have sought. It was other people who proposed that I become a management scholar and behavioral scientist; become a professor of sociology; write various works, including this autobiography and an important chapter in James G. March's *Handbook of Organizations* (Rand McNally, 1965); visit Johns Hopkins, London, Bergen, and Gothenburg; move to Dallas, Berlin, Milwaukee, and New York; and divorce my wife.

PORTLAND, 1934-1948

I was born 263 days after Mom and Dad's marriage. We lived in Portland, Indiana, a small county seat where farmers gathered on Saturday afternoons.

It was a comfortable, generally nurturing and caring community in which Jimmy Stewart and June Allison would have been at home. Almost everyone was white and Christian; and children, at least, ignored differences in wealth or ethnicity or social status.

Indeed, Portland gave me utterly unrealistic concepts of American values. When teachers explained "that all men are created equal" and that the Statue of Liberty welcomed immigrants, I had no idea how greatly people may differ, or how bitter ethnic and economic conflicts may grow. The two Jewish families sent their children to the Presbyterian Sunday School. After an election that ousted the incumbents, the Postmaster and Assistant Postmaster traded jobs again. I knew nothing of corrupt politicians. Serious violent crime was rare. When a young, unmarried woman was found dead in her garage, the police cleaned up the mess before anyone thought to ask whether it had been suicide or murder.

My family crossed social strata. Grandpa Magill became wealthy enough running a coal yard and acquiring real estate to retire at 45. However, he and Grandma lived very frugally in a small, plain house in a working-class neighborhood. There, I played with children who introduced me to comic books and country music, customs of which my parents disapproved. Grandma Starbuck inherited stock in firms founded by her father, and she lived in a large, Victorian house, one of the nicest in town. She sometimes gave us presents that were above our standard of living. Dad managed family-related businesses—first a factory that made brick and drain tile, then a bank. Thus, the upper class accepted us as fit companions, but we lived in middle-class neighborhoods.

Something about my background convinced me that it is very important to try to behave and speak honestly. Of course, I am not the first to discover how very difficult it is to be truthful, or even to know where truth lies. My statements often mean something different to me than to listeners. Not only do I choose my own words with unusual care, but I hear others' words literally. An indirect result is that I have communication problems. People get confused when I respond to their words rather than their intent, and many do not appreciate the humor I see in their words. Clichés and small talk usually strike me as funny or inane. What I speak as honest, others may hear as tactless. I also confound people by saying the opposite of what I believe deadpan. To me these inversions are ironic or satirical exaggerations, but some people take them seriously and so find them confusing or disturbing.

What conscience I have likely resulted from Mom's X-ray vision. Because she always knew when I had lied or ventured into forbidden territory, I deduced that she could see into my head and read my most secret thoughts. She also delivered swift retribution. My sister and I once agreed that we would rather be spanked by Dad because, although he hit harder, Mom's spanks made loud cracks.

I loved and admired Mom desperately. Among other things, she taught me to scorn pretension, to cherish people's eccentricities, and to believe in my abilities. Her main qualities were zest, matter-of-fact pragmatism, and physical courage. She needed courage because she had suffered arthritis since childhood, and she lived with never-ending pain.

Her parents had three daughters whom they raised to follow different careers, and they destined Mom to be an artist. She did in fact become a nationally known watercolorist, the first woman invited to join an elite club of watercolorists. However, painting was not her choice originally, and she argued that the main requirement for becoming an excellent painter, or anything else, is to work at it hard enough.

CULVER, 1948-1952

I did initiate an important turn in my life when I enrolled at Culver Military Academy. When nine, ten, and eleven, I had gone to summer camp at Culver; and I decided that I wanted to attend Culver instead of Portland High School. Militarism did not attract me, but Culver was strong academically and more familiar than schools in the East. The tuition was quite expensive by our standards, so I proposed that my parents pay my tuition at Culver instead of later paying my tuition at college. They agreed. It must have been an ambitious and confident thirteen-year-old who proffered this trade—not to mention one who appreciated a bird in his hand.

So Culver may not have made me more ambitious, but it did expose me to superb teachers and show me that I could compete intellectually at a high level. I also became a vocal soloist and prize-winning tuba player. My athletic success was less impressive. As a football center/linebacker, I hated smashing head-on into ball carriers. I competed in three-quarter-mile races for two years, and just once did I place: I took third after all but two of the other runners dropped out.

Culver introduced me to Joe Cox, who was both a kindred spirit and a complementary one. Joe conceived projects and adventures in which I shared. One time, we bought war-surplus life rafts and paddled down the Wabash River for several days. We met people who survived by selling mussels to button factories, and we discovered that the Wabash got much thicker just downstream of each town.

We also tried to replicate the experiment in which Cockcroft and Walton had first split atoms. Culver's physics teacher lent us a room, a vacuum pump, and moral support; and we built a Van de Graaff generator, accelerator tube, and high-level vacuum pump. Joe induced a glassblower at Purdue University to create the glassware. We never did split any atoms, because we graduated before our equipment worked well enough. But, our admiration won Cockcroft and Walton the 1951 Nobel prize in physics.

HARVARD, 1952-1956

Our atom-smashing project persuaded Joe and me to become physicists. Diverse scholastic achievements and high SATs brought me offers of fancy scholarships. One unsolicited offer was mimeographed and began "Dear Student." But I chose Harvard College. Joe did too, as did another close friend.

My years at Culver had been framed by America's preoccupation with anti-Communism. At Culver, of course, we spelled Communist with four letters. I saw another side when the Congressional hunts for Communists peaked during my first years at Harvard. When one committee gloatingly ridiculed an elderly retired schoolmarm, I saw demagogues running cruel witch-hunts that exploited fear and stupidity. When investigating committees demanded the firing of a physics professor who had once belonged to the Communist Party, Harvard refused. Many Harvard alumni cried outrage, and donations plummeted. It showed me that politicians and donors may not support the values that respected universities hold dear. I began to see universities as enclaves that sometimes have to confront threats from their environments.

A few years later, donations to Harvard soared after people realized how foolishly they had acted. I inferred that universities win more support in the long run if they resist threats and stand for what they believe is right.

You will see that these perceptions shaped my reactions on at least two occasions. Thus, it made a difference that I attended Harvard during those years rather than another university in another time.

My first years at Harvard were disappointing academically. Although I entered Harvard with advanced standing in several subjects, my first year produced Bs, not the accustomed As. Harvard withdrew my scholarship, and my parents faced an economic crisis. Somewhere, they found the means to pay for a Harvard education.

I had no trouble diagnosing this problem: I had studied very little. I decided that I needed more motivation, and the key to that was more challenge. Harvard took a laissez-faire approach to prerequisites, so I skipped the courses that students normally took in their second year, and enrolled in courses that students normally took in their third or fourth years. I still found myself studying hardly at all, but my grades dropped to Cs.

In retrospect, it seems obvious that I was depressed. At one point, I consulted a psychologist. He gave me a slip of paper on which he had typed: "I will get up and work today. I want to study. I want good grades." He told me to read this to myself every morning. I tried it once, shook my head in wonder, and went back to bed.

My grades did improve somewhat during my third year, and near the end of that year, I realized that I was intensely lonely. I did engineering for the radio station, I had two roommates who were very good friends, and Joe and I often took long walks around Boston, during which we concocted shrewd schemes, accomplished incredible feats, and solved the world's problems. There was no reason I should be lonely, but I evidently was.

So I married Sharlene, a girl with whom I had gone steady almost continuously since I was sixteen. My friendship with Sharlene had long been a topic of serious dispute with Mom, but I was under 21 and marriage required my parents' consent. So I visited Dad at his bank, and asked him to help me persuade Mom: I pointed out that the issue was not whether but when, and did not correct his erroneous but unstated assumption that Sharlene was pregnant.

Marriage dramatically elevated my energy level, general outlook, and performance in school. I felt socially secure and economically challenged. Rather than tasks performed for their own sake, school work became a step toward supporting my wife and building a future. Because of my rash selection of courses during my second year, I had completed the prerequisites for graduate study, and so I took graduate courses in applied mathematics and electrical engineering and earned As. I ran Harvard's electronics club, designed and built my own high-fidelity equipment, and completed an interesting project to construct a tunable filter for light.

I was still majoring in physics, but because it imposed fewer constraints than engineering. Shortly after I entered Harvard, I had read John Diebold's *Automation, The Advent of the Automatic Factory* (Van Nostrand, 1952) and Norbert Wiener's *Cybernetics, Or, Control and Communication in the Animal and the Machine* (Wiley, 1948), and developed a strong interest in computers. When IBM sent a Harvard alumnus to hire research personnel, I sought a summer job, and worked on interesting projects at IBM's Poughkeepsie laboratory in 1954 and 1955. I got to know two of IBM's senior computer designers and the professors at Harvard's computer laboratory. Thus, I determined to become a computer designer after earning a doctorate in applied mathematics.

I did not go directly to graduate study in mathematics, however, because of my stormy relation with Dad. I do not remember when our disputes began, but Dad and I argued endlessly for years. Our dinner table was a war zone. People kept telling me how brilliant my father was, but I judged him a walking encyclopedia who was not too perceptive. For one thing, he was a banker rather than a professor or scientist. He spoke and seemingly thought in clichés and mottos. It especially galled me when he described Portland's residents as "the salt of the earth." His perceptions were permeated with shoulds and oughts, but many of his guiding principles seemed to be socially acceptable facades for baser motives. For example, he repeatedly asserted that his bank's primary goal was to serve its customers, but it seemed he was describing not a goal but a mental framework he found effective with customers. Dad backed the Republicans irrespective of their candidates or positions, and he hailed Senators Jenner and McCarthy for hunting Communists. Perhaps worst of all, I felt I could never meet Dad's standards of performance, and he seemed to laugh at most of my achievements and ideas.

It was not clear to me then, of course, but Dad had good reason not to take me seriously. I insolently challenged his trustworthy mottos and questioned his cherished principles. So I was unbearable. And what had I done? Our trumpeted atom-smasher had smashed no atoms. I tried to mold plastic sheets by reusing compressors and motors out of discarded refrigerators; it took me about ten minutes to mold each piece. While working in a chemistry lab one summer, I put my wet shoes on a hot plate to dry, stretched out on a table, and did not awake until the shoes were crisp. When I tried to sell refrigerators and stoves on commission, I succeeded in selling not one, and had to become a coal man to earn money. After winning a fancy scholarship to Harvard, I lost it the first year, and racked up even worse grades the next. I not only persisted in dating a disapproved girl, I married her. I took no interest in becoming a banker. As a career, I proposed to design machines out of science fiction. Joe Cox and I spawned hair-brained investments for our parents' money: One time we asked our parents for the price of motor scooters, which we would ride back and forth from Indiana to Boston, thus saving expensive train fares. Another time we proposed that they advance us $1,500 with which to buy a derelict ship in Boston harbor: We would patch the leaks, remodel the interior, save the cost of dormitory rooms, and turn a nice profit when we sold a beautifully refurbished ship.

Although Joe did coauthor our joint proposals, I must have a knack, for I have managed to turn up similar investment opportunities throughout my life. In fact, my son has shown a similar ability.

Hoping to make peace with Dad made me postpone graduate study in mathematics and seek a master's degree in business. I had no interest whatever in actually becoming a businessman, but I thought it worthwhile to invest two years in trying to understand Dad's world. Naturally, I chose the business school that was most like a physics department and least like other business schools—Carnegie Institute of Technology. It was not even accredited.

Being bound for business school, I asked IBM for a summer job in production engineering instead of research. My brief experience in the plant-layout department left impressions that affected my career choice and my ideas about organizations.

I was to report to work at 8:18, to take 42 minutes for lunch, and to leave at 5:12. Although nice, my colleagues lacked the enthusiasm for work that I had found among researchers. Almost my only assignment was to relocate a department of forty purchasing agents, who must have been judged the least important people in the plant. I had to move these poor souls not once, but four times in eight weeks. Toward the end, they cringed whenever they saw me.

As summer ended, my department manager called me over to his desk for a performance appraisal. "Your performance has been unsatisfactory," he said, then paused significantly. "I have been checking the time cards, and find that you have averaged twelve seconds late in the morning!"

"But," I protested, "I get here before 8 almost every morning."

"You are supposed to arrive at 8:18. The minutes before 8:18 do not count and do not make up for arriving late. Early arrivals violate IBM's planning for auto traffic."

"I've also been staying an hour or two after everyone else leaves in the evening."

"That's the *other* thing I want to talk to you about. You are assigned to leave at 5:12, and you are not authorized to stay here after 5:12."

He never mentioned what I had done between 8:18 and 5:12.

CARNEGIE, 1956-1960

Business study had one effect I had sought. One sensation I had during my first two years at Carnegie was that Dad learned a lot more than I. However, relations with Dad only improved, they did not heal, for once more I strayed off into strange, impractical pursuits. Instead of carrying through with the master's program, I became a doctoral student.

Now, I did not stray on my own; I was led astray. Near the end of my first year, Dick Cyert and Jim March offered a summer job running experiments. Having no other job in sight and a very pregnant wife, I snapped up their offer. And once in the job, I did not run experiments myself. Instead I bought a stepping relay and other parts and built a machine that ran experiments automatically. It may have been the first computerized psychological laboratory.

Sometime during the summer, Cyert and March proposed that I become a doctoral student with financial aid of tuition plus $1,800 a year. So I took $1,800 a year in exchange for my ambition to earn a doctorate in applied mathematics. Talk about commitment to a course of action!

That September, Cyert invited me into his office and said he had been thinking about my comparative advantages, and he thought I ought to become a behavioral scientist. I found this an amazing thought! At Harvard, I had struggled through a required course in sociology and an elective one in abnormal psychology, but I had certainly never thought of myself as *interested* in such topics. Nevertheless, I was deeply impressed that an important professor had analyzed what I ought to be doing with my life. So I asked Cyert what he advised. He suggested I enroll in a joint curriculum that the Graduate School of Industrial Administration and the Psychology Department were initiating. Thus, I began my career as a psychologist.

I took doctoral courses for only one semester.

In February of the next year, Mom and Dad came to see us. It was their first visit since our baby was born, and it went very well. It was the pleasantest time we had spent together since Mom had first expressed her dissatisfaction with Sharlene. I was elated because it seemed the two women in my life might yet get along.

After Mom and Dad left, the phone rang in the middle of the night. On their way home, they had been rammed head-on by another auto. Mom was dead, and Dad in serious condition.

I took Mom's death hard. Aside from sorrow for her and myself, it seemed life was too short to spend it dozing in classes. I dropped all my courses, and declared that I would spend six months reading and then take the doctoral qualifying examinations.

Herb Simon and Franco Modigliani were supernovas in Carnegie's firmament. Both stood out in a faculty that was filled with brilliance, and every seminar turned into a debate between them. Their endless debate concerned the rationality of decision making. Modigliani argued that economic theory's assumptions about rationality accurately describe actual behavior, whereas Simon held that people lack the capacities to decide rationally.

Aspirations played a key role in Simon's theorizing about decision making. I wrote a paper about aspirations for a seminar about the behavioral theory of the firm, and Cyert and March reacted enthusiastically. They suggested I discuss it with Jacob Marschak, who taught me a lesson.

My paper pointed out a logical error that Leon Festinger had made in his master's thesis, but did so very indirectly ("Level of Aspiration," 1963). Marschak asked why I had not made this point more clearly.

I said, "Well, Festinger is a famous psychologist. I don't want to make him look bad, and I don't want him to get mad at me."

Marschak advised, "State your view as clearly as you can. It is hard enough to do that. It isn't your job to protect Festinger, and he doesn't need your help. He knows he can make mistakes. I doubt that he will get angry if you are right."

Carnegie made an incredible environment for doctoral students in those years. Both Modigliani and Simon have won Nobel Prizes in Economics, as has Merton Miller. At least five more of those Carnegie professors could become Nobel Laureates, and Harrison White won a similarly prestigious award in sociology. The professors had revolutionary missions—to make management scientific, to promote organization theory, to simulate human thought—and they pursued these missions seriously.

Yet, I learned as much from other doctoral students as I did from professors. For me, the main educational experience was coffee hour. All the professors and students assembled in the lounge every afternoon at 3:00, and several professors invariably arrived with topics for discussion. The master's students returned to class at 3:30, and many professors went with them. But, there were almost always small groups of professors and doctoral students who debated for another hour or so.

I passed the qualifying exams, with a major in social psychology. Then I spent two years at Carnegie not finishing two dissertations. Then I moved to Purdue and spent three years not finishing two more dissertations.

My choice of Purdue provided a lesson in academic culture as well as decision theory. I had to choose between offers from IBM, MIT, Purdue, and Stanford. Having spent four years listening to Modigliani praise economic theory, I decided to emulate it. I listed criteria that mattered to me and assigned them dollar values. I induced Sharlene, over her protests, to do likewise. Then I averaged our preferences.

Purdue had offered me $500 a year more than MIT or Stanford, but MIT and Stanford had more prestige than Purdue. I polled professors to find out how much salary one should be willing to exchange for the prestige of MIT or Stanford, or for the differences between academia and IBM. The final calculation said that, to Sharlene and me, Purdue was worth $200 per year more than MIT or Stanford.

When I reported this number to Modigliani, who favored MIT, he asked where was I really going.

"To Purdue, of course. That's how the calculation turned out."

"But," he protested, "how can you be so mechanistic?"

Purdue had made the extra $500 contingent on a completed dissertation. When evaluating offers, I had no doubt about finishing and counted this a sure thing. But I did not finish, so I never got the $500.

PURDUE, 1960-1967

I simply could not write a dissertation.

I formed my concept of a dissertation partly from professors' casual remarks. When I asked Cyert how long a dissertation had to be, he replied 200 pages. I recall asking, "All on one topic?" At coffee hour one day, Bill Cooper said the Carnegie faculty wanted every dissertation to win an award for one of the best dissertations of the year. He was exaggerating, but I accepted his injunction to aim high.

I was able to write articles, most of which I saw as chapters in a future dissertation. None of my manuscripts was longer than forty pages because I ran out of ideas. So I submitted the manuscripts, in 25-page chunks, to journals.

After five years of this, I was ready to give up. I had worked on four dissertations, none of which had panned out. An effort to simulate a 25-plant firm foundered after several months of extracting data, when I discovered that data reported to corporate headquarters differed systematically and substantially from data at plants. I did a long review article and two empirical studies relating to organizational size; but these lacked coherence, and one study yielded so few data I did not even write it up.

Only research on aspirations had gone far enough to promise an integrated 200 pages. Simon had hypothesized that people might have aspirations because these simplify decision making.[1] I had written three theoretical articles on aspirations, one of which developed another hypothesis—that people might have aspirations because these help to achieve goals quickly (1964). I designed experiments to evaluate this hypothesis. However, Simon, who was on my dissertation committee, ruled these experiments unacceptable. He and I agreed that my experiments would at best make my hypothesis more plausible, whereas he demanded evidence that my hypothesis was the only plausible explanation. I believed no one could produce such evidence for any hypothesis about mental processes, so I dropped aspirations as a dissertation topic.

Although I could see other research studies I would like to do, none promised more than one article. I had been a doctoral student for seven years, and I evidently was not destined to be a professor. You can imagine Dad's opinion of my performance. I sat around drawing floor plans and elevations, and thinking very seriously about beginning again at an architecture school.

At that juncture, Cyert telephoned. He said Carnegie might award me a degree even though I had written no dissertation. I could ask the faculty to accept my articles as evidencing an ability to do research. He believed the faculty would agree if Simon supported the proposal. Could I send him copies of my articles? I certainly could!

Off went a packet and back came another phone call. All the articles had to be typed on 8½" x 11" paper, with consecutive page numbers. That took five months. Finally, everything was ready. "What should I do?"

"Have it bound and send copies to the dissertation committee," Cyert replied.

"But, what if someone wants revisions?" I asked.

"If it's bound, they won't ask for major revisions," he predicted.

I remain grateful to Cyert and Simon for backing this option and to the Carnegie faculty for endorsing it. There must have been dissent, because at my "dissertation" defense, one professor asked argumentatively if I thought they would be setting a dangerous precedent by awarding my degree without a dissertation. I responded that I had submitted thirteen articles, almost all published; few students would choose that option.

Later, when a Purdue doctoral student asked me to supervise his dissertation, I defined the target as three articles publishable in high-quality journals. I told him that, if he and I disagreed about his work, he could submit it to journals and I would accept their judgments. I still use these criteria.

One of the articles I submitted to Carnegie was a chapter on "Organizational Growth and Development" written for March's *Handbook of Organizations*. I was fervently hoping that this would become a widely read work.

You see, when reading for the doctoral qualifying exams, I had been awestruck by the chapter about small-group experiments that Kelley and Thibaut wrote for the *Handbook of Social Psychology* (pp. 735-786, Addison-Wesley, 1954). I had fantasized that I might write something equally remarkable one day. Kelley and Thibaut had masterfully integrated hundreds of experiments, and imposed understanding on confusion. Every social psychologist simply had to read what they had written.

Knowing of my dissertation work on organizational size, March invited me to write about growth and development for his projected *Handbook*. I was elated. This was the opportunity of my fantasies. It never crossed my mind that his *Handbook* might be a dud, or that there were people who paid little attention to handbooks. I worked hard to write a landmark synthesis—sixteen-hour days, seven days a week, for eighteen months. And the effort really paid off.

I always smile when I hear a professor proclaim that success requires publishing many articles, or that empirical studies are more valuable than literature reviews. Kelley and Thibaut had shown me that one superb article outweighs many ordinary ones, and that a good literature review makes sense out of nonsense.

Indeed, I never published many of my empirical studies because they seemed worthless.

From 1957 through 1973, I thought of myself as a mathematical social scientist, and until 1967, as a social scientist who ran laboratory experiments. Despite a couple of disagreements with Simon, I aspired to do the kind of research he did. I had learned advanced mathematics at Harvard; Kelley and Thibaut had sparked a passion for laboratory experiments. My experiments mainly concerned choice behavior, but also bargaining and aspirations. In today's jargon, I was a behavioral decision theorist.

One series of experiments was especially revealing. John Dutton and I spent six years, on and off, trying to understand and simulate a production scheduler named Charlie. One winter, we focused on an estimating task he performed many times each day. We ran 577 experiments on this tiny segment of his behavior. The experiments showed us how he thought, how his thoughts could be modelled, and why an exact simulation of his behavior was less informative than an abstract model. These experiments worked well partly because we devoted an incredible amount of effort to one tiny activity and partly because Charlie himself helped us design experiments ("Finding Charlie's Run-Time Estimator," 1971).

Yet, over time, I concluded that normal experiments are not useful. Because people are so flexible and versatile, it is rarely worthwhile to show that they are capable of certain behaviors. One has to show that certain behaviors occur under realistic conditions. Yet, one cannot approximate in a laboratory the rewards and socialization experiences that occur in real-life organizations.

Furthermore, designing an experiment is much like writing a computer program. Just as a computer does only what it is told, almost all subjects strive to follow instructions and respond to offered rewards. Thus, subjects' behaviors are direct results of the instructions and reward systems. My experiments were revealing a lot about my own beliefs and very little about my subjects' properties other than obedience. I might better run computer simulations. Although complex simulations are very difficult to understand, even very complex simulations are much simpler than people.

I finally abandoned experiments after a rude shock made me take a hard look at what I was doing. Vernon Smith generously invited me to share a research grant for experimental studies of economic behavior, and I used some of this money to hire assistants who processed subjects and ran statistical analyses. One assistant spent months producing a tall pile of computer output. None of the results looked anything like my hypotheses. This was bewildering indeed for someone who thought subjects did as they were told! I diagrammed the statistically significant relations, developed a theory that would make sense of them, and began to write an article that was entirely post hoc rationale.

Yet, the dramatic differences between my expectations and the actual results nagged at me. I went back to the pile of computer output, searching for the point where results began to diverge from expectations. I found a tiny error: We had introduced corrections early on to make the four treatments comparable for later analyses. The assistant had left out a minus sign when entering one correction factor for one treatment, so he had added that correction factor instead of subtracting it. Instead of being made comparable with the other three treatments, that treatment had been turned into an outlier. But, the subsequent analyses assumed no important differences between treatments. The statistically significant findings on which I had constructed a theory were utter nonsense. I had learned a lesson about post hoc analyses and surprising outcomes from experiments.

Among the unpublished experiments were the ones on aspirations I had proposed to my dissertation committee. I had later obtained funds from the National Science Foundation to run them, but I never finished the work.

I often point out to doctoral students that prestigious schools can be hard on junior professors. My acquaintances who took jobs at MIT and Stanford never fulfilled the promise they had shown as students, whereas almost all my colleagues at Purdue went on to exceptional success.

I attribute this outcome to our supportive environment. Purdue's deans rewarded professors who did research with kind words and summer support; and they let us create a separate department of behavioral scientists. However, the supportive environment was mostly something we constructed ourselves. Initially, Don King and Dick Walton started five or six of us talking about how we could support each other. But, we all contributed to building a mutual support system, and that is one reason it worked so well. We met for bag lunches where we planned joint projects, discussed research designs, and listened to reports of findings. We read each others' drafts. We nominated each other for opportunities. We enlisted additional members. We designed and taught courses jointly and began a doctoral program. We persuaded Purdue and the National Science Foundation to build us a laboratory. One year, partly to meet them and partly to make sure they met us, we invited several well-known scientists to spend a week with us. Probably most importantly, we treated each other as if we mattered and our research mattered.

I managed the technical design of the laboratory, conceived its unique electronics, and applied for the NSF grants that paid for them. The electronic system ran experiments automatically. A direct descendant of the device I built at Carnegie, this system controlled several rooms and many devices through plug-board programming, like some computers of the 1950s.[2]

Purdue's deans broadened my education greatly because they used office and teaching assignments and joint appointments to break down specialization. At first, I shared an office with Dutton: As the deans intended, he indoctrinated me in the admirable teaching philosophies and practices of Harvard Business School. My appointments were in administrative science and economics, and I often attended meetings of economists as well as management scientists. The deans asked me to represent Purdue on a team that planned computer facilities for Indianapolis hospitals. For five years, the deans assigned me courses in business policy, managerial accounting, managerial economics, operations research, and statistics. This was enlightening, because I had taken only basic courses in accounting and managerial economics, and I had never studied business policy or operations research. Not until my sixth year at Purdue did I teach decision theory, organization theory, or psychology.

At some point, Purdue received accreditation. For the first time, I was at an accredited business school!

During my four years without a doctorate, my title was instructor. Purdue promoted me to assistant professor when Carnegie awarded my degree, and then promoted me to associate professor a year later. After I had been an associate professor one year, the Social Relations Department at Johns Hopkins invited me to substitute for Jim Coleman while he went on sabbatic leave.

Because of Coleman's great prestige, the visit gave me sudden prominence with sociologists, and Illinois offered me a full professorship in sociology. A committee at Johns Hopkins was reviewing me for another full professorship. Seeing that a move might make sense, Sharlene and I fantasized about alternatives, then I contacted Cornell. They too offered a full professorship, which looked attractive because the town seemed nice, the business school's philosophy matched mine, and I would edit *Administrative Science Quarterly*.

When I told Purdue's Dean John Day that I had two offers at full professor and was expecting a third, he said: "Come now, you were an assistant professor for only one year, and you've been an associate professor for only two years. You can't expect us to promote you from new Ph.D. to full professor in three years!" He suggested I return as a department head.

I told him, "I'm not about to turn down full professorships at Cornell, Illinois, and Johns Hopkins in order to be an associate professor at Purdue."

That rationale was a half truth, but many Americans find it more acceptable to justify actions on the basis of status or money than values. I doubt that I would have left Purdue solely for a promotion, because I really liked my colleagues, the university, and our neighborhood.

I have a half-baked theory that inducing people to move usually requires both pushes and pulls. At least all my moves have involved both.

The push was my disgust over Purdue's dismissal of Marc Pilisuk. We had been colleagues for only a year before I left for Johns Hopkins, so I did not know Pilisuk well and his case posed philosophical issues for me, not personal ones. I also had no role in his tenure evaluation because I was at Johns Hopkins and Purdue's deans and senior professors did not seek my opinions. I merely watched from afar, informed by Walton, who was actively defending Pilisuk.

A social psychologist who studied conflict resolution, Pilisuk advocated peaceful means for resolving conflicts, and he opposed the war in Vietnam. There was a flurry in the faculty when he joined a silent vigil on the quadrangle in memory of the war dead on both sides. When a colleague voiced concern that Pilisuk's politics distorted his science, Pilisuk pointed out that he had often published findings contrary to his hypotheses.

I did not agree with Pilisuk's position, nor did my closest friends. The local newspaper told us that the United States was actually fighting Chinese soldiers, not North Vietnamese. Seemingly, the United States would have to fight the expansionist Chinese somewhere . . . better in Vietnam than California. Yet, I thought Pilisuk's activities were legitimate exercises of free speech.

The New York Times brought on a crisis by publishing a letter from Pilisuk criticizing the war. One result was a letter to Dean Emanuel Weiler from a multimillionaire benefactor of the business school. Word leaked from the Dean's office that the letter complained about professors involving themselves in debates about foreign policy and patronizing leftist newspapers like the *Times*. Dean Weiler then admonished Pilisuk that he had acted unprofessionally by publishing outside his area of expertise, which was social psychology not foreign affairs. Yet, their actions said the multimillionaire and Dean Weiler deemed it proper to involve themselves in debate about foreign policy.

A few months later, Dean Weiler refused Pilisuk tenure, telling him he "did not fit in."

I got a shock when Johns Hopkins' written offer arrived—because of a communication lapse, their committee had reviewed me for associate professor. I took Cornell's offer.

CORNELL, 1967-1971

With precious little help from me, my environment had magically transformed me from an abject failure age 28 to a full professor age 32.

Cornell was great. The students were bright and hard working. The library was fabulous. I had terrific colleagues in business, sociology, and labor relations. A joint appointment in sociology helped me extend those interests. I taught computer simulation, mathematical sociology, organization theory, and research methods, and tried to learn about university administration.

Editing *Administrative Science Quarterly* (*ASQ*) publicized my name and put me into contact with respected scholars worldwide. Previous editors had been finding it difficult to attract prominent authors' best articles. I blamed this partly on the lack of a constituency and partly on the lack of a well-defined image—*ASQ* was publishing on too many topics. I set out to make it the focal journal for organization theorists, added many carefully chosen editors, and clearly followed their advice. *ASQ*'s standing did seem to rise. Submissions improved in both quantity and quality, and revenues rose modestly. However, I never fulfilled the deans' fantasy to have *ASQ* pay its overhead costs.

One reason I did not intervene in editorial decisions was the weak agreement between reviewers. The correlation between two reviewers was only .12—so low that one reviewer's opinion gave almost no information about another's. I could have raised this correlation by pairing reviewers who had more similar preferences, but that tactic would have misrepresented organization theorists' diversity. Because *ASQ*'s tradition was to avoid narrow specialization, I normally chose one reviewer with highly relevant experience and a second reviewer who should be interested but had not done similar research.

Those years brought a revolution in my relation with Dad. One day I said to myself, roughly, "You have little in common with this man. You are a professor in New York, and he a banker in Indiana. You are not trying to please other Indiana bankers, so why are you unhappy about not having this one's approval?" Thereafter, we got along much better.

Those years also introduced me to research that looked suspicious. The first jarring case involved a former friend who had written one of those prize-winning dissertations Carnegie sought. I began a book about decision making. Chapter 3 would describe my friend's remarkable study. To explain it well, I needed to understand it thoroughly. I pored over it for ten weeks, digesting every word and trying to reproduce every detail. I even interviewed the decision maker who had been modelled.

The more thoroughly I read it, the less sense it made and the more contradictions surfaced. The theory would not generate the sequences of analyses attributed to it. Neither the theory nor the analytic sequences would produce the decisions attributed to them. The decision maker said he had eagerly read the dissertation but had seen little resemblance between the theory and his thought processes, so he was surprised that the theory produced decisions similar to his. I was forced to conclude that a famous study should probably be infamous. I was so disillusioned and disgusted I threw away my book manuscript and refunded the publisher's advance ("The History of Simulation Models," 1971).

A second case also involved a dissertation. Chick Perrow sent a note, expressing concerns about the truthfulness of an article *ASQ* had recently accepted for publication. In his evaluation of the first version, Chick asked for interview evidence. Two months later, the author submitted a revision that included 700 interviews with personnel from fifty companies. But, the interview evidence seemed strangely tidy. The statistics looked like this:

	Result A	*Result B*	*Result C*
Condition 1	0%	5%	95%
Condition 2	25%	50%	25%
Condition 3	95%	5%	0%

Therefore, Chick had examined the dissertation on which the article was based, and had found no interviews. No one could conduct 700 interviews in fifty companies in two months.

I told the author we would not publish his article. He demanded a hearing. I recruited a review panel and asked the author to bring all his data to Cornell. He arrived bearing only a large deck of punched cards. We asked to see his notes from the interviews he conducted three to four months earlier. He said he had destroyed his notes after he recorded the data on punched cards. We examined the punched cards. The large deck turned out to be many copies of the same fifty cards, one card for each company. The only information on each card was the information in his article.

The review panel upheld the decision not to publish. It also wrote to the American Sociological Association, suggesting that they publish a warning about an article in the *American Sociological Review* by this author and based on these data. The Association replied that their lawyer had advised them not to publish a warning "because that would be picking out one article as an exception."

Ithaca was a lovely, neighborly town, and we owned a beautiful house. But, the house needed expensive repairs. One year, house costs plus income taxes ate up 74 percent of our income. We could not afford to replace our aging auto, which often broke down, and Ithaca became an island.

Ithaca's isolation seemed to make it hard to get advice about two of our children who had serious learning problems. Clinics in Baltimore and Boston diagnosed them as having "minimal brain damage," and prescribed drugs for both and tutoring for the older's dyslexia. We found a superb tutor, who taught the older to read; but we could not locate specialized medical or psychological advice nearby.

Another problem had surfaced while I was at Johns Hopkins and permeated our life in Ithaca: Sharlene was drunk every evening. I did not put a name to her habit or seek outside help. I just complained and waited for her to show self-discipline.

Dutton, my office mate at Purdue, had moved to Southern Methodist University, where Dean Jack Grayson was striving to build a highly ranked business school. They hired me as a consultant a couple of times, then offered me a job. Some job! The salary would double my after-tax income and make me the highest-paid business professor in the United States.

The big money looked very attractive to someone who could not repair his auto, but both Sharlene and I wanted to stay in Ithaca. I loved Cornell. We could buy a cheaper house. Nevertheless, it would be nice to convert SMU's offer into a raise. I was hoping for ten percent, twice the usual five. Twenty percent would be a triumph.

I told Dean Justin Davidson of SMU's offer. He said something like "That's a big salary."

"Well, what are you going to do about it?" I prodded.

"I'm not going to do anything about it," he said smiling pleasantly. He said he hoped I would stay at Cornell, but he would not discuss my salary.

My pride was bent, and I was angry that Davidson insisted on dictating the terms of employment. Sharlene and I debated pros and cons—Cornell's known assets versus SMU's unknown potential. As Grayson intended, I liked the distinction of being the highest-paid. I took SMU's offer.

It was one of the great mistakes of my life, because the next four years destroyed my family. It was not life in Dallas, however, that destroyed my family. I never showed up for work at SMU.

LONDON, 1970-1971

A few weeks after I took the SMU job, Derek Pugh invited me to visit London Business School for a year as a Fulbright Fellow. It appeared opportune. We were selling our house, our auto was junk, and we could store our furniture. We had never visited Europe, and it sounded exciting—good for our whole family. Grayson approved a leave of absence.

We had been in London just five weeks when we heard, at fourth hand, a disturbing tale. Roger Dunbar, whose dissertation I had supervised, was working at SMU. By letter, Roger introduced us to his sister, Joan, who had also moved to London recently. Joan became our friend and regular baby-sitter.

Then, Roger told a tale to a Canadian girlfriend, who told it to Joan, who told us. As I first heard it, the tale went like this:

> SMU's business school had hired a new Ph.D. from Yale, Eli Hipster (a pseudonym, of course). Hipster had just started teaching. He wore his hair down to his shoulders. He often went barefoot. He replaced his office door with a string of neckties. Instead of renting an apartment, he slept in his Volkswagen. He also offered to move in with professors' families for short periods, during which he would cook, inspire parties, and promote closeness. He persuaded the deans to hire avant-garde architects to create a display that would alert potential students to the business school's innovative curriculum. The display, on the school's lawn, involved a large plastic tent, strobe lights, and rock music.
>
> These eccentricities drew attention. Instead of alerting potential students, the display alerted the local fire brigade and fire marshall, who arrived with sirens wailing and demanded its dismantling. The FBI probed Hipster's connections with

> subversive organizations, but found none. The SMU newspaper printed his photo and an interview atop the front page. It quoted him as calling for revolution.
>
> The next week, two wealthy men appeared in Grayson's office and demanded that Hipster leave SMU immediately. Grayson told them Hipster had a three-year contract, but he was sure he could persuade Hipster to modify his behavior to fit Dallas and SMU. Hipster had great potential, but he needed guidance and time to adapt. The donors said they were not asking for modified behavior. They would withdraw their own $1,000,000 pledges and sabotage SMU's $160 million campaign unless Grayson got rid of Hipster before the month ended.
>
> This demand flabbergasted the deans and many professors. They were outraged and discussing mass resignation.

Farfetched as the tale was, I could not disregard it. I wrote to Dutton, asking if something like this had happened. He sent back a letter and newspaper clippings. The tale had been roughly correct, although details were wrong.[3] The wealthy donors were the chairman of SMU's Board of Trustees and the head of an organization created to raise money for the business school. The newspaper had quoted Hipster as declaring "Traditional education is shitty" and saying "bullshit" in boldfaced italics. The revolution he had sought was in teaching methods. Hipster had already left campus. No mass resignation was planned, but Dutton and others were depressed about the future.

Resigning made sense to me. Grayson and his associates had seriously misjudged their environment when they hired Hipster, and their environment had reacted harshly. Their building program would end for now, and it might be a long time before the business school could regain momentum. SMU could never attain high stature under leaders such as those who had demanded Hipster's firing. I did not want to live in a community that showed so much fear of controversy and so much intolerance of youthful deviance.

I was still a professor at Cornell, on leave because Davidson had asked me not to resign for a year. Sharlene and I went back over the issues, and decided that we'd like to go back to Cornell. I had greatly enjoyed my contacts in sociology and labor relations. Before I had left, friends in both departments asked if I'd like to work there instead of the business school. Perhaps a three-way appointment would be interesting.

I sent a brief telegram to Davidson. It said I was thinking about returning to Cornell, but I'd like to arrange a three-way appointment, and an explanatory letter would follow. I began composing letters to Davidson and others, but never posted them because a telegram came from Davidson. It said my only option was to return to the business school full-time, because sociology and labor relations had no money to pay me.

My telegram had been an error because a telegram is surprising and terse. Davidson's telegram to me had seemed brusk; probably mine seemed so to him. Moreover, all written messages leave out much information about speakers' intentions and make it difficult to iterate toward mutual understanding. Even face-to-face, Davidson and I may never have understood each other well. Joint appointments always require delicacy. I should have gotten on an airplane instead of sending a message.

Probably I should have gotten on an airplane after Davidson's telegram arrived. But I did not think of it. I felt unwanted, and I saw myself as unemployed even though I was formally a Cornell professor.

I had no energy for job hunting. I was teaching in a very demanding program for executives. Although I was doing well, teaching alone took forty hours a week. The British schools had not heard of learning disabilities. Our daughters' schoolmates called them names because they were foreigners. To fit in, they would have to become either hippies or skinheads. Mainly because we deviated from British spending patterns, we were having to import our savings from America.

We gradually adapted and learned to appreciate our environment. We enjoyed the differences between British and American, and being outside the United States became more interesting and illuminating than expected.

My colleagues at London Business School were bright, thoughtful, and nice; and I learned unexpected lessons from their research. Most gathered large-sample data via surveys, then made statistical analyses. I had advocated such studies to put organization theory on a scientific basis. Yet, close acquaintance with the research corroded my illusions. Precise-looking numbers masked an ambiguous morass of misleading labels and overlapping concepts. The strong correlations had trivial meanings that were dictated by assumptions and measures. Findings that were not trivial would not replicate, probably because they came from post hoc analyses ("A Trip," 1981).

The research group's meetings also showed me class identification and class warfare at close hand, and I began to notice these phenomena broadly in British life. I found that, when I read Karl Marx in college, I had not really understood what he was talking about. Fortunately, the British exempt foreigners unless they take on aristocratic airs.

It seemed a good idea to spend a few more years tasting the world outside America. London Business School invited me to stay, and I wanted to. I loved the school, London, and England. Yet I could not afford it. A British professor's salary covered only about half the cost of living in London with a family of five. I would have to earn as much consulting as I did as a professor—even more, because my children's problems probably required private schools. I had not entered academia to become a consultant.

I also had job opportunities in France, Australia, and Berlin. France had attracted me since I studied high-school French, but French professors earned no more than British ones. Australia seemed exotic, but moving back to the United States might be hard. So I opted for Berlin. The pay would match my salary at Cornell, I would travel widely in Europe, and I could focus on research for three years.

I heard later that Hipster got a haircut, bought shoes and suits, and became a consultant. Who knows? His clients may have included SMU's trustees.

BERLIN, 1971-1974

My years in Berlin resembled a lurid soap opera. However, one does not have to live fiction.

Germans had consulted Dick Cyert about business education, and he had drawn up plans for an institute that would serve all Europe, not just Germany. It would raise the status of business education, promote research by European business teachers, and facilitate cross-national communication.

German capitalists offered to finance such an institute, but German politicians objected to capitalists being involved in business. West Berlin was an island with no natural resources, so it needed subsidies and activities that would attract young people. Thus, the International Institute of Management became a government project in West Berlin, and one of the staff's functions was to spend their salaries there.

The first Director was an American, Jim Howell. He hired around fifteen researchers of diverse nationalities, who began work during the summer of 1971.

We arrived in Berlin and checked into a hotel. I went to the Institute to make sure our household goods had arrived. The Institute had said they would arrange shipment from Ithaca. No one at the Institute knew anything about our goods; but I should not worry, they said, as everything was in order.

Howell explained that he was leaving on a trip but he needed to talk with me, would I mind riding to the airport with him? "Of course not." In the limousine, he said, "We're not going to pay you what I told you we'd pay you. The Science Ministry in Bonn refused to approve the salary I offered you." He went on to explain that whereas the original offer had been based on the exchange rate in March, since then the dollar had lost value relative to the mark. He was negotiating my salary with Bonn, and meanwhile I would receive a conservative, temporary salary.

Gulp! My employers, a national government, had reneged on the offer I had accepted. My family was in a foreign country. Air tickets to America would cost several thousand dollars. Our household goods might be aboard a ship on the Atlantic. I had no alternative job.

I had planned to spend the first months studying German intensively, but I never began language study because I had other problems. Clowns had taken command of our household goods and were producing a comedy of errors. Each week brought a different story about why they were not in Berlin.

Our children would have to wait several years to enter the bilingual school, but officials at the regular schools wanted nothing to do with our children. They had no program for teaching German to foreigners, they said; we should send our children to the bilingual school. A school run for U.S. Army dependents let our son into a special-education class. Our daughters would have to learn German by immersion. We hired a German university student who moved into our basement, tutored the children in German, and remained available as a translator.

These issues seemed minor when Sharlene said she wanted treatment for alcoholism. The alcoholic treatment centers, we learned, had waiting lines of six months. The only English-language AA group was for young male soldiers. No one knew a psychiatrist who spoke English well enough to conduct therapy.

That was when I made another serious mistake. I should have immediately extracted my family from this disaster and moved them back to the United States. Yet, this idea never crossed my mind. I kept trying to solve the problems before us instead of changing the problems. Like one of the frogs in Bateson's fable, I had been dropped into boiling water. But, the frog jumped out, whereas I was trying to swim to shore.

I might have jumped if I had foreseen that staying in Berlin would lead me to death's brink.

The Institute's administration was frozen in a web of conflicting regulations. There was a rule against everything, including rules. Germans generally saw rules as adequate justifications, Americans as arbitrary constraints. One pattern recurred many times. A German would tell an American that such-and-such could not be done because a rule forbade it, or must happen because a rule demanded it. The American would ask: Exactly what does the rule say? Is this a good rule? Who made the rule? How can we change it or get around it?

For six months, the dollar continued declining and I continued with no contract. Then the exchange rate stabilized and Howell "offered" a contract that Bonn had approved.

Soon after, Howell resigned and departed abruptly. We were told clearly that the German Science Ministry would not approve another American Director. A different political party had taken control in Bonn, and they were asking for the Institute's redirection to fit their political agenda. They proposed that a German political scientist become Director and that the Institute focus on regional economics. The Institute's staff, including myself, spent endless hours debating its agenda and governance.

Europeans' attitudes about American empirical research shocked me. I had assumed that research involved common norms and similar activities everywhere, and my British friends did not violate this assumption. However, only small fractions of French and German professors agree with American norms. French and German professors generally laugh at Americans' empiricism. To them, American social scientists resemble hamsters running on exercise wheels—they run and run and run frantically, but go nowhere.

Despite the turmoil, I did begin research. My rudimentary German ruled out interviews and heavy reading. I had written about mathematical theories of revolutions, so I began gathering statistical data on the revolutions in

German universities a few years earlier. My experiences with computer simulation and computer applications in hospitals started me thinking about a computer program to do medical diagnosis. The German Health Administration had been evaluating drugs only for safety, now they intended to start evaluating drugs' effectiveness. Wolfgang Müller and I began helping them design an appropriate information system. These contacts brought us to the attention of doctors hunting side-effects of birth-control pills. They asked us for statistical advice. The result was a conversation that eventually became one of the most important of my life.

After several hours discussing their project, the project director asked what research we were doing. I told him I was working on a computer program to make medical diagnoses.

He probed, "Why do you want to do that?"

Thinking this was a pretty strange question from a doctor, I explained, "I want to improve medical care."

"But, diagnosis is not important to *good* medical care," he countered.

I could not believe what I was hearing. "Wait a minute," I objected. "Doctors base treatments on diagnoses, so more accurate diagnoses should produce better treatments. Computers can take more factors into account than doctors can, and computers overlook nothing."

"You're wrong in assuming that diagnoses determine treatments' effectiveness," he replied. "*Good* doctors do not rely on diagnoses."

"Yet, medical schools teach doctors to make diagnoses," I protested. "Medical education teaches doctors to translate symptoms into diagnoses, and then to base treatments on diagnoses."

"That's right. Medical schools do teach that," he admitted, "but the doctors who do what they were taught never become good doctors.

"There are many more combinations of symptoms than there are diagnoses, so translating symptoms into diagnoses discards information. And there are many more treatments than diagnoses, so basing treatments on diagnoses injects random errors. Doctors can make more dependable links between symptoms and treatments if they leave diagnoses out of the chain.

"However, the links between symptoms and treatments are not the most important keys to finding effective treatments. Good doctors pay careful attention to how patients respond to treatments. If a patient gets better, current treatments are heading in the right direction. But, current treatments often do not work, or they produce side-effects that require correction. The model of symptoms-diagnoses-treatments ignores the feedback loop from treatments to symptoms, whereas this feedback loop is the most important factor.

"Doctors should not take diagnoses seriously because strong expectations can keep them from noticing important reactions. Of course, over time, sequences of treatments and their effects produce evidence about the causes of symptoms. This evidence may lead to valid diagnoses by the time treatment ends."

I thought I spotted a weak spot in his argument. "Then, why do so-called 'good' doctors state diagnoses before patients are cured?" I asked. "All doctors make early diagnoses, even the best ones."

He said, "Diagnoses are mainly useful as something to tell patients and their families. Announcing diagnoses creates an impression that doctors know what they are doing."

At that time, I found these notions implausible. Not only were they eccentric, they said the diagnostic program I had been creating was unimportant. I continued working on the program.

Sharlene did eventually enter a treatment center. She emerged hopeful, but remained abstinent for only a few weeks. Then she took no interest in further treatment.

Next, a telephone call sent us to a hospital where our daughter was having her stomach pumped out. She had heard that a readily available pill produced wonderful effects if one took enough of them.

A few weeks later, we discovered that both daughters had hashish in quantity. They had entered a subculture that used drugs and had easy access to them.

Punch Magazine kept me sane during those months. My immediate world had become a madhouse. When I felt quite desperate, I read *Punch's* ironical commentaries on absurdities elsewhere.

Joe McGuire was assembling an anthology and asked me to survey organization theory. Stimulated by *Punch*, I sent him a tongue-in-cheek commentary titled "Organization Theory from before Ptah-Hotep to beyond Pradip Khandwalla." Writing it was therapy. A startled McGuire amended a couple of jokes that made no sense to him and renamed it "The Current State of Organization Theory."

In June 1972, I attended a conference organized to introduce American and Soviet management professors to each other. I had never ventured behind the Iron Curtain except for tourist trips to East Berlin, and the trip was fascinating and tense.

I came home ill. The flu, I thought. It got better, but then grew worse, and the symptoms seemed stronger. Again it got better and then returned. And again. And again. Each cycle produced stronger symptoms. One day in August, I realized that I was crawling up stairs because I could barely breathe.

I asked an ENT doctor if I had hay fever. The symptoms seemed stronger when I read my son bedtime stories. One of my grandfathers had asthma, the other severe hay fever, and my father hay fever. Might I be reacting to the straw in my son's guinea pig cage?

The doctor said I needed sinus surgery and sent me to a surgeon. A few days after the operation, I went home feeling good for the first time in two months.

But, after a week, my breathing problems resumed. The surgeon sent me back to the hospital. The resident doctors sent samples to a lab, which identified a bacterial infection that penicillin could cure. Massive doses of penicillin made digestion impossible, and I lost thirty pounds in two weeks. For the first time in years, I weighed what the charts recommended. The penicillin also seemed to cure my infection. I felt fine, and the doctors sent me home.

Again, after a week, my breathing problems resumed. After two weeks, I stopped breathing almost entirely. The crisis came on abruptly one evening. Sharlene and the university student bundled me into the auto and drove pell-mell with the horn blowing to the nearest hospital. I was nearly unconscious, but I remember white-coated people clamping a mask on my face and injecting my arms.

This time the doctors tried tetracycline because it killed bacteria that penicillin missed and some viruses. After another two weeks, I again went home feeling fine.

Then, after a few days, I stopped breathing almost entirely. Again a high-speed trip to the emergency room and vague images of white coats working over me.

When I awoke the next day, I lit a cigarette as usual. For twenty years I had smoked two to three packs a day. That morning, one of my doctors walked into the hospital room, pointed at my cigarette, and declared sternly, "*That* is what is killing you!"

I believed him. I put out the cigarette and have not smoked since. Thus, I found out how easy it is to quit smoking. It is very easy if you believe smoking is killing you. The withdrawal symptoms seem insignificant. I also discovered how insincere I had been the many times I had tried to quit.

Unfortunately, smoking was not really what was killing me. I suffered more breathing crises. We repeated the emergency trips.

I did not find the repetition boring, however. My doctors were running out of hypotheses and treatments. The cycles were growing shorter.

My doctors sent me to Germany's most famous allergist, whom I cherish as a prototype of ascribed expertise. I told him my hypothesis about the straw in my son's guinea-pig cage. He injected sera in my arms, looked at the reactions, and announced that I had no allergies. None at all. I pointed out that the arm with guinea-pig serum had swelled up to twice its normal diameter. The allergist said, "It is nothing significant! What do you expect after all the things I injected?"

Thereafter, I had no allergies. The ultimate authority had said so.

An editor for the Elsevier publishing company came to visit me in the hospital. He asked if I was writing a book Elsevier might publish. I was impressed by the effort he had taken, but I was busy being sick. I thanked him for his interest and promised to contact him if I did write a book. That seemed unlikely.

One day, my doctors came to see me and said I should anticipate dying. They explained they did not know why I had asthma or how to prevent it. They had no more ideas. The crises would recur. A hospital could probably revive me; but one day, I would not get to a hospital in time. So I should try to enjoy what remained of my life, which might be only a few weeks.

Having gone through eight months of escalating evidence that something was seriously wrong, I believed them and went home to die. I was 38.

I tried to figure out what to do with my remaining days, but I felt too sick to do anything useful. I did not even compose a will. I mostly stayed in bed because I had so much trouble breathing.

Sharlene watched me for a few days. Then she declared, "If you're going to die, it is not going to be at home in bed! You had better die in a doctor's office, trying to find out what is wrong with you."

I thought her heartless and unsympathetic. I also thought she was right.

I telephoned Dutton because his sister worked for a famous doctor. After inquiring, he told me to go to Mayo Clinic in Minnesota.

When I got to Mayo, I no longer had symptoms. None whatever! I was quite embarrassed and afraid the doctors would neither believe how sick I had been nor be able to figure out why.

However, tests disclosed allergies. Technicians carefully measured the amount of each substance injected, the time for a reaction to develop, and amount of reaction; then they referred to statistical tables and wrote down standard deviations. My reactions to most furs and feathers were two standard deviations above normal. My reactions to guinea-pig fur were off the chart, which stopped at five standard deviations.

I believe I have proven beyond all doubt that surgery is not an effective treatment for guinea pig. Surgery, penicillin, tetracycline, and other treatments had appeared to work solely because I was not at home, where we had a guinea pig and a cage of finches. Staying in a hotel would have been an effective treatment as long as the hotel had no feather pillows or fur rugs.

Why did these allergies suddenly manifest themselves? My hypothesis was stress. However, a researcher at Mayo examined my respiratory cells and said they had properties typical of allergy, whereas they would not have these properties with psychosomatic asthma. He conjectured that an infection picked up during my trip to the Soviet Union had activated latent tendencies.

Looking back from today, it looks wildly optimistic, but I had agreed to go to Milwaukee on my trip to Mayo. The University of Wisconsin-Milwaukee wanted to interview me for an endowed chair.

Fortunately, I arrived there in good health, and they did offer me the chair. The terms were excellent. Many of UWM's students were the first members of their families to attend college, and many held full-time jobs while they went to school. I liked the idea of a university that was offering upward mobility to working-class youth.

So did I take it? Well, yes and no. I promised to move to Milwaukee a year hence, after finishing my three-year contract with the Institute.

I had been numb to others' problems while I was ill. Sharlene had coped amazingly well, but alcohol was continuing to erode her brain. Our daughters had transferred to the bilingual school, where the one with learning disabilities had foundered in a curriculum aimed at college entrance.

Although the last sixteen months in Berlin brought no improvements for my family, they made a dramatic turning point for me. Believing I was going to die had induced serious stocktaking.

Stan Seashore was visiting in the Netherlands. We met several times, and I adopted him as a model, both positive and negative. He too had an alcoholic wife, and he spoke sadly of the brain damage she had suffered. He seemed to have been more successful than I as a father. I aspired to be as helpful to colleagues, especially younger ones. Stan had a consistent gentleness I admire but cannot sustain.

I began a practice that I commend to others who are well-known: Unless my coauthors request otherwise, I list my name last on a by-line. It makes me feel good, it eases collaboration, and my coauthors gain more from incremental publicity than I.

I had been wasting my life writing articles that few read and that left negligible long-term traces. Mathematical theories bring academic prestige, but almost no one reads them. There is a basis for European professors' skepticism about empirical research. Almost all empirical studies are forgotten as soon as they appear; and that is just as well, because they add confusion rather than clarity ("Theory Building," 1988). I wanted to write things that some people would actually read, and I wanted to leave a lasting mark.

I had grown still more critical of post hoc analyses and theorizing. I had also been mulling over my conversation with the director of the birth-control-pill project, and I had seen several versions of medical diagnosis in practice. The director's views made more and more sense.

Academic research is trying to follow a model like that taught in medical schools. Scientists are translating data into theories, and promising to develop prescriptions from the theories. Data are like symptoms, theories like diagnoses, and prescriptions like treatments. Are not organizations as dynamic as human bodies and similarly complex? Theories do not capture all the information in data, and they do not determine prescriptions uniquely. Perhaps scientists could establish stronger links between data and prescriptions if they did not introduce theories between them. Indeed, should not data be results of prescriptions? Should not theories come from observing relations between prescriptions and subsequent data?

I imagined a book that would persuade organization theorists to practice prescriptive science instead of descriptive. I wrote to the Elsevier editor who had visited me in the hospital. He said they were very interested; could I submit an outline?

The outline had eighty chapters and implied a book longer than the Bible. It would take me years to write, and I obviously could not count on living for years. Furthermore, I wanted to change practices, not publish a manifesto. Change could better be fostered by enlisting helpers—many and strategically chosen. So I proposed a book with eighty authors, a *Handbook of Organizational Design*.

Again, the Elsevier editor expressed strong interest, and asked me to identify authors for chapters. I wrote a prospectus for each chapter to define its domain and to assure that it would address prescription as well as description. I searched journals for possible authors, and fitted hundreds of names into a design matrix that took account of age, discipline, interests, imagination, and geography. Then I dispatched invitations and waited for replies.

Meanwhile, Bo Hedberg returned to the Institute after a visit home and announced that he had received a grant from his national government. Because the Swedish economy had not been growing lately, the government wanted to do something about "stagnating industries." Hedberg saw the issues in an economic and sociological frame. He wanted to find out why some industries stagnate and drive firms out of business.

I said something tactful like "Bo, you've got this thing all screwed up! The interesting question is not why industries stagnate. Technologies are always developing, people are always migrating, prices are always shifting. It's inevitable that things will change, and some of these changes will make some industries obsolete. The key issue is why do smart managers keep their firms in industries they know are stagnating? Why don't firms migrate into more promising industries when their current ones stagnate?"

Hedberg countered, "That's not realistic. Firms cannot just pick up their product lines and their engineers and plunge into new industries. Specialized skills and business connections make them captives of their environments. The firms in an industry have to evolve together. It's a problem in social policy to create incentives that keep industries vital, that keep them evolving in line with social needs and economic and technological opportunities."

Obviously we had an argument. I was saying industrial stagnation posed problems for the managers of individual firms, whereas Hedberg was saying industrial stagnation posed problems for government policies. We talked about resolving the argument by doing research together, but we would both be leaving Berlin and heading in opposite directions.

Then a letter came from Milwaukee. Did I know someone who could teach information systems and would like to visit there for a year? Hedberg agreed to do it.

After I had worked on the *Handbook* for over a year and lined up many authors, a letter arrived from Elsevier. It was signed with a name I had never heard, James Kels. Kels' letter said Elsevier was definitely not interested in publishing the *Handbook*.

Who was Kels? I telephoned him, and learned he supervised the editor with whom I had been dealing. I told Kels I would not have spent a year working on the *Handbook*, if I had not believed Elsevier was committed to it. He invited me to visit Amsterdam, and I hopped a plane.

Kels was charming and apologetic. He explained that, when he first wrote, he had not understood how far the editor had committed Elsevier; the editor had exceeded his authority. Kels and I disagreed mainly about the *Handbook*'s completion date. He wanted it done much faster than I thought feasible. I agreed to strive for his target. He said that we really ought to have a formal contract, and proffered one. I signed with a sigh of relief.

That signature later proved unwise.

MILWAUKEE, 1974-1984

Endowed chairs give freedom to people who will not take advantage of it. The Milwaukee chair provided me a good salary, a light teaching load, and discretion about what I taught. At age 40, I thought I had the kind of position professors dream of. What I had not seen were the resentments of less lucky professors and an ideological split in the business faculty.

I saw the chair as a chance to help colleagues as well as to spend time on research. I imagined a mutual-support group similar to the one we had at Purdue, and I invited all and sundry to join me in a project. We would define the project jointly and seek a grant. It came as quite a surprise that only one person besides Bo Hedberg showed interest—Paul Nystrom.

The three of us began a collaboration that extended ten years. We assembled a proposal by pooling our ideas. The National Science Foundation's budget had recently been cut, but our proposal looked good to us.

We also pooled ideas for a talk I was to make at a conference on organizational design. Hedberg contributed case studies and poetic ideas; Nystrom injected good sense and organized us. The talk went very well. Because it contained too many ideas for one article, we dissected it into two outlines: Hedberg turned one into a draft, Nystrom the other, and I rewrote the drafts. Learning to write better was a major step toward reorienting myself from a mathematical social scientist to a management theorist.

After NSF sent our proposal out for review, two or three of the reviewers wrote to us telling us how much they liked it. So when NSF rejected it, we were aghast. We had been so confident!

I consulted March, who had much experience with NSF. He said we should resubmit. I interviewed NSF's program director for sociology, then we did almost everything he specified and resubmitted.

Again, NSF rejected the proposal. This time, Hedberg interviewed the program director. After a long talk, the program director explained, "Look, you've got to understand that we're saving our money for grants to *real* sociologists." I have submitted no proposals to NSF since.

Other strange events transpired that first year. I had been appointed to hire an assistant professor of organization science, and a young English friend had expressed interest. Although he was willing to come as an assistant professor, he had 24 strong publications—more than all but a few in UWM's business faculty. I thought he represented a tremendous opportunity, so I asked the tenured professors for permission to offer him a visiting associate professorship for two years. They not only refused, they voted to hire no one in organization science. They were clearly angry. I thought their anger was a response to my proposal, but I had no idea why.

A few weeks later, without telling Nystrom or me, the other tenured professors went to the president and demanded that he replace the dean. I heard that the main accusations against the dean were two: He had long shown favoritism toward organization science, and he had given the endowed chair to an organization scientist.

Months later, two professors—but I think them outliers—told me I had disappointed them by not leading a revolt against the dean. They said they had voted to hire me because they had expected me to lead a revolt. I, of course, would never have moved to Milwaukee if I had suspected such a situation.

I began going to Al Anon, the organization for spouses of alcoholics. Then I confronted Sharlene about her drinking and told her I had arranged for her to enter treatment. To my surprise, she agreed.

Living with an alcoholic creates scars. Al Anon was remarkably helpful in sorting out my priorities, gaining objectivity, and figuring out what to do about myself. It worked largely because the participants were equals—no one was a therapist and no one was in charge.

I also met with a marriage counsellor as part of Sharlene's treatment program. After several sessions, I realized that he seemed to be saying something unexpected. I asked, "Are you telling me I ought to get a divorce?"

He replied, "You have to decide that for yourself, but it *is* one possibility. Not many marriages survive alcoholism."

The ensuing weeks were very painful because I had to look behind my twenty-year-old illusions. Was it wrong to abandon the woman I had married for life? Or was the woman I had married not this one?

I also reviewed the research on divorce and on alcoholism. No treatment was more successful than spontaneous remission. Because most alcoholics go through treatments repeatedly, this round of treatment would likely produce no more than another temporary pause in a long-term decline. I dreaded spending the end of my life with someone deranged.

April Fools' Day 1975 was memorable: That day, I went through an income-tax audit, signed divorce papers, and told Sharlene I had signed them. At least, the audit ended on a light note. During the previous year, I had lived in two countries and received income from three. Exchange rates had changed monthly. The records filled a large box. After two hours, the auditor had only found that I had deducted journal subscriptions on the wrong schedule, which had no effect on my taxes. Jokingly, he asked, "If I promise to enter into the record that you are the most honest man I ever met, will you promise to go away and never come back?"

While in Germany, Sharlene and I had kept in contact with Joan Dunbar, our baby-sitter during the year in London. Joan had remained in London, single and unattached. Sharlene and our daughters stayed with Joan when they visited London, and I telephoned Joan or took her to dinner.

Thus, Joan contacted us when she came to Milwaukee on business that spring. Only there was no longer an us. Sharlene was still in treatment, and I had filed for divorce. Joan and I began to appraise each other in a different light.

Divorce turned out a blessing for Sharlene. Although she got half our assets and alimony for a few years, the money would run out eventually. She realized she had to hold a job in order to stay off skid row. And she did. She became a counsellor in an alcoholic treatment center and never reverted to drinking.

Both of my daughters dressed like hippies, and they did not fit into the local high school, where many girls wore high heels and lipstick. The older dropped out of school as soon as she was 18, and became a school-bus driver. The younger asked to attend a boarding school that had a reputation for succeeding with problem children. I enrolled her thankfully.

Two months later, the head of the school telephoned. My daughter had been caught shoplifting in a nearby town. She would not be charged, but I would have to remove her from campus immediately. Going home, she speculated, "Now, I guess you'll have to enroll me in Riverside High School."

For a dozen hours, I had been thinking I had been too gentle and too understanding. "No, I don't," I declared. "I don't plan to enroll you anywhere! I'm tired of paying for your food and housing while you screw around. You can live at home if you pay rent, but you have to get a job and start supporting yourself."

She could have taken me to court. Instead, she got a job as a waitress, began wearing neater clothes, found a college student to tutor her, and six weeks later, passed the GED with high enough scores to qualify for early admission to the university. Two months after I had driven home an expelled shoplifter, I had a seventeen-year-old college student.

She did very well her first semester, and asked for a trip to San Diego to visit friends she had known in Germany. I bought her a round-trip bus ticket.

Except for one short visit, she never came home again. She drifted northward to San Francisco, then joined a commune that was raising marijuana in the mountains.

Joan Dunbar moved from London and in with me. She had difficulty adjusting to Milwaukee and began agitating.

Meanwhile, a couple of chapters had shown how much time it would take to edit the *Handbook of Organizational Design*, and Nystrom agreed to share the editorship. We discovered that design was not a concept that came naturally. Some authors did not want to include prescriptive ideas in their chapters. Many authors said "is" or "must" where they meant "should." Our own feelings showed that prescriptions arouse resistance unless they are phrased contingently—"In order to achieve X, one should do Y."

Bo Hedberg had returned to Sweden, where he engineered a Fulbright fellowship that he expected Nystrom to win. Hedberg persuaded the Fulbright Commission to allocate a fellowship to his department, then he wrote an advertisement for the fellowship that described the research the three of us had been doing.

Five days before the deadline, Nystrom told me he did not intend to apply for the fellowship. I had no desire to visit Sweden, but Hedberg had gone to so much trouble and might not get the kind of visitor he sought. I asked Nystrom for the application forms, thinking if I apply, I can always turn it down; but if I do not apply, I cannot change my mind later. Famous last words!

The next morning, I started to type the application. Then the telephone rang, and a static-laden voice announced cheerfully, "This is Arent Greve calling from Bergen, Norway. It is all arranged."

Who is Arent Greve? I wondered. "*What* is all arranged?"

"Your visit. The Board approved it."

"What visit are you talking about?"

"Your visit to Bergen next year. You and Johan Arndt discussed it at Indiana University last fall."

Good grief! Be careful what you say to strangers on buses. Months before, I had sat beside a Norwegian I did not know. He remarked that they were thinking about inviting someone to visit his school, and asked if I were interested. Assuming this was just idle chitchat, I said politely, "Well, I have enjoyed visiting other countries. Feel free to contact me."

The Norse gods seemed to be calling me to Scandinavia. I finished the Fulbright application. Not until after I won it did I realize that Hedberg's department would have no visitor at all if I refused to go.

Well, maybe a year abroad would scratch Joan's itches. I arranged to spend a summer and fall in Bergen, Norway, and a spring and summer in Gothenburg, Sweden.

We stopped in London on our way to Norway. Feeling romantic, I told Joan I loved her and asked her to marry me.

She asked, "Why?" Marriage would serve no useful purpose, she explained, for two who did not plan to have children.

My feelings were hurt.

In early fall, Nystrom and I received a letter from James Kels, who had moved to New York and taken our *Handbook* project with him. Kels said

Elsevier had decided against publishing the *Handbook*. He invoked two clauses that are in every contract offered by every book publisher: One clause says the manuscript must be delivered by such-and-such date. In human history, only one author ever came through on time. If another author does finish on time, the publisher can rely on the second clause. It says, in nice language, that the publisher has to like the manuscript.

Nystrom and I were in shock. The project was four years old, and we had been editing chapters full-time for eighteen months. Many finished chapters had gone to Elsevier for copy editing.

I telephoned a friend in the Netherlands. He inquired, then told me Elsevier was controlled at the top by four men: Mr. Van Tongeren supervised Kels' division. I wrote to Mr. Van Tongeren. He telephoned me and said we should not worry: He was going to New York that very week, and he would look into the matter. Two weeks later, we received a letter from Kels saying the previous letter had been in error; Elsevier would publish the *Handbook*.

Sharlene telephoned. Our daughter in California had committed suicide.

I got on a plane to America. Tears were running down my cheeks. An elderly, little Scandinavian lady sat down beside me. She watched me for a few minutes. Then, she reached over, put her hand on my arm, and said, "It will be all right. I am sure that the pilot has crossed the ocean many times before."

Four months later, Dad too died suddenly. We had made peace but never truly understood each other.

Joan's skills were in short supply, so she easily found work in Norway and had three job offers in Sweden. Yet the Swedes refused to give her a work permit. Hedberg inquired, and a labor official told him that, because Joan was unmarried, they feared she might be trying to become a permanent resident of Sweden under false pretenses.

Joan said, "Let's get married so I can get a work permit."

"That's a terrible reason to marry," I answered.

Her feelings were hurt.

Another letter arrived from Kels declaring that Elsevier would not publish the *Handbook*. I immediately telephoned Mr. Van Tongeren. A voice from Amsterdam explained that Mr. Van Tongeren retired two weeks ago.

The *Handbook* was almost complete; just a few chapters still needed revision. We wanted to find another publisher quickly, before authors withdrew their chapters and published them independently.

We feared other publishers would take Elsevier's withdrawal as a signal that the *Handbook* was risky or unprofitable. We drafted a long letter. Only one paragraph discussed the book's content; several pages discussed business issues. Who would buy it and why? What were the competing books? How many copies would it likely sell? March's *Handbook of Organizations* gave a basis for a forecast. What would be the profits? Editing *ASQ* had taught me about typesetting and printing costs.

To play it safe, we mailed our letter to 36 publishers. We were astonished when almost all expressed interest and 24 expressed strong interest. Rather than lacking a publisher, we had far too many.

Then, one publisher pointed out that we had no right to sign another contract because we still had a contract with Elsevier. Kels had not released us from the contract. Seething, we had to ask him for a release.

We decided to focus on three publishers—one prestigious academic press, one small entrepreneurial firm, and one large textbook bureaucracy. Editors from the textbook bureaucracy chartered a plane, flew to Milwaukee, and tried to induce Nystrom to sign immediately. This was their final offer they said; waiting would change nothing. He told them we were committed to negotiating with three publishers.

We told all three publishers what the others had proposed. All three then improved their proposals. Again, the textbook bureaucracy declared that they were making a final offer, but this time their credibility was zero.

One more round produced three identical offers and no basis for choosing between them. Can you guess how the textbook bureaucracy described their offer?

After doing some research by telephoning librarians and other publishers, we signed with Oxford University Press. They proved wonderful in every respect.

I believe I have learned three lessons about book publishing.

1. To publishers, books are investments made to return profits. Publishers are not interested in books' contents as such.
2. The contracts offered by publishers are written by publishers' lawyers and give rights mainly to publishers.
3. Authors should not sign contracts until their manuscripts are nearly complete. Like most people, publishers are risk averse. When they evaluate a prospectus, publishers cannot be sure when or whether an author will deliver a finished manuscript, how good that manuscript will be, in what state the economy will be at that time, or what other publishing projects will be vying for their attention. When publishers evaluate a completed manuscript, they have much less uncertainty.

When we signed with Oxford, we expected the *Handbook* to appear within a year. It took three.

With Nystrom's help, Hedberg and I eventually settled the argument begun in Berlin. Fortunately for our friendship, we settled it by agreeing that we had both been partly right. We stopped talking about stagnating environments and started talking about organizations facing crises.

Crises are indeed produced by organization's environments, although not quite as Hedberg had initially conceived. Environments change so as to obsolete markets, products, and technologies, but environments also endorse notions about how to organize that make it hard for organizations to adapt to environmental changes.

Crises are produced by organizations as well, but somewhat differently than I had conceived at first. Organizations do make mistakes, but they also strive to stabilize their environments and they blind themselves to environmental events that deviate from their expectations ("Why Organizations Run into Crises," 1989).

Hegel would have been proud of us. Our apparently contrary positions were two aspects of a more complex interpretation. Of course, such an outcome may also have been an inevitable result of our friendship, which had grown much stronger through years of collaboration.

Joan had rejected my proposal in London, and I had rejected hers in Gothenburg. Now we were back in Milwaukee, and we had lived together nearly three years. I thought I wanted to marry her, but I was not sure marriage was a good idea because people tend to put less effort into permanent relations than temporary ones. I was sure a proposal would be a turning point.

One evening, Joan queried, "What's bothering you? You've been wandering around distracted for two weeks."

I thought, well, now you're going to have to tell her what is on your mind; and if you are going to do that, you had might as well propose; and if you are going to do that, you had might as well do it the right way. I knelt at her feet and asked, "Will you please marry me?"

She paused for a moment, then said both smiling and serious, "I'm going to say yes, but first I have to think about it."

Her logic was impeccable: She did not want to leave me in doubt, but neither did she intend to jump at my proposal too eagerly.

Thus, I married our baby-sitter. The moral for doctoral students is: Choose your dissertation supervisor carefully, for he might marry your sister.

Nystrom and I became ever closer collaborators, like Stan and Ollie. Other people claimed we shouted at each other; we called it discussion. We wrote almost everything together, each doing the tasks we did best. We jointly taught many courses, each covering the topics we liked best.

I mainly taught in the Executive MBA program. In one course, the executives attacked real-life problems arising from their jobs. Alone or in small groups, they identified problems, designed change efforts, attempted the change efforts, monitored the results, analyzed what had happened, and then designed new change efforts. The problems ranged from a difficult subordinate to reorienting a division. I learned more than any of the students, because I watched 150 such efforts over ten years, but I have yet to do something with what I learned.

Hedberg reported that he had bought an Apple computer for his home. I had not known such tiny computers existed, but headed for the nearest dealer. Two hours later, we had a new member of our household.

With bloodshot eyes and unaware of my surroundings, I wrote programs twenty hours a day. Joan reacted as if I had brought another woman into the house. After two months, she demanded that we leave town for a vacation—anywhere.

After we came home from our trip, I finally opened a packet I had bought initially. It was a word-processing program, and I drafted three articles in a month. I had always found writing very hard to start: I would write the first sentence over and over for days, even weeks. With the Apple, it no longer mattered what I said first because everything could be juggled around so easily.

At IBM, I had programmed in machine language—the codes used by computer hardware. I decided to relearn machine-language programming with my Apple. Then I decided to write a word-processing program better than the one I was using. Then I decided to write a manual and to find a publisher. A large computer-users club took it on. Then it needed additions to accommodate hardware variations. Finally, *Microwriter* went on sale for $12.50.

I tried to teach information systems to executives. I believed then, and still do, that every manager should have hands-on experience with computers. They also ought to try a bit of programming in order to appreciate the difficulty of writing error-free programs. In the early 1980s, these ideas were a decade ahead of their time.

The executives rebelled. One posted on the bulletin board an article from the *Wall Street Journal* titled "Real Managers Don't Touch Computers." Their ratings of my teaching nearly set a new record—in the wrong direction.

The *Handbook* finally appeared in print—eight years after it began. The Academy of Management gave it the Terry Award as the best book on management published that year, and Oxford made a second printing. Perseverance and quality had paid off, although the intended payoffs—better science and better organizations—will take a long time and help from others.

At the University of Wisconsin, pay increases were partly across-the-board and partly for merit, with merit increases being voted by the tenured professors. UWM's tenured professors awarded me no merit increases whatever for several years in the beginning, even though I published at least as well as anyone else, my teaching ratings almost always ranked in the top five, and I served on as many editorial boards as the rest of the faculty together. Eventually, the tenured professors began awarding me small raises, and the dean intervened with additions to these. Then Wisconsin elected a governor who said universities cost too much. For four years, everyone got tiny raises. Of course, wages outside Wisconsin did not obey UWM's tenured professors or the governor.

I had visited New York University many times. Dutton had moved there from SMU, and I usually stopped to see his family when I passed through. Then Roger Dunbar moved to NYU. Through Dunbar and Dutton, I met many of the management faculty. Four NYU professors in other fields had been my colleagues in Berlin.

In 1982, David Rogers asked if I wanted to be considered for an endowed chair at NYU. I sent him my résumé but told him I was very unlikely to leave Milwaukee. My colleagues in organization sciences were terrific. We had an incredible apartment. Joan really liked her friends and her job. We both found the city of Milwaukee very comfortable.

NYU offered the chair to someone else.

The next year, Alan Meyer, a colleague and close friend, came up for promotion to tenure. The tenured professors' discussion of his case dramatized the ideological split. An economist who had not published since he received tenure observed that there were already enough high-quality professors in organization science. Karl Weick had written a letter saying Meyer's article was the best *ASQ* had published for five years and *ASQ* had nominated it for a national award. A statistician conjectured that Weick was only trying to make it appear *ASQ* published good articles; because of its lack of statistical rigor, the research did not meet minimum scientific standards. Heads nodded sagely in agreement. Ten of nineteen voted for tenure.

Soon after, David Rogers telephoned and said they were reopening the search for a chairholder. This time, I was interested. I was fed up with conflict and people who thought they looked bad because their neighbors looked good.

I visited NYU informally and met with Dean Bob Hawkins. He said the search committee had nominated me for the chair, he agreed, and he would mail me an offer before Christmas. He asked what teaching interested me most. I said I would like more contact with doctoral students. He said NYU needed that.

Christmas came and passed with no offer. In late January, Rogers reported that there would be a delay: A few professors had protested the lack of democracy in choosing me. In early March, Rogers explained that some had nominated another candidate. Both candidates would visit, then the entire management faculty would vote.

I was in a beauty pageant. I was not certain I wanted the title, but I do hate losing.

Typically, I took a risk. I noticed that the NYU professors had been asking questions about me instead of my research. Hiring, I realized, is a choice of a person rather than a project. So I set aside my planned talk and spoke about myself. I tried to be as forthright as I could, exposing my faults and mistakes as well as my successes and good fortune.

At the end of my talk, one listener excoriated me in no uncertain terms. He exploded: "I have heard Robert Heilbroner and Arthur Schlesinger tell about their lives and learned from them, but I have learned nothing from your life. You have merely wasted our time."

His attack shook me. However, other listeners realized that he had missed the point; so he had underscored the fact that I had not lectured, but spoken plainly as a person.

In late April, my telephone rang and a woman's voice said, "Dean Hawkins is calling. Just one moment please."

Hawkins said cheerfully, "I'm calling to offer you the ITT Chair. I believe you know the terms."

I replied, "No, no one ever told me the terms." One might wonder why I had not asked.

Hawkins asked, "Didn't you and I discuss the salary and other terms when we talked before Christmas?"

"No," I answered.

"Well, this is what we are offering." He named a couple of numbers.

I interjected, "Just a moment, I need to get a pencil." Mainly, I needed to digest the numbers he had stated.

Joan did not want to leave Milwaukee or to live in New York. Yet, we agreed, if I turned down this offer, we should plan on staying in Milwaukee indefinitely. People who knew I had rejected these terms would not bother making offers. NYU had a superb faculty and excellent doctoral students. Too, I figured a contestant in a beauty pageant should not withdraw after the emcee names the winner.

Ned Elton, a friend from Berlin, advised us to rent an apartment from NYU, and Joan wanted to see what that meant. I told Hawkins that we wanted to look at apartments before finally saying yes.

NYU's housing agent explained that he had two exceptional apartments to show us. The first was acceptable to us, but only three rooms, and ugly compared to our place in Milwaukee. The second apartment was gorgeous—many rooms, leaded windows, fireplace, parquet floors, overlooking a park.

I promptly declared, "We'll take it."

The agent said, "I'm sorry but you can't have it. We're saving it for one of the three deans the university is trying to hire."

"Then why did you show it to us?" I asked.

"Well," he explained, "you're important enough to see it, just not important enough to have it."

A few days after I accepted NYU's offer, Sharlene was killed in an auto accident.

NEW YORK, 1985-

I had been at NYU for about six weeks and was renewing acquaintance with Ned Elton in his office in NYU's finance department. He asked, "Would you like to go to lunch? We have a lunchroom where the economics and finance professors gather every noon, and I always grab a sandwich and eat there. It's a good place to see everybody and to find out what is going on."

I said, "Sure," and we headed for the cafeteria to buy sandwiches.

When we walked into the lunchroom, Ned jokingly announced, "Everybody, this is Bill Starbuck. He's one of the enemy."

To find out what happened next, you will have to read the next installment.

LESSONS TO LEARN

I offer one last anecdote to those who feel they have not learned enough already. It has at least four morals, probably more. It also echoes two lessons about social science research, one of them very important.

I was touring Mexico. Before departing, I read a travel guide that warned one not to drink water from faucets. So for two weeks, I carefully restricted myself to the bottled water that every room provided.

Near midnight on a very hot night in Yucatan, I drank the last of my bottled water. I took my bottle down to the desk clerk and asked if he could get me more.

He said, "I will be happy to help you as soon as I am finished, but you are welcome to get the water yourself."

"I don't mind getting the water myself," I answered. "Where is it?"

"Just fill the bottle at that faucet over there," he instructed.

"You mean this is just ordinary water from the faucet! Why do you put it in bottles?

"Tourists refuse to drink it unless it is in bottles," he explained.

PUBLICATIONS

1958

Computing machines: Rent or buy? *Journal of Industrial Engineering, 9*, 254-258.

1961

With R.M. Cyert and J.G. March. Two experiments on bias and conflict in organizational estimation. *Management Science, 7*, 254-264.

Testing case-descriptive models. *Behavioral Science, 6*, 191-199.

1962

A generalization of Terborgh's approach to equipment replacement. *International Journal of Production Research, 1*(3), 29-38.

1963

Level of aspiration. *Psychological Review, 70*, 51-60.

Level of aspiration theory and economic behavior. *Behavioral Science, 8*, 128-136.

Sales volume and employment in British and American retail trade. In W.S. Decker (Ed.), *Emerging concepts in marketing* (pp. 212-219). Chicago: American Marketing Association.

Contributions to *A behavioral theory of the firm,* by R.M. Cyert & J.G. March. Englewood Cliffs, NJ: Prentice-Hall.

With P.G. Herbst. Discussion of "Measurement of behavior structures of means of input-output data." *Human Relations, 16*, 385-389.

With J.M. Dutton. On managers and theories. *Management International, 6*, 25-50.

1964

The aspiration mechanism. *General Systems, 9*, 191-203.

1965

Mathematics and organization theory. In J.G. March (Ed.), *Handbook of organizations* (pp. 335-386). Chicago: Rand McNally.

Organizational growth and development. In J.G. March (Ed.), *Handbook of organizations* (pp. 451-583). Chicago: Rand McNally.

1966

Eve with 28 faces. *Contemporary Psychology, 11*, 119, 122.

Mathematics and the social sciences. *Tenth Muse* (Spring).

With E. Kobrow. The effects of advisors on business game teams. *American Behavioral Scientist, 10*(3): 28-30.

The efficiency of British and American retail employees. *Administrative Science Quarterly, 11*, 345-385.

On teaching business policy. *Academy of Management Journal, 9*, 356-361.

1967

With F.M. Bass. An experimental study of risk-taking and the value of information in a new product context. *Journal of Business, 40*, 155-165.

[Review of R.E. Brown's *Judgment in administration*]. *Administrative Science Quarterly, 11*, 697-699.

With J.M. Dutton. How Charlie estimates run-time. In M.P. Hottenstein & R.W. Millman (Eds.), *Research toward the development of management thought* (pp. 48-63). Bowling Green, OH: Academy of Management.

1968

Organizational metamorphosis. In R.W. Millman & M.P. Hottenstein (Eds.), *Promising research directions* (pp. 113-132). Bowling Green, OH: Academy of Management.

Some comments, observations, and objections stimulated by "Design of proof in organizational research." *Administrative Science Quarterly, 13*, 135-161.

1969

Coordination, output markets, and collective action. In M. Zald (Ed.), *Power in organizations* (pp. 312-321). Nashville, TN: Vanderbilt University Press.

1971

[Editor]. *Organizational growth and development.* Harmondsworth, Middlesex: Penguin Books.

Concerning a misspecified specification. *Sociometry, 34*, 214-226.

With J.M. Dutton. Computer simulation models of human behavior: A history of an intellectual technology. *IEEE Transactions on Systems, Man and Cybernetics*, SMC-1, 128-171.

With J.M. Dutton. The history of simulation models. In W.H. Starbuck & J.M. Dutton (Eds.), *Computer simulation of human behavior* (pp. 9-102). New York: Wiley.

With J.M. Dutton. Finding Charlie's run-time estimator. In W.H. Starbuck & J.M. Dutton (Eds.), *Computer simulation of human behavior* (pp. 218-242). New York: Wiley.

Edited with J.M. Dutton. *Computer simulation of human behavior*. New York: Wiley.

With D.F. Grant. Bargaining strategies with asymmetric initiation and termination. *Journal of Applied Social Psychology, 1*, 344-363.

1972

A critique. In T.J. Burns (Ed.), *Behavioral experiments in accounting* (pp. 458-474). Columbus: The Ohio State University.

[Review of H.C. White's *Chains of Opportunity*]. *Acta Sociologica, 15*, 298-301.

1973

With J.M. Dutton. Computer simulation as a tool for descriptive behavioral science. In W. Goldberg (Ed.), *Computer simulation versus analytical solutions for business and economic models, volume I: Simulation methodology* (pp. 257-289). Gothenburg: BAS, Business Administration Studies.

Tadpoles into Armageddon and Chrysler into butterflies. *Social Science Research, 2*, 81-109.

With J.M. Dutton. Designing adaptive organizations. *Journal of Business Policy, 3*(4): 21-28.

With J.M. Dutton. Trends in the growth and development of computer simulation. In W.G. Yost & M.H. Mickle (Eds.), *Modeling and Simulation* (Vol. 4, pp. 47-52). Pittsburgh, PA: Instrument Society of America.

1974

The current state of organization theory. In J.W. McGuire (Ed.), *Contemporary management: Issues and viewpoints* (pp. 123-139). Englewood Cliffs, NJ: Prentice-Hall.

[Review of J. Hage's *Techniques and problems of theory construction in sociology*]. *Administrative Science Quarterly, 19*, 262-264.

Systems optimization with unknown criteria. In *Proceedings of the 1974 International Conference on Systems, Man and Cybernetics* (pp. 67-76). New York: Institute of Electrical and Electronics Engineers.

1975

Information systems for organizations of the future. In E. Grochla & N. Szyperski (Eds.), *Information systems and organizational structure* (pp. 217-229). Berlin: de Gruyter.

1976

Organizations and their environments. In M.D. Dunnette (Ed.), *Handbook of industrial and organizational psychology* (pp. 1069-1123). Chicago: Rand McNally.

With B.L.T. Hedberg & P.C. Nystrom. Camping on seesaws: Prescriptions for a self-designing organization. *Administrative Science Quarterly, 21*, 41-65.

With P.C. Nystrom & B.L.T. Hedberg. Interacting processes as organization designs. In R.H. Kilmann, L.R. Pondy, & D.P. Slevin (Eds.), *The management of organization design, Vol. I. Strategies and implementation.* New York: Elsevier North-Holland.

1977

With P.C. Nystrom. Why prescription is prescribed. In W.H. Starbuck & P.C. Nystrom (Eds.), *Prescriptive models of organizations* (pp. 1-5). Amsterdam: North-Holland.

With B.L.T. Hedberg & P.C. Nystrom. Designing organizations to match tomorrow. In W.H. Starbuck & P.C. Nystrom (Eds.), *Prescriptive models of organizations* (pp. 171-181). Amsterdam: North-Holland.

Edited with P.C. Nystrom. *Prescriptive models of organizations.* Amsterdam: North-Holland.

With B.L.T. Hedberg. Saving an organization from a stagnating environment. In H.B. Thorelli (Ed.), *Strategy + structure = performance: The strategic planning imperative* (pp. 249-258). Bloomington: Indiana University Press.

1978

With A. Greve & B.L.T. Hedberg. Responding to crises. *Journal of Business Administration, 9*(2), 111-137.

1979

With J.M. Dutton. Diffusion of an intellectual technology. In K. Krippendorff (Ed.), in *Communication and control in society* (pp. 489-511). New York: Gordon and Breach.

Organisationstheorie—Mathematische Modelle einer einzelnen Organisation [Organization theory—Mathematical models of a single organization]. In M.J. Beckman, G. Menges, & R. Selten (Eds.), *Handwörterbuch der Mathematischen Wirtschaftswissenschaften* (Vol. 1, pp. 309-314). Weisbaden: Th. Gabler.

1980

[Review of *Research in organizational behavior*]. *Administrative Science Quarterly, 25*, 533-536.

1981

A trip to view the elephants and rattlesnakes in the garden of Aston. In A.H. Van de Ven & W.F. Joyce (Eds.), *Perspectives on organization design and behavior* (pp. 167-198). New York: Wiley-Interscience.

With P.C. Nystrom. Designing and understanding organizations. In W.H. Starbuck & P.C. Nystrom (Eds.), *Handbook of organizational design* (Vol. 1, pp. ix-xxii). New York: Oxford University Press.

Edited with P.C. Nystrom. *Handbook of organizational design* (Vols. 1 & 2). New York: Oxford University Press.

With P.C. Nystrom. Why the world needs organisational design. *Journal of General Management, 6*, 3-17.

1982

Congealing oil: Inventing ideologies to justify acting ideologies out. *Journal of Management Studies, 19*(1), 3-27.

[Edited special issue on] Ideologies within and around organizations. *Journal of Management Studies, 19*(1).

Epson MX-80 print-control program for the Apple II. *BYTE, 7*(3), 166-170.

Doing it with a naked Apple: Relocating machine language. *Call-A.P.P.L.E., 5*(12), 15-21.

Amplifying uncertainty. *Contemporary Psychology, 27*, 726-727.

1983

With P.C. Nystrom. Pursuing organizational effectiveness that is ambiguously specified. In K. Cameron & D.A. Whetten (Eds.), *Organizational effectiveness*, (pp. 135-161). New York: Academic Press.

Organizations as action generators. *American Sociological Review, 48*, 91-102.

Computer simulation of human behavior. *Behavioral Science, 28*, 154-165.

1984

With P.C. Nystrom. To avoid organizational crises, unlearn. *Organizational Dynamics, 12*(4), 53-65.

Microwriter //e. Renton, WA: Apple Puget Sound Program Library Exchange (A.P.P.L.E.).

With P.C. Nystrom. Managing beliefs in organizations. *Journal of Applied Behavioral Science, 20*(3), 277-287.

With P.C. Nystrom. Organizational facades. *Academy of Management, Proceedings of the Annual Meeting, Boston* (pp. 182-185).

Microwriter][+. Renton, WA: Apple Puget Sound Program Library Exchange (A.P.P.L.E.).

Columns published as The Programmer's Corner. *Icon* (1984-85).

1985

Acting first and thinking later: Theory versus reality in strategic change. In J.M. Pennings & Associates, (Eds.), *Organizational strategy decision and change* (pp. 336-372). San Francisco, CA: Jossey-Bass.

1987

With P.C. Nystrom. Fuhrung in Krisensituationen [Leadership in crisis situations]. In A. Kieser, G. Reber, & R. Wunderer (Eds.), *Handwörterbuch der Führung* (pp. 1274-1283). C.E. Poeschel Verlag.

Sharing cognitive tasks between people and computers in space systems. In T.B. Sheridan, D.S. Kruser, & S. Deutsch (Eds.), *Human factors in automated and robotic space systems: Proceedings of a symposium* (pp. 418-443). National Research Council.

1988

With J. Webster. Theory building in industrial and organizational psychology. In C.L. Cooper & I.T. Robertson (Eds.), *International review of industrial and organizational psychology 1988* (pp. 93-138). New York: Wiley.

Surmounting our human limitations. In R. Quinn & K. Cameron (Eds.), *Paradox and transformation: Toward a theory of change in organization and management* (pp. 65-80). Cambridge, MA: Ballinger.

With F.J. Milliken. Challenger: Changing the odds until something breaks. *Journal of Management Studies, 25*, 319-340.

With F.J. Milliken. Executives' perceptual filters: What they notice and how they make sense. In D.C. Hambrick (Ed.), *The executive effect: Concepts and methods for studying top managers* (pp. 35-65). Greenwich, CT: JAI Press.

1989

Why organizations run into crises . . . and sometimes survive them. In K.C. Laudon & J. Turner (Eds.), *Information technology and management strategy* (pp. 11-33). Englewood Cliffs, NJ: Prentice-Hall.

1990

With P.N. Pant. Innocents in the forest: Forecasting and research methods. *Journal of Management, 16*(2), 433-460.

Creating effective symbioses of computers and people. In K.M. Kaiser & H.J. Oppelland (Eds.), *Desktop information technology* (pp. 395-399). Amsterdam: North-Holland.

Knowledge-intensive firms: Learning to survive in strange environments. In L. Lindmark (Ed.), *Kunskap som kritisk resurs* [*Knowledge as a critical resource*] (pp. 10-20). Umeaa: University of Umeaa, Department of Business Administration.

1991

With J. Webster. When is play productive? *Accounting, Management & Information Technologies, 1*, 1-20.

1992

Learning by knowledge-intensive firms. *Journal of Management Studies, 29*(6), 713-740.

With D. Ahlstrom & J. Mezias. Impact factors of journals related to I/O psychology. *The Industrial-Organizational Psychologist, 30*(1), 51-55.

Strategizing in the real world. *International Journal of Technology Management, Special Publication on Technological Foundations of Strategic Management, 8*(1/2), 77-85.

1993

With A.D. Meyer. Interactions between politics and idelogies in strategy formation. In K. Roberts (Ed.), *New challenges to understanding organizations* (pp. 99-116). New York: Macmillan.

Keeping a butterfly and an elephant in a house of cards: The elements of exceptional success. *Journal of management Studies, 30*(4).

"Watch where you step?" or Indiana Starbuck amid the perils of Academe (Rated PG). In A. Bedian (Ed.), *Management laureates: A collection of autobiographical essays* (Vol. 3). Greenwich, CT: JAI Press.

On behalf of naiveté. In J.A.C. Baum & J.V. Singh (Eds.), *Evolutionary dyanmics of organizations*. New York: Oxford University Press.

With A.D. Meyer. Organizations and industries in flux: The interplay of rationality and ideology. In C. Gersick (Ed.), *Change in the workplace: Distinguished scholar monographs*. Los Angeles: UCLA Institute of Industrial Relations.

1994

How organizations channel creativity. In C.M. Ford & D.A. Gioia (Eds.), *Creativity in organizational contexts*. Newbury Park, CA: Sage.

With P.C. Nystrom. Leadership in crises. In A. Kieser, G. Reber, & R. Wunderer (Eds.), *Handwörterbuch der Führung* (2nd ed.). Stuttgart: C.E. Poeschel Verlag.

NOTES

I am grateful to David Ahlstrom, Art Bedeian, Dick Cyert, Joan Dunbar, John Dutton, Diane Elton, Ned Elton, Bo Hedberg, Helaine Korn, Alan Meyer, Nancy Meyer, Danny Miller, Paul Nystrom, Narayan Pant, Marc Pilisuk, Stan Seashore, and Bhatt Vadlamani for their corrections and suggestions.

1. See H.A. Simon. (1955). A behavioral model of rational choice. *Quarterly Journal of Economics, 69*, 99-118.

2. See H.L. Fromkin. (1969). The behavioral science laboratories at Purdue's Krannert School. *Administrative Science Quarterly, 14*, 171-177.

3. See R.L.M. Dunbar, J.M. Dutton, and W.R. Torbert. (1982). Crossing Mother: Ideological constraints on organizational improvements. *Journal of Management Studies, 19*, 91-108.

George A. Steiner

My Roads To Management Theory and Practice

GEORGE A. STEINER

Like the lives of most other people, my life has not been a smooth journey on one central highway. There have been many forks, twists, and turns in the road traveled. The routes taken in my scholarly work, which is the main focus of this account, have been determined by many forces. Of great importance have been personal choices motivated by teachers, friends, colleagues, classroom discussions, books and other reading matter; daydreaming; opportunities; and employment assignments. Chance, luck, and the dictates of events over which I had no control also have been responsible for paths pursued.

My academic career can be divided into two periods: pre- and post-World War II. World War II was a major fork in the road for me as it was for so many others. In both periods, especially the postwar era, I moved in and out of the academy, government, and business. Throughout, and particularly in the postwar period, I mixed theory and practice.

Prior to World War II my adult intellectual focus was economics, especially in the fields of money and banking, international monetary policy, taxation, corporation finance, investments, and current economic trends. Following World War II the central theme has been management theory and practice, especially in three interconnected areas: strategic planning, strategic management, and business-government-society relationships. My teaching, research, and consulting have been intertwined in these fields. In each field I have written textbooks which set forth new directions for teaching and research.

In this autobiography I will explain the main forces and people that led me into these fields. A few reflections on other aspects of my early life will then be presented.

STRATEGIC PLANNING

Early Interest in Planning (1929-1937)

My interest in planning began during the Great Depression of the 1930s.[1] From late 1929 to the mid-1930s this nation suffered its worst economic catastrophe. It is difficult to describe the human suffering, financial disaster, and social disruption that this crisis caused. A few facts reveal something of this extraordinary tragedy. Gross national product (in current dollars) fell from $103.1 billion in 1929 to $58 billion in 1932 at the depth of the depression. Failures of banks, savings and loans, farms, and businesses were at an all-time peak. The unemployment rate rose in 1933 to 25 percent of the labor force, a level which lasted not for days but for months. There was no federal or other unemployment insurance for the unemployed, nor was there much public welfare.

Into this world I graduated in June 1929 from Girard College in Philadelphia. My life was comparatively sheltered at Girard and it was a shock to enter the work force at a time when jobs were scarce and my relatives and their friends were becoming unemployed. I did, however, find a few part time jobs which sustained me until January 1930, when I went to work full-time on the Reading Railroad in Philadelphia. This job enabled me to enter the School of Business at Temple University. There I was exposed to the literature and thinking about the depression, its causes and what might be done to revive the nation from economic despair. The unsettling events in the environment, as I experienced them, were etched in the eager mind of a young man moving through his university curriculum.

My job at the Reading Railroad was in a roundhouse where passenger steam engines were serviced, repaired, and housed. My first job was wiping grease off the engines which was, of course, a very dirty and hot job. Fortunately, I was given a clerical job in the office after a few months of wiping engines. I was responsible mainly for keeping track of attendance and hours worked by the men on my shift, conveying messages of repairs needed on locomotives from incoming engineers to the roundhouse mechanics, and occasionally moving locomotives from one place to another at the roundhouse. Later, as the depression deepened, I also had the painful task of handing pink dismissal slips to workers who were no longer needed. It was very distressing because I knew that many of the men had been with the railroad for years and had children in universities who no longer could be supported. The cruel fact was that these men had virtually no prospects of finding another job. I remember distinctly how tears would appear in the eyes of men over twice my age when confronted with the pink slip. They did not appear to be angry but in numb shock. Thus I saw the stark consequences of our economic system's failure and wondered what had happened and what might be done to correct what I thought were economic injustices.

At Temple University I was introduced to the current literature about the economic depression and actions taken by the federal government to deal with it. Several subjects gripped my attention. One was the human costs of the depression which I had seen at first hand. Another was revelation of market system flaws that needed correction. A third was government planning to avoid human suffering, correct abuses, and revive the nation out of the troughs of depression.

Two teachers at Temple were particularly influential in arousing my awareness of contemporary economic conditions and what should and might be done to improve things. Each opened my eyes to new economic horizons and each stimulated me to read widely about the depression.

William Blaisdell, a graduate student at the Wharton School of the University of Pennsylvania, conducted a course at Temple about business organization. At the time he was studying under William C. Schluter, who was working on national economic planning. His views were published in *Economic Cycles and Crises* (Sears Publishing, 1933), a book which I read carefully. This book suggested plans to correct defects in the economic system and revive the economy while maintaining and strengthening the fundamental institutions of our free enterprise system.

Blaisdell also introduced me to the changing structure of the modern corporation and competition, subjects that have had lasting interest to me. One book that we studied was Berle and Means' seminal *The Modern Corporation and Private Property* (Macmillan, 1932). This book showed clearly that there existed substantial concentration of economic power in large corporations and that in these enterprises there was a separation of control from ownership. In virtually all of the largest companies the managers who controlled the firms held very low percentages of common stock. Stockholders were, of course, the owners of the firms and legally had control of their property. Actually, they exercised little or no control. "Passive ownership" was the phrase used by Berle and Means to define this unexercised power.

As a result of Blaisdell's classes I also became interested in the corporate holding company. This was a device used by what we might today call "financial buccaneers" to control companies with very little personal investment. A classic case was that of the Van Sweringen brothers who, through the holding company device, were able to control a dozen railroads worth approximately $1 billion with an investment of $1 million. A book by James Bonbright titled *The Holding Company* (McGraw-Hill, 1932) was assigned for me to read and report on to the class. This book explained how this method was used in the early 1930s.

Another stimulus to my thinking about the structure of American industry were the hearings before the U.S. Congress by the Temporary National Economic Committee. This committee published 31 volumes of hearings and 43 pamphlets concerning the decline of competition and the rise of economic concentration in American industry.[2] I followed the hearings and read many of the published results. I was shocked at revelations of market manipulation and monopolistic practices undertaken for personal gain, as well by the decline of competition in industry. This all was quite contrary to what I was learning about the theoretical functioning of our economic system.

Dr. John Fred Bell, another teacher at Temple, had a significant influence on my intellectual views and my life. He was the most stimulating, and in my opinion, the best teacher I have had in any university. He was a truly dedicated teacher who was always concerned with his students. I never found him unprepared in class and he always presented his materials in such a way as to fire the interests of his students.

I studied the history of economic thought with Bell. Among many major works in economics he introduced me to Adam Smith and his book *The Wealth of Nations* (first printed in 1776). Bell had enormous respect for Adam Smith and his works, which was passed on to me. He visited Glasgow College, where Smith taught and wrote, and his birthplace at Kirkcaldy, Scotland. Bell was an indefatigable digger of details and told us many personal stories about Smith. I got to know Bell and his wife intimately in later years and she once told me, in a joking sort of way, that he knew more trivia than anyone else she knew. This was true about Smith but also about other economists we studied in class, all of which made the class doubly interesting. Along with the detail, Bell was a scholar who caught brilliantly the evolution of economic thought in his book *A History of Economic Thought* (Ronald Press, 1967).

Smith's book, as is well known, revolutionized thinking about economics and economic processes. Not only did I respect the book as the foundation of classical economics, but many other things impressed me about it. One was the genius with which Smith showed how an economic system could increase the wealth of nations if the heavy hand of government restraints imposed by mercantilism England was lifted. He showed in simple language how the apparent surface chaos of an economy relieved of government controls would operate in harmony to the benefit of everyone. The book gave me a deep respect for the power of capitalism and free markets to improve the welfare of people, a respect I never lost. But I was impressed with another facet of Smith's book. Smith, the believer in a natural economic harmony, was also checked by a shrewd, somewhat cynical, and realistic Scot. While advocating throughout the book a very limited sphere of government interference in economic life, he presented one exception after another to minimal government interference. The problem of finding a proper balance between the two views puzzled me, and does to this day.

The New Deal of President Franklin D. Roosevelt, which extended from his election in 1932 to the outbreak of World War II, was a major topic among professors and students. The administration passed more legislation during its first 100 days than had ever before been experienced in a similar period of time in this country. The enactments concerned three major topics: economic relief, economic reform, and economic recovery. Here was government planning on a grand scale, addressing major issues.

As a student I studied these events. In retrospect, I did not understand all that was going on or its implications. But I did see the development of national economic plans and their implementation. In light of my exposure to individual economic hardship and eye-popping revelations of defects in our economic system, I fully understood the need to do something and applauded much, but not all, that the administration did.

The New Deal had many vehement critics. On the one hand were classical economists who decried interference with traditional market mechanisms. They asserted that if left alone the economy would recover more or less automatically. To inject government regulations into the free market, they said, would slow the road to recovery. At the other extreme were those who said the New Deal was not going far enough in dealing with current problems. They advanced new proposals, some wildly radical, that would have fundamentally changed our economic system. I did not find myself sympathetic with either extreme. I was firmly convinced of the power of the free enterprise system to benefit the nation and its people but at the same time I saw the need for substantial reforms to make it perform better. This view is reflected in my later works.

While national economic planning was of high interest to me as an undergraduate at Temple my main focus was on establishing a background to study law and become a corporate lawyer. That is why I saw the necessity to know something about economics and the structure and operation of industry. However, when I was about to graduate from Temple, it became clear that several more years in law school might seriously impair my health. I had been working mostly on the night shift at the railroad (from 11 p.m. to 7 a.m.) and carrying a full academic load, a routine that left me still in good health but physically exhausted. It was Bell who suggested that I get a master's degree at the Wharton School and then go for my Ph.D. In the back of my mind I still had the idea of getting the Ph.D., landing a job teaching, and then going for a law degree.

At any rate I went to Wharton in 1933 and got an M.A. in economics in 1934. The subject of planning was not a priority at Wharton but became one when E.M. Patterson, a famous international economist with whom I was studying, suggested that I write my thesis on international monetary policy, which I did. While at Wharton my education in classical economic theory was reinforced. I remember especially Patterson teaching me much about and respect for Alfred Marshall, the founder of the neoclassical school of economics.[3] So impressed was I that I bought with my meager funds every edition of his book. Marshall's clear exposition strengthened my appreciation of the power of the free market system and laissez-faire. I also discovered John

Stuart Mill's writings and became a fan of his. His text on economics was brilliantly argued, especially his reasons as to why government interference in economic life should be limited. Yet what struck me most about Mill was that, like Adam Smith, he was driven by his worldly insights to accept more government intervention than he would have tolerated based solely on his philosophical concepts.[4]

Following my M.A., I entered the University of Illinois to pursue my Ph.D. At Illinois I had an opportunity to teach a number of different economics courses as a half-time graduate assistant. Planning did not get my attention. It was all I could do to prepare for and teach my classes and keep up with my graduate studies. For the most part the instruction was squarely in the classical and neoclassical school of economics with one major exception. That was Frank A. Fetter, who joined the faculty as a visiting professor after his retirement from Princeton University. He enjoyed a prestigious reputation as an original thinker and critic in the general economics field. I particularly liked his strong criticism of traditional economics for not emphasizing the psychological aspects of value theory and his bitter condemnation of monopoly. Here again my conservative views about economic theory clashed with my perception of the need for government regulation to correct abuses in the economic system. All this led me to focusing my attention in economics on the pragmatic operation of the economic system and planning to improve its operation. I suppose I was turning into what was called an institutional economist.

National Defense and Wartime Planning

After completing the Ph.D. at Illinois in 1937, I taught at the School of Business at Indiana University, especially corporation finance and investments. In late 1939 and early 1940 my attention returned once again to planning, this time to planning for national defense. War had erupted in Europe in 1939 and the United States began to produce war material for Great Britain and its allies and we started to build our own defense forces. Large expenditures for defense created a number of growing economic problems, and the threats of war raised even more serious economic questions for the United States. So, several other faculty members and I thought it would be useful to introduce into our curriculum a course concerned with economic problems of defense and I was asked to conduct it. When the United States declared war in 1941 the course was called Economic Problems of War.

I invited faculty from various departments of the University to help by lecturing on subjects about which they were well qualified to speak. The course was required for all students in the school. There were about 300 students enrolled each semester. After one semester of experience with this course I decided it would be useful to compile in a small book some of the thoughts of our faculty about the impacts of and planning for national defense. The result was a book titled *Economic Problems of National Defense*. In it I wrote a chapter with the title "Industrial Mobilization Planning in the United States," my first publication on planning.

Later I decided it would be valuable to gather the individual lectures into a textbook. This I proceeded to do. At that time new agencies were being created in Washington to make and implement plans to harness the economic system to the war effort. It was natural for me to invite authorities in Washington, as well as those who taught the class, to contribute to the book. I did, and the book was published in 1942 as *Economic Problems of War*.

This book influenced my work in planning in two ways. First, it opened a new vista of comprehensive planning for war, a subject of compelling concern at the time. Second, it led me to David Novick an executive in the War Production Board. He prepared a chapter for the book on "Industrial Production Control." Later he invited me to join him in Washington which I did in June 1942.

At the War Production Board I was responsible for working with the Bureau of the Census on tabulations prepared from comprehensive questionnaires submitted by all companies in the United States using basic shapes and forms of steel, copper, and aluminum. The results were used to make allocations of these metals to individual companies. The system was founded on the idea that if the production and use of these metals could be controlled, total U.S. production could be controlled because virtually every business used these metals or products made from them. When I joined the War Production Board the system was not working effectively and was rapidly being revised. It evolved into the Controlled Materials Plan which remained throughout the war as the central production control system of the United States. I was fortunate to have had a small part to play in the perfection of this plan.

In the fall of 1943 I was inducted into the armed services and wound up as a Naval officer at the Supervisor of Shipbuilding, USN, New York. There I was involved in a different aspect of wartime planning. The Supervisor was responsible for scheduling the production of Navy ships throughout the United States. The ships ranged from cruisers and light carriers to landing craft.

Following the war, Novick brought me back to Washington to become the Director of the Statistics Division of the Civilian Production Administration, the successor to the War Production Board. The division then was preserving for possible later use an evaluation of the statistical system used to control production during the war. While there Novick and I wrote a book titled *Wartime Industrial Statistics*. This book set forth and explained the questionnaires, surveys, and statistics which were employed to control production during the war. While in Washington at this time (and later) I lectured often at the War College on national defense planning.

I was with the Civilian Production Administration from March 1946, after leaving the Navy, to September 1947 when I went to the University of Illinois as a professor of economics. I returned to Washington with the Defense Production Administration in 1951 when the United States entered the Korean War. There I became deeply involved in implementing the Controlled Materials Plan as Director of the Requirements Committee Staff. This was the place where decisions were made about the allocations of basic metals to industry by means of which industrial production was controlled. Each calendar quarter we tabulated metal requirements as reported by every company in the country that was using these metals. With these statistics, plus an enormous amount of evaluation by staff, I made decisions to balance the demand for and supply of the basic shapes and forms of steel, copper, and aluminum for all major industries in the United States. Within these balances various agencies in Washington made specific metal allocations to each company under their jurisdiction. This process took place every three months. Toward the end of 1952 I left this job to others and was named Director of Policy in both the Defense Production Administration and the Office of Defense Mobilization in the Executive Office of the President. Awesome responsibilities for mobilization planning were spelled out in the statement of functions for these two offices. I never worked harder nor made more important decisions than in discharging my responsibilities in these two agencies during the Korean War.

When the end of the Korean War was in sight it was with great relief that I returned in 1953 to teaching at Illinois. However, my interest in mobilization planning did not stop for I became a member of the Advisory Committee to the Director of the Office of Defense Mobilization, an agency in the Executive Office of the President. This assignment continued for many years.

Involvement in Long-Range Planning at the Lockheed Aircraft Corporation

After the Korean war I taught economics for one year at Illinois and then took a leave of absence in September 1954 to become the chief economist of the Lockheed Aircraft Corporation. Shortly after I arrived at Lockheed, Robert Gross, chairman of the board and chief executive officer, asked me to design for the company a system for developing long-range plans for the company. I formulated a system which was introduced throughout the company. It was the first of its type and became a prototype for similar systems in other defense companies.

In drafting the system I leaned heavily on my experiences in Washington. It was astonishing to me to discover that the fundamental planning principles and practices learned in wartime mobilization and management were applicable to a large company like Lockheed. This work led me into a major path of corporate planning which I have since followed.

The University of California Los Angeles (UCLA)

I left Lockheed in 1956 (but continued as a consultant for another decade), resigned from the University of Illinois, and joined the faculty of the School of Business (later named the John Anderson Graduate School of Management) at UCLA. There I departed from teaching economics to teaching and doing research in management theory and practice. Of course, I have continued my interest in economics but it has been subordinated to management, both public and private. This change in disciplines I found agreeable for two important reasons. Since my student days at Temple I had been more comfortable with institutional economics, which pertained to how economic organizations were structured and functioned, than with pure economic theory. Furthermore, I had had much experience as a manager in the Defense Production Administration, as staff to managers, and in strategic planning, which I knew was a significant part of management. As a result of this experience I began my teaching and research in the management area with considerable confidence.

This was especially true for strategic planning. Industry was far ahead of the academic world in this area at the time and I knew a great deal about what was going on in business and government. Indeed, it was only a predisposition to academic life that kept me from pursuing a career at Lockheed or joining a consulting firm many of which were just entering this field. As it turned out the pragmatic side of my interest was well satisfied by teaching MBA students and managers in executive programs at UCLA and other universities, plus consulting, which I was able to do under University of California policy. These activities, together with my research in planning reinforced each other.

In these years I used synonymously the words strategic planning, comprehensive planning, total planning, integrated planning, corporate planning, comprehensive corporate planning, formal planning, formal strategic planning, and long range planning. Today, these phrases are used by people in the academic world as well as in business to mean different things. At a high level of abstraction, they still mean the same thing to me. They describe a system of planning the essence of which is the systematic identification of opportunities and threats that lie in the future environment (external and internal) which, in combination with other relevant data (e.g., company strengths and weaknesses), produces a basis for a company to make better current decisions to exploit perceived opportunities and to avoid threats. It is an orderly process which sets forth basic objectives to be achieved, strategies and policies needed to reach objectives, and tactical plans and management practices to make sure that strategies are properly implemented. It is a structure of interlinked plans. The design, structure, and linkage of plans vary from company to company and from time to time in the same company.

This description fits a conceptual model that I developed in the late 1950s at UCLA and used extensively in my teaching, research, and consulting. It seemed to include that which was most essential in strategic planning and it became widely accepted and used. This is not particularly surprising because strategic planning is a decision making process which involves careful logical thinking. The model captures this concept. I believe the model was first published in an article appearing in the *Arizona Review* in April 1966.

In 1962, with a grant and financial support from the McKinsey Foundation for Management Research, Inc., I organized and conducted a seminar with seventeen directors of corporate planning of business firms and government agencies. There were also a few interested professors present. I believe this was the first such seminar on this subject. Each practitioner was asked to prepare a report for the seminar describing the long-range planning system of his company or government agency. A book of proceedings grew out of this gathering which set forth the results of the discussion at the seminar plus the papers presented. The book was published in 1963 with the title *Managerial Long-Range Planning*. This was the first book which described actual long-range planning systems in industry and government.

So well received was this seminar and so valuable was it in adding to our knowledge about strategic planning that I decided, again with the support of the McKinsey Foundation, to conduct another one concerned with strategic planning in multinational companies. With the help of Warren M. Cannon and members of the Foundation, and management consultants at McKinsey & Co., I decided to hold the seminar in Fontainebleau, France in 1964. At their suggestion I asked Olivier Giscard d'Estaing, Director General, and Roger Godino, Director and Professor, of the Institut European d'Administration des Affairs (INSEAD) to join me in organizing the conference. INSEAD specialized in training managers for multinational corporations. I was Chairman of the Conference and Cannon was Associate Chairman. His Royal Highness, Bernhard, Prince of the Netherlands was Honorary President of the seminar. There were about 100 participants. They were directors of planning staffs of large multinational companies, top managers, and scholars. We met for five days to discuss a wide range of topics important to strategic planning in large multinational companies. The seminar was held in the Palais de Fontainebleau.

The seminar was a huge success. Distinguished speakers stimulated the participants to lively discussion. Among the speakers were Prince Bernhard; Gilbert H. Clee, director, McKinsey & Co., Inc.; D. D. Otto, head of strategic planning at Philips, Einhoven, Netherlands; Henry H. Fowler, Secretary of the U.S. Treasury; Pierre Masse, president of the French Planning Commission; and Raymond Aron, professor at the University of Paris. This conference resulted in a book published in 1963 titled *Multinational Corporate Planning*. It included papers presented at the meeting and highlights of our deliberations.

I had already written a number of articles and pamphlets on the design and implementation of strategic planning systems and I was so stimulated by these two conferences and notes I had accumulated over the years about planning that I decided to write a comprehensive book on the subject. On my way home from the seminar I was invited to stop in New York to visit with the top management of American Airlines and was offered the job of vice president of strategic planning with a salary of $75,000, a rather attractive sum in those days. I remember that I was so full of enthusiasm to write this book that I rejected the offer. Had it not been for the book I might have been tempted for a few years at least to take the offer.

The book was *Top Management Planning,* published in 1969. While not the first book on strategic planning it was the most comprehensive scholarly treatment up to that time. The book was practitioner oriented and combined theory with practice. It was well received in industry and the academic world and was cited by the Academy of Management as one of the five best business books published in 1969.

My next major book on strategic planning was *Strategic Planning: What Every Manager Must Know*, published in 1979. This book is much shorter than *Top Management Planning* (383 pages compared with 795). It was written principally for executives but contained what I considered when it was written to be the best of the theory and practice on the subject. The book is mostly concerned with what strategic planning really is and is not, how to design a system most appropriate for a particular company and management, the essence of what a strategic plan should contain, and the essentials of how to implement plans once formulated. It must have filled a need, for at the time of this writing (Fall 1990) the book has gone through sixteen printings.

Throughout these years I wrote many articles on the subject of strategic planning. Some were the result of substantial research such as *Pitfalls in Comprehensive Long-Range Planning*, published in 1972. (The words strategic planning were not yet in vogue.) This research was based on 215 usable responses from chief executives, line managers, corporate planners, and other top staff officers of U.S. companies. I thought it would be interesting to compare these results with experiences in other countries of the world, and Hans Schollhammer, a UCLA colleague, joined me in conducting a similar survey among firms in six foreign countries. The U.S. survey identified ten dangerous pitfalls to avoid in doing planning. There were some variations among different countries but we found that much the same pitfalls were identified as the most important to be avoided.

Throughout the years I have been a consultant (especially for strategic planning) to many companies around the world, U.S. government agencies, and other non-profit organizations. It was my good luck to have the opportunity to serve on the board of directors of a number of companies and non-profit organizations. I have found the business and governmental worlds to be an extraordinarily rich laboratory for learning. My debt is great to people in these areas for much of my education. Aside from Lockheed there were other large companies that I tried to help design a planning system, for example, Fairchild Camera, Koc Holding (Turkey), International Telephone and Telegraph, and Central Illinois Light and Power. There were many small companies also where I was asked to help set up a planning system. There were many additional firms where I spent one day or less explaining the nature of strategic planning and how to do it. I took the position in the latter firms, incorrectly in some instances I am sure, that if the top management knew the fundamentals of strategic planning they could set up a system appropriate to their needs and operate it effectively without any outside assistance.

In 1968 I was named Chairman of the College of Planning in The Institute of Management Sciences, a post I held until 1970. While in that position I initiated a move to form an International Society of Corporate Planners. Officers of a number of other U.S. corporate planning societies joined me in forming a committee to create the international organization. William Simmons of IBM was made chairman and did much of the legwork in inducing foreign societies to join us in forming this new organization. The first meeting of the new organization was held in New York City in 1972 and I was the co-chairman. The organization has met annually ever since and is an umbrella for corporate planners around the world.

STRATEGIC MANAGEMENT

This is the second of my major fields of work. My interest in this area, like planning, began at Temple University when I first understood dimly that there was such a thing as management. Then in the War Production Board, in the Defense Production Administration, and in the Office of Defense Mobilization, I was plunged directly into a world of high-stakes strategic management. I got to know many business people in these organizations and liked the way they thought and operated. This was a rare opportunity for me since most of the executives in these agencies were from business. Then at Lockheed I found myself working intimately with top managers. Thus, at UCLA I was comfortable in changing fields from economics to management.

At UCLA I taught a number of different courses in the management area, including principles of management, business policy and strategy, and strategic planning. Teaching and research in these subjects, plus other fields such as organization theory and organization behavior, eventually coalesced into what today is called strategic management.

Aside from strategic planning my first important research in the strategic management area concerned project management. This was a new field of interest in the academic world that attracted my attention. My interest in doing research on project management began with a luncheon discussion at Lockheed with Clarence "Kelly" Johnson, whom I knew well. He had a reputation and respect in the aerospace industry for being able to design and build a prototype airplane at a time and cost from one-quarter to one-third below what was typical in the industry. We talked about how he accomplished this result in his famous "skunk works." More than a few people called Johnson a genius. He was a modest man and insisted to me that he did not consider himself a genius. He said that if any reasonably smart project manager was given a comparatively free reign (i.e., the granting of considerable authority by the government to the project manager) and followed the management principles he employed the same thing could be done.

I decided to look into this proposition and applied for and was given a research grant from the National Aeronautics and Space Administration. William G. Ryan, a UCLA collegue, joined me in the research. We chose sixteen project managers who had designed and produced a prototype of an advanced technological product in record time and cost and interviewed each one at some length. The range of contracts of these managers was from the very small to over $30 million. Each manager had different freedoms from surveillance and control by their respective government agencies but all had aerospace contracts. Illustrative of the projects were Johnson"s high flying "spy" planes (the U-2 and YF-12A), the Sidewinder missile, fire control projects, and satellites.

We discovered that all of these managers used virtually the same management principles and practices. Indeed, Ryan and I frequently joked that if we dropped a curtain between us and the project manager we were interviewing it was like talking to Johnson on the other side. All the managers attributed their success partly to the freedom from detailed government controls when they were designing and building the prototype. Following the field research we conducted a seminar with all the project managers to verify our findings. The results were published in 1968 in our book *Industrial Project Management.*

For several years I had became intrigued with identifying those factors which seemed to be most important in strategic decision making in industry. From time to time I had compiled lists of such factors and talked with my business friends about them. One of them was Ben Makela, Research Director of the Financial Executives Research Foundation, in New York. He suggested that it would be useful to ask top managers and their staffs to evaluate the importance of each of the factors on my latest list. The Foundation agreed to support the research. I prepared a questionnaire and mailed it to top managers of business firms who were asked to determine the importance of specific factors in their decision making. The response was excellent and I found, as I suspected, that a few factors were of outstanding importance in decision making in each industry, and the list varied from industry to industry. The results were published in 1969 in a small book, *Strategic Factors in*

Business Success. It seemed to me that this was an important area of research for scholars in the policy/strategy field. But very little was done until Michael E. Porter published his milestone book on competitive strategy in 1980.[5]

In teaching the policy/strategy course I used the standard textbooks. These books contained cases, generally of actual companies, and students were asked to evaluate the appropriateness of the strategies managers had adopted and to recommend strategies for the future. I was dissatisfied with these books because only a few of them mentioned results of current academic research in the policy/strategy area and then only briefly. Most were silent on the subject. I thought students were being short-changed in not having in their textbooks fuller accounts of current research. One day Frank Khedouri, a representative from the Macmillan Company, was in my office and I complained about this matter to him. He immediately wanted me to sign a contract to produce a textbook on business policy which would contain a summary of the fundamental research in the field plus the typical cases. I agreed, provided I could find a coauthor with expertise in the behavioral sciences. A few days later he called me from John Miner's office at Georgia State University and said: "George, I have found your coauthor. Here he is," and he put Miner on the telephone. I was surprised, of course. However, I knew Miner and his distinguished reputation since I had recently appointed him to be the editor of the *Academy of Management Journal*. So I agreed and we published our book, with the help of Edmund R. Gray who worked on the cases.

The book, published in 1977, was titled *Management Policy and Strategy: Text, Readings, and Cases*. It contained 19 chapters of text in which we summarized the most important research findings in policy and strategy, and intertwined them with actual industry practice. We also included 14 outstanding articles in the field, and 29 cases. The text material was also published in a separate paperback. A second edition was printed in 1982 when Gray joined us as coauthor and concentrated on the cases. A third edition with the three authors was published in 1986.

These books sold well but we decided not to prepare a fourth edition. Gray had urgent commitments in other directions and Miner and I decided it was time to do other things. We felt we had accomplished our purpose in setting a pattern for textbooks in the policy field to include results of current research. This happened and today most leading policy textbooks contain a substantial discussion of current research along with the traditional cases.

My next major research activity in the area of strategic management was undertaken at the request of The Business Roundtable, an organization of 200 chief executive officers (CEOs) of the largest companies in the United States. I was asked to prepare a report on the ways in which social and political environmental forces were changing top management tasks in large corporations. So, in 1981 I had the rare opportunity and great pleasure of interviewing 25 CEOs of our largest corporations, other top executives, management consultants, and directors of staff to CEOs. I concluded that "CEOs are spending an increasing amount of their time on problems stemming from external factors, that collectively they have changed their basic strategies that deal with social and political forces in the environment, and that they believe the requirements for a person to be an effective CEO (today and in the future) are far broader than in the past." The significance of this change, in my opinion, led me to call the book *The New CEO*, published in 1983.

BUSINESS, GOVERNMENT, AND SOCIETY

This is my third major area of teaching and research in the management field. My interest in this area, as discussed earlier, began in the depression of the 1930s, was intensified during World War II and again in the Korean War, and matured at UCLA. During the depression I had a ringside seat for watching the drama of President Roosevelt expanding the powers of government over business and the reaction of people in business to them. I saw not only the need for but the power of government to alter the behavior of many of our economic institutions, including business.

But, as I said earlier, I was ambivalent about the expanding power of government over the functioning of the economic system. As I experienced the operation of the economy in my daily working life I perceived a contradiction between the way economic theory said the system would work and how it was working in practice. There was a big difference. On the one hand I was thoroughly convinced of the extraordinary importance of maintaining the type of capitalist system we had because it was more likely than any other to maximize the welfare of the American people. But, I saw clearly the need to reform it to strengthen it. I was therefore in favor of the use of government power to improve its functioning.

The economic theory formulated in my mind was also ambivalent. In both my undergraduate and graduate work, except in a few classes, I was thoroughly exposed to classical economic theory as modified by the great neoclassicist Alfred Marshall. As I said earlier, I was an admirer of Adam Smith's laissez-faire philosophy but also of his acceptance of government regulation when needed. I learned how mainstream economists found in Smith's writings a strict laissez-faire role for government. I did not. I saw him as a sympathetic philosopher who understood the need for government to sometimes act on behalf of the downtrodden and to correct defects in the economic system. I was delighted with J.A. Hobson's famous comment that Smith's was a "baggy" system. It is possible, he said, to pick it up at various places, drop it, and find that it falls into rather different shapes. This does not mean that I rejected traditional economics. I strongly embraced it, but I did not accept it without reservations. I did not then and I do not now. I saw plenty of theoretical as well as practical justification for government action in economic life.

My ideas about the area of business, government, and society were further developed by my experiences in defense and wartime mobilization. I was exposed both theoretically and operationally to the complex interrelationships between business and government. Thus, I was delighted to be asked to teach a course on government regulation of business when I returned to the University of Illinois.

The typical government regulation of business courses taught in economics departments at that time were principally compilations of laws regulating business and their economic impacts. I did not find this approach agreeable. It seemed to me that there was much more to teaching that subject, so I set about preparing a course different from that typically taught. I studied carefully the traditional texts but did not find them satisfying. Rather quickly I decided that I wanted to teach a much broader course, one that laid a solid philosophical, economic, and legal basis for thinking about the relationships of business and government. For example, I wanted students to learn about the historical evolution of the relationship and how past events led to current relationships.

There were no textbooks available that filled the need I saw, so I began to build my course outline with books and articles. One book that came close to how I wanted to approach the subject was *Social Control of Business* (McGraw-Hill, 1926) written by J.M. Clark, a widely respected economist.[6] Clark's book, however, did not provide all I wanted in a textbook for my class so I decided to write two books. The first volume was to be a broad survey of past and present business-government relationships. The second was to be a detailed study of relationships in specific areas such as antitrust, transportation, public utilities, agriculture, and so on.

The first book was published in 1953 as *Government's Role in Economic Life*. The second volume was never written. Indeed, it took a major effort on my part to complete the last chapter of the first volume while I was in Washington, deeply involved in the Korean War. This book reflected my more mature thoughts on the business-society relationship in which I tried to reconcile and balance the theoretical economic versus the real world practical views discussed above.

It was almost twenty years before I prepared another textbook in this field. The initial stimulus was a request early in 1962 by George W. Robbins, associate dean of the School of Business at UCLA, who, as Chairman of the School's Planning and Development Committee, asked me to prepare a proposal for a new course concerned with business and society.

Robbins's suggestion was stimulated by the rise of popular demands for protection of consumer interests through federal legislation. There was widespread and strong clamor by consumers and their advocates for fewer defective products, less air and water pollution, and more controls over the use of pesticides. The movement gathered speed when President John F. Kennedy sent a special message to the Congress on March 15, 1962 setting forth a consumer bill of rights and asking for legislation to achieve them.

I submitted my detailed proposal in mid-1962 and in 1965 the faculty gave its final approval for the course, and I was asked to teach it. In preparing my first outline in December 1965 I found many relevant parts of books, and articles, but no book that would satisfy me as a basic textbook, so the outline I prepared included many articles and parts of many books. As might be expected I found a number of chapters in *Government's Role in Economic Life* to be useful. Dozens of the books and articles which I used in my first classes on business and society influenced my thinking and intellectual development in the field. Particularly influential was a little book by Joseph W. McGuire titled *Business and Society* (McGraw-Hill, 1963). This was an edited transcript of a TV series that he had prepared for broadcast in the Pacific Northwest in 1962. The subject arrangement and thrust of individual chapters in the book were agreeable to me.

As my thoughts began to crystalize about business and government interrelationships I decided to write a textbook for the course. In 1971 *Business and Society* was published. This was a comprehensive book which treated the historical evolution of the business-society relationship, the relationship in specific areas, and the outlook for the future. Included were subjects which I thought should be in a business and society text, such as changing business ideologies, business ethics, fundamental and changing social values affecting and influenced by business, environmental issues important to managers, and the social responsibilities of business, to name a few. A separate *Case Book in Business and Society* was published to accompany the basic text. The focus of the text was managment, both business and government, but it incorporated many relevant disciplines.

The second edition of *Business and Society* was published in 1975. For the third edition, published in 1980, I asked my son John F. Steiner to join me as coauthor since he was teaching this subject at California State University Los Angeles. He was a political science major in graduate school and brought this important perspective to the subject. We changed the title of the third edition to *Business, Government, and Society: A Managerial Perspective*. While one can consider government as a part of society, we decided that it should be highlighted because of its importance. With this title we also indicated that we wanted to treat the subject from the perspective of individual managers. In the fourth edition, published in 1985, we included cases in the basic text, a practice followed in all subsequent editions. The fifth edition was published in 1988, and the sixth edition in 1991.

One of the great joys of my life has been association with John in the publication of these books. The production of the first book was a little rough but our working relationships in each subsequent edition were progressively smoother. We find that we have few disagreements about most subjects treated in the books or questions concerning the writing of the book, even though we bring different perspectives to it. While our writing styles are similar I believe he writes with more felicity.

In 1970, at the annual meetings of the Academy of Management, Joseph M. Bertotti, an executive of the General Electric Foundation, and I were talking in general terms about the rapidly growing interest in the academic world in introducing new courses in curricula dealing with business and society relationships. We thought it would be worthwhile if faculty interested in this new subject could get together to exchange views. We decided to organize a conference at UCLA and invite professors who were teaching or planned to teach classes in the business-society relationship, or closely related subjects. In mind was a conference which would discuss such topics as an evaluation of current criticisms of business, the social responsibilities of business, the consumer movement, pollution issues of concern to business, what was being taught in this field, and what could be done to generate some agreement among professors about desirable course content. As academicians we knew that before a course such as this would be widely accepted in the academic world there had to be some consensus about course rigor and content.

The first conference was held in the summer of 1971. There were forty participants from the academic world and three or four people from other walks of life. We brought to this group as presenters many prominent academicians and people from business to discuss major subjects in the field. One of the popular sessions was a panel discussion of four chief executive officers of large companies about their social responsibilities. At the end of the conference we discussed what might be done to improve teaching in the area.

In preparation for this discussion on teaching I surveyed those who applied for participation in the conference and a few others, amounting to about 100 in all. I asked each one to send me an outline of the course or courses they taught in this broad field. The survey showed a wide diversity of subject matter being taught. No two outlines were alike. There were at least eight different orientations. Not in any order of importance, they were: economic, philosophical, legal, marketing, historical, urban, government, and eclectic. There were great differences in course titles. Some used cases and some did not. It was clear that course content in the field had not "jelled."[7]

The General Electric Foundation generously supported this ten-day conference which I hosted. The proceedings were published in mimeographed form (see bibliography attached).

So successful was the conference that the General Electric Foundation agreed to conduct others. In each of the next eight years comparable conferences were held and supported by the Foundation. Before each conference I asked deans of schools of business throughout the United States to nominate professors who were interested in and could profit from the conference. About 40 were then chosen and invited. For each conference I continued to serve as the coordinator and general chairman.

It is my belief and that of others that these conferences helped to create a growing agreement among those in the field about subject matter to be taught in courses dealing with the business-society relationship. Important also in the development of agreement about these courses were discussions in the Social Issues in Management Division of the Academy of Management which was established when I was President of the Academy in 1972.

OTHER ROADS

I was born on a small farm near Norristown, Pennsylvania, on May 1, 1912, the first of four children of Ellwood Heacock Steiner and Mary Elizabeth Steele Steiner. My father's family came from Oxford, England and my mother's from northern Ireland. Shortly after I was born we moved to Norristown.

I have few recollections of those early years but several stand out. One day on the farm I fell into a watering trough where milk cans were cooled and my father pulled me out. Deeply impressed in my mind is the wonderful smell of mint growing along a small brook in a lush meadow. I remember well the fragrance of apple blossoms in our orchard.

My recollections while in Norristown are sad. I remember that we children slept under layers of newspaper in the winter to keep warm and had a diet composed largely of stewed tomatoes on bread. We were poor. In October 1917 my parents died a day apart in the great flu epidemic, leaving me, the oldest, two sisters, and a brother. There was a court case over where the children would live. Several sisters of my mother wanted to keep the four children in Norristown but my paternal grandfather wanted to take us to Philadelphia. The final judgment was for my elder sister and me to go to Philadelphia and my younger sister and brother to stay in Norristown with our aunts.

It was my great good fortune to go to Girard College in 1919. Girard College was founded in 1831 under the will of Stephen Girard, who at that time was one of the wealthiest men in the United States. The school is a private institution for fatherless boys (it was not until the 1970s that girls were accepted) from seven to eighteen years of age. It is generously endowed. Those children accepted live and receive their primary and secondary education at the school for free.

Girard is located on what was a 43 acre farm outside Philadelphia at the time it was founded, but today it is well within the boundaries of Philadelphia. Both the physical facilities and the education provided are excellent. The high school had the reputation of being one of the best if not the best in Philadelphia at the time I was there. My years there were relatively carefree and I left in June 1929 in excellent shape physically and with a solid high-school education.

After graduating from Girard in June 1929 I went to live with my grandparents. I was able to find a few poorly paying jobs, such as selling magazine subscriptions, but finally landed a job laying hardwood floors that paid reasonably well. Then in January 1930 an uncle who worked on the Reading Railroad in Philadelphia got me a job there paying 44 cents an hour. This enabled me to enroll at Temple University.

At Girard I found my chemistry classes particularly enjoyable and decided to major in that subject at Temple. Unfortunately all the chemistry laboratories were held in the afternoon and I could not attend them since at that time I was on the 3 p.m. to 11 p.m. shift at the railroad. I decided to study law with the objective of becoming a corporate lawyer. This aspiration was prompted for no good reason other than that I had been captain of the Girard debating team and thought that the experience foretold aptitude for a legal career. To prepare for this career I registered as a pre-law major in the School of Business. After graduating from Temple, as noted earlier, I decided not to follow the legal path at this time and enrolled at the Wharton School with the idea of getting a masters degree and then going on for a Ph.D., an idea planted in my head by Fred Bell, as noted before. Throughout, I paid for all my expenses, including a boarding fee at my grandparents' house.

I received my M. A. in economics at Wharton in 1934 and was fortunate in getting an assistantship in the College of Commerce of the University of Illinois to pursue my Ph. D. It paid $70 dollars a month and free tuition. A few months after I arrived at Illinois it was my good fortune to be offered a job as resident faculty advisor to the Delta Tau Delta fraternity. My good friend Fred Bell also had a hand in this opportunity. He knew Paul Van Arsdell, a professor in the College of Commerce, who was the faculty resident advisor to the Sigma Alpha Epsilon fraternity and recommended me for a similar job.

Being a faculty advisor at the Delt house was a wonderful experience for me. I was given a monthly cash allowance and free board which, with my assistantship stipend, gave me affluence I had not known as a college student in Philadelphia. Being free from the continuous daily grind of working on the railroad and going to the university at the same time gave me a wonderful sense of well-being. In Philadelphia I had had no social life and suddenly found myself deeply involved in social affairs. I met my wife Jean E. Wood, who was a music major with an exceptional voice, and we were later married after I completed my Ph.D. in 1937. We have lived happily ever since.

When I was awarded the Ph.D. in economics I was offered two jobs that interested me. Frank A. Fetter was responsible for an offer from the economics department of Princeton University of $2,200. Herman B Wells, who was then dean of the School of Business at Indiana (he later became the President of Indiana University) offered me $2,400. The financial difference led me to take his offer. This was another important fork in the road for me.

At Indiana I was offered the job of Assistant Director of the Bureau of Business and Economic Research. One of my tasks was to write a short monthly pamphlet called the *Indiana Business Review* which described business conditions in the State of Indiana and its major cities. The information to do this came from responses to questionnaires we sent to people around the state. This was a great opportunity for I learned much from George W. Starr, the Director of the Bureau, and had the valuable experience and discipline of having to write the *Review* each month. Also I had a chance to write special articles for the *Review* on major policy topics of the day, plus special research reports published by the Bureau. Part of my job also was to give speeches around the state on current economic conditions. I saw this as a mixed blessing. It was a task that I thought was valuable and up to a point I enjoyed doing it. But I was nervous before making a speech which tended to give me a bit of indigestion. I remember one time I had a luncheon speaking engagement and took a number of antacid pills before lunch in anticipation of indigestion. As it turned out I took too many and burped throughout my speech! I never did that again.

While at Lockheed I was offered a full professorship of management in the School of Business at UCLA which I accepted at half the salary I was receiving at Lockheed. Also, I was made Director of the Division of Research at the School of Business, a position I held until 1972. The Division was newly created and I was the first director. It was my responsibility to stimulate research in the faculty, principally by getting outside funding, and to organize research activities. With the help of the faculty we did gradually substantially increase funds to support our research.

I also was given the task of launching a quarterly publication which we named the *California Management Review*. The idea for this journal was that of Neil H. Jacoby who was dean of the School of Business. The School of Business at U. C. Berkeley joined us in launching the magazine in the fall of 1958. I served as Managing Editor through the summer of 1960 issue and thereafter, for a number of years, was a member of the Editorial Board. This magazine has become a widely respected publication in management.

TEACHING PHILOSOPHY

The chairman of our department at UCLA asked each of the faculty in 1974 to write a statement of his or her teaching philosophy. I do not know the reason for this request. At any rate I was glad to be obliged to put my thoughts about the subject on paper. The following quotation from the statement I prepared succinctly gives my views on this matter.

> One of my fundamental objectives, in teaching especially, is to stimulate students to continue their education in the subject matter under discussion. I consider that I have failed if I have not done this. Another fundamental objective is to try to cover the subject matter in such a way that students and other audiences will retain insights, values, problem-solving tools, and approaches, which will be of major use to them in their careers. There are a number of principles which I have followed throughout my teaching career, among which are the following: I have always been highly conscientious in preparing what I have to say; in relating the materials as much as practicable to my audience; in treating my students fairly in work load, class discussions, examinations, and my evaluations of them; in meeting my classes; in being available to students; in spending time needed to meet their requirements, and in pointing out (with appropriate emphasis for different audiences) opportunities for teaching, business practice, research, and leading a quality life.

AWARDS

Rewards have been generously given to me from time to time. Among those of which I am most proud are four, as follows in chronological order. First was an LL.D. conferred by Temple University in 1963. In 1972 I was elected President of the Academy of Management. The Fellows of the Academy of Management elected me to be their Dean in 1976, a position I held for a three-year term. The Academy of Management named me Distinguished Educator of the year in 1990. Although many others were equally deserving of these awards I am deeply appreciative for having received them.

CONCLUDING COMMENTS

As I look back over my life I am reminded of Robert Frost's famous poem "The Road Not Taken." There have been many forks in my roads and the ones chosen have made a great difference in what happened thereafter. It seems to me that I have been very lucky in the people, forces, and events that helped me in my life.

In reviewing this autobiography I am astonished and a bit embarrassed at the number of I's, me's, and my's. They dot the story like raisins in a cake, but I guess that is difficult to avoid in reminiscences of this kind. Also, my recording of accomplishments seems to display an ego that I do not think I have.

My reference to self in much of this report reminds me of a charming story about President Theodore Roosevelt. He and the great naturalist William Beebe would go out on the lawn of Sagamore Hill, TR's residence and search for the faint spot of light-mist behind the lower left hand corner of the Great Square of Pegasus. When they found it they would recite:

> That is the Spiral Galaxy in Andromeda.
> It is as large as our Milky Way.

It is one of a hundred million galaxies.
It consists of one hundred billion suns,
each larger than our sun.

Then, as the story goes, Roosevelt would grin at Beebe and say: "Now I think we are small enough! Let's go to bed."[8]

PUBLICATIONS

1938

Indiana State disbursements. Bloomington, IN: Indiana University Press.
The tax System and industrial development. *Bulletin of the National Tax Association, 23*(4).

1939

The 1937 Recession. *Opinion and Comment*, University of Illinois (June).

1940

Retail trade turnover. Bloomington, IN: Indiana University Press.
[Editor]. *Economics of national defense.* Bloomington, IN: School of Business, Indiana University.
With G.W. Starr. Births and deaths of retail stores Indiana, 1929-37. *Dun's Review* (January).

1941

The defense organization of the United States. *Opinion and Comment* (June).
Federal fiscal policy in national defense. *The Tax Magazine, 19*(6).

1942

[Editor]. *Economic problems of war.* New York: John Wiley.
How to pay for the war. *Indiana Investment Bulletin, 6*(3).

1943

The production requirements plan. *Opinion and Comment* (November).
With D. Novick. The War Production Board's Statistical Reporting Experience, Part I. *Journal of the American Statistical Association* (June).

1945

Facts for war production control. Industrial Collge of the Armed Forces, Washington, D.C. (December).

1948

With D. Novick. The War Production Board's Statistical Reporting Experience, Parts II and III. *Journal of the American Statistical Association* (September).

With D. Novick. The War Production Board's Statistical Reporting Experience, Part IV. *Journal of the American Statistical Association* (December).

The influence of item characteristics on requirements determination. Industrial College of the Armed Forces, Washington, D.C.

1949

With D. Novick. The War Production Board's Statistical Reporting Experience, Parts V and VI. *Journal of the American Statistical Association* (September).

1950

Industrial production controls. *Illinois Business Review* (December).

1951

Decision making in government: A case study of material allocations under CMP. Industrial College of the Armed Forces, Washington, D.C.

1952

A program to measure maximum potential productin under full mobilization conditions. Industrial College of the Armed Forces, Washington, D.C.

1953

Government's role in economic life. New York: McGraw-Hill.

History of the Policy Development Staff of the Defense Production Administration, Mobilization Base Policy and Program Development: Historical reports on defense production (Report No. 12). Washington, D.C.: U.S. Department of Commerce, National Production Authority.

The role of government in the changing economy: Some delusions and dangers. *Economics and Business Bulletin*, Temple University, *6*(10).

Mobilization-base policy planning. *Federal Reserve Bulletin*, Philadelphia District (March).

1954

Resources allocation in mobilization. *Current Economic Comment*, University of Illinois, *16*(3).

1956

A Função Da Govêrno No Vida Econômics. Agir, Rio De Janeiro.

1958

The adequacy of government research programs in non-military defense. Washington, D.C.: National Academy of Sciences National Research Council.

Does planning pay off? In D.W. Ewing (Ed.), *Long range planning for managing*. New York: Harper & Row.

1959

With L.E. Root. Linear organization charts. *California Management Review, 1*(2).

1960

What do we know about using long-range plans? *California Management Review, 2*(l).

Civilian problems in surviving attack. *Business Horizons, 3*(1).

How to forecast defense expenditures. *California Management Review, 2*(4).

1961

National Defense and Southern California, 1961-1970. Los Angeles, CA: Los Angeles, Southern California Associates of the Committee for Economic Development.

1962

Better management through research. Graduate School of Business Administration, UCLA.

Making long-range planning pay off. *California Management Review, 4*(2).

Il Rendimento Della Programmazione D'Impress A Luingo Termine. *Revista Internazionale di Scienze Economiche E. Commerciali*, Milan, *8*(7).

How to forecast defense expeditures. In J.A. Stockfisch (Ed.), *Planning and forecasting in the defense industries.* Blemont, CA: Wadsworth.

1963

[Editor]. *Managerial long-range planning.* New York: McGraw-Hill.

1964

Why and how to diversify. *California Management Review, 6*(4).

Costs, needs and prospects of the SST. *Challenge* (June).

Program budgting: Business contribution to government management. *Business Horizons* (Spring).

La Planification Dans Les Societes Multinationales. *Economie Applique.*

1965

How to assure poor long-range planning for your company. *California Management Review* (Summer).

Problems in implementing program budgeting. In D. Novick (Ed.), *Program budgeting*. Cambridge, MA: Harvard University Press.

1966

With W. Cannon. *Multinational corporate planning*. New York: Collier-Macmillan.

Managerial methods of successful project managers with a loose rein (NASA Research Paper No. 1). Division of Research, Graduate School of Business Administration, UCLA.

The critical role of top management in long-range planning. *Arizona Review* (April).

Improving the transfer of government-sponsored technology. *Business Horizons* (Fall).

Communications and Business planning: Two vital elements in government sponsored technology transfer (NASA Research Paper No. 7). Division of Research, Graduate School of Business Administration, UCLA (February).

1967

Current U.S. trends in planning in business and government. *The European Management Review, 16.*

Approaches to long-range Planning for small business. *California Management Review, 10*(1).

1968

With W.G. Ryan. *Industrial project management*. New York: Macmillan.
Communications and business planning: Two vital elements in government sponsored technology transfer (NASA Research Paper No. 7). Division of Research, School of Business Administration, UCLA.

1969

Strategic factors in business success. New York: Financial Executives Research Foundation.
Top management planning. New York: Macmillan.
Edited with J.O. Vance. The management of technology transfer. *IEEE Transactions on Engineering Management, EM-16*(3).
Top management's role in planning. *Long Range Planning* (June).

1970

Rise of the corporate planner. *Harvard Business Review* (September-October).
Business and consumerism. *Journal of Business Policy*, University of Bradford, England (Winter 1970-71).

1971

Business and society. New York: Random House.
Profiles of the future: Changing managerial philosophies. *Business Horizons* (June).
Managing the commercial-technical enterprise. *IEEE Transactions on Engineering Management* (August).
The changing role of the corporate planner. *Managerial Planning* (June).
Business bigness: Benefits and dangers. *Business Horizons* (October).
Strategic planning in a changing environment. *RIA Cost and Management, 45*.

1972

[Editor]. *Issues in business and society*. New York: Random House.
Editor. *Contemporary challenges in the business society relationship*. Los Angeles, CA: Graduate School of Management, UCLA.
The social audit, center for research and dialogue on business and society (Paper Series No. 1). Division of Research, Graduate School of Management, UCLA, March.

Comprehensive managerial planning. Oxford, OH: Planning Executives Institute.

Pitfalls in comprehensive long-range planning. Oxford, OH: Planning Executives Institute.

Should business adopt the social audit? *The Conference Board Record, 9*(5).

Tomorow's corporate planning and planners. *Managerial Planning, 20*(March-April).

Social policies for business. *California Management Review, 15*(2).

The changing role of tomorrow's corporate planner. *Optimum, 3*(1).

1973

[Editor]. *Selected major issues in business' role in modern society.* Los Angeles, CA; Graduate School of Management, UCLA.

The redefinition of capitalism and its impact on management theory & practice. London: Aims of Industry.

The second managerial revolution: Moving toward new managerial styles. *The Conference Board Record.*

Is comprehensive corporate planning needed in your company? *Manager*, Milan, Italy.

The state of the art of corporate planning. In J. McGuire (Ed.), *The state of the art of management.* Englewood Cliffs, NJ: Prentice-Hall.

1974

[Editor]. *The changing business role in modern society.* Los Angeles, CA: Graduate School of Management, UCLA.

Business and disadvantaged minorities in the cities. *Journal of Contemporary Business, 3*(2).

Business in future society. In *Man and the Future of Organizations*, The Franklin Lecture Series, Georgia State University.

How to improve your long-range planning. *Managerial Planning* (September/October).

What should schools of businesss be teaching about business social responsibilities? In D.L. Goethie (Ed.), *Business ethics and social responsibilities: Theory and practice.* Center for the Study of Applied Ethics, Graduate School of Business Administraton, University of Virginia.

1975

Cases in business and society. New York: Random House.

Business and society (2nd ed.) New York: Random House.

[Editor]. *Changing business-society interrelationships.* Los Angeles, CA: Graduate School of Management, UCLA.

Pitfalls in multi-national long-range planning. *Long Range Planning* (April).

Proposals for a national policy assessment and action program. *Planning Review* (September).

Institutionalizing coporate social decisions. *Business Horizons* (December).

1976

[Editor]. *The changing business role in society.* Los Angeles, CA: Graduate School of Management, UCLA.

Future curricula in schools of management. *AACSB Journal* (October).

Invent your own future. *California Management Review, 19*(1).

1977

With J.F. Steiner. *Issues in business and society* (2nd ed.). New York: Random House.

With J.B. Miner. *Management policy and strategy, text, readings and cases.* New York: Macmillan.

With J.B. Miner. *Management policy and strategy.* New York: Macmillan.

[Editor]. *Business and its environment.* Los Angeles, CA: Graduate School of Managment, UCLA.

Strategic managerial planning. Oxford, OH: Planning Executive Institute.

Invente su Propio Futuro. *Direction y Control, 18* (181).

With C.W. Sprowls. Why computerized planning models fail. In H.D. Plotzeneder (Ed.), *Fachberichte und Referate/Lectures and Tutorials/Computergestutzte Unternehemnsplanung/Computer Assisted Corporate Planning.* Science Research Association GmbH, Stuttgard, Germany.

1978

[Editor]. *Business and its changing environment.* Los Angeles, CA: Graduate School of Management, UCLA.

New patterns in government regulation of business. *MSU Business Topics* (Winter).

With J.F. Steiner. Social policy as business policy. In L. Preston (Ed.), *Research in corporate social performance policy.* Greenwich, CT: JAI Press.

1979

Strategic planning: What every manager must know. New York: The Free Press.

[Editor]. *Business and its changing environment.* Los Angeles, CA: Graduate School of Management, UCLA.

Planificacion de la Alta Direction, V. I, Vo. Ediciones Universidad de Navarra, S. A. Pamplona, Barcelona.

Changing business ideologies. In M. Zimet & R.G. Greenwood (Eds.), *The evolving science of management. New York: American Management Association.*

1980

With J.F. Steiner. *Business, government and society: A managerial perspective* (3rd ed.). New York: Random House. (Formerly *Business and society.*)

1981

Politica e Estratégia Administrativa. Editora Interciencia, Editora da Universidade de Sao Paulo, Brazil.

1982

With J.B. Miner & E.R. Gray. *Management policy and strategy, text, readings and cases* (2nd ed.). New York: Macmillan.

1983

The new CEO. New York: Macmillan.

Planeacion Estrategica: Lo que Todo Director Debe Saber, Compania Editorial Continental, S. A. De C. V., Mexico.

Formal strategic planning in the United States today. *Long Range Planning, 16*(3).

1985

With J.F. Steiner. *Business, government, and society: A mangerial perspective* (4th ed.). New York: Random House.

1986

With J.B. Miner & E.R. Gray. *Management policy and strategy, text, readings and cases.* New York: Macmillan.

1988

With J.F. Steiner. *Business, government, and society: A managerial perspective* (5th ed.). New York: Random House.

1991

With J.F. Steiner. *Business, government, and society: A managerial perspective* (6th ed.). New York: McGraw-Hill.

NOTES

1. The words strategic planning were not used until the 1970s. In these early years the word planning was broadly defined in academic circles as well as in business. My interest in the depression of the 1930s was in national economic planning.
2. *Investigation of Concentration of Economic Power*, Hearings before the Temporary National Economic Committee, Congress of the United States, Seventy-fifth Congress, Second Session, Washington, D.C.: U.S. Government Printing Office, 1939. The pamphlets were issued from time to time in earlier years.
3. See Alfred Marshall (1980). *Principles of economics*. New York: Macmillan. There were eight editions of this book, the last one published in 1920).
4. See Book V, Chapter XI in John Stuart Mill. *Principles of political economy* (5th ed.). D. Appleton & Company.
5. See Michael E. Porter. (1980). *Competitive strategy: Techniques for analyzing industrial and competitors*. New York: The Free Press.
6. This book was revised later and I used his second edition published in 1939.
7. For the results of this survey see Chapter 28 in the proceedings of this conference noted in the attached bibliography, 1972.
8. See p. 234 in William Beebe (1944). *The book of naturalists*. New York.

George Strauss

Present At The Beginning: Some Personal Notes on OB's Early Days and Later

GEORGE STRAUSS

This isn't going to be a conventional autobiography. The great events of my life—my marriage and family—are hardly of interest to the wider world. The bulk of this chapter consists of some highly personal views of how what later became Organizational Behavior looked to me in the late 1940s and early 1950s, when I was a graduate student at MIT. I will then use my remaining space for a quick sketch of the next 40 years of both the field and my career.

I work in what we call at Berkeley OBIR (Organizational Behavior and Industrial Relations) and much of my work has been at the intersection of these two fields. Of the two fields my greatest emphasis has been on IR. My relationship to OB has been more of an observer than a participant—and it is an observer that much of this is written.

HOW I GOT INTO OBIR

Not long ago, Frank Schmidt of the University of Iowa asked me: "What brought you to Industrial Relations? Like most IR people, was there something special in your background?" Well, yes and no. My father was a chemical engineer whose interests included science, natural history, his garden, and much else (I used to think he knew everything), but not politics. My mother had been a nurse in the Belgian Army during World War I. The Army had sent her to this country for advanced training. Instead she met and married my father. Her interests were cleanliness, order and good cooking. Among her highest compliments was, "My, he has a good appetite."

Maybe industrial relations was in my genes: my Belgian grandfather had been a longshore boss and an active Socialist. He had sided with the union in a bitter strike at the turn of the century. When the union lost he was blacklisted and had to change his occupation. He died young, leaving behind seven children under 18, and for some time after my mother's family lived in real poverty. My American grandfather was a lawyer and later a judge, the first Democrat elected from Wilkes-Barre, Pennsylvania in decades. As a lawyer he represented the United Mine Workers and one summer spoke on the Chautauqua lecture circuit, presenting labor's case.

I grew up in Staten Island, New York during the Depression. While I was never poor or hungry myself, it was drummed into me that many people were poor and hungry (especially Belgians during the war) and therefore I should always eat everything on my plate, a lesson I haven't since forgotten. So I ate well, but felt guilty in doing so. The sight of people begging and selling apples in the street greatly bothered me. What right did I have to eat so regularly?

In the fifth grade I read *The New Russian Primer*, which contrasted the joys of a planned society with the miseries of capitalism in a depression. For a year I was a communist. But in the sixth grade I read Bellamy's *Looking Backward, 2000-1887* (Houghton-Mifflin, 1887), and so became a Fabian Socialist.

Obviously I was a rather strange kid. Beginning at age 10 I began to read the *New York Times* religiously, including the full texts of major New Deal legislation and Supreme Court decisions. The progress of the labor movement especially interested me. I remember my great thrill when General Motors signed its first agreement with the UAW. (That was a private thrill. My public thrill was when the Yankees won three series in a row.)

I went to a private school (the same one that Fritz Roethlisberger had attended some 24 years earlier). In the fifth grade while studying the Middle Ages, we made illustrated parchments with bright-colored inks. For their messages my classmates generally took conventional pieties, such as "Love Your Mother" or the Golden Rule. Mine was taken from Section 7A of the National Industrial Recovery Act: "Employees shall have the right to organize and bargain collectively...." My illustrations showed a breadline transformed into a picket line.

By high school I became more conventional. I had played football all along and finally made the varsity team (in my small school that was easy). My senior paper was not about politics at all, but was heavily influenced by the Lynds' *Middletown* (1929). Based on old newspaper files, I tried to place the early development of my school in the social history of Staten Island's 1880s. I ascribed its founding to the social-climbing efforts of German immigrants seeking to overcome their tainted association with the Island's then flourishing beer industry. A great idea, but I had little evidence. In any case I was downgraded for my great nemesis, bad spelling.

For college I went to Swarthmore (in 1940), majoring in economics and political science (both "relevant" courses) though philosophy and history were attractive diversions. I took introductory psychology, hoping it would be loaded with Freud and sex. Instead it was concerned with vision and perception. How dull! I dropped the course.

Swarthmore was a place for someone with political interests. Quickly I became active in the Swarthmore Student Union (SSU), a non-Communist liberal group which, earlier, had split with the Communist-led American Student Union over Russia's 1939 invasion of Finland. ASU had supported Russia. The Swarthmore group opposed both Hitler and Stalin, and much of our effort was spent fighting Communists. Strange as it may seem to student activists today, SSU strongly supported the allied war effort, the draft, and a larger military budget. Domestically we supported all the standard liberal causes of the time, including unions. As to campus affairs, we were against fraternities and in favor of admitting blacks (something which Swarthmore, a Quaker college, was quite late in doing). Eleanor Roosevelt was one of our heroes. In my junior year I was elected SSU chair.

Some of my limited free time I spent helping to put out the local labor weekly, sometimes working all night. Here I met local labor leaders in the flesh. Then in spring 1942, with the United States already at war, one of my political science professors, Vernon O'Rourke, decided to run for Congress against a diehard reactionary Republican (among his sins was voting against the draft). I was O'Rourke's campus campaign manager. We ran quite a campaign: bands of students pushed doorbells daily and a quarter of the entire student body took election day off to round up the votes. We lost our heavily Republican district but lead the rest of the ticket by a large margin and did better than FDR two years earlier. One thing I learned from my political activism (by contrast with that learned by the activists of the 1960s) was the value of compromise, bargaining, and smoothing feelings—not that I ever performed these arts well.

By now the war was beginning to close in. I entered the Army in February 1943, being assigned to a Miami Beach hotel for basic training. My military career was not particularly distinguished. In fact, for me the war was personally a bore. I left the United States only once, on a B-29 test flight to Bermuda to determine whether we GIs preferred normal airline food to K rations. Still I learned a good deal about a bureaucratic—very bureaucratic—organization. I picked up enough "war stories" to carry me through many lectures later on. Let me abuse you with two samples.

War Story No. 1

One of my first days at Miami Beach I volunteered for KP. Let's get the war over in a hurry, I decided, so I can get back to school. Later I could make a point in class here about motivation, public goods, etc., but what I really learned was that some people (like my sergeant) become sadistic when given a little power. After 18 continuous hours of largely make-work I never volunteered for anything in the Army again. From then on I became adept at what F.W. Taylor aptly called "soldiering."

War Story No 2

A year later I had picked up a little power myself. I was sergeant, working at LaGuardia Field, New York (living at home, taking advantage of the USO's ample supply of free tickets for New York plays) and assigned to the Office of Flying Safety. Our job was to monitor military flights in an area from roughly Washington to Boston. If weather turned bad we were to reroute these planes to safety. One hot summer Sunday afternoon I was working alone when thunderstorms broke out through southern New Jersey. Immediately (I loved the authority) I ordered all northbound planes from Washington to land at Philadelphia. Technically I did this in the name of Hap Arnold, Commanding General, Army Air Force, since the Office of Flying Safety was part of the General's staff. Unbeknownst to me, one of the planes which landed was piloted by Hap himself, flying under his copilot's name. As a Command Pilot, Hap had the right to ignore my order. As a sensible pilot, he landed. Here were all sorts of lessons here about roles, staff-line relations, and authority (French and Raven, take note).

Several hundred stories later the war was over. I was discharged at San Pedro, California, (I'd arranged this with great effort so as to collect the maximum travel pay home). Taking advantage of my uniform I hitch-hiked across country (great stories there) and returned for my senior year to Swarthmore. Then followed glorious days! The world turned from black and white to technicolor. Wonderful people to talk to. Interesting problems to grapple with. Once again O'Rourke ran for Congress and I coordinated the campus end (this time much more efficiently). Once again we mobilized most of the students. Once again we lost, but again greatly lead the rest of our ticket.

With graduation looming I had to face the real world once more. For a while I played with entering the union movement. But one of my most respected role models (the chief steward at Westinghouse) threw cold water on my cockiness. "George, my advice is you get a job in some plant (just keep your degree quiet)" he said. "If you are as good as you think you are, in a few years you will be elected shop steward. Then a few years later, if you handle your politics right, you'll be chief steward. Then, maybe they will take you onto the international staff. But don't count on it." After three years in the Army, this didn't seem promising. Instead I decided to go to graduate school, picking MIT over Harvard and Berkeley. My choice of MIT was based on Paul Samuelson's stellar performance as an oral examiner in the Swarthmore honors system and his cordial, personal letter admitting me, as contrasted with Harvard and Berkeley's cold form letters.

Vaguely I planned to study industrial relations, hoping somehow this might make some contribution to the union movement. In this I was not alone. The postwar wave of strikes had made industrial relations the country's number-one social problem. I was part of a large cohort of returning veterans who entered graduate study of industrial relations, courtesy of the GI Bill. In 1947 more members of the American Economic Association listed labor as their major interest than any other field. The professors who dated their Ph.D.s from this zesty era constituted the core of most academic industrial relations groups until recently. We saw collective bargaining as a realistic means to give the working man a new sense of dignity, to correct inequities in the distribution of income, and to improve society. The important point was that industrial relations at the time was both intellectually challenging and socially relevant ("Industrial Relations Research," 1978).

CAMBRIDGE

I was lucky to arrive in Cambridge at a critical time in OB's development. Cambridge offered a real intellectual smorgasbord. At MIT I was in the Department of Economics and Social Sciences which included both Psychology and Industrial Relations. There was similar disciplinary flexibility at Harvard where the Department of Social Relations combined Anthropology, Sociology, and Social Psychology. At MIT we graduate students were divided into As (economists), Bs (industrial relations) and Cs (psychologists). Among my fellow Bs were George Shultz, later to become a great Secretary of State, of Labor and of the Treasury, and two long-term friends, Leonard Sayles, my writing collaborator, and Ralph Bergmann, whose career has included the United Rubber Workers, the International Labor Organization, and Fresno State University.

Regardless of designation we were broadly trained. Our comprehensive exams covered three major fields (mine were economic theory, industrial relations, and human relations) and three minor fields (mine: personnel, labor law, and group dynamics). Additionally, we needed an outside department. I chose Industrial Administration (later the Sloan School), then better known as Course XV. On top of this, MIT students were allowed to take courses at Harvard, and I took advantage of the opportunity. Finally, being young and full of energy, I did a fair amount of relevant reading on my own. In short, my training was like the old Missouri River, both broad and shallow.

Our training was also very flexible. Because the field was so new, at least in Human Relations, our professors had little advantage over us. Everywhere we looked was terra incognita. As a consequence, there was a great sense of collegiality among the students and (from our point of view) between students and faculty. My dissertation chair, Charles Myers, a labor economist, was very supportive but he did little to influence my approach or choice of topics.

Though the main emphasis of this story is on what later became OB, let me first say a few words about some of my other interests and classes.

Economics

Prior to MIT the thought hadn't entered my mind that Economics and Industrial Relations might be separate fields (a lesson which some colleagues still haven't learned). Economics was formally my primary field and Economic Theory, with Paul Samuelson as instructor, was my key first seminar. Six weeks into his seminar, Paul handed me a reprint of a recently published paper. There was a flaw here, he said. I should examine it carefully. Next week we might discuss it in his office and perhaps I would like to write a reply. I wrestled with the paper all week. A theoretical piece, it dealt with selling costs and imperfect competition. Like most works of this sort its assumptions were simplistic and unrealistic. Aside from these major faults I could find nothing wrong with the argument. Sheepishly, at the appointed time, I reported my failure. Kindly and patiently, Paul pointed out the flaw. "How trivial," I thought to myself, "Who cares?" This was a critical turning point in my career. I was not to be an economist. What a relief!

Industrial Relations

Industrial Relations was another matter. Three topics were of special interest: first, labor history, (a lifelong interest); and second, the "causes of industrial peace." The National Planning Association series by this name were just being published, and these gave hope that, through effective communications, appropriate organization and, above all, trust, peaceful labor relations could be obtained. The values and solutions implied were similar to those being advanced by Human Relations.

Finally, as a budding IR man, I needed to know labor law. So, after one labor law course at MIT, I took the basic labor law course at the Harvard Law School with Archie Cox (later Watergate prosecutor) and then a seminar with Cox and John Dunlop (later Harvard Dean and Secretary of Labor). By contrast with the social science professors I had known, law school professors were viewed by their students as God-like. So when Cox had his secretary invite me to his "chambers" my fellow students were much impressed. And when he asked me to give a paper (based on my seminar work on union democracy) to the newly established Industrial Relations Research Association, I was on top of the world.

Another seminar was with Joe Scanlon. Joe, an ex-boxer, steelworker and union official, was the author of the Scanlon Plan, perhaps still the best devised plan for combining worker participation with financial incentives. In Joe's seminar I learned how to role-play collective bargaining. Yet, to my disappointment, Joe and I didn't strike it off well together. Possibly I was insufficiently sensitive to the fact that critical questions about his plan were unwelcome.

Time and Motion Study

For my unwilling minor in industrial administration I took cost accounting, controllership, and time and motion study. Only time and motion study was of note.

For those of us interested in human relations, F. W. Taylor was the devil incarnate. The same building which housed the MIT Economic Department also contained a bastion of pure Taylorism. I decided to beard the devil in his den and to take a course in time and motion study. It beautifully confirmed my worst expectations. Probably it was much the same course which Roethlisberger had taken 25 years earlier, a course he later called "pure, unadulterated nonsense."[1] As did Roethlisberger, "I took great delight in collecting…'horror stories'"[2] about how bad it was.

We learned how to hold the stopwatch and the clipboard, how to find "cooperative workers," how to use "therbligs" (Gilbreath spelled more or less backward), and above all "normalizing," how to tell whether a worker was working at, below, or above the mystic "normal" pace. We learned the latter by watching movies of women packing Necco Wafers at various speeds and guessing how fast they were working.

Quickly I learned that though Scientific Management pretended to be scientific, in fact it was highly subjective. Even today a typical union contract provides that time studies shall "be based on the time required by a qualified *normal* employee working at a *normal* pace under *normal* conditions, using the proper method with *normal* material at *normal* machine speeds." Later on, when teaching time study to unionists, in the late 1950s, I insisted that they never touch a stopwatch. That would get them into management's trap. Instead they should challenge management on every application of "normal."

For our term papers we were divided into teams of four, with instructions to find a real job, time it, simplify it, and then retime it. My three engineering colleagues quickly gained entry to a company and started timing a presumably typical job. While they were doing their calculations I talked to the operator involved. Using my newly acquired interviewing skills I learned that he worked the standard way only when the boss was around. Actually he had developed a little gadget, which allowed him to work twice as fast. Back at MIT, my colleagues did their little bit, analyzing and simplifying the job, eliminating some motions, transferring work from one hand to another, and finally cutting the allowed time by one quarter. We wrote our report. Then I added an appendix, based on my interview. We all got As. Fine, but my stupid colleagues handed the company a copy of our report, including my interview!

So my Taylorist course confirmed my prejudices. Later, as I read more about the intellectual milieu in which he worked and his quirky, convoluted personal life,[3] I developed a real interest in the old boy. The juicy details of his life have enlivened many of my lectures. Certainly there are some damning quotes in his work which can be easily taken out of context. Yet today I think he and Max Weber (the two were often linked together) had a very, very bad press. Taylor was among the first to stress and study motivation from a managerial point of view; he believed in rules (which protect workers as well as management) and so helped defang the arbitrary supervisor; further, he assumed that management could be studied—that it was a science rather than art. Indeed it might be argued that he was the father of OB. But it took years for this revisionist point of view to gain a hearing. At the time Taylor represented everything that human relationists felt wrong.

Having disposed of the anti-Christ, let me turn to the true religion, Human Relations.

Hawthorne and Harvard-style Human Relations

Much of what I knew as human relations could be traced back to a network which developed at Harvard in the 1930s, where Lawrence Henderson (a biologist) and Elton Mayo (a medical school dropout) played major roles, influencing not just Roethlisberger and Hawthorne, but Lloyd Warner, William F. Whyte, and Chester Barnard, all of whom were at Harvard during this period.

By the time I reached Cambridge only Fritz Roethlisberger and George Homans were left. Although I never had classes with either both helped me with my dissertation. Further, I was greatly influenced by the Hawthorne experiments in which both had participated. I read *Management and the Worker*[4] and some of Mayo's case studies with great care. On the other hand, his more philosophical work turned me off as quite elitist—and still does.

Hawthorne dominated the human relations field of the 1940s. Its values were the antithesis of Taylorism. Its lessons, as I saw them, were: (1) the significance of social needs; (2) the power of group standards; and (3) the difference between the Relay Assembly Test Room, where one form of supervision led to a group decision to increase productivity, and the Bank Wiring Observation Room, where another form of supervision led to output control.

Further, Hawthorne pioneered in the methodology of organizational research. The Relay Assembly Room involved a field experiment, the Bank Wiring Room applied what we now call ethnography, the observation of ongoing behavior. Hawthorne's final stage illustrated the value of nondirective listening as both a research technique and a tool for sound management. (Carl Rogers discovered the nondirective technique at much the same time as Roethlisberger; Rogers, however, used it primarily as a form of therapy—Roethlisberger used it initially for research). The methodology of the Relay Assembly Room experiment was grievously flawed, but this is irrelevant. Hawthorne gave us a new way to think about work life. Eventually it gave rise to more carefully designed research.

Except perhaps for Mayo's rather fuzzy philosophizing, Hawthorne never contributed to theory in the way that Barnard's contemporaneously published work did. This may have been related to the Harvard case study tradition. In teaching cases the instructor asks questions, for example, as to the protagonists' motivations and the possible implications of various courses of action. The purpose is for the student to learn as much as possible about the individual situation. But other than asking questions and suggesting a broad range of possible relevant factors, the case study approach is short on analytical tools for resolving problems. It is primarily inductive rather than deductive.

Counseling and nondirective listening, as practised by Roethlisberger, was in some ways merely an application of the case method. Indeed the nondirective listener was expected to behave somewhat like the case-method instructor. Clients were expected to think through their problems and develop their own solutions.

Roethlisberger taught one of the earliest "Human Relations" courses, in 1948, and perhaps the first seminar to be called "Organizational Behavior" in 1957. Arguably, therefore, Harvard and Roethlisberger were OB's founders. Nevertheless, despite the significant contributions of such luminaries as Paul Lawrence and Jay Lorsch, the field's cutting edge went elsewhere. The Harvard Business School environment was a difficult one in which to go beyond case collecting.

Applied Anthropology

Hawthorne's methodology and analytic framework borrowed heavily from an amazing variety of sources, ranging from philosophy and physiology to Janet, Pareto, and Freud. Among the more significant contributions were made by anthropologists, indirectly by Durkheim and directly by Warner, a former student of Malinowski.

Aside from the Hawthorne group there were a number of key people who were interested in applying anthropological concepts and methodologies (primarily direct observation) to contemporary society. Many were formally trained as sociologists and were allied with the then-vibrant Chicago school of urban sociologists. Some called themselves applied anthropologists and belonged to the newly formed Society for Applied Anthropology.

The work of applied anthropologists influenced my thinking greatly. The Lynds' *Middletown* and Warner's *Yankee City* series,[5] for example, taught sensitivity to status, status symbols, social (group) standards, and ethnic differences. For a while I almost automatically tried to classify people and communities by whether they were Lower-Middle, for example, or Upper-Lower. Bill Whyte's two major studies, *Street Corner Society* (University of Chicago Press, 1943) and *Human Relations in the Restaurant Industry* (McGraw-Hill, 1948), built upon this foundation. His study of status among vegetable preparers had quite an impact on me: the first thing I looked for in a factory was its status ladder. Doc, in *Street Corner*, defined for me what leadership was all about. Only recently did Bob House make me realize that there is another aspect of leadership, charisma. (Doc had charisma, too!)

The *Restaurant Industry* made another important point. The objective conditions of the job could have a major impact on attitudes and behavior. These included what we would now call job characteristics (such as Task Significance), work flow, and opportunities for communications. These insights were reinforced by the work of psychologists associated with the British Industrial Health Research Board's pathfinding experiments.[6] Pat Smith's early work was also quite relevant.[7] Together these studies laid the basis for modern Job Design. Later research did little more than confirm their findings.[8]

In my early days I attended the meetings of the Society for Applied Anthropology fairly regularly. I also wrote two articles for its journal, now called *Human Organization*. The Society's best known figure was Margaret Meade, who reminded me much of a clucking mother hen, watching us, her brood. I was delighted when she showed some interest in my dissertation. For quite a while I listed my field on questionnaires as "anthropology." What pretension! But I certainly wasn't an economist.

Group Dynamics

On the other side of the MIT campus from Economics, in a war-temporary building, was the Research Center for Group Dynamics (RCGD), sadly bereft of its founder, Kurt Lewin who died the day I arrived in Cambridge, but his spirit lived on. The RCGD, with its degree in Group Psychology, was closely linked with that of the Tavistock Institute in London and together they were in the forefront of what was then known as group dynamics.

Despite the physical distance between RCGD and my own group, I knew quite a lot of the RCGD people socially, though our groups were somewhat rivals. Once we had a touch football match: George Shultz was our quarterback and Hal Leavitt our star pass receiver. For the Dynamos Hal Kelley received the passes. Was John Thibault their quarterback? Who won? Here are critical social data I forget.

The relationship between our two groups was relatively short-lived, since RCGD had difficulty in getting permanent MIT funding and moved to Michigan sometime in 1948 or 1949. Nevertheless, the influence of RCGD on my thinking persisted.

A major distinction between group dynamics and Harvard-style human relations, was that group dynamics people were attached to an established field, psychology, and theories were important to them. Yet theories and research were expected to be more directly applicable than they are today. As Lewin put it, "There is nothing so practical as a good theory." But theory could be learned through practice, he said. "The best way to understand an organization is to change it." In short, for Lewin "action research" required that social theory and social action be closely integrated.

Group dynamics, defined broadly, made many important contributions to our understanding of leadership, democracy, group process, and resistance to change. Further it gave rise to T-groups and eventually OD. T-groups in those days were somewhat differently designed than those of later years. As we used them at MIT, there was a formally assigned role of process observer, a role which was rotated among members of the group. Early T-groups concentrated on group functioning rather than individuals. They were designed to train better committee members and chairpersons. Only later did the possibility emerge that they could be used to make not just better conference leaders, but better managers and better people as well. Eventually, it became "an all but religious exercise."[9]

Group dynamics had two important "laboratories." First there were summer programs offered at the Gould Academy, in Bethel Maine. Here T-groups took their classic form. The second was the Harwood Manufacturing Company, an Appalachian pajama plant, whose president would sometimes sign his letters, Alfred J. Marrow, President-Psychologist. Harwood was the site of many early field experiments (especially on group decision) including some conducted by Lewin, Gordon Allport, Jack French, and Alex Bavelas (who served for a while as personnel director). Some years later a different Harwood plant was the site of one of the most thorough studies of organizational change so far: Alfred Marrow, David Bowers, and Stan Seashores's *Management by Participation* (Harper & Row, 1967).

Harwood was unionized. According to Bill Gomberg, then a union official but later a Wharton professor, Marrow treated collective bargaining negotiations as a form of psychotherapy. As Gomberg told the story, Marrow once met him at the railroad station in the midst of negotiations. "The process is proceeding well," Marrow was alleged to have told him. "A great deal of hostility has been expressed and we are now going through cathexis. At this stage you will be very useful, Dr. Gomberg." To which Bill said he replied, "[Obscenity] you, you management bastard. We can't eat that crap. Give us 30 cents an hour!" Later I asked Chick Chaikin, the union's national president, what was the secret of Harwood's success. Not Alfred's psychology, Chick replied, but his brother's skill as production whiz.

I visited Bethel only for a day and I had only one class at the RCGD . This class, with Jack French, dealt with democracy, always a hot topic for me. But rather than read about the democratic theory, the class rules were that we would discuss the idea, issue by issue, and develop principles through consensus. This was to be a democratic class. After three or four sessions we got around to defining democracy. My group-dynamic classmates insisted it involved everyone going along. My opinion was that all democracy required was majority vote and civil rights—but if I were outvoted, I'd be go along, at least for the purpose of this class. No, my classmates insisted, voting would be unfair to those outvoted. We would have to reach an agreement. Obstinately I held to my position. After an hour of stalemate French "autocratically" changed the format of the class to require some *real* work. Feeling hostility, I dropped out. A bit later—in the football game, I mentioned earlier, one of the Dynamos (whose name I still won't mention) clipped me badly, preventing an intercept. Given my Freudian interest, I was sure it was no mistake.

Aside from this unsuccessful RCGD class. I took Freed Bales's seminar at Harvard, with much observation of groups through one-way glass. Here I with struggled learning how to code human interactions in terms of his twelve "interaction process categories" (e.g., "shows solidarity," "asks opinions," and the like). Despite my own inability to code interactions as fast as they occurred, this seemed a powerful instrument. It has dropped out of the literature with which I'm familiar but survives as a consultant training technique called SYMLOG.

Douglas McGregor and Human Relations

Though group dynamics and applied anthropology provided the major conceptual references for our thinking, my major organizational identification was with Industrial Relations (already discussed) and Human Relations. The Human Relations group within MIT Economics consisted of Irving Knickerbocker, Alex Bavelas, Mason Haire, and Douglas McGregor. I sat through Alex's undergraduate class, picking up a number of wonderful stories and cases based on his experience. One of these I published under our two names ("The Hovey and Beard Company," 1955) since Alex was notorious for his reluctance to publish on his own (Lewin had earlier performed a similar service for one of Alex's cases).[10]

Perhaps my most important course was with Doug McGregor. Tall, redheaded, with a little mustache, Doug looked the archetypical psychiatrist. Talking slowly, he made magnificent use of his pipe. (One of his best sessions was on "pipe work." When things got tough, he said, the trick was to let your pipe go out. By the time you have it lit again the manager you were working with will have solved his problem by himself.)

Doug's seminar gave us a chance to apply and integrate the various concepts we had learned elsewhere. But at first the seminar was quite disappointing. Doug was a nice guy and the seminar (Ec 95), titled Human Relations, was pretty central to our interests, but the stuff Doug was lecturing about most of us had read on our own (one could read the field's entire literature rather quickly). So, over coffee, some of us dissidents started planning the kind of course we would like Doug to teach. Finally three of us confronted him. "Would it possible for him to cover some of the items on our agenda?" we asked. Doug smiled, puffed on his pipe for a while, and then said, "I was worried my experiment was going to fail and that you would never take over. Great. Let's do what you want."

The course we wanted (and later Doug confided he wanted) was concerned primarily with introducing change, influencing managers to confer and delegate, and encouraging subordinates to accept responsibility. In the usual seminar we would discuss a problem, talk through the various potential forms of resistance to change, suggest alternate change strategies, and then role-play them. Typically one student would play the role of a foreman, another the role of a worker, and so on. Then we would discuss how we, as personnel people, would induce the foreman to implement our preferred strategy (often through nondirective counseling). Meanwhile one or two students served as "process observers" and would report ("feed back") periodically on what they saw happening to the group.

Sometimes we would end the seminar with fifteen minutes of "process." At times, we students (and significant others) would meet for a pot luck dinner and further "process," sometimes with a process-observer to provide feedback on our discussion of process. *Process*, the dynamics of interpersonal relations, was our greatest interest. (Consistent with this approach, my Ph.D. orals involved roleplaying: Mason Haire played a recalcitrant foreman, whom, I, as personnel director, had to straighten out.)

In short, the emphasis in Doug's course was on becoming change-agents, changing our own behavior and that of others. He trained us to be nondirective therapists on the assumption that we would either become personnel directors or at least should know how to behave as personnel directors. In this role we should stick to the "sanitary." Personality or childhood problems were none of our business: we should stick to the "here and now," the manifest rather than the latent. On the other hand, we should be aware of the possibility that others would treat us as father figures and would transfer to us the feelings they once had for their real fathers. Knowing this possibility, we should know how to avoid it. Further we should confront our own impulses to play father, a warning one of my colleagues failed to take when he became carried away in an attempt to help an emotionally disturbed student.

There was some correspondence between Doug's emphasis on training us, in a doctoral program, to be good personnel people, and the early stress in the Harvard's doctoral program on how to be a good manager.[11] To the extent that thought was given to the matter, it was assumed that to teach managers we had to be good managers ourselves (and that research was secondary). Significantly, a majority of my classmates spent at least part of their careers with companies (or, in one case, Ralph Bergmann, a union) and many, such as Shultz and Bergmann, moved back and forth between academic and non-academic pursuits.

Though today McGregor is best known for Theory X and Theory Y, these concepts hadn't been developed yet. Instead he talked about augmentative and reductive relationships. The augmentative relationship increased satisfaction and so was akin to Theory Y. Reduction led to frustration and this to aggression and other dysfunctional behavior (my McGregor notes are full of references to Dollard and Doob).[12]

Personnel

We also had a course called "Personnel," taught by Paul Pigors. For reading we were assigned Barnard as well as variety of traditional management texts, such as Alvin Brown. I found them all quite boring. Barnard was hard going and his subtleties escaped me. After Hawthorne, almost everything Barnard said seemed trite, for example, the importance of subordinates' consent. Had he provided case examples his propositions might have made greater impact.

Of greater interest we were assigned two fieldwork exercises. One required us to be a change agent and my approach was not particularly nondirective. I was assigned a section of Somerville with instructions to recruit a core of volunteers to raise money for the Community Chest. After some initial setbacks I approached the parish priest, who also proved uncooperative. I resigned myself to collecting the money myself, on a door-to-door basis. Fortunately, at a MIT lunch I met the archbishop's secretary. I told him my problem. The next day I got a call from an irate priest. "You squealed on me. You got me in trouble with the archbishop. How much do you want?" "Two thousand dollars will do us fine" I replied. ($500 had been the most ever raised in that section.) Two weeks later he delivered. Note: in a pinch I abandoned Theory Y for bargaining clout.

Even today, when the emphasis is on theory and research, doctoral candidates might gain from practical experiences such as ours.

Wage Administration

Among my more interesting courses was a Saturday morning seminar with Bob Livernash, then with the New Hampshire state personnel department and later the Harvard Business School. Bob was in the midst of a job evaluation program. He regaled us with stories about the politics and intergroup conflicts this seeming mechanical activity inevitably involved. From Bob I learned that personnel work is 20% technique and 80% implementation, a point which modern human resource texts seem to have forgotten. Bob was also a useful antidote to McGregor: as Bob's stories illustrated, personnel work requires more than being a nice guy and listening nondirectively; it requires heavy doses of backroom politics.

Further, Bob's approach (and that of Clark Kerr in work written contemporaneously) foreshadowed recent work of Jeff Pfeffer and Jim Barron (as Jeff generously acknowledges). Parenthetically, for people of my generation, very little of recent work on personnel issues by sociologists or efficiency wage theorists is at all novel. We knew it all along from the studies of the 1940s. The difference is that today's conclusions are based on quantitative analysis of massive data sets rather than on case studies, and propositions are stated more rigorously and tied to fundamental theories rather than treated as problems to be solved by practitioners.

THE FIELD IN THE EARLY 1950s

As the names of the MIT and Harvard departments indicate, the immediate postwar period was one of great disciplinary fluidity. Theory was de-emphasized. Instead the emphasis was on *integrating* and *applying* the social sciences. This period saw the establishment of the Society for the Psychological Study of Social Issues, the Society for Applied Anthropology, and the Industrial Relations Research Association, all of which I joined. All three were much concerned with the application of the social sciences and the first two published journals (*Applied Anthropology*, later *Human Organization*, and the *Journal of Social Issues*). At the same time, *Human Relations*, whose motto was "toward the integration of the social sciences," was started at Tavistock in Britain.

Human Relations was normative and optimistic. Lewin, Roethlisberger, and McGregor were missionaries, and so were we students. In our rose-colored view, the social sciences could and should be used to improve society. Soon we would have the answer to racial prejudice (Lewin's great concern), labor-management problems, economic fluctuations, and possibly even war (though I was personally far from optimistic as to the possibility of avoiding atomic destruction).

Though we were firmly convinced that most problems could be resolved through research, our research tools were fairly limited. The most important were ethnographic case studies, particularly those based on participant or non-participant direct observation. We also made use of interviews (preferably nondirective), field experiments (such as the Relay Assembly room), and laboratory experiments (as used in group dynamics). *Individual* attitudes received little attention, however. Homans called them merely "sentiments." We had no training in quantitative methods.

Consistent with our methodology our primary research focus was on groups, especially on such issues as norms, group standards, status and sociometric patterns. For us the chief lesson to be learned from Hawthorne and similar research was the repressive effect of formal organization and the liberating aspects of its informal counter part. The trick to successful management, as we saw it, was to enlist the services of informal leaders and to involve the group in solving common problems through group decision. The effective supervisor would act as an informal leader.

Externally how groups would develop would be affected by technology. Internally their operations could be improved through an understanding of group dynamics. In this way both anthropology and group dynamics could be integrated into human relations.

Our emphasis on the group level helped blind us to other issues. We were familiar with Abe Maslow's needs hierarchy and Henry Murray's concept of need achievement. Further, McGregor taught us what later became Theories X and Y. Nevertheless, human relations of the 1950s, compared with the OB of the 1960s, paid little attention to individual needs or motivation. Similarly, though McGregor and Myers were much interested in the staff role, there was otherwise little concern for the larger formal organization. Certainly ours was a closed theory approach.

Despite the seeming breadth of my training, Homans' *The Human Group* (Harcourt Brace, 1950) was as close as I got to theory. Perhaps the reason I liked Homans' book was that his theory was closely linked to cases; indeed it seemed to flow out of the cases, which was the way I (and presumably many of my colleagues) thought. As Whyte put it, "I did not develop [my] ideas by any logical process. They dawned on me out of what I was seeing, hearing, doing,—and feeling. They grew out of an effort to organize a confusing welter of experience."[13] In other words our thinking was inductive. We went from case to theory, (and not too much theory please) rather than the other way around.

MY LIFE IN THE 1950s

Now to turn back to me, personally. Obviously I did more during this period than just attend class and read books. I enjoyed the many opportunities available in the Boston area and New England. Summers I took jobs for work experience (MIT was big on this) and also to earn a little money. One summer I worked in a unionized milk bottling plant and as a nonunion construction laborer. A year later I was a unit supervisor in camp for mostly delinquent kids, supervising counselors who themselves were at least partially delinquent. As a supervisor I found that nondirective listening went a long way, but after that I was in trouble. Still another summer I was a Field Examiner for the National Labor Relations Board, learning the grimy side of labor relations.

At the NLRB I learned a cruel lesson. I was assigned an elderly secretary. Being a student of McGregor's I assumed she was bored with her job (certainly she griped enough) and that the sure answer was participation and job enrichment. So I asked her advice (based on her vast experience, as I told her) with regards to every letter and was soon delegating responsibilities to her to draft letters herself. Not long after, she blew up "Look, you're a [Grade] 7, I'm a 2. You're paid to draft these letters. I'm only paid to type up what you say. If you don't quit it, I'm going to the union." (Later, when I told Ren Likert this story, he told me "George, you pushed her too fast.")

Teaching

In my last three school years I worked as a Teaching Assistant. I taught the works, Introductory Economics (Ec 11), Industrial Relations (Ec 60), and Social Psychology (Ec 70). As TAs in Ec 60 and 70 we set our own syllabi (except for a common basic text), did all the teaching, and graded our own exams. My Industrial Relations was mostly human relations, with much role playing. The one semester I taught Psychology we all (Hal Leavitt was one of us) decided that we would teach via a T-group, perhaps the first time a T-group was taught for credit. This worked for a while, until one by one the student sections revolted. "We are tired of this democratic nonsense," they said. "The instructor should be dictator." My section was the last to revolt, perhaps not because I was such a great T-group leader but because they knew I would make a lousy lecturer.

Dissertation

By 1949, having passed my comprehensive exams (which included roleplaying), I began thinking about my dissertation. My first thought was to study several Scanlon Plan companies. Joe Scanlon showed little interest, understandably perhaps, given the nasty questions I had asked in his seminar. So I picked human relations in unions, especially local unions. In 1950 I was influenced especially by Homans's just published *Human Group*, as well as my experience with the Labor Board. I began to think of the union as a network of informal groups, much as Whyte saw Cornerville. I was interested in how leaders developed within each group, how various groups and their leaders related to each other, and how all this was impacted by the employing organization's external system, especially its work technology.

Then I had a bright idea. To examine the *development* of an informal system it might be best to study a new union. Besides entree might be easier. Fortunately I had a stroke of luck. At a MIT affair I met the national presidents of two unions, each of which was engaged in an organizing drive, one at New England Telephone, the other at Boston Edison., With their endorsement I gained entree easily.

The telephone drive came first. I took on the role of a union organizer, making house calls on perspective members. Most of my prospects were young operators and often mommy or daddy would chaperone my interview. This didn't bother me much, since daddy typically was a unionist himself and would reinforce my message. Still I made little progress. As one woman told me embarrassedly, "I don't want to join a union. I want to get married." And another explained, "I can't join. My brother is a priest." But even among the older "girls" (as they adamantly insisted on calling themselves) loyalty to Ma Bell seemed high. Gradually it became clear that the key female leaders were going to sit this one out. The union lost 2-1.

Boston Edison was different. Here the Utility Workers Union was fighting an older so-called company (independent) union. The new union's leadership had a situation well in hand and had no need for an incompetent outside organizer. But they were delighted to explain what that were doing to a sympathetic academician who shared their views and was, besides, a good listener. McGregor's training paid off.

Actually it was an ideal research site. Technically, because of Labor Board rules, the company was divided into three "bargaining units": (1) "physical," blue-collar, almost entirely male; (2) clerical, mostly female, and (3) professional, almost entirely male. Once the union won the election in all three units, as it did nicely, three separate locals were established, each with a distinctly different political life. I had a range of occupations to study, from professional engineers, through bill collectors and overhead linemen, to coal handlers. And my groups differed nicely in ethnicity, gender, age, and, above all, status.

Systematically, on the basis of interviews and various forms of written data, I developed a profile of each of the some 30 major divisions into which the company's workforce was divided: its industrial relations problems, the occupation, age, and ethnicity of its formal and informal leaders, the positions they took with regards to the competing unions, and the extent and nature of its members' union participation. I was overwhelmed with data. Today I might have entered into my computer and tested my findings quantitatively. But there were no computers then, at least not for graduate students, and I lacked the quantitative skills. So I roughly sampled my data for impressions and trends.

Boston Edison formed the heart of my dissertation, but I checked my observations with three other situations, the Ford assembly plant in Somerville, the then newly opened (now closed) GM plant in Framingham, and the three locals of the Boston Ladies' Garment Workers Union, (1) cutters, Jewish, (2) pressers, Italian and (3) dressmakers, mostly women. In all these my hypotheses worked out nicely.

What did I find? In brief, consistent with *The Restaurant Industry* status and communications opportunities were of major importance in determining "Leadership and Participation in the Local Union," my dissertation's eventual title. Within groups, high status people were more likely to participate in union activities or be elected to union office. High-status groups had similar advantages over low-status groups. Communications had much the same impact. Individuals (such as tool-crib attendants) who could easily communicate with their peers were more likely to participate and be elected. Groups, such as electrical power operators, who could easily communicate with other workers in the course of their work, also tended to hold key positions in the union. Status and communications didn't explain everything of course. There were important differences among officers and stewards in the way they conceived and played their roles as well as the functions union activity played in their lives.

The Local Union

By 1951 my dissertation was pretty well complete. Meanwhile, my MIT classmate, Leonard Sayles, had left for the Cornell Labor School to work on a project on "human relations in unions," funded by the W.T. Grant Foundation and directed by Bill Whyte. I joined the project in 1951 with a three-year appointment.

Our first task was to merge our dissertations into a single book. Though Len's dissertation was slightly more psychological than mine the two blended together beautifully. Today I can't tell which part of the resulting book, *The Local Union* (1952) was Len's and which mine. Along the way we milked our respective dissertations for at least a dozen articles, some written separately, most jointly, publishing in such journals as the *Harvard Business Review* (then considered a prestigious journal), *Industrial and Labor Relations Review*, and *The American Journal of Sociology*. In 1952 the Society for the Psychological Study of Social Issues awarded us a prize (funded by Alfred J. Marrow) for its contribution to "the scientific understanding of labor-management relations." Obviously we had a hot topic.

I spent much of the first year of my appointment at Ithaca. While there I had frequent contact with Bill Whyte, who had already influenced my work so heavily. We also occasionally saw such people as Chris Argyris, who was working on his own dissertation. But Len and I had our own project and we were pretty much alone.

Fairport

In June 1952, with two years of the project to go, I took off for another study, this time in an American Can plant in Fairport, New York. Fairport, a town of only 5,000, was pretty lonely, but fortunately the kindly union president and his wife somehow adopted me, especially for much appreciated Sunday dinners. Yet, as a study of union behavior my can plant had little to offer. The union was weak, union-management relations were placid, and no new interesting hypotheses emerged. Instead my interests turned in two directions:

How people adjust to their jobs. As my Labor Board secretary so dramatically taught me, not everyone wants job challenge. Yet many jobs are very boring. How do people come to terms with their work? Being sure that more than Mayo's obsessive reveries were involved I began asking workers, "What were you thinking about just now" (a version of a "penny for your thoughts"). "About God," one told me. "I like to think of my cans as little babies," a childless woman said. "When I put tops on them I am diapering them." (Several thousand diapers a day!)

In one department high-status women had a choice of two sorts of jobs: the first was completely routine and repetitive; the second involved considerable variety. Women who elected routine jobs were happily married for the most part; their reveries turned on family matters ("What will I serve on Sunday?"); and they viewed work as respite from screaming children. Those who picked non-routine work were generally single or had unhappy family lives. The reveries they told me dealt with changing jobs or other forms of fantasy. Obviously, personal adjustment and orientation to work were related. Further, most people made peace with their job, but at various costs to their psyche. This was a theme I was to enlarge later.

Working supervisor. My second study involved set-up men, who traditionally had served as working supervisors, coordinating and providing technical direction for work teams. College-trained foremen were usurping their functions on the dayshift, resulting in much turmoil. Meanwhile, on the largely foreman-less night shift production and quality were higher and stress-induced illnesses and accidents were lower. Later, using other material, I documented how the working supervisor's role was being eroded through much of American industry, caused in part by the ever-sharpening distinction between labor and management. Only recently, have observers noted that this distinction is much weaker in Germany and Japan, contributing to greater manufacturing flexibility in these countries.

Rochester

After a eight months in Fairport I moved to Rochester. There I began two additional studies. The first was of white-collar unions. Why were workers so reluctant to join them? How could this reluctance be overcome? How did the behavior of these unions, once organized, differ from that of blue-collar unions? Besides drawing on my Boston telephone experience, I observed a series of organizing drives (all unsuccessful) and several functioning unions.

In addition I followed closely, through a long cold winter, a bitter insurance agents' strike against Prudential. These were "five and dime" industrial agents who sold small policies, collecting their premiums monthly. Though ostensibly striking over compensation, their chief concern was what they perceived as their company's unrelenting pressure to "produce" and especially to compete with each other, for instance (according to stories told me) by holding weekly sales meetings in which the low producer of the previous week had to sit with a dunce cap in the corner. Well after the strike was over, this union had by far the best monthly meeting attendance of any union I have ever observed—over 70% month after month. Why? Because selling insurance is a lonely, frustrating job. Ninety-five percent of agents' prospects turned them down. Company meetings were even more ego damaging. The union meeting offered solidarity and to chance to exchange stupid-customer stories.

My second study was of construction unions. I spent three fascinating years with Business Agents (BAs), typically meeting one at the union hall at 6:30 AM, when he "dispatched" men to the various jobs, then driving with him through the country as he inspected jobs and resolved grievances. Often in the evening there would be a meeting, followed by drinks with the members. (I gained some six pounds through excess beer drinking).

Though I was unevenly successful in gaining these BAs' confidence, many were delighted to have someone accompany them on their rounds, someone to whom they could spill their frustrations. Occasionally I would get a late night call from a BA, just to talk over how he'd handle sticky problems the next day.

Some fifteen unions were involved, with striking differences among the occupational characteristics of their members and the way the BAs played their roles. What made these unions especially interesting was that each was an occupational community (with much intermarrying) and most were marked by internal feuds within the "family." Among the more worthwhile questions: status hierarchies and how they were expressed; the constantly changing relationships among the BAs of various unions as they cooperated for some purposes and then fought each other tooth and nail over jurisdiction; the process by which BAs decided when to "shade" the standard wage rates to save particular jobs; and the unstable power balance between BAs and their members. Since BAs controlled jobs they could punish political enemies; but if they punished too many they might lose the next election, and election fights were frequent. All this affected the bargaining process. This was rich material which is almost never examined today, perhaps because economics and sociology are now such separate disciplines and perhaps because, unless you are on a grant, it is difficult to find the time to spend endless days driving around with BAs or walking insurance agent picket lines.

Buffalo

In 1954, when my grant had expired, I went to the University of Buffalo Business School. At last *I belonged* to a community rather than merely being an observer. Buffalo, at the time, was not a research-oriented university, which meant that despite a heavy teaching load there was plenty of time for lunch and evening social activities. I quickly joined a close-knit group of friends whose interests spanned the humanities and the social sciences. One lunch we might discuss Chaucer or Joyce, the next we sampled each other's pates over wine. Since my friends did it, I even began attending string quartets and the symphony. Everybody knew everybody, and it was nice.

Not that I gave up on politics. My social set included most of Buffalo's liberals. I was active in both the local American Civil Liberties Union (this was the McCarthy era) and the campus chapter of the AAUP, serving a term as chair of each.

Contributing to my rosy memories of this period, in 1957 I got married. After a four-month European honeymoon Helene and I bought a wonderful Victorian house, had two children, and were prepared to settle down for a lifetime among our friends in Buffalo, interspersed, as we planned, with many trips throughout the world.

I enjoyed my teaching. I taught 12 hours a week in the regular day school and, to earn extra money, four extra hours Friday night for a total of seven preparation. (I flaunt these figures at my colleagues when they complain of having to teach two courses in the same semester.) Besides such topics as labor relations, labor history, and labor law I handled a three semester sequence of human relations, wage administration, and personnel administration. Showing how so slim the materials we had at the time, in Human Relations I used Whyte's *Restaurant Industry* (rejecting Gardner's *Human Relations in Industry,*[14] the field's first text, as too limited). Wage administration I renamed Incentives and Productivity, assigning Whyte's *Money and Motivation*[15] and stressing group standards, introducing change and incentive systems. For Personnel I used Pigors and Myers. All my texts were supplemented by journal articles.

None of this stopped my research, at least prior to my marriage. I went to Rochester one or two days a week to follow up on my building trades research, carrying it through three negotiating cycles. Meanwhile I was actively publishing the work I had done previously.

Personnel

Sometime in 1955 Len Sayles suggested we write a text together. It took us five years. Without giving the matter much thought we called the work "Personnel: The Human Problems of Management." We avoided "Human

Relations" because the term was under attack (see below). On the other hand, in the schools we knew, "Human Relations" was still called "Personnel." Regardless of title, our text was designed to cover the topics which are called today organizational behavior and human resources management. Since it was published in 1960 ours was not the first OB book. Hoslett, Gardner, and Leavitt came before us. But at 750 pages ours was certainly the most comprehensive.

What did it cover? Everything we knew in 1960: Maslow on needs, McGregor on motivation, Hawthorne and Whyte on groups, status, and informal leadership, Lewin on group dynamics, the British studies on job design, Michigan on supervision plus heavy doses of industrial relations and labor economics. Our general framework was McGregor's class of the late 1940s, but we added work done during the 1950s, especially by sociologists such as Blau, Gouldner, and Bendix.

There were two main differences between our text and Leavitt's beautifully organized work. First, he focussed on psychological principles; we were concerned with sociology and industrial relations as well. Secondly, we stressed the problems connected with application and implementation (something which even today most texts ignore). We viewed implementation as a political process requiring endless accommodation. Indeed an accurate title for our text might have been "Human Relations and Its Limits." Forinstance, in addition to McGregor's three forms of motivation, Be Strong and Be Good (later called Theory X) and internalized motivation (later called Theory Y), we added a fourth, implicit bargaining (a concept borrowed from Gouldner). Though internalized motivation might ideally be best, in many instances bargaining was the best one might achieve.

As it turned out, we were lucky in our choice of topics and publication date. Eventually we split the book into three different versions: one purely personnel, the second purely OB and the third combining both topics. After 30 years our various editions have sold over a half-million copies in four different languages. The last edition appeared in 1980.

In rereading the book today it seems to have stood up very well; I am surprised how much we knew in 1960 (though this may be merely an indication of how little I have learned since then). We certainly knew a lot more in the 1960s than in the 1950s.

THE FIELD IN THE 1960s

By the mid-1960s the field was beginning to jell. First, the "field" was no longer called "Human Relations." Second, it had changed greatly since 1950 and was changing still. Finally, it was rapidly becoming accepted as a key part of most business school curricula.

Human Relations Becomes Organizational Behavior

In the mid-1950s human relations came under attack from both the left and the right. From the left it was attacked by labor economists and sociologists (especially radical sociologists) who claimed that it ignored economic motivation, unions, and the class struggle; that it put the group over the individual, substituting Organizational Man for anomie; that it treated mangers as rational "elite" and workers as irrational "aborigines";[17] and that it assumed conflict was simply the result of misunderstanding, to be eliminated by discussion. (As late as 1989, in a discussion of the role of human resources management in the Industrial Relations Research Association, John Dunlop insisted on calling HRM, "human relations," which, as he saw it, was just a method of union busting.)

These attacks still sting. As someone studying human relations in unions I felt it grossly unfair to charge human relations with being anti-union. Quite the contrary. My 1948 McGregor class notes make it clear that he viewed human relations without unions as a sham. Unions were needed for participation. True, McGregor hoped for some sort of Theory Y union-management relations in which each side recognized the other's needs and that differences would be worked out through good listening. This was idealistic. It wasn't anti-union. Mayo, it is true, might be viewed as paternalistic and even a bit fascistic. Roethlisberger hoped that management would work so well that unions weren't necessary. But for him union were merely the bearers of bad news. One shouldn't shoot the messenger.

The other attack came from the right. It was best illustrated by Malcolm McNear's article, "Thinking Ahead: What Price Human Relations?"[18] Briefly the charge was that human relations was goody-goody, namby-pamby and no management could survive with just good intentions. This was the kind of criticism which management (and many economists) could accept.

The term "human relations" was out in any case. It would be interesting to study systematically what the people-oriented course was called in most business schools in the 1950s. In some it was Personnel, in others Management, but this typically included very little Human Relations. By the mid-1960s the title Organizational Behavior had taken hold, though some schools retained Management.

A Changing Field

By 1960 OB, as I will call it, was much changed from 1950 and was still changing rapidly. Important books had been published by Argyris, Likert, McGregor, and Fred Herzberg. The field had become considerably more psychological. Compared with the earlier period there was more interest in individual motivation and mental health than in group behavior; there was more concern for ego and self-actualization than for social needs. Some talked of a human resources as opposed to a human relations model.[19]

Industrial sociology as a field was dying out and organizational sociology was still to be developed. A number of earlier sociologists—Homans, Whyte, Blau, and Gouldner—were writing on exchange theory, a theory which didn't get very far in sociology, but was revived and extended by psychologists as equity theory and procedural justice.

The focus of 1960s OB was more on management than on blue-collar workers. Supervisory training was transformed into management training and then to organization development (OD). Further, the field became more quantitative and methodologically sophisticated. Survey questionnaires were widely used, especially to study supervision. Research was becoming deductive rather than inductive.

By the 1960s OB had developed a widely accepted paradigm, perhaps best articulated by Argyris and Likert. Put simply it was as follows. Workplace behavior is motivated by Maslow's needs-hierarchy. Individuals seek to satisfy progressively higher levels of need—and to do so *on the job*, not necessarily through family or community. Specifically they seek to exercise autonomy and to develop their unique personalities with freedom. Organizations, on the other hand, seek to program behavior and reduce discretion. Subordinates react to this pressure in a variety of ways, from union activity to psychosomatic illness. To keep employees in line, management must impose still more restrictions and force still more immature behavior. Thus human assets are wasted and a vicious cycle begins.

A subtle management, which provides "hygienes," such as high wages and decent supervision may well induce workers to *think* they are happy and not dissatisfied, but in fact they are apathetic. Really effective solutions include job enrichment, participative management and above all T-groups and OD.

This 1960s paradigm was even more normative and applied than early human relations. As I noted ("Human Relations," 1968), the field's key figures were crusaders. They were interested in research, not for its own sake, but because they wanted to better the human lot. They were optimistic, even utopian. Being crusaders their work was directed to managers, as well as scholars. This normative dedication also influenced the questions which these scholars asked and the variables which they considered. Likert was explicit that the causal variables with which he was concerned include only these "which can be altered or changed by the organization and its management"[20]

Finally, 1960s OB had almost naive faith that there was a "one best way" for most problems. I recall sitting next to Likert at dinner. "Ren," I asked. "Would System 4 work equally well in all cultures?" Pointing to his hotel-sticker plastered attache case, he replied. "I've been to dozens of countries throughout the world. System 4 works everywhere I have been. Sometime I may find some Hottentot tribe where it isn't appropriate. But I haven't found it yet."

The 1960s paradigm presented a glowing image of a world in which happy employees worked productivity and enthusiastically for management's goals. As I describe below, I became increasingly uncomfortable in teaching this paradigm in its unadulterated form.

OB Wins Acceptance in the Business School Core

By the late 1960s OB (or Management) had become an independent field. In most business schools it was a required course at both graduate and undergraduate levels. How this occurred still needs to be documented—and before the key participants pass away. Certainly the Gordon-Howell report played a major role. So did the American Association of Collegiate Schools of Business (though chiefly in ratifying a process almost complete). It would be useful, if someone could describe the change process in a broad sample of schools. To start the ball rolling, I describe what happened at Berkeley below.

MY MOVE TO BERKELEY

In 1960 I was invited to spend a year as a visitor at Berkeley. Having been turned down for a Fulbright in Italy, California seemed a tolerable second best (I knew it well from my Army hitchhiking days). Helene and I loved the Bay Area. With two squabbling children in the back of our VW, we explored the area thoroughly. I liked my immediate colleagues but found the University as such quite cold, compared to the intimacy of Buffalo. Then, to my surprise, given Berkeley's historical antipathy to human relations, I received an offer to stay. That posed quite a dilemma. Helene and I cherished our life, friends, and wonderful house in Buffalo. I had already turned down offers to Columbia, Chicago, and Illinois. But Berkeley, at the time, was the best IR center in the world and Berkeley's weather had much to recommend over Buffalo's, especially for growing kids.

So we vacillated. I went for long walks. I made long lists with the advantages and disadvantages of each choice. At two points I told Buffalo I would definitely return—and then 48 hours later called them to say I had changed my mind. In the end we returned to Buffalo for a year, sold our wonderful house, went back to Berkeley, lived for two years in a rented house while we agonized, took two years of sabbatical (1965-66; 1970-71) in Buffalo, and finally gave up our Buffalo dream. Crass ambition (Berkeley was more prestigious than Buffalo) triumphed. For Helene, with family in Buffalo, the sacrifice was greater.

Teaching

I was hired to be the first tenure-track faculty member to teach "Personnel." This was under the auspices of the Industrial Relations Group (Berkeley's Business School has no formal departmental subdivisions). I did this my first year, interpreting Personnel as being mostly Human Relations. In 1962 I was reassigned half-time to the Administration and Policy Group, a strange mixture consisting chiefly of decision theorists, game theorists, and management scientists The intent was that this group would provide the behavioral emphasis envisioned by the Gordon-Howell report. For a year I actually chaired the group. There I taught a required course of Organization and Administration (previously this course had been known as Business Policy). Though no one told me, I was probably expected to teach Simon. Instead I used my new textbook.

Over the next three years, after much political maneuvering, the Administration and Policy Group was renamed Management Science, the Organization and Administration requirement dropped, the Industrial Relations Group renamed Organizational Behavior and Industrial Relations, and the required undergraduate and MBA-level industrial relations courses enlarged to encompass OB. After several years of trying to teach both OB and IR in the same introductory course, the IR part was dropped. Meanwhile the personnel course was transformed into what we might call HRM today. The net result: through some Pac-Man type activity, IR obtained jurisdiction over OB, but became more OB than IR.

Finishing Up Research

Before leaving Buffalo the first time, I had started four projects, all of which I continued both at Berkeley and during my year's return to Buffalo. Each of these were based on extensive fieldwork.

The first dealt with the changing patterns of industrial relations in Buffalo's twenty largest factories. This was a period when union strength peaked and management gradually moved from the defensive to the offensive (Strauss, 1962a). The second, "Adolescence in Organizational Growth," (1974) documented the stresses which occurred as growing start-up companies shifted from informal to formal, bureaucratic organization. A third study involved purchasing agents (PAs) and their "lateral relations" with other departments, especially engineering and production scheduling ("Tactices of Lateral Relationships," 1962; "Work-flow Frictions," 1964). I was concerned with two related questions, first, how to design organizational systems so as to lessen workflow problems, and secondly, what were the bargaining and political skills required to be successful in lateral relations.

The PA research contributed to a fourth study, this time examining professionalism and the role of professional associations viewed as interest groups or quasi-(or even real) unions ("Professionalism and Occupational Associations," 1963). My focus was on engineering unions and associations, but I also looked at such groups as foremen's unions and the National Association of Purchasing Agents. My aim was to develop a conceptual scheme linking professional, managerial, white-collar, and blue-collar roles, but stressing role conflicts suffered by in-between occupations, such as engineers, whom I viewed as part-professionals, part-workers-and part-managers.

While all these studies led to publications, I was never able to develop them as extensively as I had hoped. The first two studies were designed to be longitudinal, covering five or ten years of development. My move to Berkeley left me with only three years data. As to the last two studies, having studied engineers and purchasing agents, I planned to move on other professionals, such as accountants. Other developments got in my way.

Apprenticeship

In 1962 the Institute of Industrial Relations received a large Ford Foundation grant to study unemployment. Feeling under great pressure to participate, I postponed (temporarily, I thought) my other projects.

Given my background I was at a loss as to how to study unemployment (other actually observing/interviewing the unemployed, but this had been done already). Eventually, I latched on to apprenticeship, especially in the building trades. How did presumably skilled workers acquire their knowledge? Why was apprenticeship so weak in the United States, compared to Germany, for example? What could be done to reform it?

So I spent several years trying to understand how apprenticeship worked. Aside from reading the voluminous but largely boring literature, I interviewed employers, BAs, apprenticeship coordinators, vocational school instructors and many apprentices themselves—all my standard stuff. I sat through long meetings of joint union-management apprenticeship committees, had coffee with vocational school students in their breaks, travelled with apprenticeship coordinators as they made their rounds, and spent time with BAs as they checked apprentices at work. Having exhausted the Bay Area I spent part of a sabbatical (1965-66) going through similar paces in Buffalo.

The result? A number of minor league publications (I should have set my aims higher). However, a monograph I wrote on the policy aspects of the topic got turned down (see below) and I finally gave up on a three-quarters finished book. It wasn't worth the time.

The apprenticeship study was my last empirical research. The projects mentioned earlier were abandoned. Why? In the first place, ethnographic research (which was the only kind I could do) was tremendously time consuming. You couldn't do it in a free half hour. Distances were greater in the Bay Area than in Buffalo. To make a Silicon Valley trip worth while required a complete free day—and I had few of them. Not only was I a father, but I was taking on a growing amount of administrative work. Family opportunities combined with committee work left me few large blocks of time.

Equally important, my methodology was out of date. This was illustrated by my manuscript rejection. The critical question was why construction apprenticeship was so low. According to classical economic theory, unions restrict apprenticeship in order to reduce labor supply and so raise wages. I argued that unions raised wages, not through their ability to restrict supply but through their ability to cut it off altogether by striking. More to the point, my case studies suggested that the key impediment to apprenticeship was employer unwillingness to train people who might find work elsewhere as soon as they finished their training. To the extent unions actually restricted apprenticeship it was to reduce the number of apprentices who couldn't find jobs.

My evidence consisted of lengthy interviews in two communities, extensive union records as to employment and apprenticeship numbers, and attendance at joint apprenticeship committee meetings in which the admission decisions were made. My critics said that their regressions, based on macro-nationwide data proved it couldn't work the way I said it did. My findings were based on only two cities and a small number of unions. My findings were "conjectural"; theirs were based on numbers and so had to be right.

OB IN THE 1970s

In the mid-1970s the 1960s paradigm began breaking down. The 1960s "one best way" was particularly vulnerable. McClelland postulated differences in need structures that might affect what people wanted from their jobs. Blauner, Turner and Lawrence, and Hulin and Blood found deviant work communities in which job satisfaction and job challenge were not positively correlated. Fiedler and the Ohio State studies suggested that there was no one best way to supervise. In the macro area it became quickly clear that there was no one best organization structure; this depended on the nature of the task and the environment.

As computer costs dropped, research designs became more elaborate and more variables were considered. Some concepts, such as Maslow's hierarchy proved impossible to test rigorously. With regard to others, causal relationships seemed to become increasingly complex. The relationship between job characteristics and satisfaction, for example, was moderated by a wide variety of other factors. Many conscientious OB scholars lost the confidence to give the simple solutions many managements wanted. I stopped doing consulting myself.

By the mid-1970s OB was split. On the one hand were the "scientists," on the other the "humanists."[21] A new group of younger scholars was entering the field, many trained as psychologists. They wanted to make the field more rigorous. Their success was facilitated by competition from other business school groups which encouraged OB people to appear harder, both more hard-hearted and more quantitative and scientific. By contrast with Likert, who was interested only in variables he could improve, the new scholars studied an ever wider range of variables. They were concerned with what *is* rather than what's *best*. Indeed, productivity and satisfaction were less frequently the dependent variables.

In sharp contrast to the scientists were the humanists who carried the normative optimism of the early 1960s to the extreme. For them, there was a very simple one best way: it involved sensitivity training, encounter groups, OD and the like. Consistent with the counterculture values of the period it was "as if their purposes were to create a 'Love Generation" of managers, a hippie organization in which all relations are 'trusting,' 'authentic,' and 'open'; each employee 'can do his own thing' in his own unique way, hostility can be expressed openly, and everybody works for organizational objectives—all at the same time" ("Human Relations," 1968, p. 265). Hard research was not for them.

The differences were dramatically illustrated in a meeting which David Bradford, Hal Leavitt, Ray Miles and I organized in Berkeley around 1973 of a group that later became the Organizational Behavior Teaching Society. At one point we divided into subgroups to discuss what OB should teach. One group, with Bob Tannenbaum as its guru, sat on the floor. The other, which included Larry Cummings as spokesperson, sat around a table. The reports of the groups were predictable, but still should been preserved for history. (Where was I? I think as an organizer I shuttled between the groups. I liked the Tannenbaum group's colorfulness. I was repelled by its rhetoric.)

By the late 1970s the younger idealists came up for tenure. In school after school we saw the slaughter of innocents. The humanist movement survives in only a few schools today. It is no longer a part of OB's heartland.

MY ACTIVITIES: 1970-90

Administration and Professional Work

By 1970 my glory days as a field researcher were over. Much of my time was spent administrating. I was editor of *Industrial Relations*, Associate Director and for four years Director of the Institute of Industrial Relations, Associate Dean of the Business School, and for five years member and chairman of the City of Berkeley Personnel Board. In this latter role I was the butt of more than my share of Berkeley's ideological politics as we moved into an era of collective bargaining and equal employment.

The most interesting of my committee assignments was the campus Budget Committee, a vital part of Berkeley's faculty self-governance system which made near-final decisions as to faculty appointments, promotions, and pay hikes, subject only to top administration's rare veto. Tricky judgments here: how does one evaluate scholarship in departments as diverse as drama and chemistry? It required an omniscience I lacked, but the process was fascinating.

Over the years I have been reasonably active in my primary professional association, the Industrial Relations Research Association (IRRA). Recently I served on a special "Review Committee" charged to rethink its function and role. I argued (with only moderate success) that the IRRA was too narrowly focused on labor-management relations and that we should place greater emphasis on HRM and economics. Further, we should copy much of the Academy of Management's divisionalised, broadly participative format. Having been elected IRRA president for 1993, I may be able to implement some of these ideas. Wish me luck.

Travel

Once the kids were old enough to be left alone Helene and I started travelling—over 40 countries so far. Sometime I could claim these trips had some academic purpose, other times they were frankly tourism. We have explored much of Western Europe. However, Australia and the South Seas are our favorites. In 1979 I had a Fulbright to Australia, giving some 25 lectures at 18 institutions. In 1986 we returned, this time as Visiting Professor at the University of Sydney, helping revive a troubled department (in the process learning much about the difference between U.S. and Australian-British academic administration). I am leaving for Australia again, as this is written.

Teaching

While at Berkeley I have taught almost every OBIR course offered, from Human Resources Management through introductory OB courses to Collective Bargaining, including our first graduate macro-OB course, taught jointly with Chick Perrow. My favorite is the Ph.D. seminar on the history of OB (from which much of this paper is taken).

My Collective Bargaining class made considerable use of bargaining games. Drawing on this experience, in 1984, I introduced a MBA elective on Negotiations and Conflict Resolution with a colleague. As with similar courses elsewhere this course makes extensive use of simulations, starting with bargaining over a used car and proceeding through progressively complex negotiations to a final multi-party case involving developers, environmentalists, city officials, and a mediator.

As the School's only course which permits students to develop interpersonal skills, it is popular for the same reason that T-group courses were popular in the 1960s; but this time students are taught to be tough, rather than be nice. I have mixed feelings here. I am a terrible bargainer myself. While I spend a good deal of class time on conflict resolution and integrative, win-win negotiations, it's the distributive, win-lose elements which students take away. I don't like the values I teach. Nevertheless, I enjoy the course and it's nice to be a popular teacher (even if for the wrong reasons). My ambivalence reflects a tension throughout my career, beginning at MIT. It's a tension between idealism and cynicism, between the empowering values of Theory Y and the reality that in the real world it helps to have clout. It's a tension that I have only partly resolved through my belief that unions empower.

Writing

Since 1970 my writing has consisted of a combination of review articles, think pieces and criticism. Usually too I toss in some suggestions for future research. For the most part these have appeared as book chapters or in invited journal symposia. Thus I avoid the review process.

My subjects have been rather broad (have word processor, will write). They have included performance appraisal, organization development (one of my favorites), developments in human resources generally, concession bargaining, union government, comparative industrial relations, and construction labor relations. Industrial Relations, as an academic field, is a key interest to me and I have written a set of critical articles evaluating its development and suggesting links to psychology and conflict resolution.

Criticism the OB Paradigm. In 1963 I began a series of papers asking questions about the then-dominant OB paradigm. In them I argued generally that the paradigm overstressed individual desire for autonomy and meaningful work as well as the ability of organizations to provide such work. On the other hand, it underestimated individuals' ability to adjust to routine work through various forms of social activity, game-playing, and reverie. Hitting below the belt, I argued that the paradigm "bears all the earmarks of its academic origin. Professors place high value on autonomy, inner direction, and the quest for maximum self-development...for them, creative achievement is an end in itself and requires no further justification.... [They] see little incongruity in imposing [their values] on the less fortunate" ("Human Relations," 1968, pp. 47-48).

Chris Argyris generously agreed to comment on several of these papers. His criticisms were generally quite useful but at times quite sharp. We differed quite considerably. With regards to one paper, he said "I am impressed with how freely you are willing to cite your personal view as gospel. You may be pessimistic about using intergroup in difficult situations. However, we have experimented (in preliminary fashion) with three nations who intend to go to war and have had some effect." With regards to another, "I believe you are struggling hard to be fair. However, it reads as if you are suppressing your anger (until the end). Consequently, ambivalence, hostility, bending backwards, and so on. seem to predominate." Touché.

Blue-collar blues. In the early 1970s, with a sudden concern with "blue-collar blues" and a so-called revolt against work there was a revival of interest in job redesign, job enrichment, autonomous work groups and the like. When asked to write on these topics I had a Yogi Berra déjà vu feeling. We had explored these issues thoroughly in the 1940s and they were more than adequately covered in our text and my previous writings. But for the benefit of those who hadn't read these (and for the glory of getting my name in print) I repeated them, but with new evidence. None of the standard data as to attitudes, turnover, or productivity indicated any blue-collar revolt against work, once business cycles and the composition of the workforce were taken into account. True, there had been much industrial unrest in Europe during the late 1960s, but in the United States the campus turmoil never spread to factories. Once again, professors overgeneralized from their narrow worlds.

Wasn't my somewhat cynical view toward the 1960s paradigm inconsistent with my earlier idealism? Yes and no. It was the naive, sweeping claims made by some of the protagonists which turned me off. Mine was a contingency approach. Theory Y would work in some situations, Theory X (tempered with paternalism) in others, and in almost all situations worker-management relations were determined through implicit bargaining. As I saw it, Barnard's zone of acceptance was typically quite large. Workers were neither frustrated by their jobs nor were they enthusiastic about them. A job was a job and they accepted it. Ideally all workers should enthusiastically accept management's objectives, but it was unrealistic to expect such enthusiasm to become universal.

Participation. I am not completely cynical. Workers' participation in management (WPM) has been a continuing interest. Mine is (I hope) a balanced, contingency view. Under the proper, perhaps fairly limited circumstances, WPM can improve labor-management relations and product quality and even job satisfaction and productivity. Among the main conditions are the presence of a strong union. Over the years I have looked at a variety of WPM forms, from Israeli kibbutzim to U.S. quality circles and have attempted to integrate the research, conducted in many countries and using many methods, as to the conditions under which WPM will work (and in what ways) and as to its impact on relevant actors, from rank and file workers to boards of directors and national unions. (What will I ever do with my seven file drawers of WPM notes?)

Unions again. Recently I returned to my first love, the internal life of unions. Having just edited a book, *The State of the Unions* (1991) to which I contributed chapters on union democracy and participation, my next project is to apply macro-OB concepts to union structure, but to do so prescriptively so as to be of some use to the union movement. I am also contemplating a new field study of union leadership. Back to where I started!

OB IN THE 80s AND BEYOND

By the 1980s, with humanists purged and the contingency approach wrecking the simplicities of the 1960s, OB entered a distinctly new phase—or so it seemed from Berkeley. Most of what I taught before was irrelevant. There were totally new approaches. From a micro-OB approach the world was socially constructed. Many questions were almost unresearchable since the answers depend on the contexts in which the questions are asked. Job attitudes are the result of predisposition from childhood. Leadership is almost a figment of the imagination.

The macro-level has changed even faster. In the 1950s the main macro issues were staff-line relations, decentralization, and departmentation. In the 1960s and early 1970s Perrow, Lawrence and Lorsch, Joan Woodward, and Jim Thompson brought in the impact of technology and the environment. Miles and Al Chandler tied in strategy and structure. Today the stress is on the relationship between organizations and their environment, with resource dependency, organizational ecology, and institutionalism being the rage. At Berkeley a new field of strategy is being developed, under the leadership of Glenn Carroll and Oliver Williamson. This merges bits of OB, sociology, and transactional economics.

Unfortunately little of this is teachable to introductory students looking for simple answers. Neither is it of direct help to management. Back in the 1940s the field was relevant in part because it didn't know how to be rigorous. Today rigor has largely replaced relevance—at least immediate relevance. In the long run, however, the new research may make OB more relevant than it has ever been, just as cell biology is more relevant to the physician today than are medicine dances, even though the latter were designed for immediate application.

We have gone a long way since Hawthorne. Much of the recent seminal work in both micro- and macro-OB was done by my present and former Berkeley OB colleagues, Glenn Carroll, John Freeman, Jim Lincoln, Ray Miles, Charles O'Reilly, Karlene Roberts, Trond Peterson, Jeff Pfeffer, and

Barry Staw. I can truly say that I was present, not just at OB's beginning but also at its rebirth.

PUBLICATIONS

1952

Direct observation as a source of quasi-sociometric information. *Sociometry* (February).

With L.R. Sayles. The unpaid local leader. *Harvard Business Review, 30*(3), 91-104.

With L.R. Sayles. Conflicts within the local union. *Harvard Business Review, 30*(6), 84-92.

With L.R. Sayles. Patterns of participation in the local union. *Industrial and Labor Relations Review, 6*(1), 31-43.

With L.R. Sayles. Some problems of communication within the local union. *Proceedings of the Industrial Relations Research Association, 5*, 143-150.

With L.R. Sayles. *The Local Union.* New York: Harpers.

1953

With L.R. Sayles. The local union meeting. *Industrial and Labor Relations Review, 6*, 206-219.

With L.R. Sayles. Occupation and selection of local union officers. *The American Journal of Sociology, 58*, 585-591.

With L.R. Sayles. What the worker really thinks of his union. *Harvard Business Review, 31*(3), 94-102.

With D. Wilner. Government regulation of local union democracy. *Labor Law Journal, 4*, 519-537.

Factors in the unionization of a utility company. *Human Organization, 12*(2), 17-25.

Three short cases. In G. Shultz & J.R. Coleman (Eds.), *Labor problems: Cases and readings* (pp. 155-160). New York: McGraw-Hill.

With L.R. Sayles & R.L. Sayles. Leadership roles in local unions. *Sociology and Social Research* (November).

1954

White collar unions are different! *Harvard Business Review, 32*(5), 73-82.

1955

Shop society and the union: A comment. *Industrial and Labor Relations Review, 8*, 275-277.

The set-up man: A case study of organizational change. *Human Organization, 13*(2), 17-25.
With J. Gullahorn. The field worker in union research. *Human Organization, 33*(3), 28-32.
With A. Bavelas. The Hovey and Beard Company. In W.F. Whyte (Ed.), *Money and motivation.* New York: Harpers.
Streamlining the union meeting (Bulletin). Ithaca, NY: New York State School of Industrial and Labor Relations.

1956

Control by the membership in building trades local unions. *American Journal of Sociology, 61*(6), 523-535.

1957

The changing role of the working supervisor. *Journal of Business* (July).
With L.R. Sayles. The Scanlon plan: Some organizational problems. *Human Organization, 16*, 15-23.
Business agents in the building trades. *Industrial and Labor Relations Review, 10*, 237-251.

1958

Unions in the building trades. Buffalo, NY: University of Buffalo Press.

1960

With L.R. Sayles. *Personnel: The human problems of management.* Englewood Cliffs, NJ: Prentice-Hall.
With D. Kochery. The non-profit hospital and the union. *Buffalo Law Review* (Winter).

1962

The shifting power balance in the plant. *Industrial Relations, 1*(3), 65-96.
Tactics of lateral relationship: The purchasing agent. *Administrative Science Quarterly, 7*, 161-186.

1963

Professionalism and occupational associations. *Industrial Relations, 2*, 7-32.
Notes on power equalization. In H. Leavitt (Ed.), *The Social Science of Organization* (pp. 41-84). Englewood Cliffs, NJ: Prentice-Hall.
Union bargaining strength: Goliath or paper tiger. *Annals* (American Academy of Political and Social Science), *250.*

Labor and the academicians. *Proceedings of the Industrial Relations Research Association* (pp. 234-244).

1964

Work flow frictions, interfunctional rivalries, and professionalism. *Human Organization, 23*, 137-149.

Organization man: Prospect for the future. *California Management Review, 6* (3), 5-17.

Professional or employee oriented? Dilemma for engineering unions. *Industrial and Labor Relations Review, 17*, 519-533.

1965

Apprenticeship: An evaluation of the need. In A.M. Ross (Ed.), *Employment policy and the labor market* (pp. 299-332). Berkeley: University of California Press.

With S. Ingerman. Apprenticeship, discrimination, and the law. *Hastings Law Review, 16*, 285-331.

Job training and employment. In *Background papers for the Governor's Conference on Employment*. Ithaca, NY: Institute of Industrial Relations.

AAUP as a professional occupation association. *Industrial Relations, 5*, 128-140.

1966

With L.R. Sayles. *Human behavior in organizations*. Englewood Cliffs, NJ: Prentice-Hall.

Participative management: A critique. *Industrial and Labor Relations Research* (November).

Discussion: Current status of management research. *Proceedings of the Industrial Relations Research Association 18*, 83-86.

1967

With S. Ingerman. Preparing underprivileged negro youths for jobs. *Poverty and Human Resource Abstracts* (July).

How management views its race relations responsibilities. In A. Ross and H. Hill (Eds.), *Negroes and jobs*. New York: Harcourt Brace.

1968

Apprenticeship-related instruction: Some basic issues. *Journal of Human Resources, 3*, 213-236.

Human relations—1968 style. *Industrial Relations, 7*, 262-276.

1970

With E. Rosenstein. Workers participation: A critical view. *Industrial Relations, 9*, 197-214.

Establishing representation rights: The Berkeley experience. *California Public Employee Relations, 5*, 13-27.

Organizational behavior and personnel relations. In *A review of industrial relations research* (pp. 147-206). Madison, WI: Industrial Relations Research Association.

Manufacturing organization for the future. In I. Vernon, (ed.), *Organization for Manufacturing*. Dearborn, MI: Society for Manufacturing Engineers.

With D. Bowen & P. Feuille. The California experience. In R.J. Connery & W. Farr (eds.), *Unionization of municipal employees, Proceedings of the Academy of Political Science, 30*(2), 107-123.

Minorities and apprenticeship. In N. Chamberlain (Ed.), *Business and the Cities*. New York: Basic Books.

1971

Union policies toward admission of apprentices. In S. Jacks (Ed.), *Issues in labor policy: Papers in honor of Douglas Vincent Brown* (pp. 71-108). Cambridge, MA: MIT Press.

1972

Management by objectives: A critical view. *Training and Development Journal, 26*(4), 10-15.

Discussion: Organizational behavior and personnel management. *Proceedings of the Industrial Relations Research Association, 24*, 128-129.

With H. Foster. Labor problems in construction: A review. *Industrial Relations, 11*, 289-313.

1973

Organizational development: Credits and debits. *Organizational Dynamics, 1*(3), 2-19.

Minority membership in apprenticeship programs in the building trades, A comment. *Industrial and Labor Relations Review, 27*, 93-99.

1974

Edited with R. Miles, C. Snow, & A. Tannenbaum. *Organizational behavior: Research and issues*. Madison, WI: Industrial Relations Research Association.

Adolescence in organizational growth. *Organizational Dynamics, 2*(4), 3-17.

Workers: Attitudes and adjustments. In J. Rosow, (Ed.), *The Worker and the Job* (pp. 73-98). Englewood Cliffs, NJ: Prentice Hall.

Worker dissatisfaction: A look at the causes. *Monthly Labor Review, 97*(2), 57-58.

With R. Flanagan & L. Ulman. Worker discontent and work place behavior. *Industrial Relations, 13*(2), 101-123.

Is there a blue-collar revolt against work? In J. O'Toole, (Ed.), *Work and the Quality of Life: Resource Papers for Work in America.* Cambridge, MA: MIT Press.

Alternative approaches to improving apprenticeship effectiveness. In *Apprenticeship Training in the U.S.* (Manpower Research Monograph No. 37). Washington, DC: U.S. Department of Labor.

Comment on 'job enrichment: Long on theory, short on practice'. *Organizational Dynamics, 2*(3), 43-45.

Job satisfaction, motivation and job redesign. In G. Strauss, R. Miles, A. Tannenbaum, & C. Snow (Eds.), *Organizational behavior: Research and issues* (pp. 19-49). Madison, WI: Industrial Relations Research Association.

1975

Union financial data—Symposium introduction. *Industrial Relations, 14*, 131-133.

With D. Bradford. O.B. of the future. *Teaching of Organizational Behavior, 1*(4), 3-9.

1976

The study of conflict: Hope for a new synthesis between industrial relations and organizational behavior. *Proceedings of the Industrial Relations Research Association.*

Organization development. In R. Dubin (Ed.), *Handbook of Work, Organization and Society* (pp. 617-685). Chicago: Rand McNally.

1977

With L.R. Sayles. *Managing human resource*. Englewood Cliffs, NJ: Prentice-Hall.

Managerial practices. In J.R. Hackman & J.L. Suttle (Eds.), *Improving life at work: Behavioral science approaches to organizational change* (pp. 297-363). Santa Monica, CA: Goodyear.

Union government in the U.S.: Research past and future. *Industrial Relations, 16*, 215-242.

With M. Warner. Research on union government: Symposium introduction. *Industrial Relations, 16*, 115-126.

Sex and minority leadership roles in an experiental learning class. *Teaching of Organizational Behavior, 2*(4), 330-333.

1978

Comment: Quality of working life. *American Economic Review, 68*.

Directions in industrial relations research. In *Proceedings of the Spring Meeting of the Industrial Relations Research Association* (pp. 531-536).

With P. Feuille. Industrial relations research: A critical appraisal. *Industrial Relations, 17*(3), 259-277.

1979

Can social psychology contribute to industrial relations? In G. Stephenson and C. Brotherton (Eds.), *Industrial relations: A social psychological approach*. Chichester: Wiley.

Workers participation: Symposium introduction. *Industrial Relations, 18*, 247-261.

1980

The quality of worklife and participation as bargaining issues. In H. Juris and M. Roomkin (Eds.), *The shrinking perimeter: Unionism and labor relations in the manufacturing sector* (pp. 121-150). Lexington, TX: Lexington Books.

The individual and the world of work. In *Education and the world of work* (pp. 51-59). Carlton, Victoria: Australian College of Education.

With J.W. Driscoll. Collective bargaining games. *Exchange, 5*(2), 12-20.

1981

With P. Feuille. Industrial relations research in the United States. In P. Doeringer (Ed.), *Industrial Relations in International Perspective* (pp. 76-144). London: Macmillan.

1982

Workers participation in management: An international perspective. In B.M. Staw & L.L. Cummings (Eds.), *Research in organizational Behavior* (Vol. 4, pp. 173-265). Greenwich, CT: JAI Press.

Bridging the gap between industrial relations and conflict management. In G. Bowers & R. Peterson (Eds.), *Industrial Relations and Conflict Management* (pp. 1-32). Boston, MA: Kluwer-Nijhoff.

Personnel management: Prospect for the eighties. In K.M. Rowland & G.R. Ferris (Eds.), *Personnel Management* (pp. 502-544). Boston, MA: Allyn and Bacon.

1983

In honor of Lloyd Ulman: Introduction. *Industrial Relations, 22*, 135-140.

1984

Industrial relations: Time of change. *Industrial Relations, 23,*, 1-15.

1985

Preface. In P. Gilmour & R. Lansbury. *Marginal managers* (pp. xiii-xiv). Santa Lucia: University of Queensland Press.

1986

Workers participation in management in the United States. In E. David and R. Lansbury (Eds.), *Democracy and control in the workplace*. Sydney: Longman-Chesire.

The American union decline: Why did it happen? *Hummer, 13*, 3-9.

1987

Industrial relations: What should our basic course cover? *The Organizational Behavior Teaching Review, 9*(4), 115-119.

The future of human resources management. In D.J.B. Mitchell (Ed.), *The future of industrial relations* (pp. 91-118). Los Angeles: Institute of Industrial Relations, University of California, Los Angeles.

1988

Union member attitude surveys: Content and methodological issues. *Proceedings of the Industrial Relations Research Association 40*, 159-166.

With D. Lewin. Behavioral research in industrial relations. *Industrial Relations, 27*, 1-6.

Australian industrial relations: Through U.S. eyes. *Industrial Relations, 27*, 131-148.

1989

Workers' participation and U.S. collective bargaining. In C. Lammers & G. Szell (Eds.), *International handbook of participation in organizations* (pp. 227-247). Oxford: Oxford University Press.

Industrial relations as an academic field: What's wrong with it? In J. Barbash & K. Barbash (Eds.), *Theories and Concepts in Comparative Industrial Relations* (pp. 241-260). Columbia, SC: University of South Carolina Press.

With D. Levine. Employee participation and involvement. In *Background papers. Investing in people: A strategy to address America's workforce crisis* (Vol. 2, pp. 1893-1948). Washington, DC: Commission on Workforce Quality and Labor Management Efficiency.

1990

Toward the study of human resources policy. In J. Chelius & J. Dworkin (Eds.), *Reflections on the Transformation of Industrial Relations*. Metuchen, NJ: Rutgers University Press.

Commentary: The organizing process: Contemporary challenges and union responses. *Proceedings of the Industrial Relations Research Association, 42*, 73-95.

Commentary: Understanding organizational behavior: The state of social science research. *Proceedings of the Industrial Relations Research Association, 42*, 294-296.

Participatory and gain-sharing systems: History and hope. In M. Roomkin (Ed.), *Profit and Gain Sharing* (pp. 1-45). Metuchen, NJ: Rutgers University Press.

1991

Edited with D. Gallagher & J. Fiorito. *The State of the Unions*. Madison, WI: Industrial Relations Research Association.

With D. Gallagher. Union member attitudes and participation. In G. Strauss, D. Gallagher, & J. Fiorito (Eds.), *The state of the unions* (pp. 139-174). Madison, WI: Industrial Relations Research Association.

Union democracy. In. G. Strauss, D. Gallagher, & J. Fiorito (Eds.), *The state of the unions* (pp. 201-236). Madison, WI: Industrial Relations Research Association.

Union structure: Research agenda for the 1990s. *Proceedings of the Industrial Relations Research Association, 43.*

Creeping toward a field of comparative industrial relations. In H. Katz (Ed.), *The future of industrial relations.* Ithaca, NY: Cornell University Press.

Collective bargaining and participation. In G. Szell (Ed.), *Concise encyclopedia of participation and co-management.* Berlin: De Gruyter.

The United States. In G. Szell (Ed.), *Concise encyclopedia of participation and co-management.* Berlin: De Gruyter.

1992

Workers' participation in management. In J. Hartley and G. Stephenson (Eds.), *Employment relations: The psychology of influence and control at work.* Oxford Basil Blackwell.

Commentary: Human resources management is for unions too. *Proceedings of the Industrial Relations Research Association, 44*, 44-442.

Human resources management in the United States. In B. Tower (Ed.), *Handbook of human resources management* (pp. 27-48). Oxford: Basil Blackwell.

NOTES

My thanks for comments to Ralph Bergmann, Charles Myers, and Leonard Sayles, all of whom contributed to my MIT experience—and to Eric Auchard who provided editorial assistance. My special thanks to Art Bedeian for his patience, good judgment, and sharp green pencil.

1. See p. 21 in F. Roethlisberger. (1977). *The Elusive Phenomena: An Autobiographical Account of My Work in Organizational Behavior at the Harvard Business School.* Boston, MA: Graduate School of Business Administration, Harvard University.
2. Ibid.
3. See S. Kakar. (1970). *Fredrick W. Taylor: A Study of Personality and Innovation.* Cambridge: MIT Press.
4. F. Roethlisberger & W. Dickson. (1939). *Management and the Worker.* Cambridge, MA: Harvard University Press.
5. R. Lynd & H. Lynd. (1929). *Middletown: A Study of Contemporary Culture.* New York: Harcourt, Brace; W.L. Warner & P.S. Lunt. (1941). *The Social Life of a Modern Community.* New Haven, CT: Yale University Press.
6. For example, S. Wyatt & J.N. Langdon. (1937). *Fatigue and Boredom in Industrial Repetitive Work.* Industrial Health Research Board Report 77. London: HMSO.
7. P. Smith. (1953, April). "The Curve of Output as a Criterion of Boredom." *Journal of Applied Psychology, 37*, 69-74.
8. J. Hackman & E.E. Lawler. Employee reactions to job characteristics. *Journal of Applied Psychology Monograph, 55*, 259-286.
9. K. Back (1973). *Beyond Words: The Story of Sensitivity Training and the Encounter Movement.* Baltimore, MD: Penguin; "Organization Development" (1976).
10. K. Lewin. (1948). "The Solution of a Chronic Conflict in Industry." In G. Lewin (Ed.), *Resolving social conflict* (pp. 125-141). New York: Harper.

11. Roethlisberger, *The Elusive Phenomena.*

12. J. Dollard & W. Doob. (1947). *Frustration and Aggression.* New Haven, CT: Yale University Press.

13. P. 357 in W.F. Whyte. *Street Corner Society* (rev. ed.). Chicago: University of Chicago Press.

14. B. Gardner. *Human Relations in Industry.* Chicago: Irwin.

15. W.F. Whyte. (Ed.). (1955). *Money and Motivation.* New York: Harper.

16. S.D. Hoslett. (Ed.). (1948). *Human Factors in Management.* New York: Harper; Gardner, *Human Relations in Industry*; H. Leavitt. (1958). *Managerial Psychology.* Chicago: University of Chicago Press.

17. C. Kerr & L. Fisher. (1957). "Plant Sociology: The Elite and the Aborogines." In M. Komarovski & P. Lazerfeld (Eds.), *Common Frontiers in the Social Sciences* (pp. 281-306). Glencoe, IL: Free Press.

18. *Harvard Business Review, 35*(2) (Marchg 1957), 15-21.

19. See R. Miles. 1975. *Theories of Management.* New York: McGraw-Hill.

20. See p. 29 in R. Likert. (1967). *The Human Organization.* New York: McGraw-Hill.

21. K. Back (1973). *Beyond Words: The Story of Sensitivity Training and the Encounter Movement.* Baltimore, MD: Penguin.

Eric Trist

Guilty of Enthusiasm

ERIC L. TRIST

Based on interviews between Eric L. Trist and Richard C.S. Trahair in May and December, 1989. Trahair, who teaches and does biographical research at the School of Social Sciences, La Trobe University, Melbourne, Australia, edited the interviews for this chapter.

FAMILY FORTUNES, EARLY LIFE AND EDUCATION

My father was Frederick James Lansdown Trist and my mother was Alexina Middleton. Father's family was Cornish and he was a sea captain. His family did a mix of farming and fishing and—as most families did in those parts—smuggling. In the nineteenth-century they had three clippers in the China tea trade and, coming back from China, they would take their clippers over to the Brittany coast, and smuggle French lace to sell in Plymouth. Great-aunt Rachel's crinoline provided a safe hiding place! The British navy suspected them, and forbade the family to take their ships anywhere south of a certain point in the English Channel. But my great-uncle, Phil, a very rambunctious character, said, "To hell with that!" When he took the ships south toward Brittany the British Navy went after him, seized the ships and broke them up in Devonport shipyard. Phil then went to the gold rush in Western Australia, into coastal trade, and made a fortune. He came back to England looking for my grandfather, whom he didn't find. Instead, he found another branch of the family, and they got his money. That was the end of any family fortunes on my father's side.

My mother's side of the family is highland Scot—so I'm Celt, again—and her people had a small estate in Kincardinshire. During the early period of the Industrial Revolution there was a reconciliation between her family and their neighbors who had supported opposite sides in the 1745 rebellion. My great-grandfather stood bond for his neighbor in some enterprise which went bankrupt. So again the whole family was in ruins. He started building up again, and became manager of a bleach field in Brechin north of Dundee.

My mother, who was about three years younger than my father, had been a governess in a military family in Shoeburyness where my father was stationed—that's how they met. Both parents were the youngest in large Victorian families. They were married in the 1890s, and had given up the idea of having a child by the time I came along in September 1909 when they were in their forties. They had, unofficially, adopted a cousin of mine on my father's side. Her father had been drowned at sea in the tropics. She was in her teens when I was born. My cousins were all years and years older than me.

I went to the local elementary School, St Martin's, in Dover where we lived. World War I was a very dramatic experience, very vivid to me in 1916. Bombardment and air raids all the time.

Education was the central thing in our Scottish tradition. My father was as inclined towards education as my mother, but he wasn't as emphatic. He certainly didn't want me to follow his example and go to sea, which I might otherwise have done.

I attended the local secondary school because there was not enough money to send me away to boarding school. I tended toward the arts side rather than to science, and took English, French, history and Latin, keeping geography as my science option in the sixth form. English and French literature were my favorites. My French master, Thomas Watt, was absolutely magnificent, a great personal friend, and utterly exceptional in all respects. He was my main influence at school. The other very influential master, W.E. Pearce, taught physics, and wrote a textbook, *School Physics*, which became nationally adopted.

Two special friends at school were Henry Garland, who was a year ahead of me and went to Emmanuel College, Cambridge, became a Fellow and eventually the Professor of German at the University of Exeter; the other was my contemporary, Clifford Jarrett, the most brilliant scholar I've ever known. He came top in his year in the examination for entry into Division I of the British Civil Service. He became a Permanent Under-Secretary and was awarded a knighthood.

My secondary school wasn't one where people went on to university, so my generation was the first to go to Oxford or Cambridge. I had no notion of going to a university. It never entered anybody's head at school except this French master who selected Clifford Jarrett and myself, and told the headmaster he must enter us for State Scholarships. I didn't understand what that meant. The French master explained it to me, and told us a bit what it would be like to go to university. He said that you would have a future, especially if you went to Oxford or Cambridge.

There was nothing immediately around in Dover that I wanted to do. I liked school up to the last year or two, but then I found it very provincial. I had got beyond the school, and was ready to leave in May 1927, but I had to stay on for a year to be sure of getting a scholarship.

LIFE AT UNIVERSITY

I went to Cambridge—Pembroke College—in the fall of 1928. Pembroke didn't accept me very well because I was from a Grammar School rather than a Public School, although they did take a number of people, like me, from Grammar Schools, as scholars. I didn't have a preexisting circle of friends among the college students. I didn't have the culture of people who were born well, had gone to good schools and were well off.

There was the games business, but to play you had to have a reputation of having been in a first eleven, say at cricket, somewhere that was recognized. And, of course, I didn't. Though to play for the university was beyond my aspiration, I should have like to play for the first or second team of my college, but the standards were beyond my reach. The fifth team was my level and not much fun. So I had to give up the passion for games that I once had at school. Also, I wasn't good enough to get anywhere scholastically without putting in a tremendous amount of effort and time. I had to get First Class Honours, and I had to work very hard to do that and so I dropped out of games at Cambridge. Our College was a 'hearty' college, but I wasn't one of the 'hearties.'

I had a certain interest in the stage and dramatic work. I let all that go, too, because I wasn't in the same league as others such as Michael Redgrave and Alistair Cooke. There was a tremendous amount of conversation and interaction in the societies that were newly established, such as the film society. One was over-busy, going to things, and it was often hard finding private time to work. I was not religious. I was a member of the university Labour Club, and used to go there regularly. I had several friends there, and I was known, but not well known.

I didn't have much of a social life, but managed with a small coterie of friends, including some people in other colleges. One of my best friends, Grey Walter, was at Kings College. He became very famous for work on the human brain. He was one of the people I greatly admired, and who helped me change from literature to science. Also, while I was still doing English, I was very influenced by I.A. Richards, the most famous English don at that time, who linked philosophy, literature and linguistics. With F.R. Leavis, Richards had a tremendous influence on the study of English at Cambridge, which in those days was world famous.

From September 1928 to May 1931 I read English literature. It was very exciting because of the reading, the tutors and the subject itself, which was very modern. I wrote an essay every week, but I didn't publish anything, or speak at any of the undergraduate societies because I wasn't confident enough. I went regularly to hear debates at the Cambridge Union, but I was very shy, and only listened.

After I graduated—First Class Honours in both parts of the English Tripos—I wasn't sure what I wanted to do. I thought of doing either philosophy or psychology. Through Richards I got interested in psychology, especially Gestalt psychology and psycho-analysis. I remember going to see Broad, the philosopher in Trinity, and him asking, "Why do you want to do philosophy?" I replied, "I was wondering between philosophy and psychology." And he suggested, "You read psychology. Go and see Professor Bartlett." I went, and Bartlett accepted me to read psychology which was then a Part II in the Moral Sciences Tripos.

Of course, at Oxford and Cambridge one knew perfectly well that some of the best of one's generation were there, and that quite a number were going to become famous, so one was always comparing oneself with these others. I did as well academically as anybody could, but I never thought of myself as very outstanding.

The Psychology Tripos comprised a small group where everybody knew everybody else. I was more interested in psycho-analysis than experimental stuff, but psycho-analysis was not very popular in Cambridge. You had lectures, and you read, but it was up to the scholar to involve himself. For the two years I had P.E. Vernon as my tutor. He was excellent. He didn't tell me what to do or anything and we were not really close, though he did help me with my career afterward. I read pretty broadly in experimental psychology, social psychology, and Gestalt psychology.

I was very much influenced by Kurt Lewin in those days, and there was an incident which was very negative to my future in the Cambridge psychology laboratory. I came in one afternoon, very excited, and Professor Frederick Bartlett asked, "Well, what's the matter with you?" I answered, "I've just read Lewin's article on the Galilean and Aristotelian methods." I was feeling very excited. This went against me—young Trist had shown himself **guilty of enthusiasm**, of being uncritically over-impressed, not detached enough, too involved.

I once met Kurt Lewin in Cambridge. When he left Germany, he went to Israel, and then he was invited to the United States. On his way he visited Cambridge. It was thought that he might stay for a while but that didn't happen. The last day he was there was one of the high points of my life. I was invited to tea with Bartlett and other professors. When the tea party ended Bartlett said, "Trist, you have an hour to show Professor Lewin around Cambridge before his train." I asked him, "What is it you most want to see?" He replied, "I want to see the statue of Isaac Newton." So I took him to Trinity and there was Newton's statue. Kurt stood gazing at Newton and started to gesticulate, just like the fan-tracery in the roof. This was the kind of diagram that he was doing for the book on topological psychology, which he was then writing. So, I got an advance view of what it was going to be about in front of the statue of Isaac Newton. Then, we had to rush to the train. We almost missed it because he had been so enthralled with Isaac Newton. It had started to move when we got into the station and I just managed to open the carriage door and push him in. I always treasure that memory of Lewin being thrust, by me, into a railway carriage.

I was very impressed with Bartlett as a thinker and as a teacher. His book on remembering came out while I was there, and he was elected to the Royal Society. The first psychologist ever to be so. He was, in hindsight, a great man of profound originality, but he was also an extremely pragmatic individual, and he went with the times.

The only funds for psychology that you could get at Cambridge in those days were for physiological psychology. Because I showed all the signs of becoming a social psychologist I was out.

I graduated in Psychology in May 1933. I got not only First Class Honours, but also a Distinction Star—the first time it had been awarded since World War I.

The Fellowships were highly competitive, and I think the awards themselves were given whimsically. I don't know whether they were just, although a lot of the outstanding people got them. No exam. You had a big panel interview and your referees were very important. Bartlett supported me and so did I.A. Richards. Those two together got me through.

My interview was hilarious. Sir James Irvine, the Principal of St. Andrews, was chairman that year. During my interview one of the main members of the committee, Lord Somebody-or-other, went to sleep. He woke and asked me a question I had already answered, and I wasn't quite sure how I should play it. Sir James interrupted, "The candidate answered that question while you were asleep." The whole place went up in mirth, including me. I always thought that was the reason why I got a Commonwealth Fund Fellowship. My subject wasn't in line; I was the first psychologist to get one; and what I planned to do at Yale—to amalgamate anthropology and social psychology—wasn't really of interest to any of the people on the committee.

TO AMERICA, 1933-1935

The scholarship paid my return fare, university expenses and a personal income of $150 a month, which in those days was quite handsome. I sailed in September

1933 with the other Commonwealth fellows, and found I was paid great attention to by the fund director, Edwin Bliss, because of my Distinction Star. Apparently he thought that they had got hold of someone special. The M.S. Britannic left from Liverpool, went to Cork, Galway Bay, Boston and then down to New York in ten days. Most of the passengers were very wealthy Americans so I didn't move outside the company of the Commonwealth Fellows.

At Yale I greatly admired Sapir, whom I went to study with. He was the biggest influence on my intellectual life, ever. I attended a lot of classes in psychology, went to Clark Hull's seminar as well as Sapir's. But I didn't get on very well because I didn't have any clear direction or specialization, but I knew I had to do something in social psychology. I became close friends with the then Professor of Social Psychology at Yale, Spike Robinson. But he was killed in a car accident. It was terrible.

Sapir's concept of culture was important to me. It came from the internal world of the individual, and was shared with others, and was not a fixed thing which you passively absorbed. You actively, selectively got it, so no two people got it quite the same. I was very influenced by that, and by the experience of a field trip to one of Sapir's post-doctoral people, Walter Dyke, and his wife on a Navaho reservation. They were taking down autobiographies of Navaho Indians, translating them and comparing one man's account of his culture with another's. That was what was being done at that time in Sapir's anthropology. He used to say that any language will do its stuff but you can't escape from the instrument. I was deeply bitten into by this set of beliefs and the Whorff-Sapir hypotheses.

At Clark Hull's seminar at Yale, which was where I had my initiation into behaviorism, there was an experimental situation set up such that the subject (presumed to be a child) would see a piece of chocolate in the middle of the table but would only be able to reach it by turning right around and moving in the opposite direction before finding a way to secure it. Various big noises came down to the seminar but no one—not even Lewin—could work out how to get the chocolate.

I had some time with Lewin in the United States, and I was thoroughly hooked. He was at Cornell, and then later at Iowa at the Child Development Center where the big experiments were done with Lippitt and White—the democratic climate experiments.

At Cambridge, in England, I.A. Richards had said to me that there was a very bright behaviorist at Harvard, Fred Skinner, who had written on Gertrude Stein, an interesting chap, a very nice man, and I should see him. So I went up to Boston, and Skinner took me to see his laboratory. There was more apparatus and more money in Fred Skinner's laboratory than in the whole of psychology in England. It was simply breathtaking. It took me a long time to realize what he was doing. He kept talking about a "lever" and I didn't know what a "lever" was. Eventually I managed to deduce that a "lever" was a "leever," as we pronounce it! He took me to lunch with the girl to whom he was then engaged. She was a very beautiful girl. Later we went back to his lab and he said his experiments were the most interesting thing in his life. And I said, "My God, if I were you there would be something else that would be more interesting in my life!" I was never able to embrace Skinner's views, except that I was influenced by a paper that he wrote—was it 1932?—called "The General Character of the Stimulus and the Response." It was very good and I used to teach that four years later at St. Andrews in Scotland.

I rejected the Hull seminars, but I was very interested in attending them. You had to do the politics of your ticket. The idea of graduate studies, as such, was not known in Britain, but in America it was pretty well established. And I wasn't organized for it. To get a Ph.D. I would have had to stay three years and my scholarship was for only two. Sapir nominated me because I did want to stay a third year, but I wasn't accepted.

When I was in America, like all Commonwealth Fellows, I travelled around the United States and wrote a report. In the summer of 1934, in my Model A Ford, I went south along the east coast, then west to Denver and the Rockies, from Denver down to New Mexico to Santa Fe, and then across the desert to Los Angeles. Then I went up from Los Angeles to Berkeley where I stayed for a while, and then up the north west coast and back across the mountains through Montana, to Chicago and back to New Haven.

I began to get interested in the world and politics and the Depression. It was a tremendous shock coming back from New York one night when I picked up a guy who was starving. I took him into a diner for a meal. I had never seen anything like that. This made the Depression real for me. And when I was travelling in the south that summer, there was a textile workers' strike, and several people were killed. That was a terrible thing which upset me very much. And when I was in Arizona there was big trouble in a company said to be owned by the Rockefellers. One of the organizers, a communist, was chased out of the place, and left to die in the scrub on the Navaho reservation. I was there when he was picked up. These sort of things disturbed me. I had never experienced any violence, or seen how bad it could get. Previously I had no concept of the realities of politics. Later in San Francisco I walked in a big parade in memory of the dead from certain incidents of several years before. It was a very, very moving experience.

Back in New Haven, I joined The Hunger and Strike Committee which supported strikes in Connecticut. I used to go out onto the picket line, and once I went out in the drenching rain in Hartford when there was a big arms strike. One morning we were all hosed down. The workers were very badly treated. That was the first time I was politically active, and the first time that I read any Marx, which both enlightened and confused me. I was confused by what seemed to be a metaphysic, and therefore nothing I could subscribe to. Wittgenstein had convinced us that metaphysics was 'nonsense.' On the other hand, in the Depression, Marx made every sense to me as an analyst of society.

EARLY RESEARCH IN SOCIAL PSYCHOLOGY

When I returned to England in 1935 I had a hell of a time. Just before I came back Sir Frederick Bartlett had sent one of his people to tell me that there was no job for me in psychology in Britain, not even a corner in Cambridge—nowhere! I knew Bartlett had control of all the appointments in psychology in England. Nevertheless, I went up to Cambridge to find out about jobs and I met Sir Frederick in the corridor to the psychology lab. He didn't recognize me though I had been his student for two years. Then he asked, "Look, I know you, don't I?" I replied, "Yes, I was here for two years." And then he said, "Oh, I remember now." That was how vanished I had been. That evening I was allowed to go to High Table in my College, but the Fellows thought that I was an odd joke. Going into psychology! Going to America! That wasn't their way.

Then I got a break. Oscar Oeser, whom I had met in 1932 in Cambridge, came back from Germany having finished his Ph.D. He had transferred from physics to psychology, and then gone to Germany to finish his degree. He had got some money from the Pilgrim Trust for interdisciplinary work on long-term unemployment in a Scottish area. Oeser interviewed me for the job of social psychologist in his three year project, and was interested in what I had to say about Kurt Lewin, and my political experiences of the Depression. Oscar Oeser was a committed academic and an action researcher who wanted to study unemployment and was a very enlightened social democrat at that time. So that was an enormous break for me, otherwise I would have had to fall back on my English and be a school teacher.

There were two industrial psychologists in Oeser's team who went off on their own. The economist, the sociologist and I worked pretty closely. We lived for the two major years of the project in Dundee. Occasionally we used to go over to St. Andrews where Oscar Oeser headed the Department of Psychology. He wasn't an effective organizer of our work, and the team never really worked as a complete whole.

With the economist, I was analyzing a large sample of Department of Labour records about the long-term unemployed. I had got married in the United States to a very intelligent girl, and she worked on this too.

The amount of work we had to do in finding data, and transcribing it, was monumental. The data showed that long-term unemployment—not so much unemployment itself—was due to a whole constellation of factors in Dundee. I analyzed records of juveniles' attitudes to getting jobs as the lads were coming out of school. They went to the 'low mill' in the jute industry until they were eighteen and then tried to get other jobs but met barriers in the local community. A lot of them would join the army. They would go in for seven years, come out again, and then have another big struggle to find employment.

The sociological side of their life was met by a psychological reality which bound them into long-term unemployment, and they couldn't get out. I didn't write it up, but I had analyzed the data, and I sent a report to Oscar Oeser who was going to write a book about it in Australia.

POLITICS BEFORE WORLD WAR II

I was politically involved with Spain before World War II, and with the unemployed. We knew what was coming up, and it was very, very hard to just be a psychologist. In 1938 I was beginning to get worried when I saw the Popular Front was not going to be a success in Britain. I sweated my guts out to help that one along, especially when Stafford Cripps came up to a big meeting in Dundee. But I just had no heart left to believe in these things any more. War was coming, and I had just got to prepare for war. Had Britain gone into the Popular Front in Spain the rot may have been stopped and we may not have needed to have had World War II. It was stoppable in Spain about the time of Guernica in the late 1930s. One was disgusted with one's own government in those days. It was awful. I read a book on the diplomacy just before World War II broke out. I was amazed at how everybody bluffed everybody else.

After my last year on the Dundee unemployment project at St. Andrews, I stayed on as Acting Head of the Department of Psychology. I replaced Oeser who had gone to Harvard for a year. When he came back war broke out. That period at St. Andrews was pretty rough. I was administrating this Department, never having taught in it, from September 1938 to June 1939. Then I left St. Andrews and lived in Dover with my family and my American relatives who were visiting us, and had got caught in Britain at the outbreak of war.

WORLD WAR II AND THE MAKING OF A CLINICIAN

What was I going to do in the war? I simply didn't know. I didn't volunteer for the army although I had had some association with the military in the cadets when I was at school. Then, just as I had given up trying to think about what to do with the War, there was an advertisement in *The Times* for a job in Columbia for someone with a background in English. I applied and, mercifully, was turned down. Philip Vernon, my tutor at Cambridge, who had been the clinical psychologist at the Maudsley Psychiatric Hospital, had moved into the armed services as a psychological adviser. He recommended me to Sir Aubrey

Lewis at the Maudsley, as a clinical psychologist, and Sir Aubrey accepted me. So for the first two years of the war I was a clinical psychologist in the part of the Maudsley housed in Mill Hill School, London. The first war casualties came from Dunkirk and most of the mental casualties were sent to us. In the summer of 1940 when the London blitzes started, some very frightened people came out of their rooms, ran all over the grounds and we had to go and find them.

One very interesting assignment came from the National Head Injuries Committee which was looking at similarities with what had happened in the trenches in World War I when soldiers would put their heads up from the trenches and get head injuries. I was asked to do a study of closed head injuries, especially the psychological repercussions of those injuries, which Sir Aubrey Lewis suspected might be picked up by a psychologist before being identified neurologically. I analyzed the data in great detail and gave a paper on closed head injuries at the Royal Society of Medicine. That was one of the first papers I published. My wife worked with me on it. Her family was back in America by this time.

After two years at Mill Hill I was very well experienced in clinical psychology because every kind of psychiatry was there, including psycho-analysis. It was a teaching hospital and I learned a lot from its seminars. I was one of few people very well grounded in clinical psychology in Britain at that time.

While I was at Mill Hill, people from the Tavistock Clinic, who had gone into the army, visited the hospital, saw what I was doing, were impressed and asked me to join them. I was in a reserved occupation and couldn't be released. Sir Aubrey Lewis wouldn't let me go. But no one could prevent my volunteering to join the armed services. So I volunteered and joined the Tavistock group in the army. At the Maudsley people were furious because they didn't at all approve of the Tavvy. To them I had committed treason, I was a deserter. But they could do nothing. I moved into the military because there was very much more scope there than at Mill Hill and I wanted to be with the Tavistock people. I had got stale at Mill Hill. I recommended Hans J. Eysenck as my successor and he performed incredibly well.

My wife and I went to Edinburgh where I was the psychologist for the experimental work on War Office Selection Boards (WOSBs). I then became Senior Psychologist for the whole development of WOSBs. I was a Captain, but within eighteen months I was promoted to Lieutenant Colonel.

In the WOSB experiment I worked with Majors Jock Sutherland and Wilfred Bion. The scheme was first suggested by the late Ferguson Rodger, a psychiatrist. He had the idea of a group of selectors working with a group of candidates. But the form of the Boards was developed by Sutherland, Bion and myself. A very good account of this is in Hugh Murray's article in Volume I of the history of our work—*The Social Engagement of Social Science* (SESS). My first job was to devise a psychological test program with intelligence tests, projective tests like the Thematic Apperception Test (TAT) and a life history questionnaire. At that time I had the only copy of Henry A. Murray's TAT in Britain and I kept it longer than I should out of the Cambridge library.

This was 1942 and my son, Alan, was born in Edinburgh. We were then transferred to Pierpoint Morgan's country house near London, and the family came back to London. We worked on WOSBs for three months before they became operational.

During the last two years of the war, I was the Chief Psychologist to the Civil Resettlement Units (CRUs), for repatriated prisoners of war. The CRUs were the second therapeutic community. The first, at Northfield Military Hospital, was based on a proposal by Wilfred Bion in a memorandum in 1940—the Wharncliffe Memorandum—which was never fully carried out.

In CRUs we first interviewed repatriates and escapers from 1943 onwards. Tommy Wilson conceived the scheme when doing morale studies in the Middle East; he had found that when people were separated from their relations they tended to go a bit haywire, especially after eighteen months away. Suspicions and other symptoms arose. Tommy Wilson asked for me to work on its planning and development. The aim was to devise a therapeutic community for helping repatriated prisoners of war to adjust to their home society from which they had been absent for five years. They were at first those from the German camps, most of whom had been captured at Dunkirk early in the war; later, others came from the Japanese camps. In Britain they lived in a special residence. It was very, very carefully worked out and an account of the CRUs appears in Volume I of *SESS*.

My time as Senior Psychologist in the WOSB was very exciting because I had a lot of development work to do, designing the first follow-ups and being a policy adviser. But the CRUs were probably the most exciting single experience of my professional life. It was a tremendous success and broke very new ground. I invented the terms 'social reconnection' and 'de-socialization.' I wanted to introduce a new terminology which was neutral, psychiatrically. We couldn't call these people 'patients' or 'clients,' or anything with therapeutic overtones. We had to train ordinary soldiers to do this work because there were very few technical people available in psychology or psychiatry. We had twenty CRUs with an average attendance of 240 at any one time and an average stay of one month. Also there was an extension scheme for the people who didn't or wouldn't come to the CRUs. We would visit every one of those people in their homes. Altogether it was a very moving experience.

During the war we created these social systems, such as WOSBs and CRUs, within the military for the solution of key problems that weren't solvable by ordinary military methods. I wasn't demobilized until September 1946. By this time a group had formed of young psychiatrists who had gone into army psychiatry, and, as a group, had spearheaded all of these social system creations. They drew in many other people and became known as "the Tavistock Group."

Before World War II the Tavistock Clinic had become a professional democracy. Towards the end of the war there was a postal ballot of members of the Clinic asking them who they wanted on the Post War Planning Committee. The key people in the army group were elected to that Committee, and they asked Jock Sutherland and myself to join them. From the beginning I was in on all these plans. The Tavistock Institute of Human Relations, as distinct from the Tavistock Clinic, was formed. We had a starting grant from the Rockefeller Foundation in February 1946 when the Institute and the Clinic were one. Then the National Health Service came into being in Britain, so we had to prepare the Clinic to enter that scheme and establish it as an out-patients' psychiatric facility. It was based theoretically on depth-psychology, particularly the object-relations approach in psychoanalysis. One of the first appointments was John Bowlby who was to be Head of the Department of Children and Parents. Three or four leading army psychiatrists, who weren't at the Tavistock but who were in London before the war were appointed.

Among the army group I had experienced psychoanalysis as an important way of viewing the wartime projects. We found that the object-relations approach linked the social and psychological fields. Not many of the people at this time were analysts—they were trained after the war—but they were psychoanalytically inclined people, and they had the understanding and skills which had worked in practice.

Immediately after the war we began to enter psychoanalytic training. At that time it was a rule that everybody at the Tavistock went into psychoanalysis. I am not an official Kleinian, though much influenced by her views, particularly her theory of the two developmental positions: the theory of manic-depressive states and schizoid mechanisms and the envy and gratitude theory. But I have also been very influenced by my colleague, John Bowlby, and his work on mother-child separation; by Winnicott on the concept of the facilitating environment; and by Bion and Sutherland.

As Melanie Klein aged she turned more inward and paid less attention to the environment. Meanwhile at the Tavistock we paid major attention to the environment, and became interested in social applications of psychoanalysis. As I developed, I didn't confine my attentions or sympathies to any single form of psychoanalysis. Also I became interested in Jung. I always had an independent mind in social psychology, and I tried to link it to the object-relations approach. In classical psychoanalysis Oedipus had number one place, but for me now, as the field of mother-child relations opened up, it wasn't number one.

The British government was very worried about the economy and, under Sir Stafford Cripps, formed a Productivity Committee which had a Human Factors Panel administered by the Medical Research Council. The Tavistock had three projects with the Council: the Glacier Metal project, which studied group relations in depth at all levels; a coal-mining project; and a project to develop a method for training people in postgraduate fieldwork in industry. We had six fellows for two years, one of whom was my pupil, Ken Bamforth. It was a very elaborate scheme based on experiential learning. All the fellows were in the Glacier Metal Project where they had a common field experience; they were all in some other project in the Institute; they were all in a therapy group; and, finally, they had their own group which looked at their own prejudices and problems. Universities would have nothing to do with us. There was great hostility to both the Tavistock Clinic and the Institute. How the hell we survived was a miracle.

Wilfred Bion and I were very close throughout the whole of the War and I was in Bion's original therapy group as his assistant. In the late 1940s he wanted me to go into practice with him working with groups. That was impossible for me, because I was Deputy Chairman of the Institute, committed full-time to its projects. It would have been a big mistake to join Bion because he left groups in the 1950s—which flummoxed everybody—and got completely absorbed in psychoanalysis, though he didn't lose his sense of the social field. Very few people knew exactly what group work he had done; even so all the psychiatrists in the Tavistock Clinic started taking groups. For the psychiatrists one-on-one treatment wouldn't do. They had to develop a flow of enough patients to be cost effective in the National Health Service. Developments of the Tavistock always were highly pragmatic and linked to the realities of the society. Group therapy was not, in the beginning, a theory; rather it was something we did. And nobody exactly followed Bion. He was only followed exactly in Bethel-type labs that we developed with the University of Leicester. That was when the cult of Bion—a wrong cult in my view—became established.

The first studies that led the Tavistock Institute to find an identity were in industry—the Glacier Metal Project and the coal project. The first coal study was in Ken Bamforth's original pit, and was stopped by the Divisional Board in Yorkshire because it did not wish to have attention drawn to work in autonomous groups. This was an early intimation to us of the resistance and the strength of the opposition to organizational change.

We got going again in East Midlands Division, but were again stopped when the Divisional Board wouldn't support us. So we had to go all over the British coal fields until we found, in Durham, one with a sympathetic Area General Manager. He was James Nimmo, an outstanding individual who had been at my college in Cambridge. Sir Sam Watson, Regional Secretary of the National Union of Mineworkers in the Durham Area, actively supported our work from the beginning.

The original paper on our coal project study was published in 1951. I had also delivered papers in 1950 to the Industrial Section of the British Psychological Society and to the British Association. But we weren't allowed to publish on the autonomous groups. Again the Divisional Board didn't want it referred to. We had the choice then of either playing along with the industry or not; if we had once left, we would never have got back in. So we kept our mouths shut for a time. Tommy Wilson mentioned the work in his Lewin Lecture, when the Institute, as a group, was given the Lewin Award in 1951.

Another major project was with the Family Welfare Association. In Britain with the inception of the welfare state, their previous work, which had been for the material alleviation of extreme poverty, was no longer relevant. They were besieged by people with emotional and social problems. The staff weren't able to cope with the new problems, so the head of the Association, Enid Eichholz, who had been head of the Civil Assistance Boards during the war, consulted Wilson. This led to the formation of what was first called 'The Family Discussion Group,' which later became the Institute of Marital Studies. Its methodology was developed by Michael Balint, a senior psychoanalyst; later he worked with general practitioners and with all health professionals, and marital studies became a major undertaking of the Tavistock Institute. There was also the beginning of Bowlby's world famous studies on mother-child separation and the establishment of family systems therapy. The creativeness in the early years was very, very great.

1951 saw the end of the Medical Research Council grants for industrial research at the Tavistock Institute. We weren't recognized as fit to receive funds from any British source, foundation or government, at that time. The Tavistock Clinic got extra funds from American foundations. The Rockefeller Foundation's funds went largely into the clinical field, while the new Ford Foundation funds were to go to the social and industrial field. In 1951 we had put up a proposal for a grant from the Ford Foundation which unexpectedly fell through.

So we had to do consulting for industry and find out if we could pay our way. The great project which was our salvation was with Unilever. Lord Heyworth, who was then Chairman of Unilever, had become interested in WOSBs during the war; and, because Unilever were going to expand, he had a huge problem of selection of managers. At the time there was a lot of nepotism and he wasn't going to let it continue. We developed conjointly with them what became known as the Unilever Companies' Management Development program. Selection procedures were derived from WOSB techniques and training utilized group methods and related techniques. This became the big bread-and-butter line for the Institute. Today it is a network organization, and has been developed in a most amazing way by my colleague, Harold Bridger.

Then we were asked to start consumer studies by people who had got to know us during the War. In fact all our early projects came from wartime contacts. It was because we weren't generally approved of at the time that our work had to come by that kind of route. The first consumer study we did was with Mars. I was highly involved in that one and created a concept that was both Lewinian and psychoanalytic. It was called the 'pleasure foods region,' and it referred to products, such as confectionery, alcohol, and tobacco, that were not of much nutritional value, but met psychological needs. The extended studies and theoretical development awaited the arrival of my Australian colleague, Fred Emery.

We had to do something to get a reputable name for the Tavistock Institute. Our policy was to establish the journal, *Human Relations*, with Kurt Lewin's group in the United States. His notions of action-research were parallel with our socio-clinical, action-oriented work and I was regarded as his representative in Britain. A lot of his field theory was very congenial to some of my colleagues. Establishing a connection between Lewin's group, later situated at the University of Michigan in Ann Arbor, and our work was primarily my endeavor. If I hadn't been to the United States in the 1930s it wouldn't have happened. Lewin was enthusiastic and wrote two celebrated papers for the first two numbers of *Human Relations*. He died just before they were published. His people in Ann Arbor carried on after his death.

Human Relations succeeded in establishing us internationally, especially in the United States; and it gave us an outlet for our kind of work. Its articles wouldn't have been accepted by any of the other British psychological journals. For the same reason, we also had to establish a publishing company—Tavistock Publications—otherwise Elliott Jaques's book, *The Changing Culture of a Factory*, would not have been published in 1951.

After World War II, in the early days of the Tavistock, I was the first non-psychiatrist. I was essentially a clinical social-psychologist, and nobody had my particular tradition. I was very lonely, and although I had most cooperative colleagues, I didn't have anyone that I could test my thinking with. Also I was so busy and so occupied with institution-building and policy matters, that I got out of date. I'd already had the bulk of the war period getting out of date. I was very quickly thrust into a policy-making role in the army and had been promoted very quickly. Then the Tavistock grew so rapidly that I felt I couldn't maintain myself technically to the extent that I might have done. But they weren't the only reasons. I had dreadful trouble with my personal life; my wife became very ill and eventually died. I remarried in 1959 and our daughter, Carolyn, was born in 1962.

In Britain my career had four phases. The first phase was becoming a social psychologist with the study of the social and psychological factors in long-term unemployment in Dundee; the second was really in group dynamics, which I learned during the war and afterwards in a psychoanalytic context; third came the socio-technical system ideas from the coal project; and fourth, development of the idea of socio-organizational ecology which dates from a joint paper with Fred Emery in 1965 on "The Causal Texture of the Organizational Environment."

BACK TO AMERICA—FROM 1966 TO THE PRESENT

I had developed close connections with a number of people in the United States, especially during 1960-61 when I was a Fellow at the Center for Advanced Study in the Behavioral Sciences at Palo Alto. And I had two colleagues in the Behavioral Sciences group in the Management School at the University of California at Los Angeles (UCLA). One was Bob Tannenbaum, a close personal friend of mine, with whom I trained a T-Group at Bethel. Although we used entirely different methods, we managed to complement each other, and worked very well together. Another member of the UCLA staff was William McWhinney who came over to Britain to the Department of Industry at Leeds University. I became a consultant to their studies and used to go up to Leeds University at least once a month. I liked McWhinney tremendously. When he went back to the United States he proposed me as Regent's Lecturer at UCLA in 1964. When I came back to England after that month I received a letter from the then department chairman asking if I would be interested to come to UCLA permanently.

At the time Beulah, my wife, had just been told that for her health she should live in a drier and warmer climate. After a lot of meditation I decided to accept the appointment, and for about six months I worked on it with the Tavistock people.

My appointment at UCLA started in July 1966. To go to America permanently wasn't part of my career plan, but I had been at the Tavistock since the beginning, and I felt it was time I left.

The irony of the decision to go to a drier climate because of Beulah's health appeared when one of my medical friends from London came to UCLA during the second year I was there. He said he would like to see her X-rays. He said the diagnosis was wrong, and was absolutely furious with the Harley Street specialist who had made it.

At UCLA I was professor of Organizational Behavior and Social Ecology in the Graduate School of Business Administration until 1969. I had been asked to go there by the Behavioral Science people, but I found that I wasn't in their group. I was put in a group called Management Theory, with people I'd never heard of. I was in a new country, in a new department and I didn't know the politics—so there wasn't very much that I could do.

Then Russell Ackoff from University of Pennsylvania came out with his Dean and asked me why I hadn't come over to him instead of UCLA? He was very upset and offended. Earlier Russ had come to England on a sabbatical leave and we saw a great deal of him when he played a major role with the British Operational Research Society, getting together their social science inclined group with our people in the Tavistock. Fred Emery met him and they discovered their common interest in Singer's ideas and Sommerhoff's theory of directive correlations, and began their book *On Purposeful Systems*. That was a very big development.

I stayed at UCLA from September 1966 to July 1969, working at a distance from, but in collaboration with, Lou Davis and other people. I taught a Ph.D. seminar and worked with MBAs. At UCLA they gave me a very good deal financially and, had the dean been quicker and got me a named chair, I would probably have stayed. He talked about it, but was too slow. I was also worried about my son, Alan, who had become very ill in London.

ACROSS AMERICA TO PENNSYLVANIA

You're much nearer to London on the east coast of America. So I was drawn to the east coast and in 1969 began work as Professor of Organizational Behavior and Social Ecology at the Wharton School with Russell Ackoff. I became Chairman of the Management and Behavioral Science Center at the University of Pennsylvania and had a large Ph.D. program there for almost ten years.

I started a big project in the medical school center at the University with one or two of my colleagues, and others with Russ. Very soon, I got a project at Rushton, a coal mine in Pennsylvania. We wanted to see if the methods we had developed in England's coal mine studies could be transferred to the United States where the technology and culture were different.

It was an independent mine, not part of a big outfit. Arthur Miller had become general secretary of the mine workers union. They'd had a huge tragedy and a row with the previous secretary—there had even been murders. 'Miners For Democracy' came out of all of this trouble. So I got that wave of union support. The owner of Rushton Mine was a Christian Scientist with extremely advanced social views about industrial organization. He was very charismatic and gave the project his complete support. Nevertheless, we did meet resistance to the changes we were seeking. In that project I had two staff not from the University of Pennsylvania: Gerry Susman, whom I had known at UCLA, and Grant Brown, a mining engineer from the Department of Mines and Minerals at Penn State. I used to go up there twice a month. In a way this project failed, and in a way it succeeded, and the incredible story about that is reported in Volume II of *SESS*.

Then I did the Jamestown Project in a manufacturing town in northwestern New York State. I wanted to move to another system level. Jamestown was the first small town where innovative industrial cooperation took place. This was initiated by the then mayor, Stan Lundine, who has since been in Congress and is now Lientenant Governor of New York State. I heard about this through a colleague, Neal Herrick, who directed me to Jamestown. I went up there to see them, and they became interested. So I took one of my graduate students up for the summer and we made an anthropological survey of the whole place, and presented proposals which were accepted.

In Jamestown there existed an institution, the Jamestown Area Labor-Management Committee, that was at a higher system level than the individual companies concerned. We found that having the commitment of this overall body had a stabilizing effect. Local small projects would go up and down but they would hold because of the Committee. This led me to what I called the 'function of a continuant.' I introduced the concept publicly in Oslo in 1987. The term comes from a book on logic by W. E. P. Johnson, the Cambridge philosopher, written in 1924. It was then mentioned in an article by Maurice Ginsberg in the mid-1930s. I had a new use for it, namely the need for a point of stability in a change-making organization.

One of the big troubles in change-making organizations is that they have no resources, they are very unstable, and the field that they are concerned with often just collapses. The Tavistock projects were full of this, with one or two exceptions, like the Unilever project. So I made this into a theory. It was the first time any socio-technical work had been done at the community level, while the mining project was actually the first research-funded, sociotechnical study started in the United States.

We had another big project going in the public sector. At the time there was trouble about laws like Proposition 13 in California, that is, a policy of cutting back on government expenditure. What we called Project Network comprised projects in twelve cities at that time. Again, this will be reported in Volume III of *SESS*.

Also there was a major project with a large international engineering company which spanned ten years from the early '70s. They had sixty or seventy socio-technical studies going in various places, and nothing was known about these at the center of the firm. They all failed eventually, or were phased out, except two. The first was in another country—Canada—and the second was in a new plant in the United States with new technology. But all the other projects faded even though some of them were marvelously successful for three or four years. My interest was to find out why the projects failed, and why there was no communication of the study to the center. We found that the projects had been initiated by managers who had picked up something at a conference, got things going, and when they were transferred the project would collapse. This project was published in 1982 and will be republished in Volume III of *SESS*.

In 1970-71 Fred Emery came over and we decided to put our work together in the book, *Towards a Social Ecology: Contextual Appreciations of the Future in the Present*. Unfortunately, its publication was delayed for three years because of a big row between publishers in Britain and New York. Otherwise, our book would have been out before Don Schon's *Beyond the Stable State*, and Alvin Toffler's *Future Shock*. That delay damaged our appeal very much, as did the conceptual difficulty of the work.

From 1973-74, after becoming separated from the work of Russ Ackoff, I carried on my projects at the University of Pennsylvania until 1978 when I was made emeritus.

TO CANADA

Meanwhile I had developed a long association with people in Canada. Michel Chevalier and others had known me at Tavistock, and some of them had been to the University of Pennsylvania. I was invited to go to Toronto and join the Faculty of Environmental Studies at York University as Professor of Organizational Behaviour and Social Ecology. They were interested in developing their institutional, organizational side. So from 1978 to 1985 I went there, and I was very happy.

At York I was adviser to Labour Canada. I had projects with them, and for two years was going all over the country getting very involved with people starting up Quality of Working Life (QWL) projects. We had a community group in Sudbury in northwestern Ontario, a regional project in Nova Scotia, and started Search Conferences in Alberta. My major task was to consult and advise, and set up projects and see them through.

In 1979 I found out that I had coronary artery disease. A triple by-pass operation was done in May 1983. I stayed at York University until 1985.

I went to Minneapolis for the fall term as a guest professor, at the invitation of Andy Van de Ven, Chairman of the Department of Management at the University of Minnesota. I was invited to stay but the climate made it impossible. I retired to Gainesville, Florida.

SCIENCE POLICY AND FUTURE STUDIES

I had introduced future studies at York and taught a course for two or three years which meant an immense amount of work. I was headed in that direction and that's where I ended academically.

During the '60s concern regarding recognition of, and government support for, social research had led to the formation of a Social Science Research Council in Britain. Sir Hugh Beaver, the Chairman of the Tavistock Council, wanted the Institute to take a public position on these issues and asked me to do a monograph on our experience. This attracted the interest of OECD and then of UNESCO. I became a member of the latter's committee on Research Trends in the Human and Social Sciences and produced a report on *Social Science Policy: The Organization and Financing of Social Research*. This was published in 1970 as part of the overall UNESCO study and as an independent monograph. In it I included a critique of academic individualism and an account of a new type of social science illustrated in the work of the

Tavistock—in addition to basic research and standard applied research there is a third type concerned with emerging societal problems and involving the stakeholders in projects of actively inquiring into them (cf. *SESS*).

This led me to extend my empirical interests from socio-technical projects to the wider field of social ecology and future studies.

Methodologically, I moved from action research to the search conference and then into action learning. I would start microexploratory processes in the field, then get people concerned with them, and in turn I would get involved with them. Always I believed that the methodology would lead to new insights, and that in the social sciences not everything would be found out or done by conventional methods.

In the early days of action research and action learning we couldn't always find organizations that had a 'continuant function.' Often we got support from people higher up, but that led to problems when they didn't follow through. We found, repeatedly, that the political problems of the action researcher are monumental. Otherwise every project would be a success!

Now, with Hugh Murray and Fred Emery, Beulah, and I are editing *The Social Engagement of Social Science*, a three-volume collection of writings giving an account of the work of the Tavistock Institute. The first volume was published by the University of Pennsylvania Press in June 1990 and the second in July 1993. I conceived the book in three perspectives. The socio-psychological perspective is about our studies in groups and organizations. It came from our wartime work. Then comes the socio-technical perspective which grew from work of my own in the early '50s and, finally, the socio-ecological perspective, which is more recent and expands the earlier work to wider systems. I am trying to put all the work together in one standing collection with over thirty contributors, and co-editors from Europe, Australia, and America.

Eric L. Trist
died on June 4, 1993

PUBLICATIONS

1946

With J.D. Sutherland. *Preliminary technical appreciation of the problem of selecting higher grade civil servants during the reconstruction period* (Tavistock Document No. T423). London: Tavistock Institute.

1947

With A.T.M. Wilson and A. Curle. Transitional communities and social reconnection: A study of the civil resettlement of British prisoners of war. *Human Relations, I*(1), 42-68.

With A.T.M. Wilson and A. Curle. Transitional communities and social reconnection: A study of the civil resettlement of British prisoners of war. *Human Relations, I*(2), 240-90.

1951

With K.W. Bamforth. Some social and psychological consequences of the Longwall Method of Coal-Getting. *Human Relations, 4*(1), 3-38.

1952

With A.K. Rice. Institutional and sub-institutional determinants of change in labour turnover. (The Glacier Project-VIII). *Human Relations, 5*(4), 347-71.

With A.T.M. Wilson & A. Curle. Transitional communities and social reconnection: A study of the civil resettlement of British prisoners of war. In G.E. Swanson, T.M. Newcomb, & L.E. Hartley (Eds.), *Readings in social psychology* (pp. 561-579). New York: H. Holt & Co.

1953

Some observations on the machine face as a socio-technical system (Tavistock Document No. 341). London: Tavistock Institute.

An area training school in the National Coal Board (Tavistock Document No. 342). London: Tavistock Institute.

Area organization in the National Coal Board (Tavistock Document No. 343). London: Tavistock Institute.

With E.L. Herbert. The institution of an absent leader by a Students' Discussion Group. *Human Relations, 6*(3), 215-45.

With J.M.M. Hill. A consideration of industrial accidents as a means of withdrawal from the work situation. *Human Relations, 6*(4), 357-80.

A policy appreciation of management development. London: Tavistock/ Unilever Ltd.

1955

With J.M.M. Hill. Changes in accidents and other absences with length of service. *Human Relations, 8*(2), 121-52.

1958

Work organization at the Coal Face: A comparative study of mining systems (Tavistock Document No. 506). London: Tavistock Institute.

With B. Semeonoff. *Diagnostic performance tests* London: Tavistock Publications.

1959

With C. Sofer. *Exploration in group relations.* Leicester: Leicester University Press.

On socio-technical systems. An Open University lecture jointly sponsored by the Departments of Engineering and Psychology at the University of Cambridge, November 18.

With G.W. Higgin & F.E. Emery. *Communications in the National Farmers' Union.* London: National Farmers' Union.

With H. Murray. Organisation de Travail dans les Tailles, Etude Comparative des Methods d'Exploitation Minere. *Bulletin* CERP, *8*(4).

1960

With H. Murray. Adoption Progressive d'une Organisation de Travail en Equipe. *Bulletin* CERP, *9*(2), 153-64.

Introduction. In W. Brown (Ed.), *Explorations in management* (p. 36). London: Heinemann.

Social structure and psychological stress. In J.M. Tanner (Ed.), *Stress and psychiatric disorder.* Proceedings of the Second Oxford Conference of the Mental Health Research Conference. Oxford: Blakely Scientific Publications.

With F.E. Emery. Socio-technical Systems. In C.W. Churchman & M. Verhurst (Eds), *Management Science, Models and Techniques* (Vol. 2, pp. 83-97). London: Pergamon Press.

1961

With H. Murray. Dispositions de Prendre en Vue d'une Mecanisation plus Pousee. *Bulletin* CERP, *10*(1), 36-53.

Central management courses in a large organization. London: Tavistock/ Unilever Ltd.

1962

The emergence of system theory in the study of organizations (Inaugural lecture in Tavistock theoretical series presented at the Royal Society of Medicine) (Tavistock Document No. T40). London: Tavistock Institute.

With H. Bridger. *Human relations training in Europe.* Report of the First International Meeting, IMEDE, Lausanne.

1963

With G.W. Higgin, H. Murray, & A.B. Pollock. *Organizational choice: Capabilities of groups at the coal face under changing technologies.* London: Tavistock Publications.

1964

With Sir Hugh Beaver. *Social research and a national policy for science: A paper of the Council of the Tavistock Institute of Human Relations* (Tavistock Pamphlet No. 7). London: Tavistock Institute.

Wider Organizational Networks and Their Environments. Working Paper, Third Social Science of Organizations Seminar, Pittsburgh, PA (June).

A strategy for depth research on British planning processes. Working Paper, Minnowbrook Conference, University of Syracuse (July).

The Need of the Social Psychiatrist to Influence Wider Social Networks and their Environments (Proceedings of the Sixth International Congress of Psychotherapy, London, August). *Acta Psychotherapeutica, 12*(6).

With E. Thorsrud and F. Emery. *Industrielt Demokrati.* Oslo: Universitetsforlaget.

1965

Contribution to Symposium on Community Psychiatry. *International Journal of Psychiatry, 1*(4).

With F.E. Emery. The causal texture of organizational environments. *Human Relations, 13*(1), 21-32.

1966

Sponsor's contribution to Symposium on Conflict Resolution. *Proceedings of Cambridge Conference on Operational Research and the Social Sciences.* London: Tavistock Publications.

Contribution to the Proceedings of the CIBA Foundation Conference on *Conflict in Society.* London: Churchill.

1967

The relations of concepts of welfare and development (in pre-industrial, industrial and post-industrial societies: A systems theory and socio-cultural analysis. Theme paper for the seminar on Welfare and Development Programmes, Canadian Centre for Community Studies, Ottawa (November).

Engaging with large scale systems. Paper presented at the Douglas McGregor Memorial Conference, MIT (November).

1968

The professional facilitation of planned change in organizations. In *Proceedings*, International Association of Applied Psychology XVIth International Congress, Amsterdam.

With D. Armstrong. Social science activities in eight target countries. In *Main Trends in the Social and Human Sciences*. Paris: UNESCO.

1969

Key aspects of environmental relations In B.M. Gross (Ed.), *Monograph on appraising administrative capability for development planning* (pp. 91-97). New York: Division of Public Administration, United Nations.

Social aspects of science policy. Background paper for Round Table on Social Aspects of Science Policy, University of Toronto. Senate of Canada, *Proceedings of the Special Committee on Science Policy* (pp. 4794-4820). Ottawa: Queen's Printer.

1970

Social research institutes: Types, structure, scope. *International Social Science Journal 22*(2), 322-359.

Organisation et Systeme. *R. franc. Sociol*, XI-XII. No. Spec. Analyse de systemes en sciences sociales, 123-139.

Science policy and development of research in the social sciences: The organizing and financing of social research. Section 3 in *Main Trends of Research in the Social and Human Sciences* (pp. 695-811). Paris: Mouton/UNESCO. (Also published as a separate monograph)

Urban North America: The challenge of the next thirty years. *Journal of the Town Planning Institute of Canada 10*(3), 1-20.

1971

Critique of scientific management in terms of socio-technical theory. *Prakseologia, 39-40*, 159-74.

Management and organization development in public enterprises and government agencies. In *Modern Management Techniques in Developing Countries*. New York: United Nations.

Epilogue. In C.P. Hill. *Towards a new philosophy of management*. London: Gower Press.

The human intake system: A socio-psychological and socio-ecological appreciation in a futures perspective. Management and Behavioral Science Center document, University of Pennsylvania.

1972

With C. Dwyer & T. Gilmore. *Planning and designing for juvenile justice.* Washington, DC: LEAA.

1973

Types of output mix in research organizations. In A. Cherns (Ed.), *Social science and government* (pp. 101-141). London: Tavistock.

With F.E. Emery. *Towards a social ecology: Contextual appreciations of the future in the present.* London: Plenum.

The planning process in university medical centers. Working Papers, Management and Behavioral Science Center, University of Pennsylvania.

1974

Work improvement and industrial democracy. Theme paper for EEC Conference on Work Organization, Technology and Motivation, EEC, Brussels.

Planning in an era of change and uncertainty. Keynote Address, 21st Anniversary Conference, School of Community and Regional Planning, University of British Columbia, Vancouver, BC (June).

Labor-management committees and the quality of working life in Jamestown, N.Y. Working Papers 1 & 2, University of Pennsylvania, Management and Behavioral Science Center.

With L.E. Davis. Improving the quality of working life: Socio-technical case studies. In J. O'Toole (Ed.), *Work and the quality of life, resource papers for work in America* (pp. 246-284). Cambridge, MA: MIT Press.

The new work ethic in Europe and America. The Franklin Foundation Lecture Series. Atlanta, GA: Georgia State University Press.

1975

Planning the first steps toward quality of working life in a developing country. In L.E. Davis, A.B. Cherns, & Associates, *The quality of working life, Vol. 1. Problems, prospects and the state of the art* (pp. 78-85). New York: Free Press.

1976

Engaging with large scale systems. In A.W. Clark (Ed.), *Experimenting with organizational life* (pp. 43-57). London: Plenum.

Action research and adaptive planning. In A.W. Clark (Ed.), *Experimenting with organizational life* (pp. 223-236). London: Plenum.

The culture of the post-industrial society. In R. Dubin (Ed.), *Work organization and society* (pp. 1011-1033). New York: Macmillan.

Critique of scientific management in terms of socio-technical theory. In M. Wier (Ed.), *Job satisfaction: Challenge and responses in modern Britain* (pp. 81-90). London: Fontana.

A Concept of organizational ecology. *Bulletin of National Labour Institute* (New Delhi), *12*, 483-496.

1977

A concept of organizational ecology. *Australian Journal of Management, 2*(2), 162-75.

Collaboration in work settings: A personal perspective. *Journal of Applied Behavioral Science, 13*, 268-278.

With G.I. Susman & G.R. Brown. An experiment in autonomous working in an American underground coal mine. *Human Relations 30*(3), 201-236.

1978

Employment alternatives for the eighties. Papers presented at the Urban Seminar Six on Public Enterprises and Government Agencies, Toronto Social Planning Council (November).

Developing an adaptive planning capability in public enterprise and government agencies. In J.W. Sutherland (Ed.), *Management handbook for public administrators* (pp. 389-422). New York: Van Nostrand Reinhold.

The environment and systems response capability–A futures perspective. Keynote Address at First European Forum on Organization Development, Aachen (November).

With J. Eldred & R. Keidel. A new approach to economic development. *Human Futures 1*(1), 1-12.

On socio-technical systems. In W.A. Pasmore & J.J. Sherwood (Eds.), *Socio-technical systems: A sourcebook* (pp. 43-57). La Jolla, CA: University Associates.

The quality of working life and organizational development. Keynote address, First International Conference on Organizational Development, Toronto (October).

1979

New directions of hope. *Regional Studies, 13*, 439-451.

New Concepts of Productivity. Paper presented at the Ottawa Conference on Shaping Canada's Future in a Global Perspective (August).

With S. Burgess. Multiple deprivation: A human and economic approach. *Linkage 3*, 8-9.

Adapting to a changing world. In G.F. Sanderson (Ed.), *Industrial Democracy Today*. New York: McGraw-Hill Ryerson.

A framework for analyzing the international work environment. In G.F. Sanderson (Ed.), *Industrial democracy today*. New York: McGraw-Hill Ryerson.

Employment alternative for the eighties. In *Proceedings*, Urban Seminar Six on Public Enterprises and Government Agencies (pp. 152-172). Toronto: Toronto Social Planning Council.

1980

With R. Keidel. Decline and revitalization: The Jamestown experience. In D. Morley et al. (Eds.), *Making cities work: The dynamics of urban innovation*. London: Croom Helm.

Networking for social change. In D. Morley et al. (Eds.), *Making cities work: The dynamics of urban innovation*. London: Croom Helm.

With C. Pava. *Project network—Labor management co-operation in the public sector: Developments in 10 American cities*. Management and Behavioral Science Center document, University of Pennsylvania.

The professional facilitation of planned change in organizations. In T. Johnstad (Ed.), *Group dynamics in society*. Cambridge, MA: Oelgeschlages, Gunn and Hain.

The quality of working life and organizational improvement. *Chemistry in Canada, 32*(6), 33-37.

The environment and systems response capability—A futures perspective. *Futures* (April), pp. 113-127.

1981

The evolution of socio-technical systems: A conceptual framework and an action research program. Toronto: Ontario Ministry of Labour. (Also published in A. Van de Ven & W. Joyce [Eds], *Organization design and performance*. New York: Wiley-Interscience.)

The quality of working life and organizational improvement. In R. Dorion (Ed.), *Adapting to a changing world*. Ottawa: Labour Canada.

QWL and the 80's. Closing address to the International Conference on QWL and the 80's, Toronto, August.

With D. Morley. *Children: Our number one resource*. A Report on the Saskatchewan Search Conference on Day Care, Cooperative College of Canada, Saskatoon (June).

With P. Bradshaw. *Feasibility of Q.W.L. Projects in the Sudbury Region*. Occasional Paper, Ontario QWL Centre, Toronto.

With L. Clarke. *Sudbury 2001: An evolutionary analysis*. Occasional Paper, Ontario QWL Centre, Toronto.

1982

With W. Westley. *QWL in the federal public service*. Ottawa: Labour Canada.

With C. Dwyer. The limits of laissez-faire as a socio-technical change strategy. In R. Zager & M. Rosow (Eds.), *Innovative organizations: Productivity programs in action* (pp. 149-183). New York: Pergamon.

With H. Bridger, S.G. Gray, & N. Sanford. *The early years of the Tavistock Institute*. Paper presented at the Academy of Management, History of Management Division, New York (August).

1983

QWL and the 80's. In H. Kolodny & H. van Beinum (Eds.), *The quality of working life and the 1980's*. New York: Praeger.

Afterword. In C.H.P. Pava, *Managing new office technology: An organizational strategy*. New York: Free Press.

Epilogue. In J.T. Ziegenfuss, *Patients' rights and organizational models: Sociotechnical systems research on mental health programs*. Washington, DC: University Press of America.

Referent organizations and the development of inter-organizational domains. *Human Relations, 36*(3), 269-284.

1984

Preface. In B. Cunningham & T. White (Eds.), *Quality of working life: Contemporary cases*. Ottawa: Labour Canada.

Working with Bion in the 1940s: The group decade. In M. Pines (Ed.), *Bion and group psychotherapy*. London: Routledge & Kegan Paul.

1985

Intervention strategies for inter-organizational domains. In R. Tannenbaum et al. (Eds.), *Human systems development: New perspectives on people and organizations*. San Francisco, CA: Jossey-Bass.

After-dinner Remarks. Conference on Explorations in Human Futures. Orillia, Ontario (October).

1986

With H. Perlmutter. Paradigms for societal transition. *Human Relations, 39*(1), 1-27.

Quality of working life and community development: Some reflections on the Jamestown experience. *Journal of Applied Behavioral Science, 22*(3), 223-237.

The relation of welfare and development in post-industrialism. In J. Draper (Ed.), *Commemorative volume for the Late William Baker*. (Forthcoming).

1987

Some additional reflections on working with Bion in the forties. *Group Analysis, 20*(3), 263-270.

Transitions. Discussant's Paper, Annual Conference of the International Society for the Psycho-analytic Study of Organizations, New York (October).

1989

Andras Angyal and systems thinking. In *Planning for human systems: Essays in honor of Russell Ackoff* (pp. 111-132). New York: Wiley.

1990

Edited with H. Murray. *The social engagement of social science: Selected writings of members of the Tavistock Institute. Volume I: The socio-psychological perspective*. Philadelphia, PA: University of Pennsylvania Press.

1992

With L.D. Ketchum. *All teams are not created equal—How employee empowerment **really** work*. Newbury Park, CA: Sage.

1993

Edited with H. Murray. *The social engagement of social science: Selected writings of members of the Tavistock Institute. Volume II: The socio-technical perspective*. Philadelphia, PA: University of Pennsylvania Press.

Stanley C. Vance

Up The Management Mountain

STANLEY C. VANCE

As I gaze out my study window, seeking that first magic phrase for this, my autobiography, I see a team of youngsters making like mountain goats, trying to scale the precipitous palisades of the Tennessee River across from my home. These are ambitious neophytes, seeking the thrill that comes from inching one's way up the impossible to the very top. Having just passed my 75th birthday, obviously, such sport is not for me. But, occasionally, I do scale an imaginary mountain. I usually begin in the sanctuary of my study, surrounded by the many mementoes of my long and sometimes arduous climb up the management mountain.

As I reflect upon the half century I dedicated to venturing up my own management mountain, I see a distant panoramic view of other peaks, some with deep personal meaning. I see my "Management Mt. Rushmore," bearing the likenesses of four of my closest peers—Keith Davis, "Howdy" Koontz, Dalt McFarland and Bill Newman, my old Wharton School professor. These indomitable "mountain men" have provided inspiration, recognition and scholastic camaraderie.

Proudly displayed among the trophies of my climbing days are copies of my major publications. While there is joy in these contributions, there is also a certain sadness and frustration in recalling two pink-slipped manuscripts: a family firm treatise and an advanced production management text. However, a batting average of .818 is not so bad a record!

Among the awards, certificates, testimonials, letters from gurus, plaques, and other vestiges of egomania is the sheepskin on the wall, testifying to my 1951 University of Pennsylvania Doctor of Philosophy Degree in Economics. While earning the Ph.D. was one of my most treasured accomplishments, at times

I have wondered if I should have elected the D.B.A., Doctor of Business Administration degree. But, as in so much of the historical, choice is a matter of chance and circumstance.

When I registered at the Wharton School in 1943, I was given the option of working for a M.A. or M.B.A. degree. Since my undergraduate work—except for some free-lance accounting courses—had been in the liberal arts, I naturally gravitated toward the M.A. At that time, the M.B.A., only newly gestated, had an uncertain future and lacked the aura of a liberal arts degree. The new M.B.A., also, was suspected of being money motivated. At student gatherings it was not uncommon to hear cynical liberal arts majors chanting "profits must prevail!" Even some of my staid business-prone classmates felt that profit was a dirty word and corporate life could not be anything but corrupt. Actually, the whole liberal arts crowd viewed the business-prones as Philistines and even worse, as Untouchables. As an enterprising academic greenhorn, I shied away from the Untouchable M.B.A. and slid into the Brahmin M.A. The logical extension of this route was the Ph.D.

With the benefit of hindsight, I now find nothing wrong with profits. As for following the economist route, I have no brief against economics and I seldom think of it as the dismal science. It is a worthy field where one can even win a Nobel prize. However, way back then, I seemed to prefer a more calloused hands-on approach to arm-chair rationalizing. Consequently, even though my graduate school curriculum was designed to cover the conventional M.A. itinerary, I did succeed in bootlegging an extra 42 production management credits. This was a costly and time-consuming digression but it enkindled within me a passion for understanding and preaching the gospel of productivity.

JOINING THE FACULTY CLUB

In the Spring of 1946, two events of epochal significance took place—I married and I took a teaching job at the Wharton School of Business; the first step in my management mountain climb. Regina (Gene for short) played a part in my life from pre-puberty days—we lived in the same town (Minersville, Pennsylvania), went to the same church and graduated from the same high school. We decided to get married during spring semester break at the University of Pennsylvania even though I had no job or job prospects, no bank account or tangible assets.

After a brief honeymoon, I was back on campus preparing to register for the spring term. Everyone I met that day asked if I had talked with Dean Canby Balderston (one of the founders of the Academy of Management, who later served as vice-chairman of the Federal Reserve Board). "Don't register until you meet him," was the usual admonition. Obviously, something was amiss.

What was my infraction? Was I getting the proverbial boot? With great trepidation I dragged myself to the Dean's Office, only to learn that instead of getting the boot, I was being asked to serve on the Wharton Graduate School Faculty!

A few months earlier, when contemplating graduation and marriage, I had activated my Wharton Placement Service file, seeking a production management job. I was stunned when Dean Balderston, having learned of my plans through the Placement Service, offered me an instructorship in the Geography and Industry Department. Alas, we will never know if our corporate system lost the potential of an Alfred Sloan while education gained another professor!

AMERICAN INDUSTRIES

As a neophyte instructor, I was introduced to a Wharton innovation—its basic management course, *American Industries.* This was a primer on productivity, the yardstick measuring the effectiveness of our economic system. Here *industry* was succinctly defined as "the creation of utility." This creation was effected in one of five ways: changes in form, time, place, possession and service. Fundamental to the process was the concept of *value added.* For me, the student, this course provided a wealth of facts, terms, problems, concepts; all essential for the full comprehension of how our system works. For me, the budding instructor, *American Industries* was bedazzling and challenging. There was so much I had to learn just to keep ahead of my students!

In the course, we considered the total economy and its industry and individual company segments. Economic aspects, technical/production considerations plus marketing, financial, logistical, ethical, union and political implications were integral components. As a liberal arts generalist, I really had to work my butt off to gain the fullness of this course. This concentration paid big dividends. Within five years I had completed and published my first text, with the highly original title of *American Industries* (Prentice-Hall, 1952)!

Although this text, along with a companion, *Industrial Structure and Policy* (1955), holds a prominent spot in my pleasant memories, it is not without a twinge of sadness. A few years after my authorship debut, my own Alma Mater, the progenitor of what I considered to be the "Management Koran," abandoned the individual industry nuts-and-bolts approach to the study of management. To Joseph Wharton, Frederick W. Taylor, and the host of brilliant Wharton School scientific management pioneers, this was a repudiation, an abomination.

One can only speculate as to this 180-degree turn in perspective. Could the Frederick Taylor stress on numbers, relationships, and currency of data have been beyond the cranial capacity of a new generation? Note today's continuing "softening" in pre-college education, evidenced in the precipitous drop in SAT scores; currently about 120 points below their historic highs of the 1950s. In recent international comparisons, U.S. student achievements ranked close to the bottom—13th out of 14 in Chemistry; 9th out of 9 in Biology; 10th out of 14 in Physics. In Management, the sad comparison is more evident in the marketplace than in the classroom.

Perhaps it is needless to expound on how we have been outpaced by the Japanese and even by the Asian Tigers—Taiwan, Hong Kong, Singapore, and South Korea. In the vital area of quality control, the Japanese have steadfastly bestowed the annual Edward Deming Award to firms with records of outstanding quality of product. Only in the past few years have we tried to match the Japanese reverence for SQC by setting up our comparable Baldridge Award. Ironically, even as a graduate student—48 years ago—and subsequently as an instructor, my Wharton colleagues and I studied and taught statistical quality control (SQC) long before the Japanese got into the act and took their bows.

Similarly, I remember our stress on JIT, "just-in-time" inventory control, decades before the Japanese made it fashionable. I called it "hand-to-mouth" inventory practice. I was introduced to the American predecessor of JIT at Ford's Chester, PA assembly plant while taking students on "Field Work in Industry," a follow-up course to *American Industries*. Here, in minimizing inventory costs, box cars loaded with parts, were parked adjacent to the plant. The main inventory cost was now demurrage, the incidental daily charge for the box car. The parts were then moved by conveyor to assembly. While this hand-to-mouth technique kept inventory costs low, it brought EOQ, the economic ordering quantity or lot size dilemma, to the forefront nearly a half century before the Japanese discovered JIT.

One cannot blame the sorry state of U.S. business on Wharton's retreat from the productivity-oriented *American Industries* course, yet I do feel it is symptomatic of the capitulation of hard-core specialists to windbag generalists. And yet Wharton is not alone in this retreat. Late in 1989, an article in *Business Week*, "Chicago B-School Goes Touchy-Feely" (11/27/89, p. 140), corroborated my sentiments. Chicago, long preeminent in quantitative economic research, has now added seminars in role-playing games. One, in particular, miniaturizes the course to a single word, "OH." Conversing only in OHs, the students are forced to rely on inflections to transmit thoughts. Supposedly, they are trying to learn something about nonverbal communications.

The University of Chicago Graduate School of Business, however, is distinctly a Johnny-come-lately in this respect. Back in the 1960s, Sensitivity Training, Extra-Sensory Perception, and other fun-fads were taken seriously by reputable professors and corporate training directors. The resurgence of the "touchy-feely" gimmick at Chicago's B-School is a sad commentary on university education. Wharton's shortcomings of the 1950s, hopefully, will not be repeated by Chicago in the 1990s.

Let me emphasize that this vitriol is not against *all* game playing; a number of my mementoes will testify to my contributions in management decision simulation. I am credited with writing the first commercially published business game, *Management Decision Simulation* (1960). Years later, I co-founded ABSEL, the Association for Business Simulation and Experiential Learning; served as ABSEL's second president and was its first elected Fellow.

My Wharton instructorship did not confine me to the *American Industries* course. Typically, as a bottom-of-the-totem-pole instructor, I was easy prey; a sort of factotum. In less than two years of instructorship, I covered the gamut of management courses and even taught a class in basic statistics. But of all these experiences, the most gratifying, after *American Industries*, was *Business Policy*. I considered it a great honor to work with this capstone course, particularly since it was supervised by Dr. William Newman, *The Academy of Management's* renowned Bill. I learned much and graded copious papers with a zeal approaching the sadistic. Most important, it led to a lifetime friendship with one of the greats.

THE DISSERTATION

Since I had not as yet completed a doctoral requirement—the dissertation—my preoccupation with a yeoman's teaching load could have been disastrous. I was well aware of the incidence of ABDs (all but the dissertation), and I was determined that I would never bear that tag. But I had to have a subject, research sources, and time to write.

Considering my interest in the concept of productivity, and my association with the Anthracite Coal Industry, my subject was: "A Critical Analysis of the Data and Techniques Available for Technical Capital Measurement in the Bituminous Coal Industry." Unfortunately, I was not able to critique the Anthracite industry because it had no centralized data source. On the other hand, I was able to get considerable information and cooperation from the Bituminous Coal Institute; eventually, even a job offer. My dissertation was strictly a pioneering venture, probably never to be replicated. I tried to equate manpower and electro-mechanical energy in the wrenching of coal from the bowels of the earth. Actually, I had hoped to structure a coal mining production equation.

A few years earlier, Professor Paul Douglas (subsequently Senator Douglas from Illinois) coauthored, with two graduate students, a prototype production equation for total manufacturing. Finding such an equation, I reasoned, might provide an orderly program for the inevitable manpower displacement of coal miners by mechanical cutters, loaders, and other equipment. But, as with virtually all such ambitious dissertations, mine continues to languish in the University of Pennsylvania Library stacks. The completion of the dissertation was prolonged by my acceptance, in 1947, of an assistant professorship at the University of Connecticut.

ARMSTRONG CORK COMPANY/ARMSTRONG WORLD INDUSTRIES

While at the University of Connecticut, I received a summer grant from the Foundation for Economic Education (FEE). It was an opportunity to spend a summer at Armstrong Cork Company (now Armstrong World Industries) and I was elated. Although the $300 stipend for six weeks of internship pales by today's standards, it was a big boost in the trek up the productivity trail. I was the "Schmidt" in Frederick Taylor's classic pig iron experiment. To Schmidt, the simple but sturdy Pennsylvanian, "a penny looked like a cartwheel." To me, the new assistant professor, the $300 looked like the whole cart! From this fantastic opportunity, I gleaned interviews with Armstrong Chairman Henning W. Prentiss; its President, C.J. Backstrand, and two future Chairmen, Maurice Warnock and James Binns. Since my working contacts ranged from board members and vice presidents to foremen and "hands," I even spent time in Armstrong's "hot-as-hell" training program.

Each year about fifty college graduates, many of them M.B.A.s, came to corporate headquarters for indoctrination. In addition to conventional classroom instruction, trainees spent considerable time in on-the-floor training. This included a stint in the boiler room where the trainees had to stoke the furnaces and shovel out the ashes. I labeled it the "ashes test," comparable to Accounting's "acid test." It was the "ashes test" that differentiated future Armstrong officers from the flunkees. Some elitist M.B.A.s considered removing ashes as too demeaning and refused to shovel. This was equivalent to getting a "D"—it could be averaged away but was a serious handicap to promotion.

My Armstrong program was put together by Dr. Walter Hoadley, the firm's chief economist. Among the long-term benefits of this experience was my continuing friendship with Walter. Now in retirement, Dr. Hoadley has moved from vice president at Armstrong to senior vice president and chief economist at Bank of America and thence to Senior Fellow at the Hoover Institution.

On my first day at Armstrong Cork, as I waited in the Chairman's office for my interview, I noted unusual activity—phones were ringing and aides were dashing about. Finally I was enlightened. The Korean War had just broken out and an emergency meeting of the Board of Directors was being convened. Armstrong's Board had a monumental decision to make: Should it or should it not stockpile linseed oil, imported from South America, and the most critical of raw materials in the fabrication of linoleum floor coverings. During World War II Armstrong had failed to stockpile linseed oil and almost went broke when German U-Boats created havoc with shipping. Now Armstrong faced the same dilemma—stockpiling would boost inflation and handicap our war effort while a hand-to-mouth inventory policy, though patriotic, could lead to plant closures. I was tremendously impressed by the board's expeditious decision making. Within a few hours a multimillion-dollar decision was made not to stockpile. Armstrong's board chose the patriotic, risky route.

But Armstrong Cork was more than a lesson in geopolitics. It was here that I had my baptism in corporate governance. Armstrong's Board of Directors, at that time, was basically an inside board; that is, composed of owners and officer-directors. Out of fifteen directors there were only three outsiders and they lived nearby, knew the firm, its technology, policies and problems. Consequently, it was a simple task to convene all the directors.

At the same time, Rollins College in Winterpark, Florida, was confronted with another kind of governance problem. There was serious pressure to force its president to resign. Time after time the fateful decision had to be postponed because a quorum of the trustees could not be convened. Apparently, the college's trustees were all eminent individuals but removed functionally, geographically and concernedly from the school. They were classic outside directors.

I began to wonder, could it be that outsiders, regardless of their eminence, were simply frosting on the corporate cake? Here at Armstrong I had a superb view of competent, dedicated, on-the-job directors making the key decisions. In contrast, a score of cultured luminaries could not make their big decision at Rollins. Thus began by life-long infatuation with boards of directors.

There were some unbelievable obstacles—boardroom doors were securely closed to all and the corporate "omerta" code of silence prevailed. No director was about to spill the boardroom jelly beans. Moreover, most boardroom data, even when available, defied quantification and measurement.

Five years after my Armstrong experience, I completed "Functional Control and Corporate Performance" while at the University of Massachusetts. My research was analyzed by *Business Week* (11/26/55) in a most complimentary six-column article: "Trends in Boards: More Insiders." I was extremely fortunate to have my first serious research receive such a lengthy and complimentary review. My name appeared 25 times—what greater ego satisfaction could there be?

THE DEAN DAYS

When a deanship offer came from Kent State University, I was ready. By then, at age 40, I was seasoned. Surely I had met enough academic requirements to fill the post—I had published, researched, conducted industrial seminars, and I was the advisor (in the absence of department head titles) to the small management department at University of Massachusetts.

The 1900-student body College of Business Administration at Kent gave me a splendid opportunity to practice the management that I preached. Here was a rather large university, in a geographically optimal location, yet with its business component not accredited by the AACSB. This was a challenge.

First on my agenda was the initiating of a graduate program. Strategically, the odds were in my favor. The undergraduate business enrollment of almost 2,000 guaranteed a solid base of graduate candidates. There was also minimal competition in graduate business education in Northeast Ohio—the latent demand was enormous. Within a radius of fifty miles, there were at least 10,000 qualified college graduates in the hundreds of Ohio industries.

I took to the road to ascertain and spent several weeks visiting corporate headquarters. I was pleased to find that the corporate executives shared my enthusiasm for an M.B.A. program. Thanks to Akron's rubber industry, we started off in high gear. The first class was over-enrolled and there never was a problem of too few bodies during the remainder of my tenure.

The big problem now was to recruit quality faculty along with quality pay. Initially, out of a faculty of fifty-plus, only three members had Ph.D. degrees (several accounting and law degrees were considered terminal); a sorry situation indeed. This deficiency resulted in KSU's business component not being accredited by the AACSB. Challenged by this, I began my accreditation drive by attending the annual AACSB conferences and seminars. Within a year I had recruited five new faculty members with Ph.D. degrees. My networking with deans of AACSB accredited schools, likewise, paid dividends and some of the old stalwarts are still my friends.

Contrary to what is often said, deaning is not an overwhelming, all-encompassing work ordeal. There can be considerable free time—note how many deans dig divots on local golf courses. My mode of escapism was to research and write. The work week in the CBA dean's office consisted of 5 1/2 days. George Bowman, president of Kent State at that time, always reported on Saturday mornings and expected his deans to do likewise. Since the CBA dean was the only one in the hierarchy without an assistant dean, without this luxury it meant that I had to report every Saturday. It was on these Saturday mornings that I bootlegged my research and writing. I finished two texts—*Industrial Administration* (1959) and *Management Decision Simulation* (1960).

Fortuitously, I was able to implement the simulation game at Ford Motor Company's Walton Hill Stamping Plant where I moonlighted on my free evenings, teaching several groups of engineers the fundamentals and significance of management, statistical quality control and business simulation.

Unfortunately, my deanship venture, while still in high gear, came to an abrupt end. After only four seemingly short years, I was offered an Endowed Chair and I went to the University of Oregon as the H.T. Miner Professor of Business Administration.

EX CATHEDRA

At the start of the 1960s, except for Harvard, there were very few bona fide endowed chairs in business administration. Some pseudo varieties did exist—usually the chair holder was expected to scrounge for support funds, thus becoming his/her own endower. But not so with the H.T. Miner Chair at Oregon—it was real, new, and substantially endowed. It provided more salary than I was paid as dean, and it had a liberal travel allowance. My teaching load of three-hours-per-week was flexible. Money was also available for secretarial help and graduate assistants. Ironically, my first graduate assistant, Gary Countryman, climbed a management mountain that towered considerably above mine—he became President/CEO of Liberty Mutual Insurance Company and a director of the Bank of Boston.

The Chair had other significance. It guaranteed my reinstatement as a Rotarian upon my arrival in Eugene—I had become a member while I was dean at Kent State but moving disenfranchises one. It also nudged me onto the local political scene and I was designated a Freeholder on the City of Eugene Budget Committee. Here I had the opportunity to learn a bit of civics. For example, one Good Friday our Freeholders were taken to jail where we were given a penal indoctrination. We learned, for instance, that one must be careful giving inmates items such as newspapers. The more violent could soak the papers in the commode, twist into form and make a lethal weapon.

Another time, we spent a day observing how Eugene's raw sewage was 99.8 percent purified by a recently introduced tertiary purification process. Here the effluent was transformed into potable water, much cleaner than that flowing in the nearby Willamette River.

That nibble at politics led to my serving as Resource Chairman of the Lane County (Oregon) Republican Central Committee. As such, I had the opportunity to meet national Republican figures, most notable Nelson Rockefeller, Barry Goldwater, Richard Nixon and Ronald Reagan.

THE WESTERN ACADEMY OF MANAGEMENT

Having a light and flexible teaching load plus adequate travel funds, I was able to get around, meet colleagues, visit corporate facilities, and, most significantly, to participate in professional endeavors. Fortuitously, the year before I took Horace Greely's advice to "Go West," a dynamic group of future friends initiated the Western Academy of Management (WAM). These visionaries—Howdy Koontz (UCLA), Keith Davis (ASU), Ed Flippo, and Bill Voris (Arizona), Bill Wolf (USC) and other enlightened management scholars—were the greatest group I had ever met. From my first meeting of the Western Academy of Management in Monterey, CA, I knew I had found my niche.

The Western Academy had no dues or membership based on dues. Membership was a function of loyalty, namely, attending an annual meeting at least once every three years. The annual gathering settled all matters including voting on where next year's meeting was to be held. These free souls even went so far as to vote down any and all attempts to have a formalized constitution. The membership wanted informality, flexibility, sociability, and above all, academic stimulation. Unfettered democracy in the manner of the Old West prevailed.

My big Academy of Management break came with my election to a three-year term as Secretary-Treasurer. This was a pushover post since WAM's disestablishmentarian philosophy left little for the secretary to record, and even less for the treasurer to count and conserve. Yet, this was a meaningful opening that led to the presidency of the Western Division of the Academy and a seat on the National Academy's Board of Governors.

These positions facilitated the expansion of a dynamic circle of friends. As an ancient Greek philosopher put it, "Heaven is communing with a handful of completely kindred souls." These were kindred souls and I was now in heaven!

After I moved to Oregon, I revived my interest in corporate governance. The *Business Week* thriller of former years had stimulated my academic adrenalin and now the Miner Chair provided the resources to carry on in depth. After three years of data collecting and analysis, my efforts culminated in *Boards of Directors: Structure and Performance* (1963). This was a deeper and more technical study than my 1955 *Business Week* headliner.

Now the sample was expanded to 101 of our larger corporations. These were divided into 12 industry groups and combined into two stratified samples. The study covered a forty-year time span (from 1922 to 1962), viewed in four non-symmetrical periods. For comparison purposes, I used eleven norms—six growth norms and five productivity norms. The measurements gave the study an arithmetic base suitable for further quantitative analysis.

Subjecting these data to linear regression analysis yielded interesting results—not surprisingly, the more insiders on the board, the better that firm's performance. While the regression lines varied from sample to sample, a hypothetical regression could be ventured encompassing all 101 companies. For this particular sample and time restraints, the regression read: $Y_c = 78.0 + 0.484X$ where the intercept or **a** value measured 78, and the slope or β value was 0.484. In essence, this meant that a one percent increase in the independent variable *X*, the inside director factor, yielded close to one-half a percentage point improvement in the dependent variable *Y*, the company's performance.

Applying the conventional coefficient of correlation test to the twelve industry samples showed a remarkable degree of positive correlation. Eleven of the twelve showed at least a moderate degree of correlation and three of the tests gave a remarkably high degree of correlation. There was no evidence of a negative correlation. In other words, the frequently heard statements claiming superiority for outside boards is distinctly contrary to fact. In major manufacturing enterprises, there is no quantitative evidence supporting the claim that outside boards of directors are superior to inside boards of directors. So it was then (1922-1962) and so it is today despite all the pro-outsider hype.

At first, sales of my ambitious study lagged. Then on April 23, 1964, *The Wall Street Journal* referred to *Boards of Directors* in its front-page "What's News" column. Immediately the University of Oregon Press became swamped with orders and the initial printing soon sold out.

A few months later, *The Wall Street Journal* (9/2/64) proved that lightning can strike twice. In reference to my study, it ran a very flattering lead editorial— "Battle in the Boardroom." This was a splendid endorsement of my research findings on boards of directors. In a matter of weeks, subsequent expanded printings moved as rapidly as torrid porno. This would have been very gratifying to the author except for the fact that the University of Oregon Press, like most university presses, paid no royalties!

SYNERGISTICS INTERNATIONALE

An immediate payoff from *The Wall Street Journal* editorial was a significant increase in the number of invitations to speak on corporate governance. After one such session before 400 Portland leaders, one in the audience invited me to join the board of a newly organized containerized shipping firm, Synergistics Internationale. I was flattered. I had eminent company: Portland's top corporate lawyer; the retired chairman of one of Oregon's major firms; a senior executive of Portland Port Authority and even a leading local churchman— a typical outside board.

We had interesting monthly meetings featuring all-you-could-eat-and-drink shrimp and Chivas Regal. After eight such rewarding sessions, the CEO announced that we were bankrupt. But why? Our excellent staff had produced a number of project proposals that came within centimeters of getting lucrative Federal contracts. Unfortunately, our outside board failed to realize the technology was far ahead of what the industry would accept.

I should have practiced what I preached and left corporate directing to knowledgeable insiders. Eight months after being seated, I was booted from the boardroom, setting a record for directorship brevity.

EDITOR, ACADEMY OF MANAGEMENT JOURNAL

Although no royalties were gleaned from my successful *Boards of Directors: Structure and Performance*, I was compensated in other, perhaps better ways. During the summer of 1966, I received a research grant from Standard Oil Company (NJ); now Exxon. It would keep me busy for sixteen months.

Simultaneously, while I was on sabbatical leave from Oregon, working in New York at Standard Oil headquarters, I received an invitation to serve as the fourth editor of the *Academy of Management Journal.* Dalt McFarland, the *Journal's* second editor, had been designated to "feel me out" and his letter was eventually forwarded from Oregon to Standard's offices. I was jubilant at the prospect of becoming the *Journal's* editor. I considered it to be management education's "editor laureate" and I could not hide my exhilaration from by Exxon hosts. After they had congratulated me and admitted that they subscribed to the *Journal*, someone asked, "But who reads it?"

This deflator helped shape my three-year editorial policy. I was determined to do my utmost to make the *Journal* readable and understandable to both academics and corporate executives. In my attempt to make it understandable, I did gain splendid support from the Academy's leadership. They urged the membership to submit more substantive articles. I supplemented this approach by including, in each *Journal* issue, a contribution from a corporate leader. However, this did not solve the question of who reads it—it is as pertinent today.

Another approach was my personal touch. I tried to write a friendly informal "Editorial Comment" in each quarterly issue; usually zeroing in on a topic extraneous to the *Journal's* contents. My comments covered eclectic themes such as: "The Academy and Ecumenism"; "Corporate Giving and Academic Excellence"; "Can Deans be Taught Management Principles?" This was a major departure from the practice of many editors who restrict their comments only to an introduction of the current issue's contents. This tongue-in-cheek editorial approach, while giving me some kicks, was also doing the same for others. Many Academy members encouraged me to continue in that lively vein, to give a lift to an otherwise dull publication.

It was at this juncture that the Post Office introduced Zip Codes, thereby necessitating a move from our addressograph system to computerization. Somehow this onerous task befell my devoted partner, Gene. Singlehandedly, she took up the Post Office mandate and went through more than 3,000 names of members and subscribers, checking and rechecking addresses, weeding out duplications, and adding the Zips. Then with assistance from several graduate students, the cleansed list went on the computer.

Again we had unexpected problems—the Post Office insisted that we bundle our mailings by Zips, then pack the copies in mail pouches. In primitive fashion this meant binding each of the multiple copy bundles with cord. Simple, you say. Far from it. After a few bindings the cord became a vicious hand-lacerating razor. My graduate student workers and I splattered so much hemoglobin on our bundled copies that someone referred to it as "the bloody *Journal.*" Then as a finale to our primitive mailing process, I, the honorable editor, had to transport the mailing pouches to the Eugene Post Office.

Excluding the unpaid labor of love, this ordeal actually cost my endowed chair several thousands of dollars for student help and editorial assistance. I was not the only one so encumbered—my three predecessors, likewise, labored for love. This inequity was rectified some years later when the Academy's Board began to provide the editor with an annual office budget.

Then, in an after-the-fact gesture, the Board granted the four pioneer editors—Dauten, McFarland, Gordon, and Vance—complimentary life membership in the Academy. On a dollar basis, this would mean we four would have to vie with the 969-year-old Methuselah in order to recoup our personal dollar contributions, adjusted for interest and inflation. But, of course, the honor is priceless!

The *Journal* editorship, though quite time consuming, also was most gratifying; article submissions quadrupled and quality improved. Advertising more than doubled (under Gene's watchful eye) as did our readership. Even the *Journal's* physical appearance changed, from a stapled spine to a square, making it more suitable for book shelves. Also, the shift to a larger print gained the gratitude of hundreds of aging readers with overworked academic eyes.

Now, gazing at the *Journal*, neatly stacked on my shelves, I clearly see the beautiful management panorama that hundreds of contributing authors have created. Most meaningful of this literary vista, however, are the twelve issues I presided over; each introduced by a commentary in readable prose!

STANDARD OIL COMPANY (NJ)/EXXON

While my name was not exactly a household word at Exxon, it did pop up occasionally in reference to my study on boards of directors. On May 20, 1964, Chairman M.J. Rathbone, at the company's annual meeting, quoted generously from my *Boards of Directors* and *Wall Street Journal's* review. At that time Exxon had a completely inside board of directors but was under heavy pressure from the New York Stock Exchange to have at least two outsiders on its board.

Exxon's board personified the classic thesis of Berle and Means, the separation of ownership and control. While the descendants of John D. Rockefeller retained a financial interest, they exercised no effective control. Control was centered in an all-officer inside board. This pattern prevailed in scores of prominent firms such as Alcoa, Armstrong Cork, and Bethlehem Steel. Ironically, my study in praise of inside board performance in the period

1922-1962 appeared just when Exxon faced the NYSE mandate to add outsiders or be banned from the Exchange.

Mr. Rathbone, Exxon's retiring chairman, thought there was sufficient merit in my study to push the research further. He and his board approved a sixteen-month project wherein Exxon paid my salary plus expenses. They even provided an office on the executive floor, close to the new chairman, Michael Haider. This gave me a feeling of great importance—imagine being Mr. Haider's new neighbor!

John O. Larson, Jersey's corporate secretary, was in charge of arranging my itinerary. Larson, then president of the American Society of Corporate Secretaries, had pipelines to most top corporate secretaries and had no difficulty lining up our fifty largest companies and their CEOs for interviewing. Among these were leaders such as Roger Blough (U.S. Steel, now USX), William Blackie (Caterpiller Tractor), Crawford Greenewalt (DuPont), Henry Ford II, Peter Grace, and a score of equally eminent CEOs. In the interviewing process I heard a great variety of views. My job was to synthesize these views particularly as to how valuable outsiders were to their respective boards. As the final part of my research, I wrote a detailed summary of my 115 interviews. This was solely for Exxon's board and continues to remain so.

In the past two decades Exxon's board has undergone substantial change, for which I take no credit. Two outsiders were added even before I began my company visitations, and another two before I finished the project. Today, the board is comprised of nine outsiders and only five insiders. In this transformation, Exxon has moved away from the concept of contact directors. As implied, a contact director is an officer-director serving as a resource person, an expert on some aspect of the company's business. This policy once assured that all Exxon directors served in some essential capacity. It was this individual expertise, synthesized in the board, that made Exxon number one.

Today, Exxon's contact directors have been replaced by Wall Street's Old Boys Club. Of note is Exxon's sorry record in several of its recent diversification ventures: failure at selling office automation, failure in its shale oil and tar sand gambles, and failure in its $1.2 billion Reliance Electric gamble to develop an energy saving small motor. Topping these ventures—or misadventures—is the catastrophic Valdez 10-million-gallon oil spill and the half-million gallon underwater pipeline oil spill into the Arthur Kill Waterway, a main shipping channel in New York Harbor.

To their credit, however, Exxon's directors took two big environmental steps—they named a marine scientist to the board and subsequently created an environmental watchdog post, headed by a senior vice president. Shades of the old so-effective contact directors!

During my extended stay at Exxon, I occasionally expounded on how easily a New York-headquartered firm could become the plaything of New York financiers. I must have sounded rabidly New Dealish, but it is my conviction that when boards and banks play footsie, we can begin to write corporate obituaries. Imagine my dismay when, a few years later, Exxon made a move from its long-time habitat at Rockefeller Center to a new impressive Exxon building on the Avenue of the Americas. This was solid evidence that Exxon was forever to be a handmaiden of the Wall Street gang! However, in 1989, Exxon announced it was moving its headquarters—and board—to a Dallas, Texas suburb. This was a giant step in the direction of correcting a geographical flaw which, obviously, was impeding productivity.

Even if my monumental study under Exxon's auspices continues to collect dust, I will always feel righteous about my inside-board conclusions. Regardless of my views and recommendations, I am proud of my association with Exxon and my fly-speck contribution to its board.

CONGRESSMAN WRIGHT PATMAN

Another exhilarating moment in my career occurred in Washington, D.C. on April 17, 1971. I had written an article on how Penn Central's board's behavior led to the giant railroad holding company's derailment. The article, "Penn Central—A Lesson for Bank Boards and One-Bank Holding Companies," was published in *Bankers Magazine* (1971).

Wright Patman, Chairman of the House of Representatives Committee on Banking and Currency, was impressed by this article and invited me to testify as an expert witness on hearings for HR5700, The Banking Reform Act of 1971; a bill aimed at encouraging competition in the banking industry.

Testifying on the Hill was thrilling in a masochistic sort of way. Seated on their elevated judicial benches were nineteen of the committee's congressmen. As it turned out, I was the only witness for most of the morning's session. A few of the lawmakers tried to be friendly, but most were incisive as lawyers tend to be. Also, some of my inquisitors seemed to have predispositions favoring the banking industry. However, I had my own cheering section—my wife, seated several rows behind me. Gene's contribution was to keep score, jotting the names and nasty comments of my "Torquemadas" (the bad guys) and the names of those in my favor (the good guys).

In the years following this experience, it gave me great satisfaction when one of the good guys received favorable press or was reelected; I had even greater satisfaction when one of the bad guys flubbed! Also, in the ensuing years of the great Savings and Loan debacle, I had great satisfaction recalling that some of the proposed HR5700 reforms dealt with greater scrutiny of bank directors.

My stint as a Congressional expert witness probably was not all in vain. I like to think of myself as a corporate governance Jeremiah in this case, railing against incompetent, disinterested, conniving directors. During my inquisition,

I tried to tell the Congressional Committee that a crook or dupe on the Penn Central Board was no different from a comparable inadequate on a bank board. Several Congressional banker-buddies were horrified by my remark. One even said he would never send his children to the University of Oregon for fear they might be adulterated by such views!

Unfortunately, today's record shows that out of several thousand derelict directors in the Savings and Loan ripoff, perhaps a hundred received some sort of punishment. While a handful of insiders, CEOs and their henchmen were incarcerated, virtually no outside directors were severely punished. A number of headliner cases—the Charles Keating Lincoln Savings and Loan—dragged on into the 1990s. Five prominent senators were embarrassingly if not illegally involved in Keating's high-stakes shenanigans.

Perhaps the best thing that came out of my testimony on the Hill was the 80-page transcript, recorded verbatim in the *Congressional Record* for Thursday, April 22, 1971. It remains in perpetuity among so many other monuments and memorials gracing our Capital City!

THE STOKELY CHAIR

When the climbing is good and easy, there can be no unattainable heights. By 1974 I had held the H.T. Miner Chair at Oregon for almost fifteen years. Having given it heavy wear over these years, it was now beginning to need "new Upholstery." At this appropriate time, I received an invitation to be the first to fill the newly endowed William B. Stokely Chair in Management at the College of Business Administration, University of Tennessee, Knoxville.

A new Chair is like a new car—even if the old machine still works and evokes many fond memories, you can't beat the thrill, feel and smell of the new. Naturally, the offer enticed me. Besides, Knoxville, located at the foothills of the Great Smokies, was much closer to our roots, the Anthracite Region, where both our mothers still survived. The new location was also closer to the meaningful centers of corporate governance. I could actually commute to dozens of boardrooms in a few hours. This greatly increased my span of activity and boosted my presence in the vital field of corporate governance. The new Stokely Chair was integral to every subsequent height to which I aspired. More in due course.

PRESIDENT, ACADEMY OF MANAGEMENT

My upward progression in the Academy started with my five-year officer stint in the Western Academy, topped by its presidency. Then followed three years as *Journal* editor; three more years as founding editor of the Academy's *Newsletter*, and then my election, in 1973, as the Academy's president.

Prior to my election, the Academy's officers were appointed junta-style by an informal group of mostly past presidents. Democracy caught up with the Academy in my day. There were six contenders in this first real election which, to my surprise and joy, made me the first democratically-elected president of the Academy. I had climbed my mountain—so it seemed.

Stokely Chair support, particularly a near-zero teaching load, facilitated my presidency. I had funds and time to travel and I could even write speeches for my visits to the annual gatherings of the five regional divisions. I was even invited to the Mountain-Plains Management Conference. This was a hyper-independent group of professors who refused to work directly with the Academy—theirs was the free spirit of mountaineers, plainsmen, clod busters, which I admire to this day. They felt the Academy was getting too big, too bureaucratic, and they adamantly refused to consider becoming the Academy's sixth regional division. I was honored to be the first Academy president to formally address this group of independent souls.

One of my major objectives as *AM* president was to establish a financial system and stability. In this endeavor Rosemary Pledger, Secretary—and Bob Coffey, Treasurer—both Fellows—were exceedingly helpful. These stalwarts—and others—helped me leave my mark on the rapidly evolving Academy.

My presidential day of glory came on Friday-the-13th, August 1976, at the Academy's 36st Annual Meeting at Crown Center Hotel, Kansas City, Missouri. My luncheon presidential address, attended by over 900 members—a record at that time—was on the theme of "Management Minutemen." The topic was a natural since this was the year of the United States Bicentennial. During my talk I singled out about twenty of our most dedicated management minutemen—Keith Davis, Howdy Koontz, Dalt McFarland, Joe McGuire, Frank Moore, Bill Newman, George Steiner, Bill Voris, and others—stressing how each contributed in different and inimitable ways to our discipline.

The common thread meshing all this was the Athenian concept of Entelechy, a notion developed by Aristotle, the second "president"—after Plato—of the original Academy. That illustrious Greek took three little words—*εχω* (I have) *τελος* (my goal) *ευ* (within). This belief that "I have my purpose or goal within myself" propelled our patriot minutemen two centuries ago just as it propels our management minutemen today. It is manifest in our striving to maximize ourselves, each in his or her own way. I pointed to the identity of the two Academies in their mutual search for truth and the advancement of learning through free discussion and research.

One further highlight of this meeting was my intense desire to introduce our Academy to the international scene. I invited two personal friends from abroad—Professor Ronald Edgerton, Head of the Polytechnic of Central London, and Dr. Boris Milner, Deputy Director, Institute for Systems Studies, Moscow, U.S.S.R. Dr. Milner was so impressed with the Academy, before he left, he extended to Gene and me an invitation from the All-Union Council of Ministers for Science and Technology in the Soviet Union. Without hesitancy we accepted and spent three weeks as guests of the Soviets. Needless to say, we wore the "red carpet" thin!

That visit, in 1977, took us to a dozen institutes and universities, including the Baltics. My objective was to set up an exchange program. In this respect, Mike McManus, one of the Academy's young beavers, proved to be a super star. He put together a superb proposal to present to our State Department. He also secured commitments from Corning Glass Works to help fund the exchange. I approached Control Data, International Paper, and also had encouragement from the Smithsonian and my own University of Tennessee. All signs were distinctly positive.

Then abruptly the bubble burst—my hard work and first-stage success came to naught when the Academy's Board of Governors, at its 1977 meeting, dragged its feet and then flatly refused to deal with the Soviets. As past president, I had no control over the board's agenda and found my proposal scheduled for the very tail end of the meeting. This is a familiar tactic, sure to kill a proposal. It was a bitter experience. As president during the previous year, my "troops" (the board) tended to follow me; as past president, my "troops" were charging in different directions!

This was a costly blunder, a lost opportunity for the Academy. We had been handed an invitation on a Soviet platter and we ignored it. It would have established the Academy on the international management scene. Thus we missed a chance to contribute to the transformation of Eastern Europe.

They say it takes a big person to forgive; obviously, I am not so big. I still harbor disappointment and rancor toward the board of governors, my peers, who, for whatever reasons, threw away a golden opportunity.

WILLIAM F. GLUECK

Another bittersweet memory was the untimely death of fellow-climber, Bill Glueck, at age 45. Bill was the only Academy president to die in office. I admired his talents and dedication and published his first article while I was editor of the *Journal*. Thus began an all-too-brief association in which Bill considered me his mentor.

During my *AM* vice-presidency, I had to recommend a member to serve as *Proceedings* editor for the Thirty-Fourth Annual Meeting which was to be held in Seattle, WA. Immediately my choice was Bill Glueck and the Board of Governors unanimously agreed. However, we had a dilemma. Our budget was pitifully low and we even discussed abandoning the *Proceedings*. As a compromise, the Board suggested that we cut the size and cost of the *Proceedings*. What a challenge for me!

The conventional *Proceedings* consists of a fraction of accepted articles printed in full, and lists only titles and authors of presumed second-rate papers. Now, however, considering our mini-budget and the egalitarian spirit of the 1970s, the board felt that a handful of mortals—the reviewers—should not act as supreme judges, giving few papers coverage and exposure while relegating the majority to fly-speck space. How could this be accomplished? By considering all the articles!

Bill took on this yeoman's task and spent most of the spring and summer of 1976 reading all 138 of the accepted papers, digesting each to paragraph size. This was a lifesaver for the Academy but an awful burden on Bill. Fortunately, this practice was abolished the following year. While the 1976 *Proceedings* will never measure up—by weight or dimension—with other Academy *Proceedings*, Bill's issue had "heart." He saved our *Proceedings* and in the egalitarian spirit of the times, gave every contributor equal opportunity!

Bill had a dramatic progression in academe and publishing. At the time of his death, he had five texts under contract and under way. He was elected to the Academy's Board of Governors, to FAR, to the Fellows of the Academy, and served as chairman of the Business Policy Division. He became Distinguished Professor of Management at the University of Georgia.

A few months after his death, I delivered the eulogy at Bill's Presidential Luncheon, where he would have presided. It was my saddest Academy function. I mentioned that Bill intended to talk about how modern management was gradually devolving to the Byzantine, characterized by dishonesty, intrigue, machinations, and duplicity. Yet, as Bill fondly recalled, there was something majestic and beautiful in the Byzantine culture—the icons that he loved and the brilliant mosaics. And, as I pointed out, each of us is a fragment in the management mosaic.

I concluded this sad parting with the words of Caius Valerius Catullus, the Roman poet's tribute at his brother's grave: "Frater Ave, Atque Vale," Hail Brother and Farewell!

PRESIDENT, THE FOUNDATION FOR ADMINISTRATIVE RESEARCH

The Foundation for Administrative Research (FAR) was founded in 1965 by a group of Academy past presidents, for the purpose of channeling gifts and grants, tax free, into the Academy. In order to satisfy Internal Revenue Service Section 501(C)(6) requirements for both-end tax-free status, FAR's board had to be completely independent from the Academy's board.

This IRS rule was misunderstood by some of the Academy's board members who had federalist notions for the Academy. These centralizers wanted to have direct control over every aspect of Academy life. This meant that FAR had to seek approval for all its actions from the Academy's board even though this would be in direct violation of the IRS rule. Consequently, it would mean no tax-free status for donors.

I became FAR's president at this critical juncture, in 1975, after Dalt McFarland had suffered through phase one of the impasse. When the Academy's board voted 6-3 to abolish FAR, I threatened to take the issue to the Academy's membership whereupon someone then made a motion for a second vote, reversing the first vote 3-6. FAR survived but the feud continued.

One consequence of this impasse was a go-slow policy for FAR. My board recommended low visibility with a consequent diminishing of its fund raising activities. I relinquished this dormant presidency in 1984 but remained on the board through 1988 when the Academy-FAR feud was terminated.

PRESIDENT, ASSOCIATION FOR BUSINESS SIMULATION AND EXPERIENTIAL LEARNING

In 1975, I held three presidencies concurrently: AM, FAR, and ABSEL, the *Association for Business Simulation and Experiential Learning*. ABSEL was a new and small group of 300-400 enthusiasts of business game structuring and playing. Bernard (Bernie) Keys, presently director, Center for Business Simulation at Georgia Southern University, and I co-founded the organization. While I had a keen interest in this area, having published *Management Decision Simulation* (1960), my co-founder's interest had no bounds.

While my writing and researching subsequently moved me full-force into corporate governance, Bernie continued on the ABSEL route and produced several texts and numerous papers and games in this area. Although my contribution to ABSEL was more subdued and confined mostly to panel participation, my devotion was rewarded when, in 1987, I was elected ABSEL's first Fellow. I treasure this recognition by my peer simulators.

NATIONAL ASSOCIATION OF CORPORATE DIRECTORS

Of all the would-be professions, corporate governance is probably the one in most disarray. Medicine, law and teaching have rigid entrance requirements, codes of ethics, self-policing, continued education and all other hallmarks expected of a profession, but corporate directors and boards have virtually none of these. Actually, a corporate CEO can pick a dozen people at random and declare them his board—no examination is necessary, no norms, no certification. This is the chaotic field I chose to study; beginning with Armstrong Cork in 1950, continuing with Exxon and other reputable corporations, culminating in numerous research articles, speeches, and four books on the subject.

In 1977, Stephen Cummins, John Nash, and others sought to rectify this sorry state. They initiated the National Association of Corporate Directors (NACD) which, hopefully, would provide research, publications, continuing education, regular meetings, and conferences. Ultimately, this uplifting of corporate governance would yield something akin to Certified Public Director (CPD), comparable to Certified Public Accountant (CPA) and similar certification.

I was a member of NACD's initial Directors Council on Corporate Governance. Upon NACD's juncture with the American Management Association (AMA), this became the NACD Board of Directors. My most noteworthy contributions were a series of articles published by NACD's *Director's Monthly* plus lengthy items for the *Special Report Series.* Subsequently, I was named Chairman of the NACD Editorial Board. Another interesting aspect was my appointment as the first Dean of the NACD Institute. The Institute was launched in October 1980 on St. Simons Island, GA. Although this was a great stride toward certification and professionalization, the Institute proved to be a generation ahead of boardroom acceptance. After a second attempt the following year, it was abandoned.

So good an idea as the Institute is bound to be revived; in fact, such action is currently under way. Meanwhile, the NACD continues its many other activities—publications, headed by the *Directors Monthly*, seminars with instruction by its board members, headed by President John Nash.

Capstoning these laudable activities is the annual conference. Over the years this has been my favorite. Because of many noncompensated NACD endeavors, John Nash has given me a "freeloader's ticket" to partake in these interesting events. And I do, with gusto!

DIRECTORS AND BOARDS

In the late 1970s I was enjoying a polygamous relationship with the two prime movers in corporate governance—The *NACD* and *Directors and Boards* (*D&B*). The latter was the handiwork of Stanley Foster Reed, publisher of *D&B* from 1976 through 1981, when the periodical was taken over by Hay Associates. I had the pleasure of serving both owners, first as Book Review Editor, then as Contributing Editor.

Stanley Reed was a superb entrepreneur. In addition to *D&B*, he initiated *Mergers and Acquisitions* plus other periodicals. Working control was put in the hands of his talented daughter, Alexandra, a Ph.D. (in French) who quickly mastered the intricacies of corporate governance while earning an M.B.A.

D&B blossomed but after five years it succumbed to the dynamic conglomerator, Milton L. Rock, and his Hays Associates. Then came the "reverse" synergy. In less than five years, Hays Associates capitulated to the international advertising agent, Saatchi and Saatchi. This was the classic case of the minnow, gobbled by a bigger fish which itself turned into barracuda bait.

Among my souvenirs of this era is my "Rock Apple," a beautiful crystal apple, sculpted by Corning Glass Works, with my name unobtrusively etched in the base. It was a gift from Milton L. Rock, the White Knight who was jousted out of the tourney.

PRESIDENT, NORTH AMERICAN MANAGEMENT COUNCIL

The North American Management Council—NAMCO—became successor to CIPM, the North American component of CIOS, Conseil International pour l'Organisation Scientifique. CIOS flourished for more than a half century after its inception in 1926. My wife and I still have wonderful memories of our first CIOS World Management Congress, sponsored by CIPM and David Rockefeller at the New York Hilton back in 1963. Subsequently, we participated in other CIOS triennial meetings; notably in New Delhi and Lima, Peru. But as with all beings, CIOS progressively became arthritic and barely dragged along. CIOS tried to rejuvenate its North American component, CIPM, by providing several thousand dollars in seed money.

Early in 1981, CIOS President Walter Piazza Tanguis, former Finance Minister of Peru, convened a board meeting at AMA's New York headquarters. Here he introduced me as the new—and first—president of the North American Management Council. Beginning from scratch, my first duty was to appoint a board of directors. We then concentrated on adding other institutional members to our prime booster, the AMA, and laying the groundwork for the next CIOS World Management Conference in New York which, incidentally, took place in 1989, long after I had abdicated. Coincidentally, David Rockefeller again presided over the Congress, as he had many years ago when New York played host.

When I assumed the NAMCO presidency, it was with the understanding that I would only serve for a three-year term. I did this judiciously, realizing that 800 miles separated me from NAMCO's headquarters. As I have preached during my corporate governance life, directors living at a great distance from headquarters can be a liability. Now here I was, proving my point. I enjoyed building NAMCO, but commuting to New York became a drag and I was relieved when my three years were over.

VICE-CHANCELLOR, INTERNATIONAL ACADEMY OF MANAGEMENT

In 1977, I was elected a Fellow of the International Academy of Management, a select group of 200 outstanding leaders from thirty-plus countries. This honor, together with being listed in *Who's Who in the World* in 1978, and earlier in *Who's Who in America* (1966), gave me a feeling of global euphoria.

The prime mover in the IAM was its Chancellor, Harold (Howdy) Koontz, who served from 1976-1981. As Howdy's chancellorship neared the end of its six-year term, he and Robert K. Mueller, Chairman, Arthur D. Little, Inc., and also Vice-Chancellor of IAM, urged me to become a candidate to succeed Mueller. Thus I became the new vice-chancellor.

At this juncture, I want to dedicate a few lines to the laudable, lovable, ebullient Howdy Koontz, my cherished friend and fellow mountaineer. Howdy wrote a dozen texts and scores of articles, but his *Management Principles* set the pattern for management education for the next three decades. His "Management Jungle" analogy continues to be quoted worldwide. His attributes and accomplishments could cover this entire book. Until his death, in 1984, Howdy's name was synonymous with all the progress the Academy, and the discipline, had made in the past quarter century.

Howdy's term as Chancellor of the IAM ended with Ivor Kenny's election to this prestigious post. Thus I became Ivor's Vice-Chancellor, serving from 1981 to 1987. Soon after my induction, I invited the new chancellor to visit the United States and to meet his American Fellows. We met at the New York Hilton and at the AMA headquarters. This was the first in a series of more regular meetings.

Within a year, Ivor scheduled a meeting in Ireland, his homeland, at the world-renowned Ashford Castle. The IAM Fellows, predominantly from the United States, were graciously hosted in this prestigious castle where a few months later, President and Mrs. Reagan would spend several days as guests of England's Prime Minister, Mrs. Thatcher. Our Irish hosts also extended our meeting to Dublin where the Bank of Ireland put out a big welcome. At our evening session, I, as Vice-Chancellor, had the honor to introduce Ireland's "Theosich" or Prime Minister, Garret FitzGerald.

Then, in 1983, upon the election of Taiwan's Prime Minister Sun Yun-Suan as a Fellow of the IAM, I had the honor to be invited to Taiwan to personally induct the Prime Minister. The Prime Minister seemed particularly pleased to welcome someone from Knoxville, Tennessee. It was here, many years ago, that he was employed by the TVA—Tennessee Valley Authority—as a fledgling engineer!

Indeed, we were afforded regal treatment. We were housed in the elegant Grand Hotel and were provided with a limo which flew the flags of both countries. Our visit also took us to Southern Taiwan, to Kaohsiung, where we had the pleasure of visiting with Dr. Chang Pin-Chun and his gracious wife Chin-Oh. The Changs happen to be parents of Chwen-Chuan, wife of my nephew, David Howitz.

Our R.O.C. hosts introduced us to several universities where I lectured to students and held seminars with faculty. They put on a seemingly endless series of banquets, climaxed by a formal dinner at the Executive Yuan. Here we spent an incomparable evening with key members of the Prime Minister's Cabinet and their gracious wives, first among whom was my dinner partner, Mrs. Sun Yun-Suan. According to protocol, Gene was the Prime Minister's dinner companion.

Another memorable IAM meeting took place in Armenia. It was sponsored by our eminent Soviet Fellow, Candidate Member of the Politburo and Academician, Jermen Gvishiani, and by the Council of Ministers of the Armenian S.S.R. Among the highlights of our Yerevan stay were several concerts including native son Katchaturian's Ballet, "Gaiane." Then there was the visit to the Monument commemorating the million-plus Armenians who were massacred by the Turks in 1915. And, of course, there was historic Mt. Ararat, visible from our Commissar's "Palace" suite. There was also an historic meeting with Art Bedeian's famous cousin, the state sculptor of Armenia, Hmayak Bdeyan. Before we left for Armenia, Art—now a past president of the Academy of Management—asked if Gene and I would contact his cousin whom he had never met. Upon request, our Soviet-Armenian hosts arranged a meeting.

My IAM swan song took place in Barcelona in the Fall of 1987. With the changing of the guard, Thomas Horton, President and CEO of American Management Association, assumed my Vice-Chancellorship.

DEAN OF FELLOWS OF THE ACADEMY OF MANAGEMENT

Finally, I had reached the top in less than four decades after Dean Balderston had given me the opportunity of a lifetime, to teach at Wharton. In 1984, I was elected Dean of Fellows by my 85 voting peers. The Fellows of the Academy of Management comprise slightly more than one percent of the 9,000 Academy members. I had been elected a Fellow in 1967 when Ralph Davis was Dean. Needless to say, following in his footsteps now was the ultimate achievement. I was flattered to be included with the other past deans—George Steiner, John Mee, and Bill Newman.

Being Dean of Fellows is a real sinecure. The only formality is to preside at the annual gathering of the clan. Fellows have no obligations except to attend a dinner session during the annual Academy of Management meeting. Usually this takes place at a plush club or restaurant where camaraderie prevails. If one is unable to attend, all it takes is a note to the dean to express regrets, in order to continue in good graces.

Although I have referred to the deanship as a sinecure, each dean must contend with changing circumstance. My concern was with our need to reproduce Fellows; a very stringent election process makes it difficult to gain admittance to the "club." For instance, a nominee must get a positive endorsement from at least 60 percent of the voting Fellows. Over the years, this stringency had resulted in a plateauing of Fellows to about 85 actives and 20 inactives. Considering the growth of the Academy and its number of outstanding members, it was logical and imperative to add more Fellows. My plea was for the membership to do a more conscientious job in searching for Fellow nominees in our bulging Academy membership. If not, we would be on a self-destruct course. This led to a special membership search committee, appointed by my successor.

As Dean, I tried to follow in the pattern of my predecessors. The Fellowship, as they saw it, consisted of management scholars, from all sectors of our discipline, who had made their mark. They were recognized contributors who added to the fund of knowledge through teaching, writing, researching and professional activities.

At this juncture there is no mandate that Fellows contribute more, but as we know, anyone who has tasted success can hardly be restrained from trying again and again.

EPILOGUE

At this point, as I prepare to descend from my management mountain, I find myself relaxed and fully satisfied. My euphoria comes from the feeling that I have made a number of contributions to teaching, researching, writing and professional organizations. My real pride, however, is in the depth and scope of my research in the neglected field of corporate governance where, in addition to a score of articles, I also completed four original texts. The latest of these, *Corporate Leadership: Boards, Directors and Strategy* (1983), should be a big stepping stone for future researchers in corporate governance. While I have been mostly alone in this field of endeavor, each year it is gratifying to see more and more papers on the subject being presented by young members of the Academy. It is a good feeling to be cited and quoted even when some of the new researchers do not agree with me. It is their interest that counts.

Yet, I am not resting on my laurels. I hope to carry my ideas on boards and other matters to Eastern Europe. Early in 1990, I had a call from Dr. Jonas Grigonis, Rector (President) of Vilnius University, Lithuania, reminding me that Gene and I have a standing invitation to be the University's guests. I accepted his invitation with alacrity. My big dream fulfillment there would be to help structure a top-notch graduate business school at Vilnius University plus contributing in the areas of my technical competencies; production management and corporate governance.

Alas, Gene, my plane-seat companion, having covered 35 countries with me including three visits to Lithuania, would not accompany me on this journey. She delegated her nephew, Michael J. Dabrishus, who is an Archivist at the

University of Arkansas Library, to occupy her seat next to me. This would be a golden opportunity for him to browse through sixteenth-century Vilnius University's Library and to delve into dust-entombed manuscripts of Lithuania's past.

There is even more recent archival documentation that needs to be brought to the free world's attention, such as the nefarious Adolf Hitler-Josef Stalin 1940 secret agreement to divide Eastern Europe. This Fascist-Communist plot, while never recognized by the United States and its allies has, nevertheless, been the legal instrument for fifty years of Soviet subjugation. Almost half a million Lithuanians plus comparable numbers of Latvians and Estonians were exiled to Siberia in a single decade after this diabolical pact was signed.

My intended sojourn to Vilnius, coming at a tumultuous time during Lithuania's Re-Declaration of Independence, had to be put on hold. Evidently, Gorbachev's "glasnost" did not apply to the Baltic captive nation. All foreigners were ordered out of Lithuania and visas were suspended. Even Senator D'Amato (R-NY) could not get in! But I am patient—I will outsit Gorbachev on this one!

IN RETROSPECT

In detailing my management-mountain adventures, it seemed natural for me to begin with my days at the Wharton School of Commerce and Finance. That was the turning point in my life.

Back to my chronological beginning on May 5, 1915, there were no cataclysmic events, except World War I, heralding my coming. As for my rearing, I grew up in the most unauspicious of times in Minersville, Schuylkill County, Pennsylvania; deep in Upper Appalachia's South Anthracite coal fields.

Minersville, sprawling like Rome over seven small hills, had 23 churches, catering largely to ethnic clientele, and sixty-some saloons, democratically open to all. The town population of 9,000 at its peak, was surrounded by a dozen coal mining hamlets which we referred to as "patches." Each had its own gritty mine. The mounting, spreading culm banks, slowly swallowing the host patches, testified to the industry's vigor.

In my grandparents' and parents' time, this was beautiful rolling-hill country, covered with oaks, white pine, hemlock and profusely dotted with mountain laurel. But during my time, absentee coal barons began to desecrate the land by strip mining and clear cutting the virgin forests. In effect, the Anthracite area was transformed into a Badlands after the rapacious coal barons gleaned all they could and retired to Philadelphia's Main Line.

Living in the coal fields meant frequent adjusting to the fortunes of the industry. The cyclical pattern was caused by a variety of reasons, the prime one being periodic United Mine Workers strikes. An ambitious miner could work hard during the lush periods, save a few dollars, then lose all in the prolonged strikes.

Unfortunately, my graduation from Minersville High School, in 1932, came at the abyss of the Great Depression. Although I was an honor student and ranked scholastically high in my class of almost 100, the future was grim. There were no jobs nor scholarships to be had. My father's meager income from coal mining simply could not justify sending me away to school.

Then suddenly there was a ray of hope. St. Charles Borromeo Seminary in Overbrook, Pennsylvania, began its annual recruitment for priest candidates. Tuition and board came to the almost-affordable sum of $100 per year for the preparatory years. This was my break—I could earn a degree after my fifth year. With this expectation in mind, I was glad to be accepted at St. Charles.

The country was still mired in the Depression even at the time I received my Bachelor of Arts degree in 1937. Eventually, I completed the ten-year philosophy-theology program in nine years and was ordained in June 1941. To this day I remain grateful to the Roman Catholic Church for the splendid education I received. My nine years of schooling in the liberal arts included, among other subjects, four years of Greek, two of Hebrew and four years of Psychology (presented in Latin). I also studied the language of my ancestors, Lithuanian, the oldest Indo-European language, for nine years.

However, unappreciated at the time was the Spartan/martinet discipline at the Seminary. For example, most irritating was the fact that we were not allowed newspapers, magazines, radios or movies. The only hint we had of the outside world came surreptitiously, through some of our more benign professors. Naturally, there were scores of comparable irritants. All in all, this was the perfect place for robots. It was a conformist's delight, this egalitarian, authoritarian and miserable gulag existence!

A splendid opportunity came my way while I was stationed at a parish in decrepit North Philadelphia. Seeking to broaden my horizons, I dared to apply for admission to Pennsylvania's Wharton School. The financial world had always intrigued me, perhaps because our family always seemed to lack cash! Along with President Eisenhower, we, too, were poor but deluded ourselves into thinking we were middle class. Seriously, I was always in awe of the Wharton School and its illustrious faculty.

Considering my meager beginnings and all the handicaps of growing up in a coal mining community, I must put in a plug for the American system. The opportunities are great for those who seek them. I would not, however, recommend taking the path of opportunity I took. That was a different time, a different place; hopefully, there shall never be one like it again.

PUBLICATIONS

1955

American industries. Englewood Cliffs, NJ: Prentice-Hall.
Functional directors and corporate performance in large scale industrial enterprise. University of Massachusetts.

1959

Industrial administration. New York: McGraw-Hill.

1960

Management decision simulation. New York: McGraw-Hill.

1961

Industrial structure and policy. Englewood Cliffs, NJ: Prentice-Hall.

1963

Elements of linear programming. University of Oregon.

1964

Boards of directors: Structure and performance. Eugene, OR: University of Oregon Press.
The bank vice presidency: Last stop on the line? *The Bankers Magazine, 147*(4), 45-54.
Nepotism and management succession. Faculty Study Series, University of Oregon.

1965

Management decision simulation: A computer manual. University of Oregon.
Management simulation games. *Sales Marketing News, XI*(7), 5-7.
Do boards of trustees need surgery? *The Modern Hospital, 104*(6), 105-110.

1966

Higher education for the executive elite. *California Management Review, VII*(4), 21-30.

Subject of "ivy in the boardroom." *Time* (July 1), p. 38.
Want to sit on the board of a big company? *Business Week* (July 23).

1967

Business gaming as an aid to manager development. In H.B. Maynard (ed.), *Handbook of business administration* (pp. 457-470). New York: McGraw-Hill.
Use of a performance evaluation model for research in business gaming. *Academy of Management Journal, 10*(1), 27-38.
The academy and ecumenism [Editorial]. *Academy of Management Journal, 10* (4), 326-328.
Can deans be taught management principles? [Editorial]. *Academy of Management Journal, 10*(3), 218-221.
Zip codes and management theory [Editorial]. *Academy of Management Journal, 10*(2), 104-106.

1968

The corporate director: A critical evaluation. Homewood, IL: Dow Jones-Irwin.
Corporations and culture [Editorial]. *Academy of Management Journal, 11*(4), 364-366.
Campus crisis [Editorial]. *Academy of Management Journal, 11*(3), 248-250.
Men for hire [Editorial]. *Academy of Management Journal, 11*(2), 140-142.
Corporate giving and academic excellence [Editorial]. *Academy of Management Journal, 11*(1), 6-8.

1969

With C. Gray. The impact of mergers on management theory. *Academy of Management Journal, 12*(2), 153-167.
The management of multi-industry corporations. In *Proceedings*, Academy of Management (pp. 29-44).
Chargoggagoggmanchaugagoggchaubunagungamaugg [Editorial]. *Academy of Management Journal, 12*(4), 406-408.
Professor Peregrinus [Editorial]. *Academy of Management Journal, 12*(2), 142-144.
Student power: Fact or fizzle [Editorial]. *Academy of Management Journal, 12*(1), 6-8.

1970

Business simulation gaming for teaching and research. In *Proceedings*, Oklahoma Consortium on Research Development, Oklahoma Christian College, July.

1971

Management in the conglomerate era. New York: John Wiley-Interscience.

New dimensions for boards of directors. *The Conference Board Record, VIII*(11), 533-557.

Black power in the board room: Token or reality? *Business Horizons, XIV*(3), 81-88.

Penn Central—A lesson for bank boards and one-bank holding companies. *The Bankers Magazine, 154*(1), 77-84.

Testimony as expert witness for Congressman Wright Patman, House of Representatives Committee on Banking and Currency, HR 5700, The Banking Reform Act. *Congressional Record*, April 22.

1972

Toward a collegial office of the president. *California Management Review, XV*(1), pp. 106-116.

1973

Administrators on hospital governing boards: A growing trend. *Trustee, Journal for Hospital Governing Boards,* American Hospital Association, 26(1), 20-26.

1974

From precedent through philosophy with management thought. In J.W. McGuire (Ed.), *Contemporary management* (pp. 116-120). Englewood Cliffs, NJ: Prentice-Hall.

1975

Women directors—From bedroom to boardroom. *Survey of Business,* University of Tennessee (May/June), 4-7.

Are socially responsible corporations good investment risks? *Management Review,* American Management Associations (August), 18-24.

1976

Inside versus outside directors. *Special Report,* National Association of Corporate Directors, *IV,* 1-24.
Management detente style: USA/USSR managers are gradually getting to look alike. *Survey of Business,* University of Tennessee, *11*(3), 22-25.
Potential for peoples' capitalism in corporate pension plans. *International Review of Economics & Business,* Milan, Italy, *XXIII*(7), 638-650.

1977

The Sunshine Belt: New home for corporate headquarters. *University of Oklahoma Research Bureau, 2*(1), 5-10.
Director diversity: New dimensions in the boardroom. *Directors and Boards*(Spring), 40-50.

1978

The SEC and corporate cloning. *Director's Monthly, 2*(9), 34-36.
Corporate governance: Assessing corporate performance by boardroom attributes. *Journal of Business Research, 6*(3), 203-220.

1979

Soviets free enterprise [Distinguished Guest Editorial]. *American Journal of Small Business, III*(3), 1-4.

1980

Shared executive authority: Chaos or collegiality? *Directors and Boards* (Fall), 5-10.
Springboard: The french connection. *Directors and Boards, 5*(3), 33-34.

1982

Business heroes from Homer to Horatio to Horatio to Hawley. In *The evolving science of management: A tribute to Harold Smiddy.* New York: American Management Associations.
On corporate leadership. *Director's Monthly, National Association of Corporate Directors, 6*(9), 1-5.

1983

Corporate leadership : Boards, directors and strategy. New York: McGraw-Hill.

Bank directors: Not a cavalier experience. *Director's Monthly, National Association of Corporate Directors, 7*](4), 1-4.

1984

Innovation, strategy and boards of directors. In *Proceedings*, International IIASA Conference, Laxenberg, Austria.

1985

Tennessee Valley Authority Public directors. *Director's Monthly, National Association of Corporate Directors, 9*(7), 7-15.

Detente II for directors and commissars. *Director's Monthly, National Association of Corporate Directors, 9*(2), 1-14.

1986

Interested owners. *Director's Monthly, National Association of Corporate Directors, 10*(7), 3-10.

1987

Director certification: Just down the road. *Director's Monthly, National Association of Corporate Directors, 11*(10), 8-9.

1988

RSVP. *Director's Monthly, National Association of Corporate Directors, 12*(10), 15.

1989

Boards of directors: Inside/outside, what's the difference? *Director's Monthly, National Association of Corporate Directors, 13*(12), 7-9.

1990

Is there really a difference between inside and outside directors? *Across the Board, 27*(11), 15-17.

Improvising and Muddling Through

VICTOR H. VROOM

In recent years I have been involved in the teaching of a course at Yale called Individual and Group Behavior. IGB, as it has been affectionately called by the students, is an experiential course designed to encourage personal reflection as well as mastery of psychological concepts and principles. One of the activities that has historically been a part of that course is a lifeline exercise in which students are asked to draw their lifelines, including points marking birth and death, key choice points and the external events which helped to shape them. While initially resisting the activity, it is customary for a student to derive a great deal from stepping back from the day-to-day events which are the usual focus of attention and reflecting on the large questions of the trails they have taken and of those they have yet to take.

Writing this chapter is a comparable experience for me. It has given me an opportunity to sit back and reflect on what at times seems like an incredibly busy schedule and to attempt to make sense of where I have been and where I am going. The reader is, of course, free to look for his or her own patterns in this and in other chapters which comprise this volume. One conclusion which I have reached from examining the data which follows is the paucity of long-term planning that has characterized my own career. Chance has overwhelmed purpose in influencing the choices with which I have been presented as well as the outcomes of the choices that I have made. What little planning that has occurred has been short range, like the novice chess player who looks at most two steps ahead in choosing the next move.

My Yale colleague, Ed Lindblom has given a name to this phenomenon which he feels characterizes much of organizational decision making, despite what normative theorists argue should be the case. He calls it "muddling through."[1] Perhaps I am deceiving myself or I am being unduly modest. Perhaps the astute reader will see deliberateness and the pursuit of long-range goals in the pages to follow. Perhaps in attributing my behavior in large measure to situations with which I have been confronted, I am committing what psychologists have come to call "the fundamental attribution error"—the tendency to see the causes of one's own behavior in the environment and the causes of others' behavior as residing within them. On with the tale.

I was born in the heart of the Great Depression. My father, who had been a naval officer during the World War I, was fortunate enough to maintain his employment at the Northern Electric Company in a plant that had been described to me as the Canadian counterpart of the Hawthorne Works. My mother was born in South Africa where her parents had settled after her father retired from the British Army to pursue interests in gold and diamond mining. I was the youngest of three boys—Alan was 12 years older, and Kenneth five years older than I.

As a child, I was not conscious of any scholarly ambitions or pretensions. Learning was something that came easily to me but was not something that I pursued with much passion. My passion was rather preserved for music. At about age ten my mother bought me a $25 clarinet, later to be followed by a $40 saxophone. For the next four years, the Vroom household was "treated" to an endless set of squeaks, groans, and then, ultimately, notes and chords. When I was not practicing my instrument, I was listening to recordings of Benny Goodman and Artie Shaw or Johnny Hodges and Charlie Parker. Growing up in the suburbs of Montreal during the "big band era" it was possible to see all of my favorite performers live. I was, typically, the tall kid standing by the bandstand gazing with awe at my heros effortlessly executing passages to which I could only aspire. My bedroom, in which I practiced as much as ten hours a day, was adorned with autographs of my favorite performers.

By age 15 I was, finally, good enough to be invited to join a local dance band called the Blue Knights. We all wore sky-blue blazers and navy blue slacks and played standard arrangements from the big band era. Even today when hearing Stan Kenton's *Intermission Riff*, Glen Miller's *String of Pearls*, or Tommy Dorsey's *Song of India*, I find my thoughts drifting back to life on the bandstand and my fingers revisiting the passages I have played so many times.

It was a glamorous life for a high school sophomore. The other members of the band were all in college or college graduates pursuing successful careers. For the next three years, I played at least two or three nights a week in various dance halls and nightclubs in and around Montreal. My studies suffered but not to the point of jeopardizing my high school graduation, which occurred on schedule.

I must confess to not having given much thought to what I would do after high school. My two brothers had graduated from McGill University, and one had gone on for a Ph.D. in chemistry. However, I had never regarded myself or, in fact, been regarded by teachers as "college material." To further complicate the picture, my father took early retirement from the Northern Electric Company and did not have the financial resources to pay for my college education as he had done for my two brothers.

That fact did not upset my greatly since the thing I wanted most was to play full time with a "name" band. For me that meant crossing the border to the States. To be realistic, I felt that I must start with what was called a "territory band" which moved from city to city in a region of the country, usually in band buses. The ultimate objective, of course, was to end up with a "real" name band as had my idols Oscar Peterson and Maynard Ferguson, both of whom were Montrealers who had successfully made the transition to the United States.

I gave myself the summer after my high school graduation to plan the move to the States. In retrospect I am taken with the incredible naivety with which I approached the entire process. The difficulties in obtaining a work permit or finding a band that needed a 17-year-old alto saxophonist who also doubled on clarinet, or even of learning to live away from a home that had nurtured me since birth were never confronted or successfully managed.

By late August 1949, my father had grown impatient with my lack of progress in career planning and used his local contacts to get me a job as teller in the branch of the Royal Bank of Canada less than a mile away from home. My interview with the manager and observation of the job of teller quickly convinced me that this was not for me. In desperation I sought an alternative and took the advice of a fellow member of the Blue Knights to apply to Sir George Williams College. Situated on the third floor of the YMCA building in Montreal, Sir George, now called Concordia University, had a relatively simple admissions process and, of even greater significance, had a tuition of only $250 a year—a sum that I could easily afford from my musician's income.

Sir George was relatively unique among colleges in one respect—all incoming students had to take a battery of psychological tests, including the Kuder and the Strong Vocational Interest Tests. The psychologist who presented me with my results informed me that my interests corresponded with two occupational groups—musicians and psychologists. The latter was a surprise to me. I had only the vaguest of conceptions of what psychology was all about. However, I looked forward to taking a course in that field.

The opportunity to study psychology did not present itself at Sir George. However, the core curriculum was most exciting, and unlike my high school experience, I found myself pouring more and more energy into my studies. To this I credit in large part an opening lecture by Dean Henry Hall who pointed out that a college education was one of the few things that people would pay for but would not necessarily get. In college no one would prod me to learn. What I learned would be up to me.

The source of the impact of Dean Hall's remarks is still a bit hazy to me. Perhaps it was the fact that I was financing my own education; perhaps it was the relative absence of the external controls that had permeated my educational experience to date; perhaps it was the discretion that I was to be accorded as an adult. Most likely it was all three factors that contributed, for the first time in my 17-year history, to behavior that demonstrated "dedicated scholarship."

While I continued to play music at Sir George, I found that my mind was becoming my "principal instrument." Mastery was still the goal, but notes and keys were replaced by ideas and concepts. A common theme, however, was improvisation. I was never content to parrot back the ideas and theories of others. My college lecture notes reveal a persistent pattern of recording the key ideas expressed by the instructor on one side of the page and my personal reactions and thoughts on the other side of the page.

By the end of my first year, scholarship had clearly acquired a status at least equal to that of jazz music. I sought to transfer to McGill University and, to my surprise, was accepted with full credit from my year at Sir George. At McGill I took my first course in psychology from Donald Hebb, who had just completed his landmark work titled *The Organization of Behavior* (Wiley, 1949). I was impressed both with him and with my exposure to psychology and by the end of my sophomore year had been admitted to a special honors program in that field. There were only three or four of us in that program, and we would meet weekly for lunch with "Hebb" to discuss psychological questions that we found interesting. My fascination at that time was with philosophy of science, particularly the concept of determinism and its implications for free will, religion, and individual responsibility.

My budding romance with psychology complemented my continuing interest in music. By now the Blue Knights had disbanded but was replaced by larger and more professional orchestras—this time with five saxophones, five trumpets, five trombones, full rhythm sections, male and female vocalists, and their own arrangements. The exciting, glamorous life of music continued and, in fact, enabled me to not only finance my own college career but also to pay rent to my parents in whose home I continued to live.

It was too good a life to cut short precipitously, and on graduation from McGill I elected to take a master's degree in psychology at that university. At that time McGill had just introduced two parallel tracks for graduate work in psychology. The academic track lead to an MSc and Ph.D. The professional track, which embraced both clinical and industrial psychology, lead to an MPs.Sc (Master of Psychological Science). I chose the latter path with a concentration in industrial psychology, even though I did not even know what industrial psychology was! I knew Edward Webster, who covered that subject, and he seemed like a nice-enough gentleman. Furthermore, industrial psychology seemed to offer possibilities other than academic research and teaching, which appealed to my urbane side.

In studying industrial psychology I was exposed to the works of Joseph Tiffin, Charles Lawshe, and Jay Otis. It seemed to me that I learned all there was to know about psychological testing, techniques of selection and placement, job analysis, job evaluation, and the technology of merit rating. However, to my dismay I saw little if any connection between the academic psychology on which I had labored so diligently in my undergraduate years and this new field. Industrial psychology seemed more a set of techniques than it did the application of a set of theories and concepts.

One of the ingredients of the McGill program was a set of internships in which students had an opportunity to practice their new profession in the field. My first internship was at Canadair Ltd.—an aircraft manufacturer in Montreal. There I worked on the development of weighted application blanks utilizing demographic measures to predict job turnover. I recall being upset that there was no similarity between the items which predicted turnover for Assembly Fitters "A" and those for Assembly Fitters "B." Furthermore I couldn't figure out the rationale. However, my advisors urged me not to be discouraged. They sought unsuccessfully to convince me that the important thing was not theoretical consistency but the magnitude of r^2 or variance explained.

In the late summer of 1954 after my first year of graduate work, the International Congress of Applied Psychology was held in Montreal. Among the participants in that scientific gathering were Rensis Likert and Carroll Shartle. I began hearing about the University of Michigan's organizational behavior program and the leadership research then underway at Ohio State University. Once again there seemed to be an exciting world across the border in the United States, but this time it was the world of industrial social psychology rather than the world of big band jazz!

During my final year in the master's program at McGill, I interned at the Aluminum Company of Canada in their staff training and research division. This was completely different from Canadair and helped me to form a more complete picture of this new field of which I wanted to be a part. Here I was exposed to the works of Fritz Roethisberger, Carl Rogers, Douglas McGregor, and Paul Lawrence. I had ample opportunity to read in unpublished form the latest research being conducted at Michigan and at Ohio State, and I resolved to pursue the Ph.D. degree. I applied to five schools—Michigan, Illinois, Purdue, Ohio State, and Carnegie Tech. My first choice was Michigan, and I was delighted in March of 1955 to hear that they too wanted me.

Michigan was everything that I might have hoped for in a graduate education. Here at long last was the means of integrating psychological theory with application. I majored in social psychology where I was exposed to such professors as Ted Newcomb, Doc Cartwright, Dan Katz, Jack French, and

Helen Peak. At the same time I worked in the Survey Research Center where I was concerned with applying social psychological ideas to understanding how to make organizations more effective. While he had died several years previous, the ideas of Kurt Lewin were very much alive at Michigan, and they had a pervasive influence on my thinking about individual behavior. Specifically, his reminder that behavior is a function of person and environment helped me to integrate in my own mind the social psychological emphasis on situational or environmental determinants and the prior McGill influence on individual differences. I was ready for Lee Cronbach's classic treatise[2] on the two disciplines of scientific psychology, which appeared toward the end of my graduate work.

Norman Maier was also a very strong influence on me at Michigan. My introduction to experiential learning occurred while serving as a teaching fellow in his course, Psychology of Human Relations, during my first year. His book, *Psychology in Industry* (Houghton-Mifflin, 1955), was used as a text in that course, and his constant attention to the psychological underpinnings of behavior helped to reinforce my belief that the theoretical and the practical could be integrated.

My doctoral dissertation at Michigan, *Some Personality Determinants of the Effects of Participation*, dealt with the moderating effects of two personality variables—authoritarianism and need for independence on reaction to participation in decision making. It gave tangible expression to my interest in the interaction between person and environmental variables. Sometime after the completion of my dissertation, I received a phone call from Donald Taylor at Yale informing me that my dissertation was to receive an award from the Ford Foundation in its doctoral dissertation competition and would be published as a book by Prentice Hall. Needless to say I was ecstatic, and the red leather bound edition given me by the publisher still occupies a position of honor on my bookshelf.

That recognition encouraged me to pursue a more general formulation of a theory dealing with the interaction of individual differences and situational variables. That formulation came to be called "VIE theory" or "expectancy theory" when it was published several years later in *Work and Motivation* (1964).

While I was at Michigan, my career got another unexpected boost. Norman Maier was invited to write the chapter on industrial social psychology for the 1960 *Annual Review of Psychology*. He had planned to decline since he was going to be on sabbatical leave in Europe that year. However, he knew that I made a practice of keeping up on everything that was written in the field and asked me to do the literature search so that he could organize it into a chapter on his return. I went beyond the original mandate and wrote the entire chapter. He changed barely a word before sending it off to the editors.

It was around this time that I became aware of the fact that my exchange visitor visa status obligated me to return to Canada for a two-year period. This seemed most unfortunate since at that time there were no jobs for industrial or organizational psychologists in Canada. In desperation I went to an office in the university with responsibility for international students. Together we devised a plan which they felt had a modest probability of overcoming my predicament. In the past whenever I had returned to Canada on a visit, I had in my possession a document from the University requesting a reissuance of my exchange visitor permit. This time the document referred to a "student visa" instead of "exchange visitor." (A student visa carried with it no such requirement of returning to one's native land.)

It was indeed fortunate that Ann Arbor is relatively close to the Canadian border. I recall spending a long weekend crossing into Canada at each of the border crossing routes and immediately turning around and presenting my document. Three times I received a stern reprimand from a customs official who insisted that I return to Ann Arbor to get the proper document. At the fourth try the customs official took pity on me and issued a new student visa. I was now free to enter the United States job market. I did my best to contain my jubilation until I was safely out of sight of the official lest he change his mind.

After I received my degree at Michigan, I was invited to stay on as a study director in the Survey Research Center and concurrently as a lecturer in the Department of Psychology. It wasn't something that I wanted to do for the rest of my life, but Michigan had been so good to me that I felt I could do far worse. Besides I had formed a small jazz combo called The Intellectuals, which continued to provide an outlet for my musical talents and rambunctious impulses.

I stayed at Michigan for another two years. It was a somewhat ambiguous status. On one hand, I was treated like a faculty member and invited to faculty meetings and gave colloquia and the like; on the other hand, I felt a bit like a senior graduate student who had stayed on past his time. In 1960 I received an offer from the University of Pennsylvania to join their Department of Psychology. At that time Penn's department was in a state of resurgence after many years of inbreeding. The backbone of the department was mathematical psychology with Robert Bush as chairman and people like Luce and Galanter among the full professors. The sole industrial psychologist there was Morris Viteles whose 1932 book was a classic and required reading during my McGill days.

I recall some discussion of whether I might wish a connection with the Wharton School. George Taylor, who was then the Chairman of the Department of Geography and Industry, strongly encouraged me in this direction. I recall being tremendously impressed by his range of contacts in the field of labor management relations—a field about which I knew remarkably little. However, I had been well indoctrinated by colleagues in psychology at Michigan with a disrespect of business schools which at that time was all too characteristic of faculty in the arts and sciences. I politely turned down the invitation.

While at Penn, I taught large sections of introductory psychology as well as courses in social psychology, industrial psychology, and motivation to both undergraduates and doctoral students. During this time, my major preoccupation was writing *Work and Motivation*. I should point out that I did this without a great deal of support from my Penn colleagues, most of whom felt that attempting to write a major book instead of journal articles was more appropriately a professorial endeavor rather than a task of a first-term assistant professor.

Nonetheless, I had no choice or at least felt I had none. Never before had I pursued any task (except perhaps learning to play the saxophone!) with such diligence and dedication. I spent every evening in the library and was frequently there until closing. I was compulsive about checking every reference and exhaustively surveying every item that could conceivably be relevant to my quest. Unlike my experience at Michigan, I was beginning to feel like an independent scholar. I missed the conviviality and stimulation of a group of colleagues with similar or complementary interests but relished the freedom which Penn provided me to do my own intellectual work.

One of the casualties of my appointment at the University of Pennsylvania was my part-time musical career. Such "frivolities" were frowned on by my department chair and preempted by my intellectual preoccupations. My saxophone and clarinet became relegated to a distant corner of the basement to gather dust as remnants of discarded boyhood dreams.

In 1963 my three-year contract as assistant professor of psychology was up, and I began to be wooed by several other universities. This time the most attractive alternatives were not in psychology departments but in schools of business or management. Among the chief competitors was Yale, which had Chris Argyris, E. Wight Bakke, Bob Fetter, and Donald Taylor in what was then called the Department of Industrial Administration. Yale did not then have a doctoral program, but one seemed likely to be approved in the near future.

I came very close to going to Yale because it had many attractions but, in the end, decided on Carnegie. The opportunity to work with Dick Cyert, Jim March, Harold Leavitt, and Herbert Simon was just too attractive to refuse. I might point out that I would have chosen Carnegie more quickly had it not been for the requirement that I teach master's students in their program of industrial administration. I was still a psychologist first and foremost and still believed that there was something not quite intellectually pure about the mercenary interests of those seeking a career in business!

My early days at Carnegie were filled with mixed emotions. I found myself surrounded by colleagues in economics, operations research, marketing, and accounting—each of whom had a different language and set of scholarly pursuits that I found difficult to encompass into my psychological compartments. For the first few months, I kept my office door closed and restricted my conversations with my colleagues to the exploits of the Steelers, the Pirates, or the latest office gossip. Gradually these social encounters acquired intellectual overtones, and by the end of my first year, I began to embrace the interdisciplinary exchanges which then characterized Carnegie's Graduate School of Industrial Administration (GSIA).

One of my most vivid memories of this period was a lunchtime faculty seminar on topology. My interest in this aspect of mathematics had been spurred by an apparent resemblance to some of the ideas of Kurt Lewin. A group of about ten faculty members agreed to buy a major textbook on the subject, and we devoted one lunch hour each week to exploring the subject. Each participant took the responsibility for one class. Now 25 years later, I am painfully aware of the fragility of this degree of open-minded collaboration among the disciplines. In fact the opposite—veiled hostility and at times open warfare—seems to be the norm at many schools of management.

My growing interdisciplinary bent was reflected during this period by a collaboration with Ken McCrimmon. We pursued a mammoth project aimed at developing a stochastic model of the careers of managers in the General Electric Company. It was a very large project indeed, the only one I have been involved with based solely on archival data. My principal regret is that only the earliest of our findings were ever published. Ken McCrimmon left to accept a professorship at the University of British Columbia, and the collaboration became too difficult to carry out over such a long distance.

At Carnegie I had a joint appointment between GSIA and psychology and served on the steering committee of both units. However, my major teaching commitments were in GSIA with aspiring or experienced managers. Not too long ago I came across a file containing my lecture notes from one of my early attempts to teach master's students. I read with embarrassment of my rather unsuccessful efforts to elicit their interest in the latest issues in psychological theory or to impress them with the sophistication of new psychological research methods. The lectures that had proven highly effective with Penn Ph.D. students or undergraduate psychology majors seemed to be of little interest to this new audience.

My salvation was found in a return to the experiential teaching methods, particularly role playing, which I had learned with Norman Maier during my first year of graduate study. While I rarely use role playing now, I find John Dewey's admonition that people learn by doing is fundamental to sound education regardless of the audience. Along with my adaptation to the managerial classroom went an appreciation of the legitimacy of managerial interests and later a belief that the managerial world represented a rich source of problems for research.

While at Carnegie, I had two students with whom I continue to have a strong intellectual association. One of these was Edward Deci, who received his Ph.D. not from GSIA but from Psychology. One event during the latter stages of Ed's doctoral work is suggestive of the serendipity which characterizes the research process. I had just returned from a research conference on compensation held at General Electric's Crotonville facility. At the conference I was a discussant of a paper given by Leon Festinger in which he argued, based on cognitive dissonance research, for the incompatibility of intrinsic and extrinsic motivation. As a discussant of Festinger's paper, I argued for a contrary position, which Gordon Allport has termed "functional autonomy"—that is, means become ends. One might start pursuing an activity, such as work in the pursuit of external socially mediated gratification, but end up valuing the work for its own sake.

At the conference the debate was spirited and lively, and when I returned to Carnegie, I resolved to look at the evidence in greater detail. I was delighted when Ed Deci took up the project, and he quickly embraced it, ultimately carrying out his doctoral dissertation on the subject. It is a great source of pride that Ed has continued to explore intrinsic motivation and has achieved an international reputation for his work in that area.

While he was at Carnegie, we collaborated on and edited a volume for Penguin Business Series titled *Management and Motivation*. In the 20 years following its publication, that book sold about 200,000 copies. This fact led Penguin to try to persuade us to undertake a revision. We accepted, and the revision has recently been published.

A second student was Philip Yetton. Phil had come from England to do research on the behavioral theory of the firm. He was surprised to find that very little was going on at Carnegie on that subject despite Cyert and March's book published less than a decade earlier.[3]

I had recently authored a chapter in the *Handbook of Social Psychology* (1969) in which I reviewed the empirical evidence relevant to the efficacy of participation and decision making. Below I reproduce a quote from that chapter which foreshadowed much of my subsequent theoretical and empirical work.

> The results suggest that allocating problem-solving and decision-making tasks to entire groups, as compared with the leader or manager in charge of the groups, requires a greater investment of man-hours but produces higher acceptance of decisions and a higher probability that the decisions will be executed efficiently. Differences between these two methods in quality of decisions and in elapsed time are inconclusive and probably highly variable.... It would be naive to think that group decision making is always more "effective" than autocratic decision making, or vice versa; the relative effectiveness of these two extreme methods depends both on the weights attached to quality, acceptance, and time variables and on differences in amounts of these outcomes resulting from these methods, neither of which is invariant from one situation to another. The critics and proponents of

> participative management would do well to direct their efforts toward identifying the properties of situations in which different decision-making approaches are effective rather than wholesale condemnation or deification of one approach. (pp. 239-240)

I had used that chapter in a doctoral seminar that I was conducting and expressed to the seminar participants my interest in going beyond the usual "bows" to situational relativity. Phil came to me the next day and expressed interest in the topic, and our collaboration began. For the next year and a half, we drew decision trees and tested them against scenarios which came from our joint and rather limited managerial experience. Since we were somewhat aware of these limitations, we began asking managers to describe decision-making situations in which they were involved, the process they had used in resolving them, and the outcome. Within a year our files were filled with short cases which gave us a substantially broader base for "testing" the efficacy of our decision trees.

Phil had the idea of formalizing the logic implicit in our decision trees, and this spawned the concepts of rules and the related concepts of the feasible set, both of which became important features of the Vroom-Yetton model. It was I who conceived the idea of studying the "decision trees" that managers used. This lead to the idea of a problem set—a standardized set of cases taken from our files which I thought, quite naively, would enable us to draw the decision tree used by a given manager. This rather ambitious goal required not only a relatively large number of cases but also the selection of cases in accordance with a multi-factorial experimental design. Such a design would render situational variables, which might be highly correlated in the real world, statistically independent of one another.

About a year after our collaboration began, I was granted a sabbatical leave and decided to spend it at the University of California at Irvine with my old friend Lyman Porter. Phil accompanied me, and we both devoted full time to writing and researching our model. While in California we realized that we needed much more access to data from managers in order to test our emerging notions of a problem set, and I agreed to give several seminars on participative decision making to managers in General Electric and in other organizations. To gain the cooperation of managers, I agreed to give them an individual analysis of their decision-making styles. I made this commitment knowing full well that we did not yet have a technology for carrying out that analysis but confident that a concrete deadline would spur both of us to get it ready in time.

It was during those exciting days in California that we began to realize that the research that we viewed as relevant to basic theoretical issues also had tremendous applied value. My telephone began ringing off the hook from organizations wanting to participate in the research program so that their managers could get feedback. Phil Yetton and I were very clear that we were primarily academics; on the other hand, we wished to have some control over the future development of the educational technology without sacrificing our academic integrity. The options which occurred to us at that time included (1) putting everything that we had done in the public domain or into scientific journals and monographs by which it could be accessed by our colleagues, (2) setting up our own organization which would conduct seminars and further develop the educational technology in a manner somewhat similar to what Robert Blake and Jane Mouton had done with the Managerial Grid, or (3) licensing to an existing firm the rights to use the technology. It was at this point that I made what I now view as an unfortunate error—but more of that later.

While putting on one of the early seminars on the model at General Electric's Management Education Center at Crotonville, I encountered Bud Smith of Kepner-Tregoe and Associates, Inc. and communicated some of the enthusiasm that I felt for what we were doing. Bud expressed an interest in these ideas, and negotiations began in a serious way with Kepner-Tregoe resulting in a signed contract with them in April 1972. My conception of the agreement with Kepner-Tregoe was that the models (including the decision trees, rules, feasible set, problem attributes, and the taxonomy of AI through GII) would be available for all interested parties to use in both teaching or research. Phil Yetton had the same conception. We both believed Bud Smith did too. Consistent with this view we published the model in our book *Leadership and Decision Making*, published by the University of Pittsburgh Press. Kepner-Tregoe was given an exclusive license to the problem set and feedback technology including cases, computer programs, manuals and the like. This exclusive license was subject to Phil's and my unrestricted right to continue to use these materials in our own research, teaching, and consultation.

In 1972 just after signing the contract with Kepner-Tregoe, I decided to leave Carnegie for Yale. Carnegie had been a good place for me for nine years. It had shaped my intellectual development in several important ways. I had entered as a organizational psychologist and left as an organizational social scientist with a passionate interest in management. I came as a person capable of giving a reasonable lecture; I left as a person committed to the process of education.

On the other hand, it seemed time to move on. Carnegie was not the source of interdisciplinary work that it was in the early sixties. While there were still no departments within the school, the creation of a strong group of economists who were committed to theoretical issues within economics foreshadowed similar coalitions within operations research and in organizational behavior. Furthermore, Leavitt and March had moved on to other universities; Cyert was about to become president of the university; and Simon had left the field of organizational behavior more than a decade earlier.

Yale was presented to me as being in transition. Chris Argyris had left for Harvard the previous year; Richard Hackman and Clay Alderfer, both of whom I had tried to recruit at Carnegie, were trying to keep the Department of Administrative Sciences together despite financial and organizational uncertainties.

Despite its mammoth endowment, the University had been losing money. I was asked to chair the department by President Kingman Brewster within weeks of my arrival. It was a prime candidate for budget cuts if not total elimination. The only factors in our favor were constant alumni pressure to establish a business school and, more tangibly, the fact that the University had accepted a large bequest from the Beinecke family to establish at Yale an educational unit to develop future managers.

My role as chair brought with it the responsibility to help shape the manner in which that educational endeavor would be realized. I was appointed to a task force along with the Dean of the Graduate School, the Dean of Yale College and the Director of the Institution of Social and Policy Studies to prepare a report proposing how Yale should address the challenge of management education and research.

I recall disliking intensely this sudden emersion into a strange world of power and politics. I was at a high point in my research production, and academic administration was never something to which I had aspired. I consoled myself with the observation that all parties aspired not to replicate any existing institution but rather to create something that was qualitatively different. This was a rare opportunity to leave a legacy by shaping an institution which could influence management education not only at Yale but throughout the nation.

It would have been completely impossible for me to have continued my research program were it not for a very rewarding partnership with Art Jago—a partnership which continues to this day. Art arrived at Yale as a graduate student at the same time that I did. In fact, he had called me at Carnegie to inquire whether I was planning to leave for Yale, as had been rumored. I told him of my intentions even before I had announced it to my colleagues at both Carnegie and Yale.

During the four years in which we worked together at Yale, Art and I carried out a great deal of research on the descriptive aspects of participation in decision making—most notably, research on differences between sexes in use of participative decision making and hierarchial differences in participative decision making. Perhaps our best piece of work during this period was research on the validity of the Vroom-Yetton model, which we published in the *Journal of Applied Psychology* and which represented a line of research which would be followed by many others in years to come.

My three years of administrative travail at Yale was rewarded by the creation of the School of Organization and Management and with the admission of the first class of students in September 1976. Pending the appointment of the first dean, Bill Donaldson, I had agreed to chair the first board of permanent officers, chair the search committee for a dean, and chair the committee that designed the first curriculum.

In those early days Yale's School of Organization and Management was an exciting place. The students were challenging but a joy to teach; the administrative mechanisms were highly participative and the faculty highly collegial. I recall driving home from the orientation of the entering class in 1976, which we called "community building." Clay Alderfer and I had jointly conducted that session which created a set of eight-person groups, each with their own two-person faculty advising team. I recall remarking to Clay that I had never before experienced the tremendous shared level of excitement and enthusiasm that both faculty and students felt about this joint endeavor. Is it conceivable that this level of commitment could be maintained indefinitely? With the appointment of a dean and the institutionalization of many of the norms and practices that I had sought to create in the School of Organization and Management, my administrative role declined; and I devoted my attention to developing and teaching the core course to which I previously referred, Individual and Group Behavior (IGB), and to resuming my research program.

In 1977 another unexpected event occurred that was to shape my subsequent career. One day in June I was sitting in my office when I received an unprecedented phone call from my physician at the Yale Health Plan. He had received my chest X-ray taken the previous day during a routine physical examination. He asked me to report immediately to the X-ray department. Somewhat alarmed, I dropped what I was doing and found myself spending the next two hours having my chest X-rayed from all possible angles. Finally the technician told me that I could leave. I refused until I received an explanation of what was going on. When she declined to tell me anything, I burst through a door to find a radiologist surrounded by what seemed like hundreds of pictures of my lungs taken from every conceivable angle. He too refused to give me a diagnosis but referred me to my physician who, unfortunately, had left for the day. When I threatened him with bodily harm unless he told me what was happening, he said to prepare myself for bad news.

The next day my physician confirmed the judgement—the X-rays showed evidence of carcinoma in both lungs and at a very advanced stage. An appointment was arranged two days later with an oncologist who confirmed the diagnosis. He wanted to admit me without delay to the hospital for exploratory surgery. However, lecture commitments of mine and medical commitments of his precluded the scheduling of the operation for a full week.

For the next several days, I contemplated my own mortality for the first time in my 45-year-old life. Routine events, such as watching my youngest son pitching in a Little League game, carried new meaning when watched for the "last time." I thought of all the things that had seemed important but no longer had significance and of all the things that should have been significant but had been overlooked due to pressure of work and time. In short, I resolved to spend whatever time was left for me pursuing life with a different set of priorities than I had previously.

Finally, the week was over, and I went in for the surgery. Awakening from the operation, I was given the surprising news that the tumors that had almost filled both lungs were not cancerous but rather a disease called sarcoid—a disease that had been overlooked because it rarely afflicts white males living in the Northeast. While not curable, sarcoid is treatable and has not been of further difficulty.

I describe that event in detail because of its substantial and continuing impact on how I choose to live my life. Even though the fear of imminent death was gone, my resolve to live my life differently did not disappear.

The first effect involved reconsidering a decision made almost 15 years earlier—to abandon my musical talents. My saxophone and clarinet were retrieved from deep storage and totally reconditioned. It was discouraging to hear what time had done to my lip. However, practice during the highly restricted time schedule cured all. In this case practice did not make perfect, but it did enable me to begin playing on a casual basis with a variety of groups in the New Haven area—a custom that I continue to this day. It is amazing how therapeutic it is to play an evening of jazz accompanied by a great rhythm section to an appreciative audience. Re-establishing this aspect of my identity did wonders for my sanity and served to re-establish a critical aspect of my identity.

It was in the fall of 1978 that I purchased my first serious sailboat—a 28-foot sloop called *Impulse*. I had always been inclined toward sailing, perhaps due to my father's tales of his sailing adventures (and misadventures) while growing up in New Brunswick. I was feeling somewhat guilty over time not spent with my two sons during their early years, and doing cruises seemed like a marvelous way of building the kind of relationship that I felt had been lacking.

Our cruises to places like Newport and Martha's Vineyard were in fact mutually rewarding but somewhat cramped in a 28-foot boat. So a much larger Cal 39 was purchased which my sons affectionately named *AI* after the leadership style which they professed that I used when at the helm! Since 1980, *AI* has cruised to the Maine coast, to Chesapeake Bay, to Bermuda and amongst many of the Caribbean islands. On each of these voyages, I have been at the helm accompanied by at least one and, typically, both of my sons.

During the late 1970s and early 1980s, the Vroom-Yetton model was a hot topic for research, and many investigators in the United States and abroad sought to determine its validity along with its strengths and limitations. Meanwhile, hundreds upon hundreds of textbooks published the now-familiar decision tree along with the problem attributes and the taxonomy of decision processes. One day a professor who was visiting Yale from the Peoples Republic of China showed me a textbook written in Mandarin and turned to a page in Chinese characters which I could not decipher. However, I did recognize the familiar structure of the time-efficient decision tree.

I must confess to being a bit embarrassed by the magnitude of the impact of this model. When I first wrote *Leadership and Decision Making* with Phil Yetton back in 1973, it had seemed much more like an academic exercise than a guide for practicing or potential managers. Its publication as a research monograph by the University of Pittsburgh Press pointed to the scholarly nature of the work. However, its widespread adoption in the organizational world pointed to the fact that it addressed issues of widespread concern.

By 1983 Art Jago and I became convinced that the Vroom-Yetton model had serious flaws. Our own research on the model's validity along with that of many others convinced us that it had a reasonable batting average but fell far short of the potential of such a model.

What to do about the model's problems was another matter. The Vroom-Yetton model bears some similarity to the Ten Commandments. There are seven rules, each of which takes the form of a "thou shalt not" statement. To have added an eighth rule would have meant that there would be some situations in which no action was possible. In other words, none of the five decision processes would be allowed because each would be contraindicated, albeit in a highly specific and restricted set of circumstances.

Furthermore, there were many situations in which the seven rules were of no use whatsoever since they allowed all five decision processes. To reflect what we and others had learned through research, we found it necessary to develop a vastly different model. It required a fundamental change in the old Vroom-Yetton model structure. The concept of rules and the feasible set were eliminated. In their place we substituted functional relationships between problem attributes, decision processes, and the four criteria which had been implicit in the Vroom-Yetton model—namely, quality, commitment, time, and development.

Following this realization, there was another period of intense intellectual excitement and exchange. Since Art was now at the University of Houston and I was still at Yale, we could no longer hammer out ideas face-to-face. Instead phone and Bitnet messages went back and forth on a daily basis. Gradually we evolved a new model based not on seven rules but four mathematical equations. There was little doubt in our minds that these equations would do a far better job of forecasting the actual outcome of various forms and degrees of participation in decision making than the Vroom-Yetton model it replaced. Our concern was that validity and usability were far from perfectly correlated. How could managers be encouraged to solve four equations in order to determine which process to use?

It was Art's thinking that the personal computer and the floppy disk represented the solution. He spent more than a thousand hours writing a computer program which would not only solve the equations but also provide a manager with a highly usable account of the likely consequences of the different degrees and forms of participation in a given situation. Once a person had used the software once or twice, it proved to be almost as fast as using a decision tree and a great deal more accurate.

The computer form for the model enabled us to overcome another limitation of the Vroom-Yetton model. It had permitted only two levels of each problem attribute. Questions which lined the decision tree had to be answered yes or no. Managers told us that their worlds were not dichotomous but rather decorated with "shades of grey." Embracing the computer technology enabled us to allow multiple levels of problem attributes without sacrificing usability.

Once the software problems had been laid to rest, we set about to summarize our research and thinking (which had now spanned 15 years) into book form. In the summer of 1986, Art and I went out on a cruise on *AI* to put the finishing touches to our book which we titled *The New Leadership: Managing Participation in Organizations.*

The foreword to the book was authored by Ben Tregoe, the chairman of Kepner-Tregoe. Kepner-Tregoe had been kept informed of developments involving the new model (including the software) and had expressed interest in phasing out the Vroom-Yetton model and replacing it with our new one. They extended contracts to both of us to license our new work. After much deliberation, Art and I decided not to grant them a license since the nature of their proposals as well as information gleaned from people within the firm led us to fear that with such a license Kepner-Tregoe might "shelve" the Vroom-Jago model and continue to use the Vroom-Yetton model they already had, with the possible result that the Vroom-Jago model would be unavailable for ourselves or others. In addition, I had never been happy with the job that Kepner-Tregoe had done either in developing a suitable training package based on the Vroom-Yetton model or in marketing the one that they had developed. The original ideas on which the organization had been founded—problem analysis and decision analysis—seemed to me to so dominate the culture as to leave little room for concepts invented by outside scholars.

There was great excitement at the publication of *The New Leadership* in 1988. Just prior to its publication, Art and I founded a little company which we had initially called AI Software after the autocratic term in our model. However, we should have realized that AI also signified artificial intelligence, and that corporate identity subsequently became Leadership Software. We envisioned it as a small, single-product company solely to produce MPO, the software program which Art had written to produce the floppy discs which ran the new model. Art would be the only employee, and the operation would be conducted out of his home in Houston.

This low overhead enabled us to advertise the software complete with manual and vinyl folder in *The New Leadership* at a very reasonable price. This new company was one way in which Art could derive some small economic return for his tremendous investment of time in developing the model and its applications.

My general feeling of new beginnings that characterized 1988 was interrupted violently by a visit paid by Benno Schmidt, Jr.—the new, young president of Yale—to the School of Organization and Management in October of that year. In a meeting with faculty, he announced (1) the appointment of a new dean, Michael E. Levine, who would assume office immediately with unprecedented powers (all faculty voting rights granted in the by-laws of the University were to be suspended—a condition that the university counsel later described to me as similar to martial law); (2) the organizational behavior doctoral program was to be terminated, and all non-tenured faculty in that field were to be terminated without review on the expiration of their current contracts; (3) the faculty in operations research were to be transferred to the Faculty of Arts and Sciences.

Later the new dean was to announce other changes. Community building, student participation in admissions, a weekly student/faculty meeting called liaison and the core course in organizational behavior, Individual and Group Behavior, (voted by alumni that year as the most valuable course in the school) were to be terminated. All of these changes were made without any semblance of faculty participation and debate. I was filled with such rage that I was speechless. It seemed to me that all of the things that had made Yale's School of Organization and Management unique in the world of business schools had been eliminated by one administrative act that defied comprehension.

My shock was undoubtedly heightened by the fact that I had been a member of the search committee for the dean. To be sure, that committee had not met in over six months, but our brief discussion of Levine had led me to believe that there was no support whatsoever for his candidacy. Two weeks before the announcement I had heard a rumor of Levine's possible appointment and had lunch with him in which he refused to confirm or deny the rumor. I took it upon myself to interview as many full professors (who constitute the governing board of the school) as I could find to learn their feelings about this possibility. The consensus was striking! Of the twelve professors I interviewed, all but one found Levine totally unacceptable as dean. I then had a long conversation with the president in which I relayed my findings. He thanked me profusely for what I had done, and I left the interaction greatly relieved feeling that an appointment which I felt would have been a disaster had been averted. I returned to my colleagues in a style akin to Chamberlain on his return from Munich in 1939.

The uproar following Benno Schmidt's decision has been chronicled in dozens of publications including *The New York Times, Business Week, Newsweek*, and *The Wall Street Journal.* What has been less publicized are the long-term effects. As I write these words over three and one-half years later, it is very, very, difficult for me to see any benefits accruing from these changes.

The School has been dropped from the top 20 schools in the annual *Business Week* survey; alumni in the main are disenfranchised, and most have ceased making contributions to their alma mater. Some alumni have even hired airplanes to overfly Yale graduations and the Harvard-Yale football game trailing banners critical of the president, the dean, or both. Current students, virtually none of whom knew the school before the changes, are divided on their support, but many complain about core courses taught by visitors—a practice brought about by the difficulty of faculty recruiting after the well publicized events of the past three years.

Too often we take for granted the institutional settings in which scholarship takes place. Nurturing of collegiality is a function which is either overlooked or relegated to deans or department chairs. My experience at both Yale and Carnegie Mellon taught me the fragility of these settings—of how quickly a tradition of collaboration could erode or be destroyed altogether. Yale University has a long and impressive past and undoubtedly a long future. One member of the Yale Corporation of my acquaintance has urged taking a long-term view. He counseled that Yale's traditions will enable it to recover from what I see as its current difficulties. I hope that he is right, but there is precedent for an alternative scenario. An editorial in the latest issue of the student newspaper asks how long Yale will tolerate a second-rate imitation of Chicago or Rochester within its ranks.

Less than a year after the changes at Yale a second personal disaster was to strike. A sheriff arrived at my front door to serve notice that Kepner-Tregoe had filed suit in Federal court charging me with copyright infringement and breach of contract. That was followed by a subsequent suit against Art Jago and Leadership Software. The claims made by these suits appear to be that the terms AI . . . GII as well as the problem attributes and their definitions are owned by Kepner-Tregoe and that their use by others, including me, is an infringement of their copyright. Kepner-Tregoe's motives, to me, seem obvious. The Vroom-Jago model threatened to make the Vroom-Yetton model obsolete. It would be hard for Kepner-Tregoe to justify its charges (about $300 per participant for materials alone) and its acclaimed position as market leader in this field if the product it uses was almost 20 years old and Art and I were writing about and lecturing on a vastly improved product which Kepner-Tregoe did not own. Attempts on my part to discuss the matter in a meaningful manner and reach some equitable resolution were totally rebuffed, and I found myself embarked on a course of litigation which would consume most of my time and energy and financial resources for a period of years.

To those who have not been defendants in litigation launched by a large corporation (Kepner-Tregoe was bought by U.S. Fidelity and Guaranty in the mid-1980s), I can describe the experience only with difficulty. Even though you feel certain that the charges against you are without substance, you also know that the financial costs of defending your rights are beyond comprehension. While there have been some peaks and valleys, I can honestly state that almost half my time has been spent preparing for depositions, attending depositions, searching records, and consulting with the three law firms that are representing my interests. One should add to this the "non-productive time," the sleepless nights filled with rage or self-questioning which accomplishes nothing but consumes precious energy.

Both events—the wrenching changes at Yale and the Kepner-Tregoe lawsuit—have taken their emotional and intellectual toll. I find it impossible to carve out the amount of time and space necessary to write, say, a book like *Work and Motivation, Leadership and Decision-Making*, or *The New Leadership*. Ed Deci and I have just finished a complete revision of our edited book, *Management and Motivation*, but even that edited project was delayed a year and a half beyond its expected deadline by my seeming inability to get my share of the writing done on time.

Even writing this piece which in earlier, less stressful times could have been completed in a week, was written in fits and starts—half an hour here in a hotel room followed by 45 minutes a month later while flying from New York to Atlanta. The most sustained investment of time occurred when I dictated the earliest sections to my wife and soul mate while driving from Connemara to Dublin, Ireland.

In spite of the fragmented nature of the process, I can honestly report that the task was personally worthwhile and at least mildly therapeutic. As my students in the now-defunct course, Individual and Group Behavior, have reported, reflection has been helpful in regaining a perspective on one's life.

And now the tale is over, at least for the present. Hopefully, future years will bring trails that are not only more satisfying but also more conducive to scholarship. Meanwhile it's about time to practice a few chords and scales.

PUBLICATIONS

1957

Effects of design on estimation of size of coins. *Canadian Journal of Psychology, 11*, 83-92.

1959

Some personality determinants of the effects of participation. *Journal of Abnormal and Social Psychology, 59*, 322-327.

Projection, negation and the self-concept. *Human Relations, 12,* 335-344.

1960

With F.C. Mann. Leader authoritarianism and employee attitudes. *Personnel Psychology, 13*, 135-140.

The effects of attitudes on the perception of organization goals. *Human Relations, 13*, 229-240.

A primer of leadership [Review of *Creative leadership*]. *Contemporary Psychology, 5*, 297.

Some factors affecting the perceived similarity of social objects. In *Proceedings of the 16th International Conference of Psychology*. Bonn, Germany.

Some personality determinants of the effects of participation. Englewood Cliffs, NJ: Prentice-Hall.

1961

With N.R.F. Maier. Industrial social psychology. *Annual Review of Psychology.*

[Review of *Human values where people work*]. *The Annals of the American Academy of Political and Social Science*, pp. 228, 335.

1962

Ego involvement, job satisfaction and job performance. *Personnel Psychology, 15,* 159-177.

Human relations research in industry: Some things learned. In F. Bairstow (Ed.), *Research frontiers in industrial relations.* Montreal: McGill University Press.

1963

The self-concept: A balance theoretical treatment. Unpublished manuscript, Department of Psychology, University of Pennsylvania.

With F.C. Mann & B.P. Indik. *The productivity of work groups.* Ann Arbor, MI: Institute for Social Research.

1964

With S.C. Jones. Division of labor and performance under cooperative and competitive conditions. *Journal of Abnormal Social Psychology, 68,* 313-320.

Some psychological aspects of organizational control. In W. Cooper, M. Shelly, & H.J. Leavitt (Eds.), *New perspectives in organization research.* New York: Wiley.

Employee attitudes. In G. Fisk (Ed.), *The frontiers of management psychology.* New York: Harper & Row.
Work and motivation. New York: Wiley.

1965

Motivation in management. New York: American Foundation for Management Research.

1966

A comparison of static and dynamic correlational methods in the study of organizations. *Organizational Behavior and Human Performance, 1*(1), 55-70.
Organizational choice: A study of pre- and post-decision making processes. *Organizational Behavior and Human Performance, 1*(2), 212-225
The role of compensation in motivating employees: A behavioral scientist's viewpoint. Paper delivered at the 43rd Annual Conference of the Life Office Management Association, Miami, FL.

1967

[Editor]. *Methods of organizational research.* Pittsburgh, PA: University of Pittsburgh Press.
Maslow at play. *Contemporary Psychology, 12*(2), 97-98.
Some observations on Herzberg's Two-Factor Theory. Paper presented at the meeting for the APA, September.

1968

Organizational Design and Research. Pittsburgh, PA: University of Pittsburgh Press.
With K. MacCrimmon. Toward a stochastic model of managerial careers. *Administrative Science Quarterly* (June).

1969

With L. Grant & T. Cotton. The consequences of social interaction in group problem-solving. *Organizational Behavior and Human Performance, 4*(1), 77-95.
Industrial social psychology. In G. Lindzey & E. Aronson (Eds.), *Handbook of social psychology* (Vol. 5). Reading, MA: Addison-Wesley.

1970

Some implications of research on learning for management development. In W. Goldberg (Ed.), *Göteborg studies in business administration: Vol. 1. Behavioral approaches to modern management* (pp. 74-88). Göteborg, Sweden.

The relevance of the behavioral sciences for manpower management. In W. Goldberg (Ed.), *Göteborg studies in business administration: Vol. 1. Behavioral approaches to modern management.* Göteborg, Sweden.

Edited with E.L. Deci. *Management and motivation.* London: Penguin Books.

1971

With E.L. Deci. The stability of post-decision dissonance: A follow-up study of the job attitudes of business school graduates. *Organizational Behavior and Human Performance, 6*, 36-49.

With B. Pahl. The relationship between age and risk taking among managers. *Journal of Applied Psychology, 55*(5), 399-405.

With E.L. Deci. Leadership, social value, and the risky shift. *Representative Research in Social Psychology, 2*(1).

With J.P. Campbell, C.J. Cranny, E.E. Lawler, & A.C. McKinney. The changing role of industrial psychology in university education: A symposium. *Professional Psychology, 2*, 2-22.

1972

[Review of *Leadership and management*]. In *Contemporary management: Issues & viewpoints.* Englewood Cliffs, NJ: Prentice-Hall.

1973

A new look at managerial decision-making. *Organizational Dynamics, 1*(4), 66-80.

Psychology for managers. *Contemporary Psychology, 18*(8), 391.

1974

With A.G. Jago. Decision making as a social process: Normative and descriptive models of leader behavior. *Decision Sciences, 5*(4), 743-769.

Decision making and the leadership process. *Journal of Contemporary Business* (Autumn), 743-769.

With P. Yetton. *Leadership and decision-making.* Pittsburgh, PA: University of Pittsburgh Press.

1975

With A.G. Jago. Perceptions of leadership style: Superior and subordinate descriptions of decision making behavior. In J.G. Hunt & L. Larson (Eds.), *Leadership frontiers* (pp. 103-120). Kent, OH: Kent State University Press.

Leadership revisited. In E.L. Cass & F.G. Zimmer (Eds.), *Man and work in society* (pp. 220-234). New York: Van Nostrand Reinhold Co.

1976

Leadership. In M. Dunnette (Ed.), *Handbook of industrial and organizational psychology*. Chicago, IL: Rand-McNally.

Can leaders learn to lead? *Organizational Dynamics* (Winter), 17-28.

1977

With A.G. Jago. Hierarchical level and leadership style. *Organizational Behavior and Human Performance, 18*, 131-145.

With P. Yetton. The Vroom-Yetton Model of Leadership: An overview. In B.T. King, S.S. Streufert, & F.E. Fiedler (Eds.), *Managerial control and organizational democracy*. Washington, DC: Winston & Sons.

1978

With A.G. Jago. Predicting leader behavior from a measure of behavioral intent. *Academy of Management Journal, 21*, 715-721.

With A.G. Jago. On the validity of the Vroom-Yetton Model. *Journal of Applied Psychology, 63*, 151-162.

1980

With A.G. Jago. An evaluation of two alternatives to the Vroom/Yetton Model. *Academy of Management Journal, 23*(2).

1981

Decision making in organizations: A case study in programmatic research. In J. Sgro (Ed.), *Virginia Tech Symposium on Applied Behavioral Science* (Vol. 1, pp. 199-214). Lexington, MA: Lexington Books.

Evocative theory. *Contemporary Psychology, 26*(1), 29-30.

1982

With A.G. Jago. Sex differences in the incidence and evaluation of participative leader behavior. *Journal of Applied Psychology, 67*, 776-783.

1983

Leaders and leadership in academe. *Review of Higher Education, 6*, 367-386.

1984

Reflections on leadership and decision-making. *Journal General Management, 9*, 18-36.

1985

With A.G. Jago & J.T. Ettling. Validating a revision to the Vroom/Yetton Model: First evidence. In *Proceedings of the 45th Annual Meeting of the Academy of Management* (pp. 220-223).

1988

With A.G. Jago. Managing participation: A critical dimension of leadership. *The Journal of Management Development, 7*(5), 32-42.

With A.G. Jago. *The new leadership: Managing participation in organizations.* Englewood Cliffs, NJ: Prentice-Hall.

1989

With A.G. Jago. Vom Vroom/Yetton-zum Vroom/Jago-Fuhrungsmodell: Neue Uberlegungen zur Partizipation in Organisationem. *Die Betriebswirtschaft, 49*(1), 4-17.

Forward. In E.E. Kossek, *The acceptance of human resource innovation: Lessons for management*. New York: Quorum Books.

The essential attributes of Norman Maier: A review of Norman Maier's *Psychology in industry. The Academy of Management Review, 14*(1), 104-106.

1990

Preface and introduction. In *Manage people, not personnel: Motivation and performance appraisal. Boston, MA: Harvard Business School Press.*

1992

Edited with E.L. Deci. *Management and motivation* (2nd ed.). London: Penguin.

NOTES

1. See C.E. Lindblom. (1959). The science of muddling through. *Public Administration Review, 19*, 79-99.
2. L.J. Cronbach. (1957). The two disciplines of scientific psychology." *American Psychologist, 12*, 671-684.
3. R.M. Cyert & J.G. March. (1963). *A behavioral theory of the firm*. Englewood Cliffs, NJ: Prentice-Hall.

Karl E. Weick

Turning Context Into Text: An Academic Life As Data

KARL E. WEICK

The house in which I was born stood 500 feet from the four-track mainline of the Pennsylvania Railroad, and 6 miles from the ballroom at Winona Lake, Indiana, where my mother, Dorothy, sang with my father's orchestra, Karl's Kardinals. Railroads and bands have been part of my life ever since October 31, 1936. What that has to do with scholarship on management, I hope to show.

My parents, neither of whom went to college, lived music. My mother, a French horn player whose hero was William Ravelli, the renowned director of the University of Michigan marching band, began singing professionally while she was still in high school. My father, who worked in sales for Lincoln Oil, which then became Ohio Oil, which finally became Marathon Oil, managed to keep an active orchestra together at the same time. The orchestra, a 13-piece regional band, worked the Indiana-Michigan-Chicago area and played dates such as the Culver Military Academy prom.

So it was natural that I would take up trumpet and piano at an early age, but unnatural that I would abandon them just as quickly. I seem to have imprinted on the experience of being a spectator of bands, rather than a participant. But to this day, I have never lost my fascination with the question, how can 19 musicians, without the benefit of amplification, create enough coordinated physical power at the same moment to simultaneously deafen people yet move them to experience emotional highs that they never dreamed were within their range. That's what has happened to me over and over, as Karen, my wife, and I planted ourselves in front of the bandstand, a mere 10 feet from the bell of trumpeter Cat Anderson or Bill Chase, trombonists Bobby Burgess or Jimmy Cleveland, or saxophonists Bill Perkins or Steve Marcus. From the very beginning, I was hooked on the problem of coordination and collective improvisation, although it was some time before I put it quite that way.

Early life around bands was enriched by early life around trains. The Pennsy ran through Warsaw, Indiana, the home of my paternal grandparents, as well as through Columbia City, 30 miles away, where my maternal grandparents lived. Both grandfathers were as nuts about trains as I was, or at least they indulged me as if they were. In both towns, we would go down to the station, and stand for hours, again little more than 10 feet from the action, as trains slammed through at 80 mph producing enormous suction and noise. Come to think of it, they too deafened and produced emotional highs far outside the usual range. I knew what WW II must be about simply by watching what was on the trains: trucks, tanks, troops, and ambulances. When I listened to my favorite radio program, Grand Central Station ("Dive with a roar into the 2 1/2 mile tunnel that burrows beneath the glitter and swank of Park Avenue"), I would close my eyes and see the Pennsy magically switch stations in New York City.

I had no idea that the Pennsylvania Railroad was a sprawling, powerful organization nor did I much care. All I knew was that it had the best job in the world, railroad engineer. And I also knew that train whistles in the night were not the exclusive property of country-western songwriters. Everytime a whistle blew, it felt like I wanted to be someplace else, or at least, in transit. Maybe that's why the poem *Ithaka*, which is about journeys rather than arrivals, feels just right to me at the end of the revised edition of my *Social Psychology of Organizing* (1979).

FINDLAY, OHIO (1939-1954)

We moved from Indiana to Findlay, Ohio when I was age 3. Findlay is the kind of town every kid should grow up in. Wide streets, good schools, Riverside Park, real neighborhoods, everything within walking distance, Porter's record store with a fabulous jazz section, and train stations for both the Nickel Plate and the New York Central. I saw my first diesel engine in Findlay, an ALCO PA on the Nickel Plate, when my father took up where my grandfathers left off, and took my brother and me regularly to see the trains.

The prettiest section of town was, and still is, South Main street. But, while it may have stunning houses, it was also a nightmare for a newspaper carrier like me. The houses were set back so far, that only the heavier Thursday and Friday editions of the morning paper could reach the porches when thrown from a bicycle on the sidewalk. The thin Saturday and Monday papers never had a chance of making it to the porches, and Tuesday and Wednesday papers made it about half the time. I covered the route at 4:00 in the morning, after being awakened by a clock radio tuned to Phil McKellar's all nite jazz show on CKLW. I can remember waking up to the most fascinating band sound I had ever heard. Later I discovered that it was the Sauter-Finegan orchestra's arrangement of *Midnight Sleighride*, which was so original, that RCA Victor wasn't sure whether to issue it on their classical Red Seal label or their pop label. I saw Sauter-Finegan in person several times at the outdoor Centennial Terrace in Sylvania, Ohio, and this, plus the Ted Heath orchestra, are the only groups I saw in the company of my parents.

The early morning hours were my own private territory, and that has remained true ever since. From 4:00 a.m. till about noon, life is pure gold. From noon on, reality chips away at the gold until, by 8 p.m., things often feel a good deal darker. (This essay was written between December 20 and December 28, 1990, including Christmas day, from 4:00 a.m. until noon, which leads me to wonder if I would have led a completely different life had I written about it from 4:00 p.m. until midnight.)

While growing up in Findlay, I wasn't much of a student and I'm sure I got into Wittenberg College only because they pretty much had to take high school graduates who went to the Lutheran Church. My most vivid recollections of my teens are of fascinating work experiences in the company of sympathetic, patient, hardworking adult males. I gave color commentary on sports broadcasts over WFIN with sportscaster Claire Meekins. I co-announced record shows with Jim Travis. I was an assistant to Charlie Conley, photographer for the local newspaper. I was a camp counselor, under the guidance of Sam Richmond. These people were models who gave me a long leash, feedback at a pace I could absorb, and a second chance when I really screwed up. For example, at Boy Scout camp, I was in charge of instructing 150 campers a week in the art of safe, competent axemanship. During one demonstration, while I was splitting a piece of wet wood, the axe slipped and cut my left index finger to the bone. I reflexively stuck my finger behind my knee, clamped the knee back to slow the flow of blood, matter of factly said to the campers, "Okay, what did I do wrong?," and then fainted. Sam Richmond didn't fire me. The next week I was in charge of instructing 150 campers in the art of safe, competent knot tying ... which is harder than it looks when you have only 9 fingers available.

If I had to designate a single reason why I wound up in psychology, it's because I was so impressed as an adolescent with the man my mother worked for, George W. Crane, who wrote a national column called the *Worry Clinic*. Crane was energetic, a fascinating conversationalist, a dynamic speaker, the center of attention wherever he went, a person who loved to try new things, and very funny. Who wouldn't want to be like that! So, at an early, impressionable age, I simply decided that Dr. Crane was who I wanted to be. He called himself a psychologist. So I wanted to become a psychologist. It was as simple as that. None of this "I want to be a psychologist because I like people" stuff. I liked jazz more than I liked people. But I liked Crane's performances even more. So I fell in love with form rather than substance, and chose psychology with the implacable logic, if it's good enough for him, it's good enough for me. What is astonishing is that I never once revisited or questioned that choice. Even to this day.

My brother Jim appears to have had a similar experience. While on a camping trip at the Philmont Scout ranch in New Mexico, he was kicked by a horse, suffered a severely fractured arm, and Dr. Burress of Albuquerque, New Mexico, the doctor who took care of him, made a vivid impression. I think Jim right then and there simply said, "I'm going to be a physician," and that was it. He too never reviewed the matter again.

WITTENBERG COLLEGE (1954-1958)

From Findlay, I went to Springfield, Ohio, which was on the New York Central, to attend Wittenberg (now) University, where I promoted and staged concerts by the Dave Brubeck Quartet and the Les Brown Orchestra. Brubeck came to Wittenberg, with Paul Desmond, just two weeks after he had appeared on the cover of *Time* magazine, which guaranteed a sellout. One week before the concert, I had conducted a seminar in Koch Hall at which I gave people some in-depth background on jazz and Brubeck, and played samples of what they would be hearing. The intent was to make the concert an educational as well as aesthetic success. Three hundred people turned up for the seminar, one of whom was an AD Pi pledge from Mansfield named Karen Eickhoff.

I didn't go to Wittenberg to ride trains or listen to jazz, although at times I wasn't sure what I did go for. But that puzzlement did not last for long, because of the incredibly good Wittenberg faculty. At Wittenberg, the professors were the kind of people I wanted to become, which meant that their profession, also started to look attractive. Floyd Nave, professor of geology, became the person with whom I sorted out everything from how I could remove a D on a final examination for which I studied while announcing an all-nite record show, to whether or not I should depledge the Lambda Chi fraternity (I did). Robert Remsberg in philosophy had a staggering amount of patience for those of us who could not figure out what the great philosophers were talking about, but had the uneasy feeling that it was important. Ex-Marine William Coyle brought *Madame Bovary* and other classics more alive than any person I have met since then.

But the psychology department, with George Dudycha, Virgil Rahn, and Roland Roselius was home. Dudycha was the writer and the systematic thinker, Rahn was the psychometrician and clinician (which is why my first RA assignment at Ohio State was to write test items for the Ohio State

Psychological Examination), and Roselius was the experimentalist, just then finishing his Ph.D. in educational psychology at Ohio State with John Horrocks. Roselius was my continuing source of a realistic job preview for what life would be like if I went on for a Ph.D.

I have often suspected that when I decided to go for a Ph.D, the life in academia that I envisioned was modeled very closely after the life I saw at Wittenberg: easy conversations at frequent intervals between faculty and students, earnest discussions of weighty issues while seated around the fireplace at a professor's home, fascinating things to read, humanities as the foundation of everything, easy movement among disciplines, and the discovery of patterns among seemingly unrelated elements. The world I envisioned was a world of teaching with incidental research, a world that is quite different from the one in which I now live. Maybe Allport's concept of functional autonomy really works.[1] I conducted research in order to teach, but over time, doing research became an end in itself and I lost sight of the original instrumentality. But not quite.

There is a mixture of wistfulness tinged with anger when I see people get turned off to the world of ideas when their window on this world is an overworked researcher. I suspect that my longstanding fondness for the world of Wittenberg is most visible when I write articles which teach rather than present new evidence, and when I give speeches that do the same thing. Not only do the speeches let me teach, but they also let me re-enact my days as a radio announcer and experience something of the excitement surrounding improvisation and one-night stands that I associate with jazz musicians.

I formally met the Karen Eickhoff who came to the Brubeck seminar when I was an announcer at WIZE. She introduced herself as a radio announcer on station WBLY, which was our main competitor. As an announcer, she was far more adventurous than I was. For example, under the airname "Cruisin Susan" she announced from a helicopter hovering over the Clark County fair, from school playgrounds, and while driving in a station wagon, whereas I was simply squeezed between two turntables downtown trying to sound clever while I spun the same records she did. During that period she gave a stunning performance as Laura in the College's production of *Glass Menagerie*. I saw the play both nights it was staged (the second night I sat beside Dean of Students Hulda Sallee) and I knew this was the most talented, exciting person I could ever hope to meet. We got "pinned" (after de-pledging I joined a group called Dorm League) on the Snyder Park golf course, engaged when I hid her engagement ring inside a '46 Dodge and gave her a set of clues as to where it was, and married by Professor Remsberg in Weaver Chapel on Friday December 13, 1957. We had a day and a half honeymoon at the Biltmore Hotel in Dayton, Ohio and then came back to study for final exams on Monday morning.

One of our first joint decisions centered on the question: Where should we go to graduate school? Karen had finished her student teaching just the day before we were married, and wanted a position where she could teach English and drama. I wanted a Ph.D. program where I could get a Ph.D. degree in industrial psychology, so that I could mix together consulting and teaching—don't forget Dr. Crane the applied psychologist. I applied to three places, Purdue, Ohio State, and Bowling Green. I had my heart set on Purdue and the other two places were simply backups. Purdue turned me down and I thought the world had come to an end. Roselius talked up Ohio State, which had accepted me, so we decided to go to Columbus feeling okay, but not thrilled.

OHIO STATE (1958-1962)

Columbus was on the southern branch of the Pennsylvania railroad, the portion running between St. Louis and New York, which meant I could relive most of my Warsaw experiences again. The demands on time and money imposed by grad school, meant that jazz did not dominate our life, although we did have some fascinating contacts with it. We saw the short-lived Gerry Mulligan big band, the equally short-lived Kai Winding trombone quartet, and the longer-lived, more powerful, Ohio State Lab band, which was then directed by Ladd MacIntosh. Lab band concerts were held on Sunday afternoons, and that was our main break from grading and writing papers.

The first year at Ohio State, writing test items, and taking miscellaneous courses toward the Industrial Psychology degree, did little to raise my spirits. But then several events happened which built a fire under me.

I had heard rumors that Harold Pepinsky, a professor of counseling, was the most demanding advisor in the department, had a million different interests, was an active researcher, and worked closely with his advisees. Pep's ability to spot nonsense was legendary, and while he was basically a kind person, he was also an impatient person. I gathered my courage, made an appointment to see if I could work with him, and failed to impress him on my first try. But I kept trying, by attending his courses and his research meetings and by writing papers for him, until finally he agreed to take me on as a research assistant to study the topic of research team productivity. Doing research, on research, for someone new to research, is downright terrifying. Pep kept just the right blend of terror and support in the project so that we all worked all the time at our limits.

The work I did with Pep, and his research associate Mary Moll, consisted of a series of in-depth interviews with members of a research team who were designing a heart valve, and two groups at Battelle working on semi-conductor problems, one group reputedly being more productive than the other. The question was, what separates more from less productive teams? To answer this question we paid very careful attention to the way people talked about their work and partitioned it into tasks and antecedents. Each mention of a task was treated as a separate unit and we built a cognitive and linguistic structure for their talk, which I now think looked a lot like a cause map.

The task that most intrigued all of us was one which we variously labeled facade maintenance, impression management, and simulated productivity. We found that a significant amount of time and activity on all three teams was devoted to giving the impression that the group was being productive, rather than to doing the work itself. We were sensitized to this dynamic because all three of us had just read a fascinating monograph which was being circulated in offprint, by an unknown person who couldn't even seem to spell his first name correctly, Erving Goffman. We were reading what was to become *Presentation of Self in Everyday Life*, and in true Pepinsky fashion, we saw evidence everywhere of the phenomenon we had just been reading about (e.g., when we read Miller, Galanter, and Pribram's *Plans and the Structure of Behavior*, we saw TOTEs everywhere).

To this day we still have not resolved the debate concerning the relationship between feigned productivity and actual performance. The argument for a negative relationship says that people with low competence and lagging performance, use more impression management to paper over this deficit. The argument for a positive relationship says that impression management gets sponsors off the team's back and allows people to do the work that really needs doing. This line of argument suggests that people with high competence engage in more impression management.[2] Also intriguing was the possibility that, if people act their way into meaning, then going through the motions of being productive might create the very productive action whose absence spurred the simulation in the first place. The seeds of my own long-term interest in issues of meaning, language, enacted realities, social construction, loose coupling, and creativity all seem present in these early struggles to see if teams were productive because of or in spite of, monitoring by their sponsors.

The pedagogical point is that Pep took me backstage in the research enterprise right away, gave me hands on experience almost immediately, and treated my ideas as just as worthy of consideration as were his own. I tried to create the same climate for my own students when I left Ohio State, and was successful doing so at Purdue and Minnesota. But after Minnesota, I seem to have drifted away from that style, partly because I took on shorter projects that required more thinking and less data collection. As the style of my work and writing became more distinctive, it became harder for me to involve students actively in what was an increasingly private activity. What was I to do, have them hang around and watch me read? Or write? Or wad up pages of manuscript that didn't work? Or respond to a question which, no sooner had I asked it than I heard the answer in my own head and rudely ignored their answer? There have been people, both faculty and students, who fit beautifully into the somewhat cramped world I have just described. But, on balance, things seem to work best for everyone when I serve as the "outside" person on dissertations chaired by someone else.

My work to this day shows the extent of Pepinsky's influence. He is fanatic about clear, graceful writing, he reads everything he can get his hands on, the bibliographies of his papers have a startling range of citations, he is eclectic and interdisciplinary, he has a longstanding interest in language and productivity, he always wants to know what's new, he has ties to Minneapolis, his wife gives him some of his best ideas, he is a therapist at heart, and half of the time people have no idea what he is talking about. If that doesn't describe me, I don't know what does. I feel sorry for anyone who tries to tackle academia without a model like this.

While Pep was the most enduring reason that Ohio State turned around for me, there were other events that proved to be significant. The Psychology Department decided to require that all graduate students attend a year long proseminar. Each professor in the department had one week (three sessions) to present the best material he thought his specialty had to offer (Emily Stogdill, the only woman, didn't present). The reading list was staggering (e.g., Lauren Wispe assigned both volumes of the *Handbook of Social Psychology* for his week on social psychology). What we saw, week after week, were passionate experts and fascinating lines of work. We literally saw the whole field of psychology at one sitting in its most compelling form. That never happened again and probably couldn't happen again. I'm sure others came out of that course perfectly willing to return to their specialties, but the proseminar, plus Pep's example, Wittenberg's liberal arts tradition, and George Crane's broad interests combined to make me a militant generalist. I wouldn't have it any other way.

Ohio State was good for me in still another way. I tried out a variety of programs within psychology including, the counseling program where I did an internship at the VA hospital in Chillicothe, the clinical program, the social psychology program which, during my four years had four different heads—Wispe, Bonner, Rosenberg, Kiesler—and finally, I ended up in a degree program which Ohio State built specifically for Genie Plog and myself, called Organizational Psychology. No such program had existed before. The people who administered our doctoral exams included Pepinsky (counseling psychology), Rotter (clinical psychology), Briggs (engineering psychology), Shartle (industrial psychology) and Bonner (social psychology), an assortment of people whom only a generalist would love.

My dissertation had an equally implausible start. Bob Rosenthal, who is now at Harvard, was then teaching clinical psychology at the University of North Dakota and had been invited to Ohio State to teach George Kelly's courses while Kelly was on sabbatical. Rosenthal was excited about his own research on experimenter bias, which was just then beginning to appear in print. And he was also excited about a new book by Leon Festinger called *A Theory of Cognitive Dissonance*. We read the book in Rosenthal's seminar and I loved the ideas. Since Pepinsky was interested in productivity, it was a simple matter to ask, what effect does dissonance have on productivity?

I mulled this question over and just when it was time to design my dissertation research Pep left for a sabbatical year in Norway. Milton Rosenberg, not a fan of Festinger, then agreed to supervise the dissertation. But Milt resigned from the department abruptly when Ohio State refused to allow a controversial speaker on campus. Meanwhile I kept doing pilot work and then data collection for the main study, which Doug Crowne then agreed to supervise. While Karen cranked an ancient Friden calculator for hours doing statistical analyses, I wrote and rewrote drafts which Crowne worked on with great care. I had no idea at the time how much I must have disrupted Crowne's already frantic life as he worked to strengthen his upcoming tenure case, but he never once refused to help. The one saving grace is that the resulting dissertation was judged the best dissertation of the year in the American Research Institute (ARI) national competition, thereby vindicating some of Doug's efforts.

We started our family in Columbus, although that too had its absurd moments. I was sufficiently nervous about getting to the hospital, especially since delivery was expected during snowy December, that I kept practicing the drive to University Hospital, which is quite remarkable when you consider that it was located just seven blocks from our apartment on West Lane. Nevertheless, when Karen went into labor at 3:00 a.m., and I started to back the car out of the garage, I turned too sharply, snagged the left front tire on a board sticking out of the side of the garage, ripped the tire open, and immediately rendered the car useless. Near hysteria I ran back into the house, called a cab, and we sat on the porch until it finally came. From then on, things went OK except that everyone on the obstetrics staff thought everyone else had notified me in the waiting room, that our son Kirk had been born with a normal delivery in the morning. They hadn't. And suddenly at 3:00 p.m. in the afternoon, this dawned on them and they gave me the good news. What one's imagination can concoct, seated in a hospital waiting room for 11 hours with no news, is frightening. To this day, I have an aversion to ringing telephones and I suspect it goes back to hearing the phone in the waiting room ring so many times with news for everyone but me.

As if all of this were not enough absurdity, I was hired by Purdue, the place that had rejected my Ph.D. application, to teach industrial social psychology.

PURDUE (1962-1965)

When we moved to Purdue, we moved close to the New York Central and the daily James Whitcomb Riley train to Chicago. Once each year, in April, the Psychology Department took over the lounge car and partied all the way up to the Midwestern Psychology Association meetings in Chicago, and then quietly tried to regroup all the way back after the convention. But for sheer adventure, there was nothing to equal the antiquated equipment on the Monon, which also ran from Lafayette to Chicago, over a route which had no conceivable commercial value that any of us could detect. The sensation was almost that of being on a tourist line or an amusement park concession, a sensation which was heightened because the train ran right down the middle of a main street in Lafayette. Jazz in Lafayette consisted mainly of occasional road shows, the best of the lot being the Stan Kenton-Four Freshmen concert, which was extraordinarily tight because they had just finished a recording session at Butler University in Indianapolis. Since we had our hands full with a rapidly expanding family the fact that jazz was in short supply did nothing to dampen the quality of life.

I could not have found a better place to start a career. The psychology faculty were unusually receptive to a brand of industrial psychology that was not typical Tiffin and McCormick textbook material. I taught training, but I taught it as a problem in attitude change and persuasion. In many ways that was a model for my teaching thereafter, namely, an applied topic is taught using disciplinary language and findings and experiments, rather than practice, as examples. My first talk at Purdue was to a graduate group called PAGSIP. I talked about jazz improvisation as a model of group interaction, complete with recordings and photographs. (Shades of my Brubeck shtick at Wittenberg.)

Not only were the people in psychology receptive to new material, they were also a tight-knit community who enfolded us. Ben Winer used to take Karen and our children, and Irene Stephens and her children, to watch trains come and go at the local station. Don King, who had the office opposite mine, taught me everything I know about teaching and even took the time to sit in on and critique many of my classes. Ken Michels mentored me on doing research and publishing. Several of us—E.J. Asher, Mark Stephens, Don Brown, and sometimes Ben Winer—golfed together regularly. This was the last time I played golf because, as my career unfolded, "there wasn't time for it." Mark Stephens, who had been Doug Crowne's advisor, helped me with my writing. And Bob Perloff filled the Pepinsky role as, day in, day out, he would come bounding in, reprint in hand, and puff, "Hey, have you seen this yet?" Usually I hadn't, which meant my scholarship got better every time Bob appeared.

I had an office next to the graduate student bullpen area, which enabled me to meet and work with Mike Malone, Don Penner, Gordon Fitch, Jack Larson, Ed Ryterband, Abe Tesser, and Dick Bootzin.

Penner, a graduate student who loved to tinker, taught me the upside of method centered research. We would build an apparatus and then ask, what psychological problems does this pose for a group, and who has talked about these problems before? We did this, for example, when we combined the fishing reels used in Triplett's classic social facilitation studies with an Etch-A-Sketch tracing task, into a device which, in one place, created conditions of group competition and cooperation. This same method-driven style of inquiry appeared later at Minnesota when Dave Gilfillan and I studied model cultures using the common target game and Perry Prestholdt and I studied dissonant rewards using a device adapted from research with pigeons. The most recent incarnation of this same strategy is found in one of my favorite chapters, an article on reverse simulation ("Utilization as Reverse Simulation," 1983). I argue that lab technologies represent social designs which should be exported to the real world (we should simulate the laboratory in the real world, not the real world in the laboratory).

I also developed close ties with faculty at the Krannert Business School, which at that time, in one of those rare fortuitous gatherings of talented people, included Richard Walton, Bill Starbuck, Vern Smith, Mike Driver, Jack Sherwood, and Marc Pilisuk. Starbuck got me my first major writing assignment, the chapter on lab experimentation in March's *Handbook of Organizations*. The chapter was originally assigned to John Lanzetta, but as the publication deadline for the handbook came closer and closer, Lanzetta suddenly had to bow out. March was stuck, he asked Bill what he should do, Bill said I have this colleague down the hall who runs experiments and might help, so Bill brokered an inquiry to see if I would be interested. Since I knew nothing about laboratory experiments with organizations, I said, "Sure, I'll write the chapter." How else would I learn about the topic? I dropped everything, wrote the chapter in record time, and instantly created a partial "identity" for myself.

Dick Walton took me on my first, and very nearly my last consulting engagement at Dalton Foundries in Warsaw, Indiana. There was intense conflict in the foundry between foremen and workers and Walton, fresh from his work with Bob McKersie, had been called in to improve conditions. I personally tried to improve conditions by teaching Fritz Heider's balance theory to the foremen. During the drive back to Lafayette, Dick conveyed, with enormous tact and support, the message, "nice try but ...."

Professionally, several things fell into place during the time we were at Purdue. Six months after I got there, while going through the mail one morning, I opened a letter from Pittsburgh and inside it was a check for $1000 and a letter from John Flanagan congratulating me on writing the best dissertation of the year in psychology. At first I thought it was a joke because I didn't even know the dissertation was under consideration. I ran over to the Home Ec cafeteria where I knew Ken Michels, Vic Deneberg, and Mark Stephens often had coffee at that hour and sure enough there they were. All three attested that the letter and check were indeed not a hoax, which felt great for all of two hours, after which I then began to be troubled by the thought, "Okay, now what do you do for a encore?"

Before receiving the ARI dissertation award, I had written up the dissertation research with Mark Stephens' help, submitted it to the *Journal of Abnormal and Social Psychology*, and Dan Katz had rejected it on the basis that it was a minor piece of dissonance research. But then something happened that I have not seen happen again to this day. One of the referees, Arthur R. (Bob) Cohen, wrote to Katz saying that he had been troubled by his negative evaluation of the manuscript, as a result he had restudied the manuscript, he discovered that he had missed the point of the work, the point was highly significant, and that he wanted to reverse his recommendation and urged Katz to reverse his decision. Katz did, sent me the correspondence with Cohen, and said he would be pleased to publish the work. This incident had a big impact on me and informed much of my editing philosophy later at *Administrative Science Quarterly* (*ASQ*). I actually didn't realize this possible linkage, until the moment I began to draft this paragraph for this essay.

As a result of the dissertation award, I was invited to give the Psi Chi invited address at the Midwestern Psychological Association in Chicago. I chose to address the scathing criticism of dissonance theory that was then being circulated by Chapanis and Chapanis, and I did so in a speech titled "When Prophecy Pales" (1965). The title is still one of my favorites. Up until the point where I gave the speech, I was not part of any inner circle of dissonance researchers since I came from Ohio State of all places, which didn't even have a social psychology program, and the dissonance people were clustered at Duke, Minnesota, and Stanford which had strong programs. But my remarks were one of the first public statements to rebut the researchers from Johns Hopkins, the audience in Chicago was filled with dissonance researchers, and Elliot Aronson was one of the most enthusiastic about the speech, which may have been one reason I was offered a position at Minnesota a year later.

The Psi Chi speech is interesting to me simply because it seems to show a developing voice, and already shows a style which seems to characterize much of my writing: humor, unexpected connections, unusual literature citations, an upbeat ending, strange examples, tacit propositions to be tested, and thinly veiled advice that we all need to beware of sluggish imaginations, all of which lead half of the audience to ask, "What does this have to do with dissonance theory?" and the other half to say, "Now that's dissonance theory!" My work seems to generate more bimodal reactions than does that of most people with whom I compare myself, and the Psi Chi speech seems to have set this pattern in motion.

Purdue was distinctive personally, as well as professionally. Our second son Kyle was born one month after we arrived. This time I didn't puncture a tire to add to the drama. Instead, I was teaching the Harvard Business School Slade case to MBA students when my secretary walked into class, said your wife is in labor at St. E's (St. Elizabeth's), and, totally flustered, I asked the class to predict whether it would be a boy or a girl, which they did (a boy). And then, and this is the truth, I turned to the class and said, "Hey, I have an idea. Why don't you vote on whether you think it will be a boy or a girl?" They laughed me out of the classroom and out of the building, and on to the hospital.

Since we had two children when our third son Kris was born in 1964, we had made elaborate advance plans to have an instant baby-sitter when Karen went into labor, so that I could take her to the hospital. Unfortunately, we did not prepare for the contingency that we would call the baby-sitter at 3:00 in the morning. When we did call, she woke out of a deep sleep, mumbled, "What time is it?" and promptly fell back asleep, with the phone off the hook. Whistles and shouts didn't rouse her, so Karen went off to the hospital alone. I got a sitter four hours later, but by that time Karen was in the recovery room. She was in a bed next to a gigantic window, the sun was shining, so was she, and Kris looked as if he knew he was welcomed.

MINNESOTA (1965-1972)

The move to Minnesota represented a high point in both trains and bands. My first real contact with Minneapolis came when Marv Dunnette called me during a party at Joe Tiffin's house, and said that if I flew up to Minneapolis immediately, a house in Prospect Park had just come on the market which he thought was ideal for us. I did, and he was right, but while the lawyer was driving me back to the airport after contracts were signed, a tornado hit the edge of Minneapolis, the sky over the airport was a frightening mess of lightning, and I got out and took a cab right back downtown to the Burlington railroad station and bought a roomette to Chicago. I sat in the dome car late at night, and watched the storm, feeling more content than I had in a long time. That was the first of many trips shuttling back and forth between Minneapolis and Chicago, most of which I took on the Milwaukee Road. I was on a first name basis with the crews, the ticket agents, and knew the route and the schedule the way most people know the road to their house. On all the runs, the Milwaukee used their beavertail observation-parlor cars, which were unmatched for comfort and viewing.

Jazz in Minneapolis was terrific, and ranged all the way from a get down dirty blues piano player at Big Al's, a club located just 10 feet from the Milwaukee Railroad tracks, to the Don Ellis big band which had made Minneapolis its home base. The Buddy Rich band made several appearances, during one of which we witnessed a relative rarity, namely, in his exuberance, Rich pushed his foot pedal completely through the head of his bass drum and the concert came to a halt until they could locate a new head. Needless to say, Rich was not at a loss for words while awaiting the repair.

Jazz orchestras were enough in the air that Dave Gilfillan, Tom Keith, and I thought it was a good time to see what effect musicians' expectations of the quality of music had on their execution of the music. We designed a true field experiment which showed clearly that musicians, who thought they were about to play a high quality piece of new music, were more attentive and exerted more effort when they actually rehearsed the music, which resulted in a better sounding tune, compared to musicians who worked on the identical piece of music, but thought it had been written by a journeyman composer.

The study was a clear and convincing demonstration of a self-fulfilling prophecy, although you would never know it by reading the published report in *Sociometry*. For some reason, I did not think that a clear example of a collective self-fulfilling prophecy was "enough" theory to surround the evidence, so I wrote a much more elaborate introduction using McGuire's theory of persuasion. I very nearly strangled a simple, clear study that made one solid point worth making. Since I wrote up this study after we had moved to the business school at Cornell, my hypothesis for this strange behavior is that I was uneasy about the move out of a psychology department. I overcompensated for this uneasiness by hauling out every bit of psychology I had ever learned to reassure the psychologists (and myself) that I was still one of them. My overcorrection very nearly ruined a perfectly good study. Fortunately, people ignored the McGuire trappings, saw clearly what was going on in the orchestras, and extracted the key point—expectations enact the conditions of their own validity.

At Minnesota I tried to work in both the Social Relations Lab and the industrial psychology program, but the center of gravity was in social psychology because Aronson had just left to go to Texas. It did not dawn on me until many years later that I probably used up industrial psychology's recruiting slot in the department, but they got less from me than they expected. For my part, I was awed by working in the same lab where Hal Kelley, Festinger, Aronson, Dana Bramel, Schachter, Darley, and Willerman, had been. I hoped some of this aura would rub off if I simply put in lots and lots of hours in the same setting.

The Minnesota department once again was a community. Within three blocks of our house lived Marv Dunnette, David Campbell, Jack Yellott, Milt Trapold, Bill Fox, Bruce Overmeier, Paul Meehl, Jack Darley, the poet John Berryman, ethologist John Tester, and mayor Art Naftalin. Everyday I walked two miles to get to the University which must be why, when I got to Austin, Texas, I discovered I just couldn't stand the heat and why, when we moved to Cornell from Minnesota, I honestly told people I was moving south because Minnesota was too cold for me.

At Minnesota I had wonderful on-the-job-training in laboratory experimentation from Elaine Walster, Ellen Berscheid, and Norm Miller. I still think the model culture study which Dave Gilfillan and I published in 1971 is the best experiment I've ever been associated with, and it has just as much currency now for issues of succession, organizational learning, and level of analysis as it had when published.

The first edition of *The Social Psychology of Organizing* was written at Minnesota. This short book was intended to be part of an introductory text for social psychology which would be formed by a stack of paperbacks, each written by an authority on some aspect of social psychology. Without ever checking this out, I assumed that freshmen would love new theory (e.g., the second cybernetics), old theory (e.g., social evolution), counter-intuitive ideas (e.g., people discover their plans only after they accomplish them), new concepts (e.g., ethnomethodology), and new twists on old concepts (e.g., fate control), as much as I did.

Consequently, I wrote a short, dense account of the ways in which the things I then found fascinating were interwoven. I simply assumed that what I wrote had obvious relevance to organizations since it obviously was about the people who worked in them. The "fascinated" reader was left to fill in the details and examples. Those assumptions were innocent, if a bit naive, but they worked. The book was not a big seller in the Kiesler series, that honor went to Phil Zimbardo as it has ever since, but it built a steady following, in part because it stood conventional wisdom on its ear—students love to be counter-intuitive—and because it seemed to support quite different presuppositions, which meant teachers and researchers alike could impose their own imprint on the argument. Davis has since demonstrated that this combination,[3] which I inadvertently stumbled onto, tends to be associated with "classic" works.

My third book, *Managerial Behavior Performance and Effectiveness* (1970), which was co-authored with Campbell, Dunnette, and Lawler at Gull Lake, was written in three weeks using what I still feel is the ideal vehicle for collaboration: intense activity, division of labor, daily feedback, know each other more fully through work and play, no interruptions, family is part of activity which mutes guilt and indignation, you see an end in sight, there is daily competition for quality and quantity of output, and each learns how the other is thinking and can blend with and anticipate that thinking. John Campbell worked much longer than three weeks to smooth the transitions, produce a consistent style, and enrich the citations, but the core was in hand when we all left the cottages and headed back toward the Twin Cities.

Near the end of our stay at Minnesota (1969-1970) Mauk Mulder wanted to learn more about simulating organizations in the laboratory, so he invited us to Utrecht, The Netherlands in 1969. He and I organized a research team, which included Pieter Veen, Jan Rietsma, and Din Binkhorst and built a simulation. However, in achieving realism, we built something that was almost impossible to run.

To a train lover, the Netherlands is heaven. The trains are frequent, fast, clean, punctual, and the equipment is varied. To get to the Institute in Utrecht from our house in Doorn, I used to hike two and one-half miles through a dense woods to the station at Maarn, which is on the main East-West track to Arnhem and Germany, and be within a half an hour of a departure, no matter when I arrived.

My interest in music continued and Binkhorst, who played tenor in the Utrecht Jazz Orchestra, invited me to join him at a rehearsal since there wasn't much music to hear. I did, and I kept going back because I started to see patterns across rehearsals even though I couldn't understand a word of what people said. I checked out the apparent patterns with Din, and then we developed an interview format which was designed to elicit the musicians' own maps of patterns so that we could compare them to our own hunches. All of this happened because earlier, we had been sitting around at a research meeting, talking about Maruyama's second cybernetics, when it dawned on us that respondents rather than observers could draw Maruyama's cause diagrams. To test this possibility instantly, we each drew a Maruyama-like map of the research meeting that had unfolded up to that point. Not only did we draw similar maps, but we identified a sequence of events which formed an amplification loop and which had repeatedly caused us trouble in past research meetings. That's when we really got excited. So it was an unanticipated hunch during a research meeting, coupled with an unanticipated trip to a rehearsal, which paved the way for our study of cause maps ("Cognition in Organization," 1977).

As a family we watched the United States landing on the moon while sitting in the lounge of the Pabst hotel in Doorn; heard about Cornell's guns on campus episode on Armed Forces Radio; and re-entered the country shortly after the Kent State massacres.

Soon after we returned to the United States and Minnesota, Tom Dyckman, an accounting professor at Cornell, heard me give an address to the American Accounting Association in New Orleans. In the speech I chided behavioral accountants for their timid experiments and naive assumptions about mediating psychological processes. Since Tom did some work of the kind I was criticizing, he initiated more discussions with me after the meetings and raised the possibility that I might want to move to Cornell. The idea of working in a business school with a joint appointment in psychology, was intriguing. Furthermore, Karen and I were increasingly nervous about the drug culture which was moving into the Minneapolis inner city schools, we were short-handed in social psychology and it became harder to justify organizational problems as mainstream social and, to a small town boy from the Midwest, the Ivy League looked like the big time. So we packed three boys plus luggage plus our cat "Charlie" into a tiny BMW 2002 and headed for the Finger Lakes.

We decided that a change from a public to a private institution might just as well be accompanied by a change in lifestyle, so we bought a 40 acre working farm just outside Trumansburg, New York (home of the Moog synthesizer), and 14 miles from the Cornell campus. While Karen and the boys gradually accumulated goats, pigs, rabbits, sheep, and calves, we all learned about farming through brute trial and error (e.g., although sliding barn doors appear to be very heavy, the slightest bit of wind can lift them off their track and float them through the air a considerable distance, calves can jump through open windows, newborn lambs prefer a warm kitchen to a cold barn).

CORNELL (1972-1984)

Trains and jazz took a different, some would say more symbolic, form when we moved to Cornell. We lived just one-half mile from the roadbed of the Lehigh Valley (the tracks had been ripped up): we could see, looking North across Lake Cayuga, a daily coal train which inched up to the Milliken Station powerplant at a maximum of 5 miles per hour; and we often took guests to dine at the old Lehigh Valley station. But to see and board a real train, we had to drive to New York Central tracks in Syracuse. Jazz also was more elusive. Our sons formed a short-lived group called Echelon which had the sound of Chicago. We once heard a concert by the Glenn Miller band (you take whomever you can get) in the Ithaca Theater after the heating system failed. The failure meant that the warm moist air coming out the bells of each instrument condensed into steam. A hot trumpet solo, literally, produced smoke on each sustained notes, which was the most fascinating visual effect I had ever seen in music.

My first exposure to the Cornell culture was Urie Bonfenbrenner's somewhat blunt version of what life there was like. He said in essence, you wouldn't be here unless you were really good; now all you have to do is more of what got you here and let the rest of us do what got us here. Compared to Purdue and Minnesota, that sounded a lot more anomic than what I had been used to. Maybe that was what the Ivy League was all about.

The place didn't prove to be quite that harsh. But the amount of interaction with colleagues did go down somewhat, partly because there simply were fewer of them. Tom Lodahl, Art Kover, Dave Smith, and I were the OB group, and within a short time, all three had left.

ASQ filled much of this void and its authors and reviewers became a substitute set of colleagues. Caroline Violette and then Linda Pike as managing editors, Howard Aldrich as associate editor, and Sam Bacharach as book review editor, became the main people I interacted with face-to-face, along with three doctoral students—Michel Bougon, Lance Kurke, and Carl Homer—and two accounting people, Bob Swieringa and Dyckman.

ASQ became a prominent part of life at Cornell although I had not intended it that way. When I agreed to go to Cornell, my only condition to Dean Davidson was that I not have to edit *ASQ*. Four years later I was editing *ASQ*, due to a series of circumstances neither he nor I could envision. I have already written about the *ASQ* experience extensively in Cummings and Frost.[4]

There is always a great deal of speculation about how much influence an editor can exert over the content of a journal. During my tenure as editor, I can count eight changes that I made and they are among the smallest events imaginable in publishing. You can see these changes if you compare Issue 1 of Volume 22 (which is the last issue my predecessor, Tom Lodahl, edited) with Issue 2, Volume 30 (which is the last issue I edited). You will find eight differences in Volume 30:

1. inclusive page numbers on the spine;
2. a list of former editors at the bottom of the title page;
3. book reviews listed on the back cover;
4. a complete bibliographic citation at the bottom of the first page of each article;
5. retrieval information at the bottom of each page of each article;
6. biographical information about the authors;
7. the name of the school which published the journal added to the front cover; and
8. A notice to contributors inserted in each issue.

And that's it. What I have to show for nine years of hard work are eight changes in appearance.

Yet, small as those changes are, they have tangible effects. They make it easier to retrieve articles (1, 3, 5), easier to cite articles (4), easier to submit appropriate articles (8), easier to follow up articles (6), easier to see the continuity and legitimacy of an emerging field (2), and easier to identify a single place as a center for organizational studies (7). These changes make it easier to use *ASQ*, which means more readers will skim it, more librarians will be urged to purchase full runs of the journal, more readers will want to have their own copies, and better work will be submitted which amplifies each of the other changes. Thus, small events can make a difference.

I have had other invitations since *ASQ* days to edit journals, all of which I turned down. I did so because I need more time to work on my own writing, because I continue to edit anyway since I get on average of 20 manuscripts a month on which people would like comments, I serve on several editorial boards, and I have an obsession that all of my students write all of the time and their writing deserves careful attention.

I wrote three pieces at Cornell which I still like: "Small Wins" (Tom Peters' dissertation where the idea of small wins originated remains a gold mine of ideas); "Psychology as Gloss" (my view of application which is modeled after the figure of biblical exegesis, something that I learned from the Methodist minister in Trumansburg, Tom Lang) and "Systematic Observational

Methods." I worked full time for an entire sabbatical semester on the observation chapter and wrote it during the winter on the shores of frozen Lake Cayuga, heated by a wood stove which was cast in the shape of a cathedral. The chapter has a more playful tone than is common for handbooks, and that tone may reflect my attempt to compensate for the unrelenting grayness of an Ithaca winter. Had I written the same chapter in Austin, Texas, it might well have sounded like a generic handbook chapter. I'm glad for the unique tone because I think it breathes some life back into methodology.

Life at Cornell became a lot more complicated as I became less and less able to control a growing addiction to alcohol. I now realize that I showed all the classic symptoms, the move to Cornell being perhaps the telltale search for a "geographic cure." Blackouts became more frequent through the mid-1970s until, during a visit to Minneapolis in February 1978, I talked to Milt Trapold and Ellen Berscheid, both of whom had become active in chemical dependency work in the Twin Cities. Milt ran down the list of symptoms of alcoholism, I copied them down without saying a word, Milt said "I think those symptoms fit you," I still didn't say a word, and then I said "thank you," and walked out of Ellen's office. I flew back to Ithaca and the next morning sat down at the kitchen table with Karen, handed her the list of symptoms I had copied and said, "read this, I think I'm an alcoholic." Before we got up from the table I had decided to go into treatment, Karen called Milt who got me into the St. Mary's chemical dependency unit right away, and we told the boys what was up when they got home from school. Dean Davidson, Hal Bierman, and Caroline Violette at Cornell all gave me unqualified support for the decision and made it possible for me to leave classes and *ASQ* for an indefinite period.

I had my last drink on the flight to Minneapolis. Milt picked me up at the airport and drove me around for awhile because I was too frightened even to speak. He got me calmed down, helped me check in to the hospital, and that's the last familiar face I saw until Karen and the boys came for "family week" six weeks later. That week was hardball, with everyone prodded and then helped to get hold of all the ways in which my drinking had made their lives much tougher, how tired they were of covering up and making do, and yet, how there was still a spark to build on, if the drinking stopped. Completely. It had to be hard for our three teenage sons, especially coming from a small town, to participate in the sessions. They could have refused, but they didn't. Their courage helped me regain mine. Through the skillful work of Marge Marquis, a group of no-nonsense patients all of whom signed my copy of the AA *Big Book*, and AA itself, I started a process of recovery and left the hospital after eight weeks.

Ellen visited me the final day of my stay at the hospital, and heard me say publicly that the Serenity Prayer was the most profound set of words I had ever heard, and that it was to be my guide from then on. Having said that,

I hugged Marge, hugged Ellen, took a cab to be airport, and flew back to Ithaca, for the first time ever, without a drink in my hand. The next day, when I walked into my MBA class, I said simply, I want to tell you where I have been the last eight weeks, what happened to me, and what I learned. I pulled no punches, fielded intensive questions for two more hours, and that was that.

Without alcohol as a buffer, I feel life's sharp edges more vividly, socializing is a lot more work, anger is a chronic threat to composure, and having fun is a measured rather than explosive activity. But I know what's going on, I know more quickly when I am about to lapse into bad habits although that doesn't make it any easier to avoid them, and I know that if I forget to take it one day at a time, I'm in deep trouble. As the phrase says, my goal is progress, not perfection.

Ithaca felt isolated, both geographically and intellectually. It takes an effort for people to get in and out. I have had my most harrowing flying experiences going into Tompkins County Airport and vowed always to fly out of Syracuse, which is no less harrowing because of wild weather from Cortland, New York north to the airport.

After Kris graduated from high school, Karen and I decided to sample life somewhere else, and accepted an invitation to spend the year (1983-1984) at Seattle University, whose provost, Tom Longin, had served on the Trumansburg school board with Karen. This short-term move to the tracks of the Great Northern railroad, and the jazz sounds of George Cables, Kenny Barron, and Bud Shank, opened our eyes in several ways. I realized that, had it not been for reading *ASQ* manuscripts, my grasp of ideas would have been even more dated than it had become. At Seattle University, year-long conversations with members of the business school advisory board, night school teaching of motivated MBA students, and my own ambitious reading program, enriched by superb theater, regular jazz performances, and walks along Elliott Bay resulted in one of the best theory pieces I have ever written ("Sources of Order in Underorganized Systems"). And we also realized that with just the two of us, the opportunities available in our surroundings were now much more crucial.

So, when Jim Dyer and Bill Cunningham at Texas made us an offer in February, we decided to accept it. During the year in Seattle, we realized how much more stimulation a city bigger than Ithaca could provide. And Texas was at the height of the boom period, and their enthusiasm and rah-rah attitude was refreshing. The prospect of colleagues my own age, George Huber, Reuben McDaniel, and Brian Graham-Moore, was a promising change from working strictly with junior faculty and doctoral students. Eight years of *ASQ* editing was beginning to take its toll, although I misjudged how much I would miss that action once John Freeman took over. And besides, Texas was "exotic."

TEXAS (1984-1988)

Railroads in the Southwest were a whole new unfamiliar set of names for us. We lived close to, jogged alongside, and rode trains on the former tracks of the Missouri Pacific, which runs right down the middle of Route 1 in Austin. Jazz, in a city known for Willie Nelson and Austin City Limits, was spotty, although when it came in the form of Carmen McRae, Lionel Hampton, Sarah Vaughan, or Rick Lawn directing Bob Mintzer and the UT Lab Band, it energized and reaffirmed.

Some of my writing had become sloppy at Cornell. The arguments were not as tight or as fully developed as they should have been and they involved poses and affectations which I sometimes mistook for evocative messages (e.g., blindspots in organizational theorizing, affirmation as inquiry). McDaniel and Huber, both former engineers, and both students of decision making, came down hard but constructive on my casual arguments derived from the organizing model, and they helped me make the arguments more substantial. In doing so, they didn't convert me to their views, however. My "Cosmos vs. Chaos" (1985) paper, for example, argues that the information technology of which Huber is so fond, can harm rather than help decision making. My argument would not have been as forceful or as stripped of flowery images, had it not been for their inputs and arguments.

I met Harry Wilmer, Director and Founder of the Institute for the Humanities in Salado, Texas, because he wanted some advice about what to do with the Institute's increasing size. Our talks enlarged, Karen and I were invited to join the institute, and eight times a year, at 4:00 on a Sunday afternoon, we heard people like the poetess Naomi Nye, sleep researcher Alan Hobson, and author Maya Angelo, present the best they had to offer. Their remarks were followed by an hour of questions and answers which ranged from "What is your sister like?" through "What do you think of Texans?" to "What is the ontological status of that concept?"

Wilmer is probably the most impressive person I've ever met: a Jungian analyst who worked with Vietnam veterans, a promoter of film festivals, a person whose network has incredible scope (e.g., he was one of the trainers of psychiatrist-jazz pianist Denny Zeitlin at Langley Porter), and an unassuming, candid, kind human being who is enormously creative. The Institute played an important indirect role in the writing I did while at Texas. Each Institute seminar drew me out of whatever narrowness had accumulated up to that point in my own thinking and may well have functioned just like those proseminars did back at Ohio State.

For example, Item 49 on my résumé, under the heading Chapters in Edited Volumes, has the title "Small Sins and Large Evils." It's not the kind of item you'd expect to find on the résumé of a person in organizational behavior, but it's on there because it represents one of the many ways in which the projects at Wilmer's Institute for the Humanities inform my work. Wilmer organized a major symposium on the concept of evil, which later was turned into a Bill Moyers special on PBS. My job was to summarize the symposium, and in preparation, Karen and I read and discussed everything we could find about the topic of evil. She wrote a bibliography and extracted key quotes, while I kept trying to tie the often esoteric discussions to the more familiar world of psychology where I felt more at home.

My effort to pull the two domains together is reflected in this short paper which was in the program given to all participants, and reprinted in the book published from the proceedings. To this day I still have the feeling that in trying to psychologize the concept of evil, I gutted it of much of its evocative power. That can happen, when social science and the humanities try to make common cause, but it is no reason to stop trying. I am encouraged in my efforts to work with these two domains, by my colleague at Michigan, Mayer Zald, who works this interface with more confidence, more eloquence, and more wisdom, than I have yet been able to bring to the problem. If I simply listen more attentively, Mayer may yet help me tap a voice that has been dormant since Wittenberg.

Collaborative papers with people like Larry Browning, were easy at Texas, but collaborative research was a lot harder, partly because key researchers such as Huber and Jim Dyer were already tied closely into the high-tech scene in Austin. Karlene Roberts at Berkeley, who has been one of my most valuable and durable friends, stepped into this breach. She asked me to join her and Todd Laporte in a unique effort to see what might be common among air traffic controllers, nuclear power plant operators, and nuclear carrier crews. In each case, these were people with enormous responsibilities to avoid errors, who had to operate complex technologies which they did not always understand fully. Publication of Perrow's book *Normal Accidents* lent some urgency to the gatherings. The meetings of researchers with representatives of these three groups were a model of how the university-industry interface ought to function. I credit Roberts' continuous communication with everyone as the key which made things work.

The meetings were often dazzling. An air traffic controller would begin to describe a problem, only to have a military person say, we had the same thing happen too and here's what we did about it. All of which of course were data for those of us looking for patterns. The group met on the carrier Carl Vinson, at the Diablo Canyon reactor, and at the en route air traffic control facility in Fremont, California. In each setting, we talked research and practice in the morning, walked out onto the floor to test hunches informally in the afternoon, wove the fragments together over dinner, and reviewed, at our next gathering, what the previous week's "insights" looked like now that we had some distance from them.

I found the problems of high reliability organizations fascinating for several reasons. First, they were a new kind of organization, and its always more fun for me to break new ground than to rework old ground. Second, these were important organizations to understand because they could kill people, lots of people. Third, they were macro units which could be decimated by the stress they created at the micro level. Fourth, they seemed to be mechanistic structures that worked well in turbulent environments, something that theory says shouldn't happen. Fifth, they focus, intensify, and provide new material for old debates concerning centralization versus decentralization, autonomy versus control, professionals versus division of labor, and human intervention versus automation. And sixth, in a world of growing interdependence and competition, issues of reliability blur into issues of quality. Thus, reliability may well be the issue of the '90s.

Why did we leave Texas for Michigan? I may be too close to this decision to understand it fully. It has been the decision I review more often than has been true of other moves in my life. At the time we left, it seemed like the right thing to do. Texas was declining as rapidly as it had ascended earlier in the '80s. Pressures on the legislature for budget cuts generated some powerful rhetoric concerning how unimportant higher education was to the state, something about which we had been uneasy all along. Recruiting for the OB group had gone badly because people had legitimate questions about the quality of the public schools.

Both Yale and Michigan offered chairs when they learned that higher education in Texas was in trouble. While we were tempted to go to Yale, there were simply too many unresolved puzzles in the negotiations for us to say "yes." Instead, impressed by Ann Arbor's bookstores, summer art fair, and concerts, and excited with the prospect of being just down the street from Bob Zajonc, Dick Nisbett, Mayer Zald, Bob Kahn, Michael Cohen, Martha Feldman, and in the same school with Bob Quinn, Kim Cameron, Noel Tichy, Rick Bagozzi, and Janet Weiss, we said "yes" to Michigan.

The decision made the front page of the Austin paper as part of an article about the exodus of senior people from Texas. Soon thereafter the legislature became somewhat more generous toward the University—which change then, of course, made the negative setting I had chosen to leave, less negative, which then plants a small seed of doubt. It did not help matters that, having decided to go to Michigan in June 1987, we then decided to finish out the fall semester in Austin. Post-decision dissonance was considerable when Black Monday (10/19/87) and the crash of the local real-estate market, both occurred while we tried to sell a house. Nevertheless, we left for Michigan and, as if it were intended as an omen, we heard a National Public Radio interview, while driving north along Route 69 in Indiana, in which the interviewee, a person who had spent all of his life on the road, said that the three cities in the U.S. with the most going on were San Francisco, Boulder, and Ann Arbor.

MICHIGAN (1988-PRESENT)

Both trains and jazz proved to be alive and well in Ann Arbor. The Michigan Central train station, which now houses the Gandy Dancer restaurant, remains one of the most attractive in the United States, there are three trains a day to and from Chicago, and Karen and I often greet the morning train while we walk next to the tracks in Gallup Park. We have been exposed to a whole new set of musicians in Ann Arbor, people like Sonny Rollins, Steve Reich, and Phillip Glass, all of whom have demonstrated the power of improvisation to enrich one's life and add subtlety to it. And we've seen once again people like Ella Fitzgerald, the Modern Jazz Quartet, and Joe Williams, whom we last saw at the Guthrie Theater in Minneapolis. It's as if Ann Arbor picked up, where Minneapolis left off.

Perhaps the most enjoyable jazz experience I had after moving to Michigan, happened at Disneyland. At Steve Kerr's urging, I joined Todd Hostager and David Bastien in a demonstration seminar on jazz at the August 1988 Academy of Management meeting. Pete Christlieb and three other musicians, none of whom had played with each other before, agreed to meet for the first time, and create jazz, while members of the Academy looked on. What we hoped was that listeners would see and hear the gradual development of cohesion, mutual accommodation, and cooperation that characterizes jazz. What people actually saw and heard was a seamless performance, in which the only uncertainty was the first note of the first selection, *Shiny Stockings*. No one knew whether the first note would be the first note of the melody or an introduction that would pave the way to the first note of the melody. It was the former, but you had to be a genius to hear how everyone hedged their bets until the puzzle was resolved. What threw me was that this was the first time I had ever heard this tune played in a group this small. During the seminar, the musicians admitted that they shared my surprise, but this seemed simply to have inspired them even more to pay close attention to one another, and make it work.

At Michigan, I am the Rensis Likert Collegiate Professor of Organizational Behavior and Psychology, which is the first chair I've held named after an academic whose work I know.

Michigan has an unusual set of dynamics, all of which are in play. It has a young faculty which means mentoring overload, underdeveloped networks for placement, and modest time for and interest in community building. Organizational psychology is in a period of transition as big names such as Pelz, French, Katz, Kahn, Tannenbaum, and Georgopoulos retire. In Austin, the undergraduate program drove the business school (at one time 9500 undergrad majors), whereas at Michigan, the executive program drives the school. In either case, the place of scholarship and research can be uncertain given the overwhelming demands for teaching resources.

What Michigan has going for it is some stunning success at recruiting (Dutton, Sandelands, Meyerson, Caproni, Ashford, Walsh, Pentland) and a strengthening university-wide program in organizational studies, supported by the Rackham Graduate School and guided by the most seasoned, humane, informed senior person I've ever worked with, Mayer Zald. There is also a reaffirmation that doctoral education is central to the intellectual power of the group.

I've done some of my best writing at Michigan: an analysis of the Tenerife air disaster, an analysis of organizational learning, a reinterpretation of the variable of technology, extension of the idea of cause maps to the larger sensemaking tool of cartographic myths, a co-authored extension of the loose coupling concept with Doug Orton, a reconceptualization of organizational design as a process of improvisation, and the AMR best article of the year winner, "Theory Construction as Disciplined Imagination." Let me say more about the "best article" since, in a way, it is some closure on my question at Purdue, "What do you do for an encore?"

At Minnesota, Ellen Berscheid and I used to speculate about what it would be like to win a major award from a professional association. The scenario we returned to most often was one in which there would be a brief ceremony, followed by a brief reception, and then, as the last person wandered away, we would flop down, alone, look around at the crumpled napkins, and ask, "Is this what it was all about?"

I had a chance to test these speculations when, on August 18, 1990, I received both the award for the best article of the year in the *Academy of Management Review* (AMR) and the award for lifetime contributions to the field of management scholarship, at the Academy of Management presidential luncheon. The juxtaposition of the two awards suggested that, while the career may have been successful, it was not yet over. The awards meant a great deal, but fifteen minutes after I received them, I was back at work as a participant in a symposium on renewal. None of this quite fits the poignant scenario Ellen and I concocted.

Equally as gratifying as the awards, have been three symposia at Speech Communication Association annual meetings organized to celebrate the 10-year anniversary of *The Social Psychology of Organizing* (November 16, 1980), 20 years of contributions (November 3, 1984), and 20 years of *The Social Psychology of Organizing* (November 20, 1989). Some of my richest friendships have come from the communication community: Putnam, Eisenberg, Pacanowsky, Browning, Hawes, Rogers, Smith, Bantz, Goodall, Jablin, Johnson, Redding, Tompkins, and Monge. One of the biggest unexpected disappointments in the move to Michigan, was its underdeveloped program in communication. I didn't know this in advance because I simply assumed that a university of Michigan's stature would be well covered in this area and I never asked anyone whether this assumption was accurate (just as I had assumed that Texas granted sabbatical leaves only to find after getting there that it didn't).

So what's next? Is Michigan it, or will the restless musician manque resurface and we hit the road again? Can we Austinize Ann Arbor? Or do we simply know the Midwest too well to ever call it exotic? One of my secret passions is to write a book called the *Exotic Midwest* which culls its many quirks and shows that it has just as much warrant to be called a separate nation, as does Texas. I suspect it could be done. Especially if believing is seeing.

CONCLUSION

When I looked back over the preceding chronological account, I was struck by the fact that it was filled, less with the texts I generated, than with the contexts in which they were generated. The preceding account is more about people, events, and settings than about ideas, sustained projects, and burning questions. Why? I think part of the answer is that my style of work is basically reactive. I get my ideas from my surroundings, which means I am never away from work, which means that I spend most of my time turning context into text. Anyone who knows me, knows that my shirt pocket is always bulging with 3 x 5 cards, knows that there is a reporter's pad in my coat pocket, and knows little about my face since its always turned down toward the notes I'm writing. I listen closely for phrases that suddenly connect up all kinds of stuff I've been carrying around in my head. In a sense, I am like a bricoleur who makes do with whatever resources are at hand, to complete whatever project is at hand, a skill I first learned in discussions with Harold Garfinkel.

To know my contexts, therefore, is to know my work. For example, in looking back over my work in preparation for a recent Harvard symposium on the future of OB, I was struck by the frequency with which I seem to study what happens when people don't understand what is going on. My concern is not déjà vu (I've been here before), but rather, vujà dé (I have never been here before and I have no idea where I am). Consider the evidence. I study interpretation, sensemaking, equivocality, stress, dissonance, and crisis behavior, all of which are associated with the question, what is going on here? I advise people to become more complicated so they can sense more of the complications in their worlds. I sound like a cartographer manqué because I keep looking for maps and my favorite story is one in which people find their way out of the Alps using a map of the Pyrennes. I define technology as material relations that exceed human comprehension. Seemingly ineffective organizational acts such as hypocrisy, ambivalence, and galumphing surprise us by having unexpected benefits. Small stuff can be satisfying and sensible. And events only makes sense after the fact.

It is all well and good to say I'm interested in how people cope with complexity, but that interest is anything but idle curiosity. Apparently I never survived my first encounter with bewilderment, and my professional life represents one long Zeigarnik effect to gain some closure on that raw, open-ended initial experience.

Small wonder that I keep looking for ideas, tactics, and determinants of sensemaking at a micro level of analysis. My work is no less problem-focused than that of anyone else. It's just that the problems I focus on are more private, closer in, and more hidden by theory-based overlays. But the question—What does it all mean?—is certainly not my question alone, which explains why I feel my analyses have generality. Also, since the problem is close in, I have no shortage of data. Everything I do is empirical. However, I am also deeply mindful of the sentiment attributed to Freud that the only trouble with self-analysis is countertransference.

The chronology of my living is one long tale of loping from puzzle to puzzle, just as the chronology of my writing is one long tale of how people cope with cosmology episodes. The two worlds merge because I cope by writing, whether it be on 3" x 5" cards, in a journal, or free associating at a word processor. And since that's the way I cope, it's not especially surprising that in my work I presume everyone else copes the same way, by asking, "How can I know what I think until I see what I say?" The world writes its way into a more sensible existence just as I do. No big deal. But then, as Bergson said, "A true philosopher says only one thing in his lifetime, because he enjoys but one contact with the real."[5]

In 1988, two students at Wharton, as part of a class assignment, had to interview me and write up my life. I sent them my essay on eccentric predicates to prime the interview ("Careers as Eccentric Predictates," 1976). Their first observation, based on the essay, stunned me: "You make it sound so easy." Easy? Not quite. We've moved too often, worked too hard, cut too many ties, stuffed too many feelings, to call it easy. The impression of ease is simply my effort to cope, to take myself less seriously, to own up to fallible judgment, to remind myself that I can control inputs but not outcomes, to entertain, to whistle in the dark, to keep going, to head off depression. This has been a perennial problem in my writing. My narrative style is to look for the ironic, the humorous, the human, and in doing so, seem to miss the dark side. I know there's that side. But I also know that, if there is any validity to self-fulfilling prophecies, it makes less sense for me personally to look for that dark side.

If I had it to do over, would I do the same thing again?

If careers are retrospective constructions, then this seems like a senseless question. Would I do what again? Stumble around until John Lanzetta gets in a jam, and I get recruited because I'm just down the hall, to write an authoritative chapter on lab experiments, which I know nothing about? Make strong statements such as, I'll never edit *ASQ*, so that four years later I can do just that? Give a speech about commitment while I negotiate a move from Texas to Michigan?

But suppose someone doesn't buy all this retrospective stuff and says, you're evading the question. Would I become a professor of organizational psychology if I had it to do over again? A professor, yes. Of organizational behavior? I'm not sure. Next time around I'd be tempted to shift either toward a field with a higher paradigm such as neurobiology or a field with a lower paradigm such as literary theory. A field such as OB, which has a low paradigm with pretensions to a higher paradigm, is a maddening set of contradictory pressures that seem to balance off one another. Moves toward a higher paradigm call forth the complaint, you're mutilating the phenomenon. Moves toward a lower paradigm call forth the complaint, you're blurring the phenomenon. To mutilate or to blur. Both seem a far cry from, to explicate and to err. Come to think of it, much of what I do right now is more like literary criticism than neurobiology. Which means, the second time around might well look just like the first time around.

Except... I can see myself being just as happy advancing the throttle of the Broadway Limited as it edges out of Union Station, or just as happy improvising a 5th chorus of *Satin Doll*, as I am happy right now improvising sentences about an academic journey. So long as Karen is willing to be part of the next time around, I'm perfectly content for us to make it up as we go along, just as we did this time.

PUBLICATIONS

1961

With H.B. Pepinsky. The simulation of productivity in organizations. *Personnel Administration, 24*, 18-24.

1964

The reduction of cognitive dissonance through task enhancement and effort expenditure. *Journal of Abnormal and Social Psychology, 68*, 533-539.

1965

With H.B. Pepinsky, J. Riner, & M. Moll. *Productivity in organizations: A metatheory of work and its assessment.* Columbus, OH: Ohio State Research Foundation.

When prophecy pales: The fate of dissonance theory. *Psychological Reports, 16*, 1261-1275.

Laboratory experimentation with organizations. In J.G. March (Ed.), *Handbook of organizations* (pp. 194-260). Chicago: Rand-McNally.

1966

The concept of equity in the perception of pay. *Administrative Science Quarterly, 11*, 414-439.

With D. D. Penner. Triads: A laboratory analogue. *Organizational Behavior and Human Performance, 1*, 191-211.

With D.Knapp & D. Knapp. Interrelations among measures of affiliation. *Journal of Social Psychology, 69*, 223-235.

With D.D. Penner & H.G. Fitch. Dissonance and the revision of choice criteria. *Journal of Personality and Social Psychology, 3*, 701-705.

Task acceptance dilemmas: A site for research on cognition. In S. Feldman (Ed.), *Cognitive consistency* (pp. 225-255). New York: Academic Press.

With H.B. Pepinsky, J. Riner, & M. Moll. Research team productivity. In R. Bower (Ed.), *Studies on behavior in organizations* (pp. 135-156). Athens, GA: University of Georgia Press.

1967

Dissonance and task enhancement: A problem for compensation theory? *Organizational Behavior and Human Performance, 2*, 189-208.

Organizations in the laboratory. In V. Vroom (Ed.), *Methods of organizational research* (pp. 1-56). Pittsburgh, PA: University of Pittsburgh Press.

Promises and limitations of laboratory experiments in the development of attitude change theory. In C. Sherif & M. Sherif (Eds.), *Attitude, ego-involvement, and change* (pp. 51-75). New York: Wiley.

1968

With P. Prestholdt. The realignment of discrepant reinforcement value. *Journal of Personality and Social Psychology, 8*, 180-187.

With B. Nesset. Preferences among forms of equity. *Organizational Behavior and Human Performance, 3*, 400-416.

Systematic observational methods. In G. Lindzey & E. Aronson (Eds.), *Handbook of social psychology* (rev. ed., pp. 357-451). Reading, MA: Addison-Wesley.

Processes of ramification among cognitive links. In R. Abelson, E. Aronson, W. McGuire, T. Newcomb, & M.J. Rosenberg, & P. Tannenbaum (Eds.), *Theories of cognitive consistency* (pp. 512-519). Chicago: Rand-McNally.

The Panglossian world of self-justification. In R. Abelson, E. Aronson, W. McGuire, T. Newcomb, M.J. Rosenberg, & P. Tannenbaum (Eds.), *Theories of cognitive consistency* (pp. 706-715). Chicago: Rand-McNally.

Trans-level experimentation. In B.P. Indik & K. Berrien (Eds.), *Individuals, groups, and organizations* (pp. 216-232). New York: Teachers College Press.

1969

The social psychology of organizing. Reading, MA: Addison-Wesley.

Laboratory organizations and unnoticed causes. *Administrative Science Quarterly, 14*, 294-303.

With D.D. Penner. Discrepant membership as an occasion for effective cooperation. *Sociometry, 32*, 413-424.

Social psychology in an era of social change. *American Psychologist, 24*, 990-998.

1970

With J. Campbell, M. Dunnette, & E.E. Lawler. *Managerial behavior, performance, and effectiveness*. New York: McGraw-Hill.

The ess in stress: Conceptual and methodological problems. In J. McGrath (Ed.), *Social and psychological factors in stress* (pp. 287-347). New York: Holt, Rinehart, and Winston.

The twigging of overload. In H.B. Pepinsky (Ed.), *People and information* (pp. 67-129). New York: Pergammon.

Retrospect in tasks. In B. M. Bass, J. Haas, & R. Cooper (Eds.), *Managing for accomplishment* (pp. 88-100). Lexington, MA: D.C. Heath.

1971

With D.P. Gilfillan. Fate of arbitrary traditions in a laboratory microculture. *Journal of Personality and Social Psychology, 17*, 179-191.

Group processes, family processes and problem solving. In J. Aldous, T. Condon, R. Hill, M. Straus, & I. Tallman (Eds.), *Family problem solving* (pp. 3-32). New York: Dryden.

Improving organizational theory. In M.W. Frey (Ed.), *New developments in management and organization theory* (pp. 11-26). Amherst, MA: University of Massachusetts Press.

1972

Critique. In T.S. Burns (Ed.), *Behavioral experiments in accounting* (pp. 257-273). Columbus, OH: College of Administrative Science, Ohio State University.

1973

With D.P. Gilfillan & T. Keith. The effect of composer credibility on orchestra performance. *Sociometry, 36*, 435-462.

1974

Amendments to organizational theorizing. *Journal of Academy of Management, 17*, 487-502.

Middle range theories of social systems. *Behavioral Science, 19*, 357-367.

Conceptual tradeoffs in studying organizational change. In J. McGuire (Ed.), *Contemporary management: Issues and viewpoints* (pp. 244-251). Englewood Cliffs, NJ: Prentice-Hall.

1975

With D.P. Gilfillan. The sway and decay of tradition. *JSAS Catalog of Selected Documents in Psychology, 5*, 189-190.

The management of stress. *MBA, 9*(October), 37-40.

The future of work: The reward for the individual. *Industrial and Labor Relations Report, 12*(1), 26-28.

1976

Educational organizations as loosely coupled systems. *Administrative Science Quarterly, 21*, 1-19.

Careers as eccentric predicates. *Cornell Executive, 2*, 6-10.

Reply to Ross Stagner comments on "The management of stress." *MBA, 10*(2), 18-19.

With M. Bougon & G. Maruyama. The equity context. *Organizational Behavior and Human Performance, 15*, 32-65.

1977

Laboratory experimentation with organizations: A reappraisal. *Academy of Management Review, 2*(1), 123-128.

With M. Bougon & D. Binkhorst. Cognition in organizations: An analysis of the Utrecht Jazz Orchestra. *Administrative Science Quarterly, 22*, 606-639.

Organization design: Organizations as self-designing systems. *Organizational Dynamics, 6*(2), 30-46.

Enactment processes in organizations. In B. Staw & G. Salancik (Ed.), *New directions in organizational behavior* (pp. 267-300). Chicago: St. Clair.

Reward concepts: Dice or marbles? In T.H. Hammer & S.B. Bacharach (Eds.), *Reward systems and power distribution: Searching for solutions* (pp. 33-55). Ithaca, NY: New York State School of Industrial and Labor Relations, Cornell University.

On repunctuating the problem of organizational effectiveness. In H. Pennings & P. Goodman (Eds.), *Organizational effectiveness* (pp. 193-225). San Francisco: Jossey-Bass.

1978

The metaphors of business. *Cornell Executive, 4*(2), 2-4.

Some challenges for future group research: Reflections on the experience in psychology. In R.T. Golembiewski (Ed.), *The small group in political science: The last two decades of development* (pp. 482-504). Athens, GA: University of Georgia Press.

Spines of leaders. In M.W. McCall & M.M. Lombard (Eds.), *Leadership: Where else can we go?* (pp. 37-61). Durham, NC: Duke University Press.

Cognitive processes in organizations. In B. Staw (Ed.), *Research in organizational behavior: An annual series of analytical essays and critical reviews* (Vol. 1, pp. 41-74). Greenwich, CT: JAI Press.

1979

Social psychology of organizing (rev. ed.). Reading, MA: Addison-Wesley.

With E. Webb. Unobtrusive measures in organizational theory: A reminder. *Administrative Science Quarterly, 24*, 620-659.

Some thoughts on normal science and Argyris's Model I and Model II. In J.G. Hunt & L.L. Larson (Eds.), *Crosscurrents in leadership* (pp. 88-96). Carbondale, IL: Southern Illinois University Press.

Overview of second conference on behavioral experiments in accounting. In T. Burns (Ed.), *Behavioral experiments in accounting: II* (pp. 413-422). Columbus, OH: Ohio State University Press.

1980

Blindspots in organizational theorizing. *Group & Organizational Studies, 5*(2), 178-188.

The management of eloquence. *Executive, 6*(13), 18-21.

Middle range themes in organizational theorizing. In C. Pinder & L. Moore (Eds.), *Middle range theory and the study of organizations* (pp. 392-407). Boston, MA: Martinus-Nijhoff.

1981

With Robert Swieringa. Interfaces between management accounting and organizational behavior. *Exchange, 6*(3), 25-33.
Psychology as gloss. In R. Kasschau & C.N. Cofer (Eds.), *Psychology's second century* (pp. 110-132). New York: Praeger.
Evolutionary theory as a backdrop for administrative practice. In H. Stein (Ed.), *Organization and the human services: Cross-disciplinary reflections* (pp. 106-141). Philadelphia, PA: Temple University Press.

1982

Affirmation as inquiry. *Small Group Behavior, 13*, 441-450.
Administering education in loosely coupled schools. *Phi Delta Kappan* (June), pp. 673-676.
With Robert Swieringa. An assessment of laboratory experiments in accounting. *Journal of Accounting Research, 20*(Supplement), 56-101.
Management of organizational change among loosely coupled elements. In P. Goodman (Ed.), *Change in organizations* (pp. 375-408). San Francisco, CA: Jossey-Bass.
Rethinking research on decision making. In G. Ungson & D. Braunstein (Eds.), *Decision making: An interdisciplinary inquiry* (pp. 325-333). Boston, MA: Kent.

1983

Stress in accounting systems. *Accounting Review, 58*, 350-369.
Contradictions in a community of scholars: The cohesion-accuracy tradeoff. *The Review of Higher Education, 6*(4), 253-267.
Misconceptions about managerial productivity. *Business Horizons, 26*(4), 47-52.
With R. Daft. The effectiveness of organizational interpretation systems. In K. Cameron & D. Whetten (Eds.), *Organizational effectiveness: A comparison of multiple models* (pp. 71-93). New York: Academic Press.
Utilization as reverse simulation: Making the world more like the laboratory. In R.H. Kilmann, K.W. Thomas, D.P. Slevin, R. Nath, & S.L. Jerrell (Eds.), *Producing useful knowledge for organizations* (pp. 494-520). New York: Praeger.
Organizational communication: Toward a research agenda. In L. Putnam & M. Pacanowsky (Eds.), *Communication and organization: An interpretive approach* (pp. 13-29). Beverly Hills, CA: Sage.
Managerial thought in the context of action. In S. Srivastava (Ed.), *The executive mind* (pp. 221-242). San Francisco, CA: Jossey-Bass.

1984

Small wins: Redefining the scale of social problems. *American Psychologist, 39*(1), 40-49.

With R. Daft. Toward a model of organizations as interpretation systems. *Academy of Management Review, 9*, 284-295.

Theoretical assumptions and research methodology selection. In F.W. McFarlan (Ed.), *The information systems research challenge* (pp. 111-129). Boston, MA: Harvard Business School Press.

1985

Cosmos vs. chaos: Sense and nonsense in electronic contexts. *Organizational Dynamics, 14*, 50-64.

Systematic observational methods. In G. Lindzey & E. Aronson (Eds.), *Handbook of social psychology* (3rd. ed., pp. 567-634). New York: Random House.

A stress analysis of future battlefields. In J.G. Hunt (Ed.), *Leadership and future battlefields* (pp. 32-46). Washington, DC: Pergamon-Brassey's.

Sources of order in underorganized systems: Themes in recent organizational theory. In Y. Lincoln (Ed.), *Organizational theory and inquiry: The paradigm revolution* (pp. 106-136). Beverly Hills, CA: Sage.

Editing innovation into *Administrative Science Quarterly*. In L.L. Cummings & P. Frost (Eds.), *Publishing in the organizational sciences* (pp. 366-376). Homewood, IL: Irwin.

Editing a controversial manuscript: A case study. In L.L. Cummings & P. Frost (Eds.), *Publishing in the organizational sciences* (pp. 650-656). Homewood, IL: Irwin.

Editing a rejection: A case study. In L.L. Cummings & P. Frost (Eds.), *Publishing in the organizational sciences* (pp. 774-780). Homewood, IL: Irwin.

The significance of corporate culture. In P. Frost, L.F. Moore, M.R. Louis, C.C. Lundberg, & J. Martin (Eds.), *Organizational culture* (pp. 381-389). Beverly Hills, CA: Sage.

1986

With L. Browning. Arguments and narration in organizational communication. *Journal of Management, 12*, 243-259.

The concept of loose coupling: An assessment. *Dialogue*, American Educational Research Association (December), pp. 8-11.

With M.G. Bougon. Organizations as cause maps. In H.P. Sims, Jr. & D.A. Gioia (Eds.), *Social cognition in organizations* (pp. 102-135). San Francisco, CA: Jossey-Bass.

1987

With R. Swieringa. Action rationality in managerial accounting. *Accounting Organization, and Society, 12*, 293-308.

The fine tuning of graduate education. *Organizational Behavior Teaching Review, 11*(3), 44-47.

With J.D. Orton. Academic journals in the classroom. *Organizational Behavior Teaching Review, 11*(2), 27-42.

Organizational culture as a source of high reliability. *California Management Review, 29*, 112-127.

Perspectives on action in organizations. In J. Lorsch (Ed.), *Handbook of organizational behavior* (pp. 10-28). Englewood Cliffs, NJ: Prentice-Hall.

Substitutes for corporate strategy. In D.J. Teece (Ed.), *The competitive challenge* (pp. 221-233). Cambridge, MA: Ballinger.

Interpretation-based decision aids. In M.A. Tolcott & V.E. Holt (Eds.), *Impact and potential of decision research on decision aiding* (pp. 61-63). Washington, DC: American Psychological Association, December.

1988

Enacted sensemaking in crisis situations. *Journal of Management Studies, 25*(4), 305-317.

Small sins and large evils. In P.B. Woodruff & H.A. Wilmer (Eds.), *Facing evil* (pp. 83-92). Peru, IL: Open Court.

Area introduction and overview. In Y. Ijiri & R.L. Kuhn (Eds.), *New directions in creative and innovative management* (pp. 127-130). Cambridge, MA: Ballinger.

1989

With L. Kurke & E. Ravlin. Can information loss be reversed? Evidence for serial reconstruction. *Communication Research, 16*(1), 3-24.

Mental models of high reliability systems. *Industrial Crisis Quarterly, 3*, 127-142.

Loose coupling: Beyond the metaphor. *Current Contents, 21*(12), 14.

Theory construction as disciplined imagination. *Academy of Management Review, 14*(4), 516-531.

On relevance. *OBTS News and Commentary, 6*(3), 1-2.

Organized improvisation: 20 years of organizing. *Communication Studies, 40*(4), 241-248.

With L. Berlinger. Career improvisation in self-designing organizations. In M.B. Arthur, D.T. Hall, & B.S. Lawrence (Eds.), *Handbook of career theory* (pp. 313-328). New York: Cambridge University Press.

Theorizing about organizational communication. In L.M. Porter, L.J. Putnam, K.H. Roberts, & F.M. Jablin (Eds.), *Handbook of organizational communication* (pp. 97-122). Beverly Hills, CA: Sage.

With R. McDaniel. How professional organizations work: Implications for school organization and management. In T. Sergiovanni (Ed.), *Schooling for tomorrow* (pp. 330-355). Rockleigh, NJ: Allyn and Bacon.

With J.D. Orton. One way transfers and organizational cohesion. In J. Anderson (Ed.), *Communication yearbook* (Vol. 12, pp. 675-687). Beverly Hills, CA: Sage.

1990

Styles of scholarship: "Tonight let's do Thompson." *Journal of Organizational Change Management, 2*(2), 18-21.

The vulnerable system: An analysis of the Tenerife air disaster. *Journal of Management, 16*(3), 571-593.

With J.D. Orton. Loosely coupled systems: A reconceptualization. *Academy of Management Review, 16*(2), 203-223.

With L.E. Sandelands. Social behavior in organizational studies. *Journal of the Theory of Social Behaviour, 20*(4), 322-345.

Technology as equivoque: Sense-making in new technologies. In P.S. Goodman & L. Sproull (Eds.), *Technology and organizations* (pp. 1-44). San Francisco, CA: Jossey-Bass.

Cartographic myths in organizations. In A.S. Huff (Ed.), *Mapping strategic thought* (pp. 1-10). London: Wiley.

In Press

The non-traditional quality of organizational learning. *Organization Science.*

With L.D. Browning. Fixing with the voice: A research agenda for applied communication. *Journal of Applied Communication Research.*

The management of closeness in Jungian training societies: An organizational analysis. In H.A. Wilmer (Ed.), *The experience of closeness and Jungian therapy*. Peru, IL: Open Court Press.

Jolts as a synopsis of organizational studies. In R. Stablien & P.J. Frost (Eds.), *Doing exemplary organizational research.*

NOTES

1. G.W. Allport. (1937). The functional autonomy of motives. *American Journal of Psychology, 50*, 141-156.
2. A mechnism somewhat like this is explicated in J.W. Meyer & B. Rowan (1977). Institutionalized organizations: Formal structure as myth and ceremony. *American Journal of Sociology, 83*, 340-363.
3. See M.S. Davis. (1986). "That's classic!": The phenomenology and rhetoric of successful social theories. *Philosophy of the Social Sciences, 16*, 285-301.
4. See pp. 366-376, 650-656, and 774-780 in L.L. Cummings, and P.J. Frost. (1985). *Publishing in the organizational sciences.* Homewood, IL: Irwin.
5. Cited on page 115 in H.R. Wagner (1983). *Alfred Schutz: An intellectual biography.* Chicago: University of Chicago Press.

William Foote Whyte

From Participant Observer To Participatory Action Researcher

WILLIAM FOOTE WHYTE

I began my research career under the influence of those advocating a complete separation of basic research from action. In my Harvard days, this was reenforced by the conviction of Lawrence J. Henderson, Chairman of the Society of Fellows, who believed that society lost nothing from this separation since sociologists did not yet know anything worth applying. In my first study (*Street Corner Society* 1943) I tried to hew to this puristic line, but my urges toward social reform propelled me into action on at least two occasions. I persuaded a social work executive to hire a man I called Doc, a corner boy leader, instead of trained social workers to manage a store front recreation center, and I organized a march on City Hall to protest the city's neglect of our district.

For many years, the commitments to science and to social reform coexisted in my mind and psyche in a state of unresolved tension. I began the street corner study as what I now call *participatory research*; two men (those I called Doc and Sam Franco) moved beyond the roles of key informants to become active collaborators in the study. But this was not *action research* since the study was not designed to reach any particular action goals. Later I abandoned my puristic commitment to science and engaged in various *action research* projects. But these were not *participatory research*; my colleagues or I used research subjects as sources of information, but we sought to control the research process. Finally, in the late stages of my career, I arrived at my own resolution of this tension between science and action in a research strategy some of us call *participatory action research*. In this strategy, one or more members of the organization we study participate fully with us in all stages of research, from design to data gathering and analysis, to report writing, and on to actions growing out of the project.

That tension is now resolved for me as I have become convinced that *participatory action research* (PAR) provides one way—and a very powerful way—to advance both science and practice. This autobiography traces the evolution of my research career along these general lines.

In the second and third editions of *Street Corner Society* (1955, 1981) I presented accounts of my experiences in my first field project, and in *Learning From the Field* (1984) I included accounts of fieldwork experiences in a number of other studies. I will summarize such accounts here but give more attention to the overall framework of the development of my thinking and writing over the years.

FAMILY AND CHILDHOOD

I come from a solidly upper-middle-class, professional family. One grandfather, William Foote Whyte, was a doctor, the other grandfather, James H. Van Sickle was a school teacher and then superintendent of schools in Baltimore and Springfield, Massachusetts, where I was born.

My parents, John Whyte and Isabel Van Sickle met on fellowships in Germany where they were both doing graduate work in German language and literature. She gained a masters degree, he went on to the Ph.D. and a career in college teaching. I grew up in an atmosphere emphasizing intellectual and cultural values and deemphasizing the pursuit of money. Wherever we lived, our walls were lined with well-filled bookcases. The books remained with us like treasures long after they had been read.

When I was a teenager, I brought a girlfriend to visit our home. As soon as she entered the apartment, she remarked, "My, all those books. Are they yours or did they come with the apartment?" My father thought that was one of the funniest things he had ever heard.

While recognizing that big business executives were more affluent than the Whytes and enjoyed higher social positions, my parents looked down upon businessmen as narrow-minded money grubbers, in the image of Sinclair Lewis's *Babbitt*. Long ago I came to recognize that many business and industrial executives have wide ranging and creative minds, but still the family influence may explain in part why I have always felt more at ease in dealing with workers than chief executive officers.

Organized religion never played a role in our family life. John Whyte had grown up in a family of church-going people. In fact, he claimed that he used to go to Presbyterian church or Sunday school five times a day on Sunday and that he had stored up enough church to last the rest of his life.

In race and ethnic relations, I was inoculated against anti-semitism by my heritage, since I am one-eighth Jewish (as far as I can sort it out, the mix is one-fourth Scotch, one-fourth Dutch, three-eighth English and one-eighth Jewish.)

Prejudice against any race was regarded as evil in my family. Mother took pride in the fact that her father had substantially upgraded the Negro schools in Baltimore, which had been a dumping ground for incompetent white teachers.

My parents were politically liberal to radical. In 1920, to protest Woodrow Wilson's abandonment of his vision of "peace without victory" through his "Fourteen Points" in the punitive Versailles Treaty, John Whyte voted for Warren G. Harding, but mother voted for the Socialist candidate, labor leader Eugene Debs.

That one Republican vote became something of a family joke thereafter, as the Whytes consistently supported Democratic candidates and were strongly committed to Franklin Roosevelt and his New Deal. My parents wanted me to love my country but to show that dedication through a commitment to social reforms to make it an even better country.

The intellectual atmosphere of the Whyte house did not crowd out interest and participation in sports. My father was a crack doubles player in tennis and talented enough in baseball to be offered a position on a semi-pro team. He took me to national tennis championship matches and a Yankee baseball game—to see Babe Ruth and Lou Gehrig hit home runs. While I did play on my college tennis team, I did not have the natural athletic ability of John Whyte.

I am an only child, and my parents were particularly concerned not to "spoil" me and make me too dependent on them. They always emphasized that I should think for myself and do what I thought I should do, even in the face of conflicting opinions of influential people. That need for independence may have been reinforced by the disruption of our family life when my mother came down with tuberculosis at a time when I was just beginning first grade. While she was away at a sanatorium in Colorado for over a year, I was farmed out first with my Van Sickle grandparents, and then with my father's sister and her family. I was well treated throughout this period, but it was not the same as being in my own family.

John Whyte had had to switch from teaching German when that department was shut down in N.Y.U.—and throughout the country—in the World War I hysteria. He was then working as the Research Director of the National Association of Creditmen, and his two week summer vacation was the only time he could be with me except for brief visits. (He went back to teaching later in 1925.)

When my mother was able to return in 1924, we moved to a home in Caldwell, New Jersey, but for a year she was confined to a sleeping porch, and I could get no closer to her than the door of that porch.

EDUCATION

Ideologically, my parents were committed to public schools, but in the 1920s a reform movement called "Progressive Education" was sweeping the country, and my parents and especially my mother were caught up in it. I was not unhappy in the Caldwell Public Schools. I had friends among my classmates, and I found I could do well academically without strain, but my parents were unhappy with the traditional, rigid classroom. When a like-minded group of parents formed Caldwell Country Day School, my parents persuaded me to try it out, and one day there persuaded me to stay.

In contrast to the rows of desks and seats screwed to the floor, in the new school I was in an open classroom with movable desks. We also had smaller classes and teachers who seemed to be more interested in us.

For three years at the Country Day School, my most vivid memories are of the weekly Council Ring, in which the children showed each other the drawings or paintings we had done, recounted something special, or read aloud things we had written. For that program, I began writing an endless story about a young boy who left home to escape from oppressive parents and had adventures on the road from Florida up the coast and eventually to the Azores Islands—that destination attracting me when I suddenly discovered that the Atlantic Ocean was not just empty water. I enjoyed writing, and the pupil response encouraged me to believe that I could write what others would want to read. I decided then and there that somehow I would make writing a career.

Some woman speculated that the story indicated that my own parents were rough on me, and I was taking out my feeling against them in this way. Nothing could have been farther from the truth. My parents were so good to me that I could not think of running away from home myself, and yet I seemed to need some kind of adventure. I realized even then that my social world was limited, and I felt a need to broaden it out.

After going back for one year of high school in Caldwell Public Schools, the Whytes moved to Bronxville in Westchester County. My parents cast about within commuting range of Brooklyn College for a public school with a good progressive reputation. That led us to Bronxville where I settled in for the last three years of high school. That school was rewarding to me not only for its innovative and flexible educational program, but also for the opportunities it provided beyond school work.

In my senior year, I reported school news for my home town paper, the Bronxville Press, which came out on Tuesdays and Fridays. There I worked under editor Paul Lambert, the best boss I ever had. He gave me few compliments but constantly offered me opportunities to expand my vision and responsibilities. In addition to news coverage, I wrote two weekly columns, one on sports and one, "The Whyte Line" on any topic regarding Bronxville education. By this time I had finished requirements for four years of French and was advanced enough in other studies to have substantial blocks of free time. I began visiting classes in the elementary school, from kindergarten through the sixth grade. Teachers were initially surprised, but, after my articles had begun to come out, I learned that some of them were unhappy, when I did not visit their classes. After each class, I would ask the teacher to explain what she had been trying to accomplish and where the lesson of the day fitted in with the general program. I was fascinated with this experience in open and highly flexible classrooms in which pupils focused on group projects in which they were learning things that were traditionally taught in more highly structured and sterile ways.

Since this progressive program was still highly controversial in Bronxville, Superintendent Willard W. Beatty was naturally worried when he learned that a potential loose cannon was roaming about among the children and teachers, but, at the end of the series he told me I had written the best account he had read of the kind of education he and the teachers were trying to develop. He then reprinted the columns in a Bronxville School's Bulletin under the title of "Bill Whyte visits the Elementary School" (1931).

The work I did on that series was much closer to the kind of field work I came to do professionally than anything I did in college.

Between high school and college, I spent a year with my parents in Germany, 1931-1932. When I was taking my leave of Paul Lambert, he invited me to write a weekly column from Germany. I was surprised and pleased. But now it occurred to me that I might be worth a raise from my previous 8 cents an inch rate. I proposed 10 cents, and he accepted. Of course, I did not make as much money in the year abroad as when I was filling a page every Tuesday, with additional stories coming out in the Friday edition. One month I had reached a peak of over $50, which in 1931 was a lot of money for a boy my age. The money was gratifying, but the work meant much more to me than that. Beyond job satisfaction, I learned how to write fluently enough to turn out a high volume of copy by Sunday night for a Tuesday school page. The experience protected me ever after from having writer's block. Whenever I think I have something to communicate, the task of putting it into writing seems easy.

In Germany, I moved around some with my parents, but then, when they were in Munich, they settled me in a boys' boarding school in the mountains in Partenkirchen, which was to become the cite of the 1936 Winter Olympics. The purpose was not to advance my formal education but to enable me to develop greater fluency in German as well as more understanding of German culture.

This was a period of extreme tension in Germany, with the Nazis on the rise and other parties trying to prevent them from taking over. The faculty of the school was sharply divided between pro- and anti-Nazi so that they had had to make a rule that they would not discuss politics. This ban on arguments did not limit their willingness to talk to me, and I began interviewing both sides and reporting what I learned in a column called "Personally Conducted." Finding Hitler at that time an unknown quantity in the United States and generally regarded as so unbalanced that it was hard to imagine him coming to power, I set about background reading of biographical accounts and other writings on German politics. My columns were not entirely devoted to the political struggle. I was also writing on personal experiences and friends that I had met before and was renewing acquaintance with, or friends I made in the school.

SWARTHMORE COLLEGE

My parents picked the college I was to attend, and I did not object. They were attracted to Swarthmore when they heard its President, Frank Aydelotte, speak at a Bronxville P.T.A. meeting. His description of the Swarthmore Honors Program suggested to them the freedom and stimulation that I would thrive on, and it sounded good to me.

After their sophomore year about half of the students were admitted to the Honors Program. For the next two years we would have no classes but work entirely in small seminars, which met once a week and often in the home of the professor. Each semester we had only two seminars, totaling eight for the two year period. Three or four of them were in our major subject and the others were divided between our two minors. There were no quizzes or examinations in the seminars, but we all prepared for final examinations by outside examiners.

Many years later, Swarthmore was to establish a Department of Sociology and Anthropology. My introductory class in psychology did not lure me in to go on to study social psychology, which might have appealed to me more. I majored in economics and minored in political science and American history. Besides tennis, writing was my main extracurricular activity. I was active in literary circles and became editor of the college literary magazine.

For its influence on my subsequent career, a seminar in Government and Business with Clair Wilcox was most important. For my second paper, I had to choose a topic in government finance. None of the proposed options interested me, so I asked permission to write on financing New York City. Wilcox told me that I would have to proceed at my own risk because he knew very little about that topic and could only steer me to one book that had been written some years earlier.

I read that book and then arranged to get away from college several days before the beginning of the Christmas vacation, to spend some days in the New York Municipal Library. Mainly I went after the documents, but I did interview one or two of the city government department heads.

Wilcox was impressed enough with the paper to think that it might interest Thorstein Selin, editor of a bulletin series for the American Academy of Political and Social Science. Over several weeks of the second semester, I reorganized, expanded, and rewrote the manuscript. It came out in 1935 as a bulletin, *Financing New York City*. Thus, my first academic publication was in the field of economics.

By this time, I knew I was on a fast track to somewhere, but I did not know where. *Financing New York City* attracted attention in New York and Albany and seemed to offer strong possibilities of a job in government finance in that State. That was gratifying, but I was not much interested in government finance. That was just one of the areas on which I had to write a paper, and New York City financing was the aspect that appealed to me most. I was still very much interested in a writing career, but I had no idea how to get started, while earning a living.

President Aydelotte, then chairman of the Rhodes Trust, assumed that I would apply for a Rhodes scholarship. When he heard that I had no such intention, he invited me to lunch to try to change my mind. He stressed the cultural advantages of two years of Oxford with time off for travel on the continent. I replied that, through my family I had already had such advantages with four trips to Europe, mainly to Germany but also with time in France, Holland and England. I felt I needed to get to know my own country better. My father had heard of the recently established Society of Fellows of Harvard which offered very attractive three year juinior fellowships, with a maximum of freedom to the fellow. Students were not allowed to apply, but my professors got me into the running.

The impetus for establishing junior fellowships was the belief of retiring President A. Lawrence Lowell and Professor L.J. Henderson that Ph.D. programs had become too highly mechanized and that Harvard needed a fellowship that would allow young scholars complete freedom to map out their own academic programs. All of the facilities of Harvard were open to us, but there was one restriction: the junior fellow was not allowed to work on a Ph.D. program. This was later relaxed, but I'm glad that the rule was in place in my time. That rule gave me the freedom to discover what I wanted to do the rest of my life.

When I began at Harvard, I had only the vaguest ideas of what I would study and how I would carry out the study. In Swarthmore, a weekend program of the American Friends Service Committee for a group of students in a Philadelphia slum district settlement house had got me interested in urban slums and fitted in with my general commitment to improving the welfare of the underdog. At Harvard, I knew only that I would study a slum in Boston. Still considering myself an apprentice economist, I thought at first in terms of a study of slums and housing. My associations with social anthropologist junior fellow, Conrad M. Arensberg, along with my interest in fiction writing (that I was not yet prepared to abandon), led me away from that plan.

Arensberg had recently returned from the study of an Irish rural community, and I was excited by his accounts of the methods that he used and what he had been finding out. I also was fascinated with the theoretical and methodological work he was doing with Eliot D. Chapple on the quantitative study of human interactions.

As I followed these interests, I soon realized that I was not going to be an economist and began thinking of myself as a social anthropologist. At this point, I was thinking of a community study like the Lynds' *Middletown*.

I was eighteen months into my field work before I really found out what I was doing. During that period, I was meeting people in groups, always assuming that I was establishing those contacts in order to learn about the larger structures and the social processes in the community. It was only toward the end of that time, faced with the challenge of reporting something to the Society of Fellows to justify an application for renewal of my three year term, that I realized that the real focus of my study was on the groups I had been coming to know and their relations with the larger structures of politics and the numbers racket.

Fortunately for me, through all this exploratory period, I had been following Arensberg's advice: whatever the occasion, I should observe what was going on and later record my observations in as full detail as my memory would allow, without being concerned as to the meaning of each event. Now, as I reviewed my notes and wrote up what I had learned about the groups I knew best, I had at last a sense of direction.

After the early weeks of exploratory work in the solidly Italian-American district of the North End of Boston, I had moved from Harvard's palatial Winthrop House to rent a room in the home of an Italian family that ran a restaurant. For two years, that was both my home and office base within the warmth of the Orlandi family.

In June 1938 until the end of my study in July 1940, I lived in a reconditioned North End apartment near the waterfront with my wife, Kathleen King Whyte. She was just getting started in a commercial art career, having sold two book jackets to New York publishers. She was willing to take the chance that she could continue this work in Boston—a belief that proved to be unfounded—but, in any case, she wanted to share the adventure of this social exploration with me. The remaining months in the North End were devoted to some extension of my fieldwork but primarily to writing the first draft of *Street Corner Society* (1943). Kathleen worked closely with me on that, becoming informally my editor.

GETTING THE DOCTORATE

To begin graduate work at the University of Chicago, we arrived with a draft of my doctoral thesis in my trunk. Arensberg had directed me to Chicago, to work with social anthropologist W. Lloyd Warner. Since he had an appointment in sociology as well as anthropology, he could be my major professor in either department. The doctoral requirements in the two departments indicated that there was a substantial overlap between the subdiscipline of social anthropology and what was called social organization in the sociology department. I decided in favor of sociology because I could get what I wanted in either department, but what I did not want to take time to study seemed more difficult to learn in anthropology, which required some competence in physical anthropology and archaeology. I decided to make social anthropology my minor and remain on the borderline between the two disciplines, as I have ever since. I should add that a major influence in supporting my sociological interests was Everett C. Hughes, but he also shared my social anthropological inclinations, being active in the Society for Applied Anthropology, and becoming its President. Warner and Hughes were my chief mentors in graduate work.

When we were suddenly bombed into World War II in December 1941, I wanted to get through the doctoral program as fast as possible and managed to finish up the following late spring. Since Joyce, our first child, had been born in our last month in Boston and Martin was due to appear in November, in 1942, I was not tempted to shift gears and try for a military commission.

INDUSTRIAL RESEARCH IN OKLAHOMA

When I took up my first teaching job at the University of Oklahoma, Sociology Department Chairman W. B. Bizzell assumed that I would want to study Indians, since there were representatives of 43 tribes in that State. I told Bizzell that I would like to do something more directly related to the war effort. Bizzell happened to know the founder and still chairman of Phillips Petroleum Company, and wrote me a letter of introduction to him. At the time, social research in industry was practically unknown to most executives, so Frank Phillips was puzzled when he granted me two minutes time before the start of a meeting of his Board of Directors. He asked me two questions: "Are you a lawyer?" "Have you had any experience in the oil industry?" I answered in the negative to both questions, but at least Phillips passed me on to his employment manager (the top personnel title in the company at that time). From that unpromising beginning, several weeks later, I managed to work my way into a study in the Phillips Oklahoma City plants converting natural gas into gasoline.

Until we left Oklahoma the following June, I spent two days a week in the field with the oil workers and the local management people. The experience fascinated me and persuaded me to devote most of the rest of my career to research in industry.

Phillips then was still a young company, only about 25 years old, but growing rapidly toward becoming one of the "seven sisters." I thus had an opportunity to study the stresses and strains in employee relations that developed through growth from highly personalized relationships between top management and workers to a large bureaucracy. To add interest to that scene, a C.I.O. union was making serious inroads in the company's hold on its workers. As I got to the point where most workers trusted me, I was able to gain an inside view of what swayed them in the midst of a hotly contested organizing campaign (1943).

I might have continued another year at Oklahoma, but students were thinning out, and I felt increasingly uneasy about being on the sidelines in the war crisis.

TIME OUT

My problem seemed solved when I was offered a job at Harvard in the program for training officers for military government for the planned invasion of Italy. I was to teach half time and devote the other half to research on Italian culture. That opening disappeared when, at the point of beginning work at Harvard, I came down with polio contracted in Oklahoma. After six weeks in Massachusetts General Hospital, Kathleen managed to accomplish the almost impossible task of working out arrangements for transporting me by train from Boston to Penn Station in New York and from there on to Georgia Warm Springs Foundation, about seventy miles beyond Atlanta. There followed a period of about 10 months of recuperation and physical retraining to adjust to a left leg practically lifeless and a right leg with less than half its original strength.

WITH THE COMMITTEE ON HUMAN RELATIONS IN INDUSTRY

When I was getting strong enough to contemplate going back to work, there was an opening at the University of Chicago to work with the Committee on Human Relations in Industry on a study in the restaurant industry.

We moved to Chicago in late May of 1943. I had research assistants, but, although still weak from polio, I wanted to get into the fieldwork myself. For three months I spent two days a week doing fieldwork with Stouffer's Restaurant in Chicago's Loop. A fascinating new world was now opening up for me: a production organization that was also a service organization. I interviewed members of management but spent most of my time interviewing waitresses in their free time between the noon meal and the evening meal, concentrating on the tensions involved in serving customers in a restaurant devoted to fast service, under conditions of inexperienced staff and considerable nervous tension.

Putting my own fieldwork together with the skillful interviewing and observation of Margaret Chandler and Edith Lentz, I wrote my second book, *Human Relations in the Restaurant Industry* (1948) and probably one of the best articles I ever wrote, "The Social Structure of the Restaurant" (1949).

Before Eric Trist focused our attention on the need to study Socio-Technical Systems, that was what, in effect, I was describing and analyzing, but I did not have the wit to recognize the significance of the approach or to give it a name. Why did I fail to recognize the theoretical significance of what I had done? I think it was probably because, though fascinated at the time with the world of restaurants, I somehow felt the factory was at the heart of what I should be studying.

I date the beginnings of organizational behavior research in industry to the Western Electric program, in association with Harvard University, in the 1920s, but, long before the appearance of the path breaking *Management and the Worker*, Western Electric had abandoned any systematic social research program, to go off on a tangent with the personnel counseling program—which I called later (1978) a "monumental misunderstanding" of what should have been learned from the early studies of the relay assembly test room and the bank-wiring room. I attributed this tangent to Elton Mayo's fixation on "obsessive reveries" suffered by workers on monotonous jobs, as he emphasized in his own books and as I learned from him in a seminar in 1937.

By the time the Chicago program began, organizational behavior research had long been dormant in the Harvard Business School, while the professors were gathering case materials for teaching. The Committee on Human Relations in Industry was the first organized university program to move into this void, soon followed by E. Wight Bakke's Labor-Management Center and Charles Walker's Technology Project at Yale and a group led by Douglas McGregor at M.I.T.

I felt privileged to become a junior member of such a committee. As a graduate student, I had known some of the members, and I admired and liked them. W. Lloyd Warner was chairman of the committee and Burleigh B. Gardner was its executive secretary, the only faculty member working full time on a research program, besides me. Other members were Everett C. Hughes, Allison Davis and Robert Havighurst (of the Committee on Human Development), Frederick Harbison (economics), and George Brown (Business School). I shared an office with Burleigh.

We were also fortunate in having graduate students with a good deal of industrial experience. I particularly enjoyed working with Donald Roy, Orvis Collins, and Melville Dalton, with whom I shared an interest in worker reactions to individual incentive systems. My restaurant project led directly to another project and another book, published much later (1965). My talk on the restaurant study at the Radisson Hotel in Minneapolis led to a request from Vice President and General Manger, Byron C. Calhoun to help him find a new personnel man. Since he had had three men in that position within the past year, it seemed to me that simply recruiting a new person was unlikely to be helpful. After some discussion, he agreed to an action-research program. Meridith Wiley, a student in our program, took the position of personnel man, and Edith Lentz moved to Minneapolis to do full-time field work, reporting to Wiley and me. I made monthly two-day visits to the Radisson, and in between Edith (and occasionally Meridith) came down to discuss the work with me. I did some consulting, but mainly worked through Wiley (supported by Lentz's field data) in getting work group meetings set up with supervisors and also interdepartmental discussions to smooth out some of the most severe friction points.

During this period (1944-1948) I also got involved in studies of union-management cooperation, first with S. Buchsbaum and Company and the International Chemical Workers Union (1946) and, during my last months at Chicago, with a plant of Inland Steel Container Company organized by the United Steel Workers (1951).

At the time, we were under fire from some academic critics as "managerial sociologists," and my interest in union-management cooperation was taken to mean finding ways of getting the union to go along with management. That was not what I had in mind. I was searching for ways in which the two parties could meet on an equal basis and work out their problems. Critics assumed that management people were being guided by our research. On the contrary, we had considerable difficulty getting any management people interested in our studies.

In those days, it was even difficult to gain access to any plant for field work. There were two common responses to any access request. Either things were going so smoothly that management did not want to introduce any outsiders who might ask workers how they felt about the job in such a way as to make them find reasons to be dissatisfied or else the situation was so tense that the introduction of any outsider could precipitate an explosion. There was an occasional personnel man who took an interest in our work, but most of them seemed to be looking for some kind of gimmick. I would be told "What we want you to do is tell us how we can make workers feel that they are participating." When we explained that we were not into impression management and that the only way to make workers feel they were participating would be to involve them in some significant decision making, that would be the end of the personnel man's interest.

We did encounter one important exception to that generalization: James C. Worthy of Sears Roebuck and Company. He worked closely with the Committee on Human Relations in Industry and particularly with Burleigh Gardner and Lloyd Warner. I found him a man of real intellectual interests in our field, and we came to regard him as if he were a research colleague as well as a personal friend.

Even the six companies that initially supported the program with $3,600 each for a year were at first unwilling to have any research done in their plants. For the first year of the Committee, Burleigh Gardner had to guide the research through having students interview miscellaneous workers in their homes about what made a good job or a bad job. Perhaps the executives were interested in picking up ideas that might help their companies to reduce absenteeism and labor turnover in a period of critical war time manpower shortage, and perhaps they simply felt gratified to have the opportunity to have dinner every six weeks with the professors to discuss high level semi-philosophical aspects of human relations. In any case, $3,600 a year was a trifling amount to be spent or wasted.

In 1946, Burleigh Gardner left the University to found Social Research Inc., and I became Executive Secretary of the Committee. I had now been advanced to associate professor and continued with research as well as teaching a course and working with students, but I was not happy with my responsibilities in managing the Committee's program. We continued to be dependent upon financial support from a number of companies. I did not feel comfortable going after management money, nor was I very good at it.

EARLY YEARS AT CORNELL

In the summer of 1948 I moved from Chicago to take up a professorship in the recently established New York State School of Industrial and Labor Relations at Cornell University.

At first I worried about leaving a university in the heartland of industrial America to go to the semi-rural environment of Ithaca in upstate New York, but I found compensations not only in living conditions but also in working opportunities. My job called for half-time teaching, so I was able to allocate a couple of days a week to fieldwork, and in that early stage of the school, we had unlimited access to state cars to get us to research sites. Elmira and Corning were only an hour's drive from the campus. I would get together with students for each trip. Away from the distractions of the office, on the way to the site, we would discuss what we were going to do. Returning home, we would talk over what we had found out and try to figure out what it all meant.

At Cornell, I was in on the formative stages of the new school, the first and only college offering a bachelor's, a master's, and a Ph.D. in Industrial Relations. After the founding of ILR in 1945, a number of other universities set up graduate programs in industrial relations, but all of the others involved joint appointments with professors having their basic appointment in a disciplinary department such as economics or sociology or psychology.

At Cornell, Alexander Leighton, who was instrumental in working out the appointment for me, had a joint appointment in the Department of Sociology and Anthropology, but otherwise nearly all of the professors had full-time appointments in ILR, as I did.

At the time, there were no formal departments established. I joined the so-called Human Relations unit along with Leighton. A couple of years later, when he moved over to full time in sociology and anthropology I assumed the leadership of that unit, which many years later came to be called the Department of Organizational Behavior.

Our school was founded in 1945 in response to the beliefs of state legislators, led by Irving Ives, that labor conflict was one of New York State's key problems, and the leaders of labor and management were not sufficiently well-informed about collective bargaining to be able to work out their problems peacefully. Nevertheless, ILR was widely suspected of radical tendencies, and, in those early days, when we were still in temporary quarters, some people in management referred to us as "the Kardboard Kremlin," even though, of course, nothing like collective bargaining existed in the Soviet Union.

Leighton had established a pattern of semi-weekly evening meetings in his home for professors and graduate students working with us, along with spouses. When he moved across the campus, Kathleen and I continued that custom, which provided a valuable base for developing mutually stimulating relations between professors and students.

In the years 1948-1954, while I was active in fieldwork in Elmira and Corning with my students, I devoted most of my energies to getting field projects started with students. Chris Argyris' first book grew out of his doctoral thesis on an Elmira plant, where we worked together. Leonard Sayles and George Strauss came into our program after getting their doctorates at M.I.T., and we worked closely together on studies of local unions, financed by a grant from the Grant Foundation. Their book, *The Local Union*, was widely regarded as the first field study that gave an inside view on the divisions and rivalries within local unions, along lines of occupational and ethnic differences.

European post-doctoral fellows, Peter Atteslander from Switzerland and Friederick Fuerstenberg from Germany, worked with me on studies in the Steuben Division of the Corning Company. In this period, we had the first graduate student from Japan, Hideo Kawabuchi. He was with us only for one year but was so captivated by what he was learning about human relations in industry that he returned home to found the Japan Human Relations

Association—they use the English title untranslated. The JHRA grew to become very active in spreading the human relations gospel, which was taking a much stronger hold in management circles in Japan than in the United States at this time.

In this period, while I was active in the field with my students and research associates, my writing was based primarily upon earlier field projects (1951, 1955). What is probably my best book on industrial relations, *Money and Motivation* (1951) presented an interpretation of worker response to individual piece rates, along with some discussion of more broadly-based incentive systems. That was based primarily on my Chicago work with Orvis Collins, Melville Dalton, and Donald Roy but adding two Cornell cases written by Frank Miller and Leonard Sayles, along with George Strauss' interpretation of an earlier case of Alex Bavelas (never published by Bavelas).

In developing a new course introducing students to field research, in collaboration with Urie Bronfenbrenner, Steven A. Richardson, and John Dean, I was frustrated in my search for realistic accounts of the personal experience of field workers who had participated actively with the subjects of their study over extended periods of time. What little the writers had reported seemed to me to reflect their conclusions after the study of how they should have gone about it rather than revealing their earlier fumbling efforts, along with the personal anxieties of learning how to participate and study at the same time. There seemed to be a conspiracy to suppress information and ideas that did not fit into some logical and straight-forward framework. Since I believed that beginning students would be encouraged by learning about the errors of their predecessors, who had nevertheless produced useful studies, I dug out my North End notes and wrote the appendix for the second edition of *Street Corner Society* (1955). In so doing, I did not spare myself the embarassment of reporting on my blunders and even on such unethical and foolhardy conduct as voting four times in a congressional election. I also reported that my earlier plans for the study bore little relation to the final product and that I had been 18 months in the field before I knew what I was doing.

Apparently that appendix added greatly to the value of my first book. By 1955 sales of the first edition had practically dried up, but then the second edition led many professors of sociology or social anthropology to adopt the book for introductory courses or research methods courses. By the 1960s I began to hear the book that had attracted little attention when first published being described as "a sociological classic." By now it has been translated into Spanish, Italian, Chinese, and German.

BEGINNING TO EXPLORE LATIN AMERICA

I was due for my first sabattical year in 1954-1955. That provided a welcome opportunity for a change of scene. Whereas in my earliest industrial studies, everything I learned seemed new and exciting, by this time I seemed to be seeing familiar patterns over and over again. This led me to wonder to what extent the conclusions I was reaching were culture specific to the United States or to what extent they would apply to the same industries in different cultures.

In the course of casting about for research and financing opportunities abroad, I narrowed the choices to four locations: England, Norway, Quebec, and Venezuela. England I eliminated, thinking its culture too close to our own for comparison purposes.

Norway I eliminated because, although I knew my colleagues would be fluent in English, I wanted to be able to talk to workers in their native language. I was not put off by the challenge of learning Norwegian, but that ability would only broaden my opportunities in one small corner of the globe. (If I had anticipated the exciting Scandinavian developments in worker participation beginning in the 1960s, I might have made a different decision.)

Quebec and Venezuela offered very similar opportunities. In northern Quebec, I would have been studying industrial relations in the Arvida plants of Aluminum Company of Canada (Alcan). In Venezuela I would be studying industrial and community relations with the operations of Creole Petroleum Company (a subsidiary of the company now called Exxon) in the Lake Maracaibo region. In Arvida, higher line management was almost exclusively English Canadian, whereas workers, foremen, and general foremen where generally French Canadian. In Creole's Maracaibo operations, higher line management was almost exclusively from the United States whereas workers and foremen were Venezuelans, and some Venezuelans were beginning to move up to general foreman. Both companies offered budgets to supplement my half year Cornell salary and funds for research and secretarial assistants.

The balance was so even in other respects that we made our decision on the basis of climate. Although we did not look forward to the mean 85 degree fahrenheit temperature, year around, night and day in Maracaibo, we decided we would rather be hot than cold. (In the pleasant summer climate of Arvida in 1956, I did have the opportunity to carry on inter-ethnic relations studies, with three French Canadian professors from Laval University.)

We sailed for Maracaibo in late August 1954. During the preceding six weeks, I spent two hours a day or so by myself learning Spanish, working with books and records earlier developed at Cornell. By the time we landed, I had reached the point of being able to ask my interview questions but was often still at a loss in understanding the answers.

When oil was discovered on the eastern side of Lake Maracaibo in 1913, that semi-desert area had been practically unsettled. By this time, the city of Cabimas had a population of over 50 thousand, but still had no municipal water system. As in some other Latin American countries, the government of Venezuela had neglected the provinces, concentrating revenues and public works in and around the capital city of Caracas. All tax revenues except local fees were collected by the central government, and local officials thus were dependent on very stingy handouts from Caracas.

The Creole company camps, with wire fences surrounding them, were a prominent enclave of relatively easy living, compared to Cabimas and other towns on that side of the Lake. The company had provided water, gas and electricity and in general had been acting in the role of an unelected local government for Creole employees and families. The company had also provided relatively well built homes in three interrelated camps, for the management (largely American) for supervisors, and for workers and their families—all Venzuelan in the latter two categories. Unfortunately, from the beginning, the company had been charging only a trivial amount for the rental of worker and supervisory apartments. Therefore, workers and supervisors could save very little through moving out, and Creole recognized the need to provide an enormous financial subsidy to encourage such movement. The company had reason to believe that workers and supervisors were not happy with living in the camps, and so it seemed a good idea to learn how the Venezuelan men and women felt about living conditions. Furthermore, the enclaves were becoming a political issue among Venezuelan intellectuals and middle-class people in other areas who resented their enclave nature.

The study of attitudes of the Venezuelan inhabitants of the company camps obviously called for a survey and thus pushed me into methods for which I was poorly qualified. To be sure, I had learned something from supervising Cornell theses, but now I was entirely on my own.

Isabel Peraza de Morse, the Venezuelan wife of an American engineer, proved to be a very skillful interviewer in developing the background information regarding worker attitudes and in applying the survey personally from house to house.

As we had expected, our respondents were not happy with living in company camps, but they felt trapped by the availability of essential public utilities and the nominal rentals.

The personnel chiefs, who had arranged for my project, seemed pleased with the reports on supervisory and community relations and our concluding discussions with other management people in Caracus—with one exception. Besides the reports that I had promised, I volunteered one more, which they had not asked for: a report on the Creole Personnel Program. The personnel people took great pride in their generous fringe benefits and their safety program, but I was impressed with the lack of any constructive involvement between the personnel men in the field with relations between expatriate management and the Venezuelan supervisors and the workers. That report was greeted with some apparent embarrassment in Caracas, and thereafter I was never asked to do anything for Creole or for the parent company.

My year in Venezuela did not lead to another book, but it did have two long-run payoffs. By the end of that year, I was fluent enough in Spanish to get along well in conversation and to understand what was said to me in interviews. That year also hooked me on Latin American Studies so that I began reading, thinking, and discussing Latin American topics in the expectation of further involvement in that region.

CORNELL: 1955-1961

In the years 1955 to 1961, my involvement in field work was limited to an Alcan summer project in Arvida, Quebec, and getting a project started in Corning Glass Works in the Steuben Division. The Steuben project provided me with a case study of a well nigh extinct type of operation in modern industry: teams of skilled craftsmen making fine glass objects by hand and simple tools, but that only led eventually to a chapter in the first text book I attempted. *Men at Work* (1961) had a very modest initial sale and soon petered out. (Seven years later, I tried again with *Organizational Behavior: Theory and Practice* [1968], which suffered the same fate as my first try. I came to the conclusion that my style of research and theoretical analysis had gone out of style in the face of competition from writers who concentrated on stating hypotheses based upon statistical analysis of population aggregates.)

In this period I took on two new responsibilities. In 1956, I succeeded Robin Williams as the Director of Cornell's Social Science Research Center. This was a half-time job, and I arranged to attract Henry Landsberger, who had received his Ph.D. in our program earlier, to become half-time Assistant Director, devoting the other half time to the ILR Department of Organizational Behavior.

The mission of the Center was to stimulate interdisciplinary discussion and communication across the campus and to assist young scholars planning their research and research proposals. This meant exploring campus interests to find topics or problem areas that might attract an interdisciplinary group interested in talking and working together. Probably the most memorable project we undertook in that period was a faculty seminar on the theories of Talcott Parsons—a project into which I was dragged reluctantly. It was Landsberger's idea. When he asked me, "Bill, do you think there might be some interest in an interdisciplinary seminar on the theories of Talcott Parsons?" I replied, "My God, I hope not—but maybe you ought to find out." I had always liked Talcott, but I found the writings of America's leading sociological theorist almost impossible to understand and not worth the effort of understanding. Nevertheless, when Henry found interest among a very able faculty group, ranging across the campus from sociology and social psychology to political science, economics, and philosophy, I felt obliged to participate myself. The seminar went on for two years, meeting every two weeks in the home of one of the professors, and ended with the appearance of Parsons to answer his critics—or dodge their questions. The project did result in a book, *The Social Theories of Talcott Parsons*, with Max Black, the eminent philosopher of science serving as our editor. I contributed one highly critical chapter, whose main theme was that, although the word "action" appeared in the title of most of Parsons' books, actually Talcott was not focusing on action but rather on the actor's "orientation to the situation." I saw his actors constantly in rehearsal but the curtain never rising on the action.

The second new activity in this period was the editorship of *Human Organization* (1956-1961, 1962-1963). I took on this responsibility in response to a phone call from Margaret Mead. For the last several years, Eliot D. Chapple had served as editor, and the Society for Applied Anthropology was headquartered in his New York City consulting office, paying half the rental. I was aware of the growing dissatisfaction among the members with the leadership of the Society, but I had no idea of the severity of the problems until I found them lodged with me at Cornell.

Margaret had tried to reassure me, stating that the Society was financially solvent—which was not true, but Margaret was simply ill informed about the actual condition. Her confusion arose from the fact that the Society had a grant from the Grant Foundation to publish what was called The Research Clearing House, which undertook to survey the literature to provide abstracts of the most relevant articles related to applied anthropology. Money allocated to that special purpose was still in the bank account but not available to finance *Human Organization* and the general expenses of the Society. When we sorted out the figures from the New York office, we discovered that, if all the bills were paid, the Society would be over a thousand dollars in the hole.

I was able to persuade the Foundation officials to allow us to terminate the Clearing House and use the remaining funds to strengthen the general budget. This relieved the financial crisis for the moment, but *Human Organization* was more than three issues behind in its quarterly publication schedule, which naturally diminished the interest of members in paying their dues.

I had been told that the Society had a membership of about 1,500, but, when we eliminated all those who were more than one year behind in payment of dues, that figure dropped to about 1,100.

Since the Center job had already given me a half time release from a regular teaching load, I did not ask for or receive any additional released time for the editorship. The School of Industrial and Labor Relations provided no direct financial subsidy for the Society, but we operated out of my office and thus saved substantially over the rental that the Society had been paying in Manhattan. Later (1964) I was elected President of the Society for Applied Anthropology, but it was clear that the editorship of *Human Organization* was a far more important position for the Society. The editor was not only responsible for putting out the quarterly journal but also had to manage the finances and the membership operations of the Society. An old friend, who was an accountant, volunteered to reorganize the accounting system and simplify it so even I could understand it.

For editorial assistance and to handle the business affairs, I called on one of Cornell University's hidden resources: talented but underemployed faculty wives. I was fortunate in having Laura Holmberg, Katrina Morse, and Marian Tolles work with me.

Unlike most academic journals, *Human Organization* introduced each issue with an editorial page or two, giving the editor free rein to express his or her views. I welcomed this opportunity and tried in my first issue to sound the clarion call to the members to indicate that the Society was beginning a come back. Nevertheless, it was apparent, even with the new editorial board, improvements would come too slowly to save the Society unless we undertook some special promotional projects.

The first promotional project arose out of a summer workshop I conducted jointly with social anthropologist Allen R. Holmberg on "Human Problems of U.S. Enterprise in Latin America." Holmberg was much more knowledgeable than I regarding Latin America, having been deeply involved in applied research in Peru beginning in 1948 with what became the famous Vicos project, which involved transforming a semi-feudal hacienda into a self governing community. We put together Holmberg's background knowledge of Latin American culture and his interpretation of the significance of the Vicos experience with my own research background in Venezuela to put out a special issue on "Human Problems of U.S. Enterprise in Latin America."

We promoted the special issue to American companies with major involvements in Latin America, offering a discount for ordering a hundred copies or more. So as to assess the potential market before printing, I spent some time in Manhattan, calling on high-level personnel people in various firms and thus signed up enough orders to justify substantial expansion of our normal pressrun. Taking a deep breadth, I ordered a pressrun of 5,500 copies. (Eventually, we did sell almost all of those copies.) I look back upon this project with mixed feelings. On the one hand, it was vital to the survival of the Society, but, on the other hand, the implicit message was that, if the leading American executives of American owned firms understood the culture and developed good human relations with the nationals inside and outside of the company, the company and the host nation could live happily ever after. I realized later that, important as cultural sensitivity and understanding may be, the foreign domination of the industry of a nation constitutes a political problem that good human relations do not resolve.

This project also provided us with a strategy to expand the membership and increase our revenue. We circulated to former members the promotional piece on this special issue, and that brought some of them back. We followed the same formula several times later—but without special promotions to business. With each special issue, we sought to enhance the value of membership to those already with us and at the same time tried to sell individual copies of that issue and gain new memberships. Later we added a monograph series which was distributed free to members and also used to promote individual copy sales and new memberships. We also secured a grant from the New World Foundation to finance a special issue celebrating the 25th anniversary of the founding of the Society for Applied Anthropology.

Although I pinchhit for my successor as editor, Robert J. Smith of the Cornell Anthropology Department when he was away on sabbatical (1962-1963), I look upon the years 1956-1961 as my time of major responsibility. I was happy to end that period with *Human Organization* caught up in its publication dates and an unexpended balance of over $11,000 in our bank account. I enjoyed the new experience of the editorship, but I was glad to move on to other things.

INVOLVEMENT IN PERU

By 1961, I was due for another sabbatical year. In studying relations between management and workers in Venezuela, it was impossible to sort out to what extent worker reactions were resultants of the hierarchial situation or to what extent they might have arisen from intercultural problems between Venezuelans and Americans.

I now wanted to do some case studies in a Latin American country in firms where both management and workers were Latin Americans. Through Holmberg, I had become particularly interested in Peru. I had assumed that he would be pursuing his rural development research, and I would be operating in industry, and the two streams of research and interest would come together to provide a broader understanding of the society and culture of the nation. Guided by Holmberg, I made two brief exploratory visits to Peru in the summers of 1958 and 1960.

Planning to study "Human Problems of Industrial Development" in Peru, I secured a Fulbright Fellowship and a grant from the National Institute of Mental Health, thus making it possible to extend our time in Peru over 14 months—an academic year and two summers. Our two older children were now in college, but Lucy and John came with us to Lima. Since San Marcos National University was in political turmoil, the Fulbright Commission got me an office in the National Engineering University, in the Department of Industrial Engineering. The project was well financed. I had four student research assistants and a bilingual secretary and another one who proved to be one and one-half lingual.

I had made contacts with management people in my brief summer trips, and now I found the major opening to field sites through IPAE, the Peruvian counterpart of the American Management Association. IPAE sponsored a luncheon club of a limited number of members who got together every two weeks, and I managed to get myself invited to one of their sessions. In the drinks before lunch, Robert R. Braun took me aside and asked about my plans. When I had finished my account, Bob expressed great interest and volunteered to be an informal advisor. He explained that he was then interim manager of IPAE and had his own consulting business on the side, but he did not have all his time occupied, and he said he would be glad to work with me.

I soon recognized that I had come upon an invaluable resource. He had interviewed me in Spanish, but Bob Braun was tri-lingual. He had come to Peru from Vienna after finishing high school. He had worked as a management consultant and had been in charge of the Price Waterhouse subsidiary in Peru. He had had extensive experience with Peruvian owned and managed firms and also with German, English and American firms. He was highly sensitive to cultural differences and was an invaluable guide not only to contacts that I needed to make but also how to win the cooperation of management people.

Our first case studies were carried out through personal interviewing and observation on the job, but then Bob pushed me into a survey research project with Empresas Electricas (Lima Light and Power Company). Lawrence K. Williams had recently come into ILR's Department of Organizational Behavior, following extensive experience with the University of Michigan's Survey Research Center's project with Detroit Edison. This provided an opportunity to adapt the Detroit Edison survey to gather comparable data from its Lima counterpart. That project led to our first cross national comparative publications. ("Supervisory Leadership," 1963; "Do Cultural Differences Affect Workers' Attitudes," 1966).

The case studies of industrial companies and my broadening contacts with management people impressed me with one striking aspect of Peruvian culture. With very few exceptions, Peru's industrial entrepreneurs were either immigrants or sons of immigrants. Peruvian culture did not value the entrepreneurial role in industry or business. In the children's history books, the heroes were military leaders who had failed gloriously, losing their lives in battles already lost. Achievement motivation was not to be found in those books.

The press reported business news of the companies, but notably absent were feature stories about how an industrial leader had started out with little money but indomitable drive to succeed and had managed to build a large and prosperous organization. There had been such individuals in Peru, but their children and grand-children would have been embarrassed to be reminded that the entrepreneur had started from such a humble beginning.

Such reflections lured me toward undertaking a study of Peruvian culture, but how does one study the culture of a nation? In the 1950s, several of my colleagues in the Sociology Department at Cornell had carried out a study of the values of college students in a number of American universities. I asked

Rose Goldsen for a copy of the questionnaire. Graciela Flores, who proved to be the ablest and most enterprising of the four student field workers, assumed primary responsibility with me for designing the Peruvian survey instrument and later applying it in the field. Since student career choices had generally been made before they entered the university, we decided to apply the survey to male high school seniors. (I regretted later that we had not surveyed females also, but the public high scools were segregated and I assumed that, in any case, the males would be more likely to work in industry.)

In the United States, it would have taken some days of diplomacy to work out any arrangement to apply a survey to a high school class, and we would have expected to be turned down in some cases. There was no such problem in Peru. The Ministry of Education had a small educational research unit, and I visited the head of the Instituto Pedagogico Nacional to get his advice on our project and interest him in it. The advice was valuable in sorting out public and private schools by status. The collaboration was even more important. We had only to tell the Instituto Director what school we wanted to survey next, whereupon he would pick up the phone and say that the Ministry of Education was carrying out this important survey and he would like us to have access to a class of high school seniors at nine o'clock on a particular morning. The most resistant school director said that ten o'clock would be more convenient. In this way, we carried out two or three surveys a week, finishing up 12 Lima schools within a month. We then arranged to carry out the same survey in several provincial cities. These high school surveys provided us with fascinating comparisons by social class, indicating that the public school students showed substantially more achievement orientation than those in the higher status levels—but they also were more inclined to seek work from the government than those at the elite level, who were more attracted to business management. We also found important differences between Peru and our American college students particularly in the dimension we called *faith in people* or *trust in one's fellow man.* Americans showed much more tendency to be trusting than the Peruvian students. The project also won for Graciela a fellowship to study for a year at Cornell, where she continued working with Rose Goldson on the high school value studies.

By now I had become so immersed in Peruvian culture and development to move me to write up an ambitious plan of research for a book that would pull together what I was learning from industry and the values study with what I was learning from Allen Holmberg's rural research. That plan won for me a Research Career Award from the National Institute of Mental Health, providing $25,000 a year salary support over a period of 15 years, 1964-1967, taking me conveniently to my sixty-fifth birthday, at which time I expected to retire. The award was designed to free me from all teaching and administrative obligations so that I could concentrate on research. The grant more than covered my salary for the first few years, and later the ILR School made up the difference. I elected to continue teaching one semester each year, but the Award enabled me to devote much more time to Peru than I could have done otherwise.

By 1964, Allen Holmberg was terminally ill with leukemia, so I could no longer count on him to further my knowledge of rural Peru. I was moved to get into rural research myself even more by the election of President Fernando Belaunde Terry in 1963. While we were living in Lima, I followed the 1962 presidential campaign with avid interest and became a rooter for Belaunde. In that election, he came in about half a percentage point behind Victor Raul Haya de la Torre, with former president and dictator Manuel Ordía close behind the two leaders. The Belaunde forces claimed fraud, but, in any event, the military leaders would not stand for a government of Haya and the APRA party. They intervened to annul the election and announced a rerun in 1963. Belaunde won and assumed office in July of that year.

Belaunde had been Dean of the College of Architecture, with a background in city and regional planning. One of his main campaign pledges was a program of land reform and rural development.

The Belaunde election stirred me to devise what now seems like a grandiose plan. In addition to established government programs, Belaunde was organizing something like the American Peace Corps, inspiring Peruvian University students to channel revolutionary and reformist zeal into helping communities move ahead.

I assumed that this government campaign would bring about major changes in the country side. Therefore, it seemed important as soon as possible to get down a base line study of a number of rural communities and then manage to go back three to five years later to study those same communities, under conditions reflecting the changes stimulated by the government program. The only way to lay down such a base line in a hurry was to carry out surveys. The plan called for intensive interviewing and observational studies, in the same communities after the surveys had been completed.

Lawrence K. Williams became codirector of this enterprise for Cornell. He and I worked together drafting a preliminary version of the questionnaire, and he thereafter had the primary responsibility for guiding the survey operations and the survey data analysis.

To start field operations, I sought out one of Peru's leading anthropologists, José Matos Mar, who had long been professor at San Marcos, the leading public university. Matos had recently received a grant from Belaunde's government to set up the Instituto de Estudios Peruanos (IEP). For the summer vacation period between university semesters, January—March 1964, he would have a dozen advanced undergraduate students doing fieldwork in the Chancay Valley along the coast about an hour's drive north of Lima. Matos agreed to have his students pretest the questionnaire and then carry out the first village surveys with the revised instrument. Throughout this program, Cornell had financial support from either the National Science Foundation or the National Institute of Mental Health, so we were able to finance my trip to Peru and provide the students with some modest stipends to supplement what they were receiving from IEP. I spent some days with Matos and students in the Chancay Valley, discussing research methods and working with the students on the pretest and on the revised questionnaire.

The arrangements with Matos and the San Marcos students worked so well as to encourage me to extend the scope of our studies to a number of other communities on the coast and in the highlands, working with and through professors and students of sociology or anthropology in provincial universities close to the areas of study.

Before the end of 1964, we had carried out surveys through the universities at Cuzco, Arequipa, and Huancayo in the highlands, and through the University of Trujillo on the north coast, giving us a total (with the Chancay villages) of 26 surveys.

It was exhilarating to move so far so fast, but we soon realized that we were headed for an enormous fiasco unless we substantially scaled down the scope of our operations. We recognized several problems. In the first place, I had had the vision of using this research program not only to gather data for Cornell but also to contribute to the education in survey research methods and in field work for students in five universities. While we were able to carry out the initial surveys according to this plan, it became evident that the diplomatic and political problems of dealing with and through so many universities were overwhelming. In addition to working out the arrangements in each university, we had to contend with the widespread ideology which made working with Americans appear like collaborating with Yankee Imperialism. Then the surveys went much faster than the anthropological community studies, so that we ended 1964 with rather sketchy and inadequate anthropological field reports. I also became concerned about the rather limited value that the students were gaining from the initial survey operations. We had worked out arrangements to get the questionnaires onto IBM punch cards through facilities in the Ministry of Health. I did have some discussions with students, inviting them to consider what the marginal percentages might mean in one community or another. They were unable to speculate on those figures.

If we were not to be caught in the trap called "academic imperialism," we would have to bring Peruvian students and professors into all stages of the research process. This meant having someone competent in survey analysis located in Lima to work with them.

Our initial financing would not support such a program. I delivered a paper at a meeting of the American Anthropological Association, where an official of the Advanced Research Projects Agency in the Pentagon heard it and wrote me to express interest in this type of research.

I had worked out an arrangement with Matos to make the IEP the headquarters of a joint program in which he would become co-director along with Larry Williams and me. Early in 1965, on the way to Peru, I stopped in Washington to check the prospects of financing. The ARPA official assured me that no secret reports would be required by ARPA—nothing beyond what we would routinely report to any private foundation. Furthermore, ARPA would make its decision on our proposal within two months or less. If we had sought additional financing from NSF, NIMH, or private foundations, we would have expected to wait 9 to 12 months for an answer.

In Lima, I discussed the ARPA possibility with Matos. We both would have preferred almost any other source of funds, but Matos decided that it would be possible to continue an expanded joint program, provided that the ARPA funds were used for Cornell staff and expenses, while the NSF grant supported our Peruvian associates.

Within less than a month of submitting the ARPA application, we received a substantial grant. This enabled us to establish Oscar Alers in Lima as Cornell's research associate, and to bring back to Peru from M.I.T., where he had been involved in some survey research, Julio Cotler, a very talented Peruvian sociologist.

Meanwhile, at Cornell, Larry Williams and I were jointly teaching a seminar on our Peruvian studies, getting our students involved in analysis of our survey data, as a means of preparing them for thesis research later in Latin America. An Italian graduate student, Georgio Alberti, joined this seminar and then went on to carry out his own thesis project in Peru's Mantaro Valley. He then remained in Peru, succeeding Alers as our research associate.

In 1966, we encountered a crisis that threatened to wipe out our program. The Camelot scandal erupted in Chile. This involved a research program financed indirectly by the U.S. Army to study the conditions favoring counterinsurgency in developing countries. In sounding out key people in countries where such research might be done, its academic sponsors did not reveal the underlying counterinsurgency purpose. A Norwegian sociologist, who was familiar with the plans, happened to be in Chile at the time. When he disclosed the Pentagon financing, the public scandal resulted in the cancellation of the Camelot program.

This greatly heightened Latin American suspicions about any project financed by the United States and particularly anything financed by the Pentagon. Following my further discussions with IEP people, a previously inactive member of their Board of Directors leaked the information about Pentagon financing for our rural community studies. I believed that our program was basically different from Camelot. Our village studies had not been designed or financed by the Department of Defense in the first place. ARPA had only come in to provide additional support to a program that Cornell and IEP had jointly designed, and none of us had any interest in contributing to knowledge about counterinsurgency. Nevertheless, Matos and I were attacked vigorously in several stories in the newspaper of the APAA Party. Furthermore, I was described as a mysterious figure who had no connection with any American university. (Of course, it would have been easy for anyone who really wanted to know to find out my university connection.)

It now became evident that we could not continue utilizing ARPA funds—which we had only begun expending. I got Cornell University to return the unexpended balance of the ARPA grant, much to the annoyance of ARPA officials, who presumably had never had money turned back to them before.

Now we had to fall back entirely on the NSF grant, which had been scheduled to carry us through 1967. With our expanded program, our NSF funds would run out by the end of 1966. I put in new proposals to both NSF and NIMH.

In November 1966, I made what I thought would be the last visit to our IEP program, and Matos and I talked nostalgically about how happy our working relationship had been and how sad it was that it could not continue. In early December, I got a call reporting that NSF had approved the proposal, but NIMH was also prepared to approve our proposal. Which grant would we prefer? I had never before suffered such an embarrassment of riches. Since NIMH could approve three year grants, whereas NSF was limited to two years, we decided to go with NIMH.

We were now in a position to move ahead with more intensive anthropological studies among selected villages and with the 1969 resurvey program. We scaled down the number of villages for further anthropological study and the resurvey from the original 26 to 12, where we had the best data from our previous research. To simplify our diplomatic and management problems, we now concentrated our collaborative efforts within IEP. For the resurveys, we had an experienced IEP researcher in charge of the fieldwork in each regional study, under the general direction of Giorgio Alberti, while we continued to depend on students from the regional universities for most of the survey interviewing.

Georgio Alberti and I then teamed up to pull together what we were learning about research methodology and rural development through a book, *Power, Politics, and Progress: Social Change in Rural Peru* (1976).

What did we accomplish in our long Peruvian involvement? I see the outputs in three categories:

1. *An exceptional record of long-term international research collaboration.* Somehow, in a period of rising Peruvian concern over Yankee domination, we managed to sustain a mutually fruitful research partnership for 12 years. Our program produced a large number of research publications—until near the end, much more in Spanish than in English. Many of those publications came to be used in university teaching in sociology and anthropology in Peru. When we were unable to recruit graduate students to

work with us, we learned that advanced undergraduates could perform superbly. Furthermore, five of them established such a record with us to win fellowships to study for masters or doctors degrees in Cornell or English universities. When they started formal graduate work, they were ahead of the national students, since they arrived on campus with Spanish drafts of what would become their theses.

2. *Integration of research methods.* We found that we could indeed add value to surveys or to anthropological studies through combining the two methods. For example, this enabled us to clarrify relations between conflict and cooperation in communities. It had been generally assumed that perceived cooperation and conflict in community projects represented a single continuum, so that a community whose residents perceived it as high in cooperation would also see it as low in conflict. In other words, there would be a high negative correlation between perceived conflict and perceived cooperation. On the contrary, we found that both for 1964 and 1969 the correlation between perceived conflict and perceived cooperation was practically zero. We were studying two independent dimensions of perceived community life. There were villages perceived as high in cooperation and low in conflict or low in cooperation and high in conflict, but there were also villages that were perceived higher than the average scores for the sample in conflict and cooperation and others that were lower than the average perceived scores in both dimensions. Furthermore, when we laid this pattern out against the anthropological studies of these same communities, the survey findings made sense. This finding led us to rethink the nature of conflict and cooperation in peasant communities. If this reorientation had arisen solely out of the anthropological reports of our fieldworkers, we would not have trusted their reports enough to question the single continuum model. When the data from the two methods supported the same conclusion, we felt on firm ground.

3. *Recognizing the myth of the passive peasant.* Like so many scholars who had gone before us, we had been assuming that our peasant communities were so locked into their traditional cultures that they would be unable to improve their economic welfare, unless they received some impulse from outside to overcome their resistance to change. In fact, it was the expectation that the Belaunde government would be supplying this impulse that had led us to the design of our rural studies. Although the Belaunde administration did indeed attempt to provide the impulse, the Congress was controlled by an opposition coalition which did everything possible to block this rural development program. Nevertheless, in the period of our studies (1964-1969), in many of these communities there was internal dynamism that produced significant changes quite independent of programs developed from the outside. This finding led us to focus more closely on such internal forces.

FROM COMMUNITIES TO AGRICULTURAL RESEARCH AND DEVELOPMENT

As we were analyzing and writing up our rural research, we continued our relationship with IEP, spending two months each year from 1970 to 1976 in Lima. Through that period, I was shifting my interests toward studies of agricultural research and development in Peru and elsewhere in Latin America.

At Cornell, Franklin Long, Professor of Chemistry, had secured an Agency for International Development grant to support a Program for Policies for Science and Technology in Developing Nations, and he asked me to join an interdisciplinary group ranging across the natural sciences, engineering, and the social sciences. Thinking of how I might contribute, building on past research, it occurred to me that I could shift the focus from the rural community to the organizations designed to support agriculture: research, extension, farm credit, and so forth.

In Peru, I began getting acquainted with the International Potato Center and the national research and extension agencies. With Kathleen, I followed this exposure with two or three week visits to CIMMYT (International Maize and Wheat Improvement Center) in Mexico and CIAT (International Center for Tropical Agriculture) in Colombia. Then focusing more on national level programs, we got involved in shortrun field studies in Guatemala, Honduras, and Costa Rica.

At Cornell, I found myself involved with a group of social scientists and plant, animal, and soil scientists, who were coming to the same conclusion regarding the impacts of the "green revolution": the new high yielding varieties of wheat and rice had enormously increased the yields of those crops, but small farmers had generally benefitted little unless they had access to irrigation. That posed the research problem: how to reshape some aspects of the agricultural R&D process so that small farmers could share more fully in the fruits of scientific advances.

Within the Rural Development Program of Cornell's Center for International Studies, I teamed up with Damon Boynton, a plant scientist, to develop a faculty seminar focused on this research problem and then leading eventually to a book (1983). This brought together chapters by sociologists, political scientists, economists, plant and soil scientists, and agricultural engineers. (Kathleen had the responsibility of editing the volume so as to make the varied pieces understandable to nonspecialists in any of the disciplines.)

STUDYING EMPLOYEE OWNERSHIP AND WORKER COOPERATIVES

1976 marked the end of our involvement in Peruvian research, and yet the topics I focused on at home were in a sense a continuation of work done in Peru.

In 1970, the self-styled Peruvian "Revolutionary Government of the Armed Forces" decreed a program to reform private industry through requiring companies to turn over to their employees, in the form of stock, a percentage of their annual profits, and also to have employee representation on their boards of directors. Although I was not confident that this program would usher in worker participation in management, this clearly represented a major change, bound to have an impact on private industry. We secured a grant to carry out a series of case studies on the impact of "the industrial community," as the Peruvian government called the institution being established under its decree ("The Industrial Community in Peru," 1977).

Back home, with some colleagues, led by economist Jaroslav Vanek, I became involved in efforts to develop nonprofit organizations to promote the creation and support of worker cooperatives. Several years later, I got caught up in the growing interest in employee stock ownership plans (ESOPs), as Senator Russell Long led through Congress a series of measures providing government incentives to firms that shared stock ownership with employees. The ESOP program was basically different from what had been attempted in Peru, in that managements were not forced to cut employees in on ownership but were provided with financial inducements to do so.By the mid 1970s, I became aware that, in a number of cases, workers were undertaking to buy their company or plant that was being shut down.

During the 1976 political campaign, I talked to Ithaca's Congressman Matthew F. McHugh about the possibility of devising legislation that would support this jobsaving strategy. McHugh expressed an interest and suggested that I also seek the interest of Congressman Stanley N. Lundine from Jamestown, New York. With some graduate students, I had already been involved with the Jamestown Area Labor-Management Committee, created by Lundine when he had been Mayor of the city. Furthermore, through this initiative, I had not only met Lundine but also had renewed an old acquaintance with Eric Trist, then with the Wharton School of the University of Pennsylvania. Trist had helped JALMC to build its consultation and facilitation program with advanced graduate students from Wharton. Cornell's research associate, Chris Meek, managed to work out a collaborative relationship with them and participated actively in the Jamestown program ("The Politics of Worker Ownership," 1983).

In a meeting of a review committee for NIMH, I encountered Joseph Blasi, who was to become a key figure in my work with Congress on employee ownership. Congressman Peter H. Kostmayer of Bucks County, Pennsylvania, had offered Blasi a full-time position on his congressional staff. Then Director of the Project for Kibbutz Studies at Harvard University, Blasi declined the offer but made a counterproposal. He would work for Kostmayer one day a week in Washington, as social policy advisor, if the job did not entail any routine administrative duties in the Kostmayer office. A young man of Italian descent, Blasi had done research for his doctoral thesis as a participant observer in an Israeli kibbutz. Blasi expressed enthusiasm for developing legislation to advance employee ownership as a means of saving jobs.

In the spring of 1978, Congressmen McHugh, Lundine, and Kostmayer teamed up to introduce into the House of Representatives the Voluntary Job Preservation and Community Stabilization Act. Thanks to the support of our congressmen, their staff people and Network, a lobbying organization of Catholic nuns, that bill picked up cosponsorship of about one out of every six members of the House of Representatives. A more important gain arose when Corey Rosen, a staff member of the Senate Select Committee on Small Business learned of our bill through reading the Congressional Record. This led him to Joseph Blasi and completed the major linkages in what I called our Academic-Activist Network.

The bill our congressmen introduced in 1978 never did become law, but later Corey Rosen drafted the Small Business Employee Ownership Act, which passed congress and was signed by President Carter in July 1980. In the Reagan landslide that fall, Senator Gaylord Nelson was defeated, and Corey Rosen and his wife, Karen Young, both lost their staff positions with the Senate Select Committee on Small Business. Corey and Karen then founded the National Center for Employee Ownership, which has become an influential organization for advancing the cause through research, publications, and conferences.

By 1975, I was shifting my focus of research from ESOPs toward worker cooperatives and particularly toward the Mondragón cooperative complex in the Basque country of Spain. I learned first about that extraordinary set of worker cooperatives and supporting organizations through a clipping from a London newspaper that I chanced to see on the bulletin board of Jaroslav Vanek's office. At this time, conventional wisdom held that, whereas other types of cooperatives could be successful, worker cooperatives were not a viable form of economic organization. The Mondragón experience contradicted this judgment. The first worker cooperative was founded in 1956 by 5 young men and 18 fellow worker members. From this small beginning, the Mondragón movement expanded until by 1990 it was to include approximately 100 worker cooperatives with over 20,000 members. From the early days, the worker cooperatives have been linked together through a cooperative bank, a research and development cooperative, a set of the democratically governed educational institutions, specializing in engineering and business administration, and were also linked with a thriving chain of worker-consumer cooperatives, governed jointly by consumers and workers.

It had also been commonly believed that for worker cooperatives to survive, they would have to occupy special niches in the economy not of interest to powerful private firms and would be limited to rather low levels of technology, for the lack of capacity and member willingness to invest in modernization. Mondragón gives a lie to this judgment also. Ulgor, the first and still largest of the Mondragón cooperatives, has long held the number one position in the Spanish market in the production of stoves, refrigerators, washing machines, and dishwashers. A number of these firms appear to be at the cutting edge of modern technologies, and Mondragón cooperatives have been far more successful in the export market than the average Spanish private firm.

As soon as I learned about Mondragón, I resolved to go there in search of the forces that had made possible this extraordinary socioeconomic development. The opportunity arose in 1975 when I was invited to Israel to participate in a management seminar program. Along the way, Kathleen and I stopped off in Spain and got our first exposure to Mondragón. Little more than a year before his death, we had the opportunity to meet the most extraordinary individual of my experience, the founder and chief designer of the Mondragón cooperative complex. José María Arizmendiarrieta was a Catholic Priest who, upon being turned down by his superior on a request for church support to do graduate work in sociology, was dispatched to begin his duties in the small city of Mondragón in 1941 (population of about 8,000 at that time). In his seminary studies, he had concentrated more on social and economic development than on theology, and he was familiar with the literature on the weaknesses of worker cooperatives. He was a man who combined a penetrating social vision with a very pragmatic sense of the practical realities of economics and technology. He never had any formal authority in any of the Mondragón cooperatives, yet in the early days he had the key ideas regarding how a worker cooperative should be structured and governed and how cooperatives should be linked together to provide a mutually supporting interorganizational network.

In 1975, I was too involved in finishing up the Peruvian program and in research and writing about ESOPs at home to make a commitment to Mondragón, beyond a preliminary article ("The Mondragón System," 1977). At the time of our first visit, the Mondragón complex was still expanding rapidly, but by the early 1980s Spain was mired in a recession that had hit that country harder than most industrialized nations. The Mondragón cooperatives were now struggling to hold their own. In October 1983, Kathleen and I got back to Mondragón for three weeks. We found that the cooperatives were coping far better with the recession than the average private firm. For several years, their growth had halted, and yet, with a variety of mutually supporting programs, they had managed to keep unemployment among their members to less than one percent. Furthermore, they were in the process of basic reorganizations which were to enable them to resume expansion by 1984.

Toward the end of our stay in Mondragón, I invited a small group of cooperative officials, who had helped us in our research, for a feedback session, which I offered simply as a matter of reciprocity, without any thought of going farther in our Mondragón research. When I had concluded, José Luis González, Personnel Director of the FAGOR group of cooperatives, surprised me by saying, "Why don't you write up a research proposal to continue working with us?" At age 69 and just having worked my way through a major research program in Peru, I was not thinking of launching a new one in Mondragón. Still, I was fascinated with Mondragón and wanted to respond in some way.

At Cornell, I put my problem to Davydd J. Greenwood, who was not only director of our Center for International Studies but also a leading authority on Basque culture and economic organization. He informed me about the Spain-United States Committee for Education and Cultural Exchange, and suggested the possibility of getting support for a joint program involving Cornell and the Mondragón Cooperative Complex.

Grants from that Committee supported two years of inter-institutional collaborative research and enabled Kathleen and me to get back to Mondragón for additional studies in 1985 and 1986. In the same period, Greenwood became actively involved with members of the FAGOR cooperative group, particularly through month-long seminars in July of each of those years, in which he was teaching about social research methods and theories but also getting the seminar members into research on their own organizations. This program supported Kathleen and me in our further studies, leading to our jointly authored book, *Making Mondragón: The Growth and Dynamics of the Worker Cooperative Complex* (1988).

By 1990, I thought we had put Mondragón behind us, but we had been hearing that the leaders of the cooperative movement were carrying out major reorganizations to strengthen the cooperatives in competing in the European market, after 1992, when all tariff protectection for Spanish industry would be eliminated. That led us back to Mondragón for a five day visit in April 1990—and to contemplation of a new edition of our book to deal with the major changes that are already under way.

WHAT DOES AN EMERITUS PROFESSOR DO?

Becoming an emeritus professor would give me more time to write, but I did not want to be entirely divorced from the university program. It occurred to me that the Extension Division might be a likely location within which to fit applied industrial relations research and I went about trying to find a way to do it.

In the Extension Division, I met Director of Management Programs, Donald Kane, and he introduced me to Peter Lazes, who had arranged to bring the Xerox labor and management people off-site to have some training sessions at Cornell. Kane and I sensed that this was an unusual situation, in which Xerox and the Amalgamated Clothing and Textile Workers Union were going far beyond the usual boundaries of labor-management cooperation.

What excited us particularly was the development of a social invention to meet a crisis in which management was prepared to save millions of dollars through shutting down production departments and "outsourcing" the threatened products. Guided by Lazes, company and union agreed to set up what we are calling *cost study teams* (CSTs) to work full time for six months to try to find potential savings that would match vendor's prices and keep the production and jobs at Xerox. This social invention worked so well that it stimulated even further collaborative efforts and also led to an extraordinary employment security clause in the 1983, 1986, and 1989 contracts: no worker with three or more years seniority would be laid off.

This was my first direct exposure to what we now are calling *participatory action research* (PAR): Lazes, a social psychologist, had led the parties toward the CST projects and helped to train the CSTs in problem solving methods, but the figures on cost savings were entirely developed by the practitioners.

When Kane and I found Lazes interested in quitting independent consulting to join in a university program, we began to figure how this might be done.The opening came with the shut down of the Lackawanna plant of Bethlehem Steel Corporation. That was outside of the jurisdiction of Steven Allinger, who was on the staff of the Higher Education Committee of the New York State Assembly, but he had come from Lackawanna and was concerned as to what might be done. He wondered if an employee buyout might be a possibility. When he couldn't find anybody in the state university system, outside of Cornell, he called an old friend from Lackawanna, the UAW union leader who had organized Cornell's service employees to ask if Al Davidoff knew of anybody at Cornell who knew something about employee ownership. Davidoff knew an employee who knew a student, Edwin Houser, who was working on a thesis with me dealing with an employee buyout. That led Allinger to me.

Before following up, I checked to learn that Bethlehem had not invested any substantial amounts in Lackawanna since 1935, which indicated that this was a lost cause for employee ownership. Still, Houser and I went to Albany to orient a group of Assembly staffers on employee ownership—without trying to promote it for Lackawanna.

Several weeks later, Allinger came to the Cornell campus with a fellow staffer to consult with a group of us, including the Director of Extension. By now he was willing to write off Lackawanna and was thinking more broadly: wouldn't it be a good idea if New York State had some way of helping firms in difficulties before shutdown plans were announced?

Allinger went to work on a bill to provide ILR with funds to participate in interventions that would help labor and management to become more competitive. The first year the bill did not pass, but a year later, supported by Lazes' lobbying efforts, the bill did pass, enabling us to set up Programs for Employment and Workplace Systems (PEWS).

Reflecting on the Xerox case, in which practitioners were active participants in the research process, excited our interest in further development of *participatory action research* (PAR). In Mondragon I played a minor role in a project Davydd J. Greenwood developed with the FAGOR group of worker cooperatives. With Jose Luis Gonzalez, Personnel Director of the FAGOR group, Greenwood developed a project focusing on the culture of the cooperatives and the role of the Personnel Department within this culture.

That led to my editing an issue of *American Behavioral Scientist* (May/June 1988) dealing with the Xerox and FAGOR cases, along with earlier work along the same lines, as a means of demonstrating the scientific as well as practical value of PAR.

In my earlier studies of agricultural research and development in Latin America, I had encountered a number of cases which I now recognized involved small farmers as active participants in the research process and, therefore, could also be called PAR projects. That realization led to my next (edited) publication, *Participatory Action Research* (1990), expanding on the ABS issue with additional industry cases and a series of cases on agricultural research and development. Then, to provide my own interpretation of the development of participatory processes and structures in industry and agriculture, I wrote *Social Theory for Action* (1991). That book aims to pull together what I have learned regarding participatory structures and processes (or the lack of them) since I began my first field study in 1936.

SOME FINAL REFLECTIONS

What did I accomplish in this long career?

I have dealt so far primarily upon my research and writing, which, I suppose, will be the primary basis for determining the reputation I leave behind me, but I have also had substantial involvement in other activities.

Although I used my primary commitment to research to reduce my teaching obligations, in fact I did enjoy teaching. I found I was particularly good at encouraging graduate students to get out into the field and providing some fieldwork guidance. I never sought to dictate what a student should study and took pride in the fact that those who worked closely with me did not conform to a pattern that I set for them.

In large undergraduate and graduate classes, I would like to think that I was at least an average teacher, but I confused many students because I was constantly trying to reshape what the major readings stated to conform with what I wanted them to say. I made it a point never to teach from an old set of notes and always tried to bring in what I was learning from recent field projects. Still, I always felt somewhat guilty, thinking I could have been a better teacher if I had devoted more time to teaching.

I did only a very limited amount of consulting with industrial or other organizations and never felt that I was very good at consulting. For me, the most rewarding consulting experiences were focused on questions of research programs and policies. Here I served on the President's Committee on Research for the Prudential Insurance Company (1960-1964), and from 1965 to 1972 on the Subcommittee of Research of the National Manpower Advisory Committee of the U.S. Department of Labor. I was chairman of that Subcommittee from 1968 to 1972.

I was interested in the research program of the Prudential, but I confess that the most rewarding part of that assignment was the opportunity to get together with a very interesting group of professors. Among them were economists John Kenneth Galbraith and William Baumol, sociologist Paul Lazarsfeld, political scientist Harold Lasswell, and my former student, Chris Argyris.

In the Department of Labor, I was brought in (at the suggestion of staff psychologist, Richard Shore) as a means of trying to broaden the base of DOL research, which had grown up primarily in the Bureau of Labor Statistics, dominated by economists. I should note that this broadening effort was fully supported by some of the leading economists in the Department, and, of course, the effort extended far beyond me. Whatever I contributed had a minimal lasting impact, since the Reagan administration drastically reduced the Department's research budget.

I have been honored by my colleagues, being elected President of the Industrial Relations Research Association (1963), The Society for Applied Anthropology (1964), and the American Sociological Association (1981). Still, I seem to occupy a peculiar position, being recognized as a person of some importance through my publications, yet they nevertheless seem to be outside of the mainstream of academic discourse. As I have already noted, my two attempts to write organizational behavior texts never achieved any popularity.

In all three associations, I sought to reform the annual meeting. As President I laid down the ground rules: that professors should talk and not read their papers aloud, since I had found such paper reading the dullest form of human performance. The effort did a little good for the meetings for which I was responsible, but after that the academic culture reasserted itself.

For ASA I began my duties when it appeared that the Reagan administration was pushing for big cuts in social science research budgets. I worked closely with ASA chief executive officer, Russell Dynes to help mobilize the Consortium of Social Science Associations, which has since become an effective lobbying group.

I take special satisfaction from a very unorthodox activity for a professor: working closely with congress on employee ownership legislation, linked directly with my own research on the emergence and spread of employee ownership. In influencing public policy, I was only a minor player, but I enjoyed the sense of being involved in a movement that might reshape the economies of my own and other countries.

As I reflect upon my research, I see myself engaged in two career long quests: to find better ways to link research with practice, and to discover behavioral uniformities in a variety of settings.

I began as a participant observer, with no interest in survey research. I then found that my scientific quest would be strengthened through surveys but especially through combining surveys with field interviewing and observation. After my first field study, I abandoned my commitment to pursuing "pure" science but did not find ways, that satisfied me, of combining research with practice until the mid-1980s, when I began to work out my own version of *participatory action research.*

Both my scientific and practical interests led me to focus on studies of *participation.* Early in my industrial studies, I recognized the importance of worker participation in the United States, but then I wondered whether this was simply a function of U.S. culture. That led me to studies of industry in other cultures.

As I got involved in Peru and then in other Latin American countries in rural research, I was excited to find participation an important variable in linking research to practice among small farmers. I then took up the challenge to extend the analysis of participation from industry to agriculture.

My latest book, *Social Theory for Action: How Individuals and Organizations Learn to Change* (1991), pulls together what I have learned from the pursuit of both quests: to find scientifically legitimate ways of linking research to practice and to discover behavioral uniformities across a broad range of social and cultural settings.

PUBLICATIONS

1931

Bill Whyte visits the elementary school. *Bronxville Schools Bulletin, 18.*

1935

Financing New York City. *The American Academy of Political and Social Science*, Bulletin #2.

1939

Race conflicts in the North End. *The New England Quarterly, 12*(4), 623-642.

1941

Corner boys: A study of clique behavior. *American Journal of Sociology, 46*(5), 647-664.
The social role of the settlement house. *Applied Anthropology, 1*(1), 14-19.

1943

Street corner society. Chicago: University of Chicago Press.
A slum sex code. *American Journal of Sociology, 49*(1), 24-31. (Bobbs-Merrill Reprint Series, No. 312)
Social organization in the slums. *American Sociologocal Review, 8*, 34-39.
A challenge to political scientists. *American Political Science Review, 37*(4) 692-697. (Bobbs-Merrill Reprint Series, No. 117)

1944

Sicilian peasant society. *American Anthropologist, 46*(1), 65-74.
Age-grading of the Plains Indians. *Man, 54*(53-70), 68-72.
Can the social sciences be useful? *The American Scholar* (Summer), 346-355.
Vocational education in industry: A case study. *Applied Anthropology, 3*(4), 1-6.
Pity the personnel man. *Advanced Management, 9*(4), 154-158.
Who goes union and why? *Personnel Journal, 23*(6), 215-230.

1945

With B.B. Gardner. The man in the middle: Position and problems of the foreman. *Applied Anthropology, 4*(2), 1-28.

1946

[Editor]. *Industry and society*. New York: McGraw-Hill.
Politics and ethics: A reply to John H. Hallowell. *American Political Science Review, 40*(02), 301-307.
With B.B. Gardner & A.H. Whiteford. From conflict to cooperation: Buchsbaum Case [Special issue]. *Applied Anthropology, 5*(4).
With B.B. Gardner. Methods for the study of human relations in industry. *American Sociological Review, 2*(5), 506-512.

1947

Solving the hotel's human problems. *The Hotel Monthly.*

Union-management cooperation: A Toronto case. *Applied Anthropology, 6*(3), 1-9.

1948

Human relations in the restaurant industry. New York:McGraw-Hill.

Incentives for productivity [Bundy Tubing Company]. *Applied Anthropology, 7*(2), 1-16.

1949

Semantics and industrial relations. *Human Organization, 8*(2), 4-10.

Patterns of interaction in union-management relations. *Human Organization, 8*(4), 13-19.

The social structure of the restaurant. *The American Journal of Sociology, 54*(1) 302-308.

1950

With J.T. Dunlop. Framework for the analysis of industrial relations: Two views. *Industrial and Labor Relations Review, 3*(3), 383-401.

With S. Garfield. The collective bargaining process: A human relations analysis: I—IV. *Human Organization.*

1951

Pattern for industrial peace. New York: Harper and Brothers.

Money and motivation. New York: Harper and Brothers.

Observational field work methods. In M. Jahoda, S.W. Cook, & M. Deutsch (Eds.), *Research methods in social relations* (Vol. 2, pp. 129-150). Dryden: The Dryden Press.

Organization and motivation of management. In W.F. Whyte (Ed.), *Industrial productivity* (pp. 94-109). Madison, WI: Industrial Relations Research Association.

Social science and industrial relations: How management can use the human relations specialist. *Personnel, 27*(4), 258-266.

Small groups and large organizations. In J. Rohrer & M. Sherif (Eds.), *Social psychology at the crossroads* (pp. 297-312). New York: Harper and Brothers.

1952

Economic incentives and human relations. *Harvard Business Review, 30*(2), 73-80.

1953

Leadership and group participation. *New York State School of Industrial and Labor Relations, Bulletin 21.*
Modern methods in social research. Office of Naval Research.

1956

With A.R. Holmberg. Human problems of U.S. enterprise in Latin America [Special issue]. *Human Organization, 15*(3), 1-40.
Human relations theory. *Harvard Business Review*, 34(5), 125-132.
Problems of industrial sociology. *Social Problems, 4*(2) 148-160.
Engineers and workers: A case study. *Human Organization, 14*(4), 3-12.

1957

Human relations in industry. *The Delphian Quarterly, 40*(2).

1958

With J.P. Dean. How do you know if the informant is telling the truth? *Human Organization, 17*(2), 34-38.
Interviewing. In N. Adams & J. J. Preiss (Eds.), *Human organization research* (pp. 352-374). Homewood, IL: Dorsey Press.

1960

With E. Hall. Intercultural communication: A guide to men of action. *Human Organization, 19*(1) 5-12.
Applying research in human relations. *Management Record* (June).
Who does what with whom, when, and where? *Swarthmore College Bulletin* (October).

1962

Applying behavioral science research to management problems. In G. Strother (Ed.), *Social science approaches to business behavior* (pp. 125-140). Homewood, IL: Dorsey Press/Richard D. Irwin.

1963

With L.K. Williams. *Supervisory leadership: An international comparison.* Symposium 33, 1-8. C.I.O.S. International Management Congress XIII.

Culture, industrial relations, and economic development: The case of Peru. *Industrial and Labor Relations Review, 16*(4), 583-593.

Toward an integrated approach for research in organizational behavior [Presidential Address, Industrial Relations Research Association]. *IRRA Proceedings, 32,* 2-20.

1964

On 'street corner society'. In E. W. Burgess & D. Bogue (Eds.), *Contributions to urban sociology* (pp. 256-268). Chicago: University of Chicago Press.

High level manpower for Peru. In C. Myers & F. H. Harbison (Eds.), *Manpower and education: Country studies* (pp. 37-72). New York: McGraw-Hill.

1965

Men at work. Homewood, IL: Irwin-Dorsey.

With E.L. Hamilton. *Action research for management*. Homewood, IL: Irwin-Dorsey.

A field in search of a focus. *Industrial and Labor Relations Review, 18*(3), 305-322.

Common management strategies in industrial relations—Peru. In W. H. Form & A. A. Blum (Eds.), *Industrial relations and social change in Latin America* (pp. 47-69). Gainesville, FL: University of Florida Press.

1966

Analogies and images: Thoughtways of foreign policy. *The Nation* (May).

With R.R. Braun. Heroes, Homework and Industrial Growth. *Columbia Journal of World Business, 1*(2), 51-57.

With L.K. Williams & C.S. Green. Do cultural differences affect workers' attitudes? *Industrial Relations, 5*(3), 105-117.

With J. Matos. *Proyecto de Estudios de Cambios en Pueblos Peruanos* [*Project for the Study of Change in Peruvian Communities*]. Instituto de Estudios Peruanos.

1967

With J. Matos. Models for building and changing organizations. *Human Organization, 16*(1/2), 22-31.

With S. Kellert & L.K. Williams. Culture change and stress in rural Peru: A preliminary report. *Milbank Memorial Fund Quarterly, 45*(4), 391-415.

With G. Alberti. The industrial community in Peru. *The Annals, 431*(May).

1968

Toward an integrated theory of development: Economic and non-economic variables in rural development. Ithaca, NY: New York State School of Industrial and Labor Relations.

Imitation or innovation: Reflections on the institutional development of Peru. *Administrative Science Quarterly, 13*(3) 370-385.

With R.R. Braun. On language and culture. In H. S. Becker (Ed.), *Institutions and the person* (pp. 119-138). Chicago: Aldine.

Must you tell a 'funny story'? *Columbia Journal of World Business, 3*(4), 85-87.

Reflections on my work. *American Behavioral Scientist, 12*(1), 9-13.

1969

Organizational behavior: Theory and application. Homewood, IL: Irwin-Dorsey.

Dominacion y cambios en el peru rural. Instituto de Estudios Peruanos.

Reflections on my work. In I.L. Horowitz (Ed.), *Sociological self images: A collective portrait* (pp. 35-49). Beverly Hills, CA: Sage.

The role of the U. S. professor in developing countries. *American Sociologist, 4*(1), 19-28.

On the application of behavioral science research to management problems. *Indian Journal of Industrial Relations, 5*(1), 3-27.

Rural Peru—peasants as activists. *Trans-Action, 7*(1), 37-47.

On the cultural pattern of the academic meeting. *The Subterranean Sociology Newsletter, 3*(2/3).

Building better organizational models. In G.D. Somers (Ed.), *Essays in industrial relations theory* (pp. 109-122). Ames: University of Iowa Press.

1972

Pigeons, persons and piece rates. *Psychology Today* (April), pp. 68-69, 98-99.

On the utilization of the behavioral sciences in manpower research. In I. Berg (Ed.), *Human resources and economic welfare* (pp. 272-298). New York: Columbia University Press.

Organizations for the 1980s. Man and future of organizations. *Franklin Foundation Lecture Series, 3*, 9-27.

1973

Organizations for the future. *Annual volume of Industrial Relations Research Association.*

1975

Organizing for agricultural development. New Brunswick, NJ: Transaction Books.

Peruvian paradox: Military rule and popular participation. In *Chile and Peru: Two paths to social justice*. Kalamazoo, MI: The Institute of International and Area Studies.

Conflict and cooperation in Andean communities. *American Ethnologist, 2*(2), 373-392.

[Conversations: An interview with William F. Whyte 1975]. Interviewed by W. F. Dowling. *Organizational Dynamics, 3*(4), 51-66.

1976

With G. Alberti. *Power, politics and progress*. New York: Elsevier.

Methods for the study of conflict and cooperation. *American Sociologist, 2*(4), 208-216.

1977

With A. Gutierrez-Johnson. The Mondragón System of Worker Production Cooperatives. *Industrial and Labor Relations Review, 31*(1), 18-30.

The emergence of employee-owned firms in the U.S. *Executive* (Spring).

Potatoes, peasants, and professors: A development strategy for Peru. *Sociological Practice, 2*(1), 7-23.

Toward a new strategy for research and development agriculture: Helping small farmers in developing countries. *Desarrollo Rural en Las Americas, 9*(1-2), 51-61.

1978

Extradepartmental enterprise. *Transaction/Society, 15*(3) 22-25.

Organizational behavior research: Where do we go from here? In E.M. Eddy & W. L. Partridge (Eds.), *Applied anthropology in America* (pp. 129-146). New York: Columbia University Press.

In support of voluntary employee ownership. *Society, 15*(6), 73-82.

The elusive phenomena [Review essay on the memoirs of Fritz J. Roethlisberger]. *Human Organization, 37*(4), 412-419.

1979

On making the most of participant observation. *The American Sociologist, 14*(1), 56-66.

1980

With J. Blasi. From research to legislation on employee ownership. *Economic and Industrial Democracy, 1*(3), 395-415.

With D. McCall. Self Help Economics. *Society, 17*(4), 22-28.

Confronting the conglomerate merger menace. Statement submitted to the Committee on Small Business, Subcommittee on Anti-Trust and Restraint of Trade, House of Representatives, 96th Congress, 2nd Session, February.

1981

Participatory approaches to agricultural research and development. Ithaca, NY: Rural Development Committee, Cornell University.

Street corner society (3rd ed.). Chicago: University of Chicago Press.

With J. Blasi. Employee ownership and economic democracy. *Courses by Newspapers*. San Diego: University of California.

1982

With J. Blasi. Worker ownership, participation and control: Toward a theoretical model. *Policy Sciences, 14*, 137-163.

Social inventions for solving human problems [Presidential Address, American Sociological Association]. *American Sociological Review, 47*(1), 1-13.

Winners and losers. *Cornell Executive, 8*(3), 24-26.

With C. Rosen. Employee ownership: Saving businesses, saving Jobs. *Economic Development Commentary, 18*(1), 16-19.

With J. Blasi. Worker ownership and public policy. In F. S. Redburn & T. F. Bukss (Eds.), *Public policy for distressed communities* (pp. 177-192). Lexington, MA: Lexington Books.

1983

Worker participation and ownership: Cooperative strategies for strengthening local economies. Ithaca, NY: ILR Press.

Higher yielding human systems for agriculture. Ithaca, NY: Cornell University Press.

Worker participation: International and historical perspectives. *The Journal of Applied Behavioral Science, 19*(3), 395-407.

With J. Blasi & P. Mehrling. The politics of worker ownership in the United States. In C. Crouch & F. Heller (Eds.), *International yearbook of organizational democracy, organizational democracy and political processes* (pp. 637-654). New York: Wiley.

1984

Learning from the field: A guide from experience. Beverly Hills, CA: Sage.

1985

Employee ownership: Lessons learned. *Industrial Relations Research Association Proceedings*, pp. 385-395.

Employee ownership: Yesterday, today, and tomorrow. *ILR Report, 22*(2), 7-15.

1986

Philadelphia story. *Society, 23*(3), 36-34.

On the uses of social science research. *American Sociological Review, 51*(4), 555-563.

1987

From human relations to organizational behavior: Reflections on the changing scene. *Industrial and Labor Relations Review, 40*(4), 487-500.

1988

With K.K. Whyte. *Making mondragon: The growth and dynamics of the worker cooperative complex.* Ithaca, NY: ILR Press.

1989

[Editor]. Action research for the twenty-first century: Participation, reflection, and practice [Special issue]. *American Behavioral Scientist, 32*(5).

With D,J. Greenwood & P. Lazes. Participatory action research: Through practice to science in social research. *American Behavioral Scientist, 32*(5), 513-551.

Advancing scientific knowledge through participatory action research. *Sociological Forum, 4*(3) 367-385.

1990

[Editor]. *Participatory action research.* Beverly Hills, CA:Sage.

The new manufacturing organization: problems and opportunities for employee involvement and collective bargaining. *National Productivity Review, 9*(3), 337-348.

New ways of organizing industrial work. In R.S. Peck (Ed.), *To govern a changing society: Constitutionalism and the challenge of new technology* (pp. 169-183). Washington, DC: The Smithsonian Institution.

Value of joint programs underestimated [Critique]. *Labor Research Review, 14*, 87-91.

1991

Social theory for action: How individuals and organizations learn to change. Beverly Hills, CA: Sage.

From Practice To Theory: Odyssey Of A Manager

JAMES C. WORTHY

Any contribution I may have made to the development of management thought has grown chiefly from efforts to understand and explain human behavior in complex organizations in whose management I was directly involved. Particularly during my Sears years, I was aided greatly by opportunities to collaborate with creative scholars pursuing ambitious scholarly goals. My own input to these endeavors was hands-on experience as a practicing manager, dealing with practical problems of organizational effectiveness.

Because my career has alternated between government, private business, and education, I have worked in a variety of organizational environments. I served two tours with the federal government in Washington, once as Assistant Deputy Administrator in the National Recovery Administration in the early years of the Roosevelt New Deal, and again twenty years later as Assistant Secretary of Commerce in the rather differently oriented Eisenhower period. My work in private business spanned twenty-three years with Sears, Roebuck and Co., where I rose to the position of vice president, and ten years as regional partner of an international management consulting firm serving clients in many different business and institutional settings. On retiring from that position in 1972, I was appointed professor of public affairs and management at the newly-established Sangamon State University in Springfield, Illinois, a post I held until reaching the state's mandatory retirement age in 1978, when I joined what has since been named the J.L. Kellogg Graduate School of Management of Northwestern University as professor of management. Over my years in business and education, I have been a director of a number of corporations and I continue to serve as a consultant to a limited number of business and academic institutions. In addition to my career responsibilities, I have been active in numerous political, civic, and professional affairs, notable among which were services related to the governance of public higher education in Illinois. Most of the writing I have found time to do has been on managerial aspects of the activities in which I have been engaged.

In this account, I have given special attention to work done at Sears, Roebuck during the years 1938-1952, not because later work was uninteresting or unimportant, but because whatever contribution I may have made to management theory grew largely from work done during this period. My years prior to that time, of course, shaped the values I brought with me to Sears, and my experiences during the years that followed further broadened and matured my thinking.

EARLY YEARS

The eldest of four children, I grew up in a small village named Glenwood about twenty miles south of downtown Chicago. My family moved there in 1916, when I was six; we were part of the migration from southern Appalachia, where Worthys had lived since before the Revolution, drawn by the northern industrial boom of the World War I. During the war my father did fairly well, but in the years immediately following he went through several periods of unemployment and a succession of temporary jobs before finding work as a utility man on the maintenance crew of a factory in nearby Chicago Heights, a job he held until his death twenty-five years later in 1948.

Glenwood (population then about 350, now much larger) was a satellite community of Chicago Heights, a heavy-industry city of some 15,000 at that time. Glenwood was a working class town of modest single-family homes. Most adult males (few women worked outside the home) were either semi-skilled or common laborers in not always steady jobs. My parents considered themselves "middle class," which might not fit the way that term is used by social scientists but accurately described my family's position in this particular community. There were certainly some who were better off than we, many who were poorer, and some who were just plain "no account."

Chicago Heights, four miles to the south where I went to high school, was also largely a working class town, with an "upper class" of factory managers, independent businessmen, lawyers, and doctors, and a "middle class" of teachers, shopkeepers, and office workers employed in local establishments; far more numerous were factory hands, with gradations ranging from skilled through semi-skilled and unskilled. Lowest on the scale were the sizable numbers of recent immigrants from central and southern Europe, and blacks from the rural south. The various areas of the city were clearly defined in terms of ethnicity and social status, with the lower orders concentrated on the east side of the railroad tracks; the "right" and "wrong" sides of the track were well-defined categories. One section of the east side was occupied almost exclusively by Italian immigrants; something of the economic conditions prevailing in that community is suggested by the fact that even in the so-called prosperous twenties the area was known as "Hungry Hill."

Early in life I began to learn about jobs and working for wages. My first paying job, at age six, was carrying water for a threshing crew harvesting oats on a farm near the village. At eight, I had a paper route and experienced the thrill, in that day before radio or television, of bringing news of the Armistice to the people of the village. I remember running along Main Street, calling "Extra! Extra! The war is over!" at the top of my voice, and people rushing from their doors to grasp the paper from my hand.

Most summers during my grade school years were spent working on nearby farms. During high school summers, I held jobs in a lumber yard and factories in Chicago Heights; in my spare time, I built a thriving business making wooden trellises for local gardeners. Although I found time for sports and other recreational activities, I took working to earn much-needed money (that went into a family pool) as part of the natural order of living, and most jobs I really enjoyed.

Education: Elementary and Secondary

Neither my father or mother had much in the way of formal schooling—perhaps the equivalent of sixth grade, certainly nothing more. Both read a good deal, my mother chiefly the Bible (often aloud) and my father mainly current periodicals and the daily newspapers. His prime interest both in reading and conversation was politics, in which he was active as a local Democratic leader. We had a home library of perhaps twenty-five or thirty volumes of classic American literature purchased in sets from door-to-door salesmen.

For a small, far from opulent community, Glenwood had a remarkably good elementary school staffed with three fine teachers; I remember each of them warmly after all these years. I was equally fortunate in my high school experience in nearby Chicago Heights. I had an inspired English teacher with a gift for making literature come alive, and a series of able math and science teachers who opened my eyes to wide and exciting fields of learning. My grades were good enough to earn membership in the National Honor Society. I also took part in numerous extracurricular activities, including football (captain in my senior year), wrestling, drama, public speaking (winner of several interscholastic contests), and student government (culminating in election as "mayor"); with these, together with study and part-time jobs, my high school years were busy.

One thing troubled me all through those years: what I wanted to be when I grew up. At various times I toyed with the ideas of becoming a lawyer, an engineer, a politician, a government worker, a businessman, a teacher—all fields to which I felt, and to some extent still feel, a strong attraction. Circumstances resolved the issue for me. At the time I graduated from high school, there simply was no way I could afford the cost of college; I decided, therefore, to work for a year or two and save enough money to at least get started on the higher education both my parents and I were anxious for me to have.

The year following high school graduation, I worked for the Public Service Company of Northern Illinois (now part of Commonwealth Edison) as an outside collector. This was 1928 and the country was awash with optimism. Businessmen, political leaders, and economists were talking about the final conquest of poverty and the advent of "perpetual prosperity." My work as a bill collector exposed me to a different side of life. In those days, electric bills for small homes were usually around $3 or $4 a month, and families who fell behind on those modest amounts were likely to be in straightened circumstances. The district where I worked had enough such families to require five full-time collectors. There was considerable unemployment in this highly industrialized area, especially among blacks and immigrants. Though far fewer in number, some of the delinquent accounts were white collar households whose breadwinners had held presumably secure positions but had been "laid off," a fate I had assumed was mainly that of manual workers. While the sample covered by my rounds was small, I saw enough cases of poverty and economic distress to raise doubts in my mind about the "good times" in which we supposedly were living.

Northwestern University

In the spring of 1929, despite having been out of school for a year, I had the remarkable good fortune of receiving a unique scholarship from Northwestern University. It was one of the first to be awarded under a program established by a multi-million dollar grant from Frederick C. Austin, a retired manufacturer of road-building machinery, to prepare young men for careers in business.

According to the university announcement, scholarships were awarded on the basis of "scholarship, leadership, character, and health" to those applicants "who in the judgment of the university have the greatest potential capacity for proficiency in business. The proficiency here contemplated is to be measured in terms of public service rather than by the accumulation of private fortunes." The scholarships provided full room, board, and tuition for four years at Northwestern and a year of study and travel abroad. At today's level of education costs, it was the equivalent of about $75,000, by far the most generous undergraduate scholarship ever offered by any university up to that time and perhaps up to this.

More important than the financial provisions was the educational program itself. Walter Dill Scott, president of the university, saw in the substantial grant from Mr. Austin an opportunity to break new ground in higher education for business. To that end, he named a board of advisers comprised of deans and faculty from various schools and departments to supervise the program, with Dr. Earl Dean Howard as chairman. Howard was both a professor of economics at the university and head of labor relations for Hart, Schaffner and Marx (now Hartmarx Corporation), the large men's clothing manufacturer in Chicago. He was widely known and respected in management, labor, and academic circles. Years before, as a young man just starting his academic career, he had played a central role in helping resolve the bitter 1910 Chicago garment workers strike and subsequently had been a key figure in the development of structured relationships between management and organized labor in the clothing industry. As a professor, he had established a reputation for innovative curriculum development and effective teaching. Scott judged him to be especially well-qualified to design a program that would integrate the studies of the scholars with the world of business.

The university planned to award ten new scholarships a year; the first ten scholars, among whom I was one, enrolled in the fall of 1929. We were a diverse group from a variety of family backgrounds ranging from working- to upper-middle-class (scholarships were awarded without regard to financial need). At nineteen I was the oldest member of the group; the youngest was sixteen. To foster a sense of group identity and common educational purpose, we were forbidden to join fraternities and required to live together in contiguous rooms in one of the men's dormitories (in later years we would have our own house). Living together proved to be one of the significant values of the program because it was easier to organize group social and learning activities, and the close, day-to-day interaction of the scholars was itself a rich learning experience.

We were given wide latitude to choose courses that fit our individual needs and interests, and a number of unique courses were designed for our benefit. We were encouraged to take more work in English literature and composition than was usually required for other than English majors. For me, English turned out to be the most interesting, enjoyable, and "practical" of all my studies. The writing requirement gave me greater facility in the use of language, and literature gave me insight into character, both of which have proved invaluable ever since.

Important among the special courses designed for our benefit were several taught by Professor Howard himself. He employed two interesting techniques in his teaching. One was the Socratic method of probing and sequential questioning which forced students to think through the implications of their answers, and the other was his emphasis on the central importance of "attitudes of mind." To Howard, people's attitudes toward things were more important in determining their behavior than the things themselves. He maintained that the only way to understand behavior—social, economic, political, or other—was to understand the influences that shaped the attitudes behind the behavior. All this seemed unnecessarily abstract at the time. Looking back, I think I see in Howard's teachings the beginning of my later interest in studying what employees thought about their jobs and the companies they worked for, a line of inquiry that led to fruitful speculation.

We met frequently with faculty members in their homes or had them as guests in our quarters; while this was not course work in the usual sense, it was an ongoing educational experience of the highest order. Most notable were our weekly meetings at Professor Howard's home. The stuff of the meetings varied. Sometimes the discussions were essentially academic, dealing with questions raised in our courses of study. More often the subject was a critical public issue, or an important current event, or the state of the economy. In those depression years with long breadlines and massive unemployment, a recurrent theme was the bitter apposition of idle factories and idle workers, and the questions these raised about governmental policies and the justice and workability of contemporary economic institutions. Many of these meetings were attended by special guests, typically well-known figures with firsthand knowledge of significant contemporary problems. Some of these were leading Chicago area businessmen, but Howard was careful to invite from time to time individuals who were critical of business. One of these I remember vividly: Whiting Williams, who met with us five or six times in 1930 and 1931.

Williams had been chief of labor relations for a Cleveland steel company. Concerned and puzzled by the labor unrest following the World War I, he decided to learn what was troubling workers by becoming a common laborer himself and leading an itinerant worker's life. A series of forays of this kind convinced him that the problem lay more with management than with workers and that the only road to industrial peace lay through changing the minds and methods of *employers*. Williams decided to devote himself to that task through writing and lecturing. He was a close friend of Earl Dean Howard, and when his travels brought him to the Chicago area he welcomed Howard's invitation to meet with our group.

His topic always had something to do with what workers were like, what they thought about their jobs and their bosses, and how they reacted to the kinds of things that happened on the job. He was a master storyteller and a superb mimic of the jargon and dialects of the men with whom he worked; he had the ability to make the people and the circumstances he described vividly real to his audience. Years later, when I read Mayo and Roethlisberger, I felt I was in territory not altogether unfamiliar; now, after sixty-some years, I can recognize that Williams exercised considerable influence on my thinking after I entered the business world.

My college years, 1929-33, were the period of the Great Depression, but in the special world of campus life there was little personal exposure to its hardships. My visits home, however, brought me into direct contact with some of the human costs of that economic disaster. My father was one of the fortunate ones. For much of the time he worked only one or two days a week, but unlike many of his neighbors he had a regular paycheck, however fluctuating and meager it may have been. Hunger, real hunger, was common among people I knew. Public assistance in those days was unknown, and what little help there was for the destitute came through locally organized volunteer efforts in which both my mother and father were leaders. Through my family, I had a more direct personal knowledge of the ravages of the depression than most of my fellow students.

Following my junior year, I took the year of study and travel abroad that my scholarship provided. I chose to study problems of European unemployment, which gave me further exposure to the gross inequities of contemporary society. To provide bases from which to operate, I registered successively for one term each at the universities of Bonn, Vienna, and Oxford. At all three locations, I engaged chiefly in library research and discussions with faculty, but in Vienna this was supplemented by a considerable amount of time spent in working class neighborhoods in the company of a Viennese friend who was an active Social Democrat (later executed by the Nazis). The sight of unemployed men idling listlessly on street corners, ragged children playing in side streets, and dispirited housewives cooking meager meals in Spartan kitchens is vividly etched in my memory. I saw little evidence of the light-hearted gaiety for which the city is famous.

National Recovery Administration

On returning to Northwestern in May 1933, I learned that my mentor, Earl Dean Howard, had aided in drafting the National Industrial Recovery Act, keystone of President Roosevelt's economic program, The legislation was passed by Congress in mid-June, and soon thereafter Howard, because of his part in writing the act and his long experience in the clothing industry, was appointed deputy administrator of the National Recovery Administration, responsible for developing and administering codes of fair competition for the garment industries. He invited me to Washington to serve as his office assistant while he was getting his new job organized; in September I would return to finish my senior year at school.

I accepted with alacrity what I thought would be a summer job. Soon after I arrived, however, Howard suffered a heart attack and was incapacitated for several weeks. Now, well over a half century later, it is difficult for current generations to comprehend the sense of desperate urgency that pervaded Washington and the country at the time. The economy was flat on its back.

At NRA, we firmly believed that chaos and possibly violent revolution loomed unless our agency could get the wheels of industry turning again—and soon. In Howard's absence there were appointments to be kept, meetings to be held, papers to be signed. I simply did whatever was necessary to keep the office running. By the time summer was over, I had been promoted from office assistant to the far more responsible position of Assistant Deputy Administrator, a post I held for the remainder of the life of NRA. I did not return to Northwestern or complete my baccalaureate degree until some years later, but my three and a half years at NRA, still in my early twenties, gave me a level and quality of administrative experience few people are likely to have before their forties.

I learned a great deal at NRA. Most of the apparel industries were highly unionized, and the task of writing the labor provisions of their codes was often one of negotiating a collective agreement and then translating its terms into the legal form of a code. I was concerned only tangentially with the writing of the trade practice provisions because these were worked out chiefly between the industry associations and the NRA's legal staff. I knew something about labor history from my studies at school, but now I gained intense direct experience with unions, their leaders, and the realities of labor-management relations. My role in the writing of codes was largely that of a mediator, tempered by care to observe and comply with NRA policies. Unfortunately, those "policies" were often confusing or contradictory, and in some important areas nonexistent.

The first chief of NRA was General Hugh S. Johnson, a colorful character but inept administrator. He was followed by more competent leadership, but the promising new enterprise got off to a bad start from which it never recovered. Flawed over-all direction and the absence of clear policies provided a field day for special interests. In the crisis atmosphere of the time many self-serving provisions were written into the codes and acquired the force of law. Price-fixing was commonplace, in fact if not in name, and efforts were made to control commercial and industrial practices in far too great detail. At the end of NRA's short life, the official compilation of codes with their related supplements, amendments, and executive and administrative orders filled twenty-two volumes with 15,756 pages of closely-packed rules, regulations, and procedures, plus a twenty-third 587-page index volume, all intended to govern the day-to-day affairs of American business. What started as a great crusade to put the economy back on its feet became an administrative nightmare. I emerged deeply skeptical of the capacity of government to manage the country's economy.

Although much of what I learned at NRA about organization and management was negative, it was nonetheless valuable. Fortunately for the country, the Supreme Court in 1935 found the Act unconstitutional and the agency was disbanded. I was one of a small group kept on for another year to help write the history of that mismanaged initiative of the early New Deal.

The only lasting benefit of the National Industrial Recovery Act grew out of its famous Section 7A, which guaranteed workers the right to organize and bargain collectively. That provision was retrieved from the wreckage and formed the basis for the Wagner Act. This benefit was not without cost, but the net gain to the American economy and American society was substantial.

SEARS, ROEBUCK

From my life experiences to this point, and particularly from my long association with Earl Dean Howard, I had developed a keen interest in management-employee relations and a determination to pursue a career in that line of work. On leaving NRA toward the end of 1936, I found a position as personnel manager for a Milwaukee department store. When this job proved disappointing, I sought and secured a position in the corporate personnel department of Sears, Roebuck and Co., where I started in February 1938.

I was attracted to Sears because it was a rapidly-growing company that offered excellent prospects for advancement, and because its reputation as a good employer held promise for the kind of career I was seeking. I was not disappointed on either count.

Originally only a mail order company, Sears under General Robert E. Wood had branched into the retail business in 1925. The company in 1938 employed about 60,000 people divided among ten mail order plants, a dozen or so factories, and nearly 500 retail stores scattered from coast to coast and from border to border. (The number of stores and employees grew substantially in the years that followed.) From the beginning, the new retail business grew rapidly and experienced severe growing pains, especially during the depression years. By the time I joined the company, basic merchandising and operating policies had been hammered out and a stable organization structure was in place.

Wood's Management Philosophy

Largely through trial and error, General Wood had evolved a philosophy of decentralized management to which he was firmly committed. Most stores reported directly to headquarters in Chicago, with no intervening district or regional levels of management. Within a broad framework of policy, local managers operated with a very large measure of independent responsibility and authority.

For a military man (West Point 1900, quartermaster general in the World War I), General Wood had a curious distrust of hierarchical organization. He stated his philosophy of management in a remarkable memorandum written in October of 1938. He had appointed a committee of senior executives to review the experience of the stores during the sharp 1937-38 recession, and the committee had proposed closer inspection of store practices and a set of stringent controls to keep managers from repeating mistakes made in the difficult preceding months. In his memorandum, the General demurred:

> No organization is perfect, even the most efficient one. The easiest thing in the world is to find weaknesses in a large organization. The natural human tendency for the men at the top and for the bright young members of their staff, if they discover a weakness, is to set up a system of checks and inspection that will obviate the weakness, forgetting that in most cases the remedy finally turns out to be worse than the disease. While systems are important, our main reliance must always be on *men* rather than on systems. If we devise too elaborate a system of checks and balances, and have too many inspectors going out as representatives of the parent organization, it will be only a matter of time before the self-reliance and initiative of our managers will be destroyed and our organization will be gradually converted into a huge bureaucracy.
>
> I have faith in the great majority of our managers. I believe they will work out their own salvation with a relatively small amount of supervision from the officers and the staff. While system is important, I repeat that our main reliance must be on men rather than on systems, and the proper selection and training of managers is the most important work of the officers and the retail staff.

The highly decentralized organization Wood had in place by this time reflected this philosophy, which I found much more in tune with my own emerging ideas, especially after my experience with NRA's abortive trial of centralized management of the economy. Wood recognized that for real decentralization to work, it was necessary to make administrative provision to assure that key positions, such as store manager, were filled by well selected and carefully trained people. For very practical reasons, this meant a strong headquarters personnel department. I joined that department just as it was beginning to take form under the leadership of Clarence Caldwell. Responding to the challenge laid down by Wood, Caldwell saw the need for developing a rational and coherent body of principles and a strong factual base for the company's personnel policies and manpower planning programs. This, he knew, would require a research and planning function within his department, and I was hired to organize and head that activity. This placed me in a strategic position to participate in and help fashion a human resources management program that came to be widely recognized as one of the most advanced and effective in American business at the time.

My responsibilities grew to include the design and administration of the wage and hour policies, employee benefits, training, executive development, and employee relations programs of the far-flung and rapidly expanding Sears organization. The World War II and Korean War periods created serious personnel problems for Sears, in the resolution of which I was closely involved. As the scope of my work grew, I took care to strengthen my original research and planning base, which became an effective tool to aid in managing my widening areas of activity.

Unlike some of his contemporary chief executives, Wood recognized that a widely dispersed organization of mail order plants and hundreds of retail stores, all operating with a high degree of local autonomy, required that administrative means be provided to minimize friction and divisiveness between employees and management, to maintain high morale, and to motivate superior individual and group performance. To Wood, good employee relations was simply good business. It was an article of faith with him that if the company treated its employees fairly, paid them well while they were working, and made reasonable provision for their retirement, these policies would more than pay for themselves. And they did, as witness Sears' record of growth and profit under Wood's 30-year stewardship. That record rested squarely on Wood's brilliant marketing strategy, but the strategy itself was strongly buttressed by Wood's ability to mobilize the enthusiastic support of all ranks of personnel within the vast Sears system.

Wood's concern for fair treatment of employees was reflected in the attitudes and practices of his subordinates. I had not been in my original personnel research and planning position long when one day Caldwell was called to meet with the company's new president, T.J. Carney. Because Caldwell knew what Carney wanted to talk about, he took me with him. (Wood had recently been named chairman but continued as chief executive; Carney, formerly operating vice president, had been named president but functioned as what today would be called chief operating officer.)

Carney told us that he felt uncomfortable in his new position and spoke at some length explaining that when he was general manager of a mail order plant he could walk through the building, stop to talk with employees, find out how people felt about their jobs, and if there were problems straighten them out. When he became operating vice president in charge of all ten mail order houses, he could still visit and walk through the plants, maybe not as often as before but often enough to feel he had a good idea of what was going on.

"But here I am, president," he said ruefully, "sitting in this big office in Chicago with no earthly way to get out and talk to the thousands of people who work for us in hundreds of different places all over the country, and it bothers me to be so out of touch with our people." He had merchandise condition reports and P&L statements to tell him how well managers were running their stores but nothing to tell him how they were doing where people were concerned. "Now you're a couple of bright guys," he said, leaning toward us for emphasis, "and I want you to figure out some way to keep me informed on that important part of my job."

Caldwell and I returned to his office and talked for a long time. Our discussion ended with Caldwell telling me to put aside everything else I was doing and concentrate on the new task Carney had given us.

The Houser Surveys

It seemed clear to me that the best way to find out how employees liked their work and whether they had complaints was to ask them. For this purpose, we retained an outside firm, Houser Associates, which had considerable experience with employee attitude surveys. By the end of 1939 a number of experimental surveys had been made, and the results were encouraging. Carney—and Wood, who followed these new developments with interest—felt that we had made a good start and that the surveys were giving them at least some of the information they wanted. The project continued on a gradually expanding basis until Pearl Harbor, when it was suspended for the duration of the war.

We were gratified to learn that, generally speaking, employees thought well of the company. Analysis of questionnaire responses revealed that 72 percent thought Sears was either "one of the very best" places to work or "better than average"; 95 percent said they would rather work for Sears than for "almost any other company" they knew. Responses to other questionnaire items were similarly favorable. Nevertheless, some of the results were worrisome

Initially, the surveys were undertaken for the simple, straight-forward purpose of finding out how well employees liked their jobs, their bosses, and their working conditions. The questionnaires covered everything in the working situation thought likely to concern employees, with space for comments and specific complaints. It was assumed that if dissatisfactions were discovered their causes could be identified and corrected and all would be well. That assumption proved only partially valid.

Houser Associates' approach was essentially that of traditional market research: to count the number of people who respond in various ways to a series of questions. The questions themselves, and particularly the comments and complaints section, did uncover things that needed fixing and steps were taken to right them. But beyond that, the results were enigmatic in many ways, What, for example, was a "good" score on certain points? Was a 65 percent favorable response to a question about employee discounts equivalent to a 65 percent favorable response to a question about rates of pay? Obviously not, but how to evaluate the relative significance of responses to different kinds of questions? Why should people in shipping and receiving think less well than salespeople of identical employee benefits? One of the statistical devices built into the questionnaires was a "morale score," a measure of employees' overall satisfaction with their jobs and the company. It was puzzling to find marked differences in the scores of different employee groups in the same store since these were people who were working under identical company policies and the same local management. Beyond specific complaints and a few fairly superficial points, there was often great uncertainty as to just what the tabulation of responses meant and what, if anything, management could do about them.

I was familiar, of course, with the then-limited standard literature on management, but there was little there to help explain what we were finding. Seeking answers, I began to broaden my reading and in the process discovered Chester Barnard, Mary Parker Follett, and above all Mayo and Rothlisberger and Dickson through whom I learned something of the work that had been done at Western Electric's Hawthorne plant. (Strangely, that plant was less than three miles from Sears' corporate headquarters, but little was known at that time in the Chicago business community about the pioneering work that had been done there.)

By singular good fortune, sometime in 1942 a young man applied to me for a position. This was David G. Moore, who had earned a master's degree in sociology at the University of Illinois and who had worked at Western Electric for Burleigh B. Gardner doing research on Hawthorne's employee counselling program. I was impressed with Moore's ability to describe work relations phenomena in terms that were unfamiliar to me but made sense, and he for his part was fascinated by some of the data I showed him on our employee attitude studies. There was a good fit, and I hired him.

Moore began to organize in new ways the mass of data that had been assembled and logical constructs began to emerge. There were fairly wide ranges of responses within all employee groups, but significant variations in central statistical tendencies among groups organized by age, sex, length of service, type of work, level of authority, size of store, economic base of city, geographical region, and other factors. As the data began to be more meaningful, intriguing questions emerged around the fact that different groups of people had markedly different attitudes toward precisely the same things.

Why, for example, should women consistently have higher morale scores than men, employees in smaller stores higher than those in larger stores, employees in Georgia and Alabama higher than those in New England, employees in small towns higher than those in large, heavy-industry cities? As the analysis of statistical data continued, it became increasingly clear that while company policies and supervisory practices were important and in some cases needed to be improved, something more was at work. We began to move away from relatively simplistic cause and effect analyses, focussing instead on the relationship between employee expectations and their actual experience on the job. This proved to be a far more fruitful line of inquiry.

THE COMMITTEE ON HUMAN RELATIONS IN INDUSTRY

As Moore and I discussed the implications of these new analyses, Burleigh Gardner's name came up frequently and I asked Moore to arrange a meeting with him. Gardner by that time was no longer with Western Electric but on the faculty of the Graduate School of Business of the University of Chicago. He was executive director of the university's recently-formed Committee on Human Relations in Industry, an interdisciplinary group organized largely on Gardner's initiative, whose members were drawn from the departments of anthropology, sociology, psychology, and education as well as from the business school. The group members' common interest was the application of behavioral research to industrial organizations, and the committee's primary purpose was to conduct cooperative research with area employers. Sears became an early supporter, and the largest, of the committee and its work. Other collaborating companies included Container Corporation, Inland Steel, Libby, McNeil & Libby, Raddison Hotel Company, the National Restaurant Association, and a number of other interesting but smaller and less well-known organizations.

Chairman of the committee was social anthropologist W. Lloyd Warner, formerly of Harvard, who had worked with Mayo and Roethlisberger at Western Electric, where he was the chief designer of the Bank Wiring Room Study. Early in his career, Warner had conceived the notion that the study of primitive man could shed light on the problems of modern man. To that end, his first major scholarly effort had been research on an aboriginal tribe in Australia. Upon his return to the States he became involved with the work at Hawthorne, and his experience there reinforced his earlier speculation that rich possibilities lay in applying the concepts and techniques of social anthropology to the study of the behavior of people at work in a modern industrial community. In developing this line of thought, he was strongly influenced by A.R. Radcliffe-Brown and Emile Durkheim.

The Bank Wiring Room study focussed on internal relationships within the plant. Warner tried to extend the study to include community influences on Hawthorne employees, but it quickly became clear that the Hawthorne area, not far from the heart of metropolitan Chicago, was much too large and complex for the kind of in-depth research he had in mind. Instead, he selected Newburyport, Massachusetts, a smaller, more autonomous, more stable community. This study produced the famous "Yankee City" series, a milestone in the literature of social anthropology. Burleigh Gardner, also a social anthropologist, worked with Warner on the Newburyport study and played a key role in the parallel "Deep South" project conducted in Natchez, Mississippi.

Gardner and Warner were interesting and stimulating people to work with, and I developed firm and lasting friendships with both. One of the things that impressed me about Gardner from the beginning was his respect for workers. I often heard him remark on the pleasure he found in watching an operator at a lathe, a serviceman quickly finding and correcting the malfunction in a home appliance, a typist's fingers dancing over her keyboard. Warner had a similar empathy, although at a more impersonal and abstract level. My years of association with both of them were among the most rewarding of my life.

From the Bank Wiring Room Study at Hawthorne emerged the notion of industrial organization as a social system, and that idea and its related concepts were deepened and enriched by the Yankee City and Deep South studies. Concepts dealing with the social organization of the workplace and the social codes, customs, and sentiments developed around the work itself, as well as the status of the work group in the larger social system of the community, cast new light on what we at Sears were finding in our attitude surveys. The kinds of work people were doing strongly influenced their interests and their relationships with others in the work system. The relationship between attitudes and kinds of work was especially clear in the Sears studies because of the similarity of jobs and work systems from one company unit to the next.

As a matter of fact, explanations of survey results based on concepts such as these proved more readily understandable to seasoned Sears executives than many of the ideas then current in standard management literature. Like Moliere's *bourgeois gentilhomme* who had been speaking prose all his life without knowing it, these executives had been "practicing" social anthropology all along. The idea of social class and differences in class behavior made sense to them. They might not have been familiar with the term "status symbols," but they knew the difference between corner offices and those down the hall. They recognized the importance of anniversary celebrations even if they had never heard of "rites of passage." Although this was long before the idea of "corporate culture" became popular, they knew what was meant by the admonition, "That's not the way we do things at Sears."

They understood things like these because they had lived with them all their working lives. Anyone who rises to a position of managerial responsibility in an intricate system of organizational and personal relationships must perforce learn to use many of the principles that comprise the corpus of social anthropology, whether they recognize them as such or not. With this "knowledge of acquaintance," use of concepts drawn from social anthropology made it easier to explain to Sears executives what was being found in the surveys.

During the war years the company suffered heavy personnel losses, both to war industries and to the armed services, and all but the most essential activities were sharply curtailed. Short staffs notwithstanding, General Wood directed his headquarters departments to devote all the time they could spare from immediately essential duties to preparing for the peace to come; "postwar planning," in fact, became a high priority activity. Anticipating a period of rapid business growth following the war and the likelihood of extensive organizational restructuring as the nation converted from a war to a peace economy, the personnel department was instructed to prepare for the heavy demands that would be made upon it. In particular, we were to give special attention to the need for maintaining the high levels of employee morale that top management considered essential. The attitude survey program had already proved a useful tool in this respect, but experience had demonstrated the need for considerable refinement. The first major collaborative effort between the company and the Committee on Human Relations in Industry was the redesign and improvement of that program.

A New Approach

Warner, Gardner, and their associates had extensive experience with interviewing as a fact-finding tool, and Gardner had been closely involved in Western Electric's famed interview-based employee counseling program. Face-to-face interviews conducted by skilled interviewers using non-directive techniques have many important advantages over questionnaires as a means for gathering information on the nature and sources of difficulties in management-employee relationships, and they had been used to good advantage for that purpose at the Hawthorne plant.

At Sears, we had a different problem. We wanted to include not just employees working in a single plant, but those in hundreds of operating units—retail stores, mail order plants, offices, warehouses, and factories—widely scattered over the entire United States. An interviewing program with any significant degree of coverage would have been prohibitively expensive and painfully slow, even if enough skilled interviewers could have been found or trained to do the work. Attitude surveys based on carefully framed questionnaires, on the other hand, were far less expensive and could cover much more territory in far less time.

Working with Gardner and with Warner's help and encouragement, we combined the two techniques. A simplified questionnaire was developed in which employees could record their attitudes toward the company in general, the local organization and its management, their immediate supervisors, compensation, working conditions, and so forth. Unlike the questionnaires used by Houser Associates, the function of the new instrument was not so much to gather explicit information as it was to ascertain the degree of employee satisfaction or dissatisfaction with critical aspects of their employment relationship. For this purpose, the comments and complaints section provided especially useful clues for further inquiry. The questionnaires were used as a kind of "geiger counter" to identify areas of difficulty, and the interviews to probe the nature and source of the difficulty. In this way it was possible to concentrate the attention of the interviewers on those areas where their more refined but expensive techniques could be used to best advantage. Combining questionnaires and interviews in this way gave us the advantages and avoided the disadvantages of both.

The scope of the surveys was expanded to include the functioning of the operating unit as a whole (store, plant, etc.) and the total pattern of activities and formal and informal relationships that comprised the unit. In recognition of this broader purview, the surveys were rechristened "organization surveys." Rather than seeking simply to uncover areas of dissatisfaction, the purpose became the analysis of strains or cleavages within company units that might impede their function as well as impair employee relations. Determining levels of morale served chiefly as an aid in locating problem areas for closer study by a field survey team.

Although Gardner contributed significantly to the design of the new program, the training of survey teams, and the interpretation of results, the field work was done by members of the Sears personnel staff. Based on his extensive contacts with rank-and-file employees during the planning phase of the program, Gardner was sure that they had enough confidence in management's motives that it was not necessary to use the committee's staff or retain an outside firm to administer the questionnaires and conduct the interviews. Gardner and Moore simply trained Sears people to do the work. This proved to be a wise course, not only for cost purposes but because serving as members of survey teams was exceptionally valuable experience for management trainees and future personnel executives.

Social Research, Inc.

Sears' initial work with the Committee on Human Relations soon expanded to a variety of other areas of concern to Sears management, and our demands placed heavy burdens on the committee. Meanwhile, we grew increasingly impatient with the procedural delays of working through university channels. Weeks and sometimes months were consumed in proposal writing and securing necessary clearances before important projects could get underway. We were primarily interested in solving problems, and time was often critical. Partly at my urging, Warner and Gardner early in 1947 established an independent consulting firm, Social Research, Inc. (SRI), with Warner as chairman and Gardner as president. To help them get started, I signed a contract underwriting basic expenses for the new firm's first two years of operation.

Gardner severed his connection with the university to devote full time to the venture, but Warner continued at Chicago until moving to Michigan State in 1959. Gardner was succeeded by William Foote Whyte as executive director of the committee. Whyte, formerly a junior fellow at Harvard where he had done significant work on the social organization of working class youth (published as *Street Corner Society*) had joined the committee staff in 1944 and had participated actively in the Sears work even before assuming the responsibilities of executive director. He left Chicago in 1948 to accept a professorship at Cornell. One of the committee's significant achievements was Whyte's *Human Relations in the Restaurant Industry*. Different in many ways from both Gardner and Warner, Whyte shared their empathy for the men and women who do the unglamorous parts of the world's work, and he too became a warm personal friend with whom I have stayed in rewarding contact for the more than forty years since he left Chicago.

With Whyte's departure, the Committee on Human Relations in Industry was disbanded. It had operated for a period of only five years but those years had been remarkably fruitful, especially in demonstrating the utility of applying the concepts of social anthropology to the practical problems of business and industry. Those concepts themselves were greatly enriched by exposure to modern forms of economic and social organization rather than simply those of primitive societies which had previously been the discipline's primary focus of attention. Not least important, the work of the committee laid much of the foundation for what became the organization behavior subdiscipline of management science. We at Sears took what I always felt to be justifiable pride in the part our company had played in the committee's productive life.

The work and influence of the committee did not die with it. No longer burdened by university red tape, Sears' work with Warner and Gardner, and for a time with Whyte, grew apace. Some of the more significant of that work during the years 1947-53 included studies of special problem groups such as low status employees, commission salesmen, warehouse workers, and veterans returning from military service. A study of relationships between the company's sources of supply and its buying organization was particularly useful, as was an analysis of internal relationships within the buying organization itself. A study of the social class backgrounds of upwardly mobile employees helped refine the company's recruitment and executive development programs. All told, an extensive number and variety of projects were undertaken in cooperation with Gardner and SRI for the purpose of improving the effectiveness of the company's organizational and managerial practices and for enhancing the quality of management-employee relationships.

Between 1946 and 1952 when I was granted a leave of absence to join the Eisenhower administration in Washington, organization surveys were conducted in nearly 500 company units employing, in total, over 100,000 people. These units included retail stores, mail order plants, parent departments, warehouses, and factories. Types of employees covered were likewise diverse: sales and clerical personnel; manual, technical, and professional workers; supervisory employees; and executives. The size of units ranged from fewer than 25 employees to over 10,000, and their geographical distribution corresponded fairly well with the geographical distribution of the U.S. population.

Under Moore's leadership and with Gardner's aid, the staff developed high orders of analytical skill, and learned to use the questionnaire results much as a doctor uses tests as an aid in diagnosing patient ills. At one point, we considered developing a typology of organizational malfunctions analogous to the typological constructs of psychiatrists, a possibility suggested by the frequency with which profiles of questionnaire and interview data tended to form patterns that grew familiar, and the tendency of certain kinds of problems to occur in identifiable syndromes. Unfortunately, because of workload pressures this idea was not pursued, although the ability to recognize regularities significantly enhanced the skills of the survey teams.

SURVEY RESULTS

The Sears surveys proved valuable in many ways. They were a singularly useful means for uncovering and helping correct problem situations. They provided management with rare insight into and understanding of the actual state of affairs within the very large and widely dispersed organization into which Sears by that time had grown. They produced a comprehensive body of factual knowledge by which management was able to refine and improve personnel policies to meet the rapidly changing conditions of the postwar period. But their most important contribution may have been the message they carried to employees: Clearly, management wanted to run the business in ways that served employee's needs as well as the company's. The survey program developed into a highly useful administrative tool, and with modifications is still a significant feature of Sears' widely admired personnel system.

In addition to its other values, the program developed into one of the company's most effective general executive training programs. After a survey was completed and its results analyzed, the leader of the survey team would meet with the executive responsible for the unit and his staff and review the findings. The local executives would then be questioned as to what interpretation might be placed on the findings, and a discussion would follow as to the best methods for dealing with whatever problems had been uncovered. The survey "report" generally consisted of a memorandum to the manager saying, in effect, that "in our meeting we agreed that such-and-such things required attention and that such-and-such action would be taken." The local executives were thus intimately involved in identifying problems and designing solutions. It was an interesting example of the "case method" of teaching, with the considerable pedagogical advantage that the "case" was not some other company but the unit for which the executives themselves were personally responsible. The learning results were impressive.

Research Findings

In trying to sort out and evaluate the broad variety of influences at work in concrete situations, it became strikingly apparent that there is no simple explanation for any given state of employee morale. Rather, both our surveys and special studies disclosed the existence of complex interdependent factors that combine in subtle and intricate ways to produce a given degree of employee satisfaction or dissatisfaction. Existing levels of morale, whether high or low, seem to reinforce the factors producing them, thus tending to keep good morale good and poor morale poor. For this reason, despite sincere and vigorous action, management often found it hard to bring about perceptible improvements in problem situations. The reverse was also true: local organizations were often able to survive poor leadership without too many scars or too much impairment of operating efficiency, at least for relatively short periods.

As with the prewar Houser surveys, the new, more comprehensive approach found that employee attitudes were significantly influenced by both internal and external factors. Internal factors included quality of supervision, job status, work pressures, differences between goals of employees and management, tensions arising from hierarchical relationships, and disruptions caused by changes in management, company policies, job methods, and systems of rewards. It was interesting that only in isolated instances was compensation of much significance as a negative factor. It was basic Sears policy to keep wage rates on the high side of prevailing local scales, and where compensation was found to be a source of dissatisfaction the cause usually proved to be a local slip-up in the implementation of that policy. The company enforced strict standards on employee hours and working conditions, and little dissatisfaction was registered on those scores.

Pervasive "external" factors were also found. There were significant variations between groups by age, sex, length of service, type of work, level of authority, size of store, economic base of city, and geographical region. Whereas differences such as these had before been puzzling, with the new approach they became more understandable. Younger employees newly started on their careers tended to have different expectations from their jobs than their older colleagues. The higher levels of morale generally prevalent among women appeared to be explainable by differences in social roles that were more sharply differentiated in the 1940s than they are today. Levels of morale in retail stores tended to be higher than those in warehouses and factories, apparently because of greater ideological agreement between salespeople and management. Closer ideological affinity also helped explain the higher morale generally prevalent in more rural as compared with more industrial areas, and among employees with higher- rather than lower-ranked jobs.

Less readily apparent were the reasons for consistent differences by size of company unit, but these too yielded to the new type of analysis. Employees in smaller units worked in a simpler social environment. They had a much better opportunity to get to know each other so that cooperation and coordination could develop on a more personal basis and be less dependent on impersonal systems and controls. In terms of human relations concepts, more of the total work of the unit could be accomplished through the informal organization with less reliance on the formal. Individual jobs took on more meaning and importance because their relationship to other jobs and to end results could be more readily seen.

One of the things the new surveys disclosed was that every management action has two dimensions, one "technical" and the other "symbolic." The technical dimension is the objective nature of the action; the symbolic, the meaning imputed to the action. Everything management does is evaluated by workers in both dimensions: what it is and what it means.

For example, analysis of employee responses to the surveys underlined the fact that wages and salaries were not only sources of livelihood but important factors in employees' sense of personal worth (shades of Whiting Williams!). Rates of compensation reflected to employees management's opinion of each person's value to the organization. It made a vast difference whether pay scales in a store or other unit were pitched high or low by prevailing community standards, or whether rates for a particular job were high or low in comparison with other jobs in the unit. Because of their symbolic dimension, it was critically important to workers, even more than to management, that salaries be orderly, "make sense," be "fair." The surveys indicated that by and large the company did reasonably well on these points. In those instances where local practice fell short the adverse reactions were all too apparent.

By the same token, physical working conditions played a rather different role than customarily thought because they carried significant symbolic meaning. Employees wanted good equipment, pleasant and attractive places of work, and well-maintained washrooms, but because these were expected they could never in themselves build a well-motivated organization. Their absence, on the other hand, could cause problems. If employees were discontented with any aspect of their relations with management, they were likely to seize upon and magnify any shortcomings in their physical environment. They could tolerate situations they knew were difficult for management to correct, but where annoyances appeared unnecessary or unjustified they were likely to interpret the condition as evidence of management's lack of concern for them as people. The poor working conditions were tangible evidence of management's attitude and this was what employees resented.

Organization Structure

In retrospect, much of the most significant of Sears' work with both the Committee on Human Relations in Industry and Social Research, Inc. dealt with the structure of organizations and how people related to that structure and to one another. The conception of an industrial organization as a social system led directly to interest in organization structure. For the study of structure, Sears offered rich opportunities.

Sears by 1950 was a very large organization composed of many discrete units widely distributed over the entire United States and much of Latin America and Canada. There were several different kinds of units, including retail stores, mail order plants, catalog sales offices, service centers, warehouses, offices, and factories. In size, local units ranged from very small to fairly large. Especially significant from a research point of view was the company's philosophy of decentralized management that permeated the entire system.

Note has already been taken of the extreme degree of decentralization in effect in the latter part of the 1930s, when I joined the company. The pattern of nearly five hundred retail stores reporting to a single officer in Chicago was modified in the 1940s with the establishment of five U.S. "territories," each headed by a territorial vice president to whom reported all stores and mail order plants in a defined geographic area; even so, the degree of decentralization remained far greater than was generally true of chain stores and other multi-unit business organizations.

Just as the overall organization structure was highly decentralized, so too was the structure of many of the constituent units. Early in our research, we began to distinguish between "tall" and "flat" organization structures (the terms "vertical" and "horizontal" were also used). Tall structures were those with multiple levels of supervision and relatively short spans of control; flat structures were those with fewer levels and wider spans. Even after the five territories were established, the total retail system was an example of an extremely flat organization: 52 stores in the smallest territory and 260 in the largest reported directly to single vice presidents (1950 figures), and there were only two levels of management (three for stores in the same metropolitan area) between the president of the company and the store managers. The parent merchandising organization with 44 senior executives reporting to the merchandising vice president was another striking example of flat organization structure. Sears gave short shrift to the then-prevalent theory that spans of control ("spans of management" in later parlance) should be kept as short as possible.

The degree of centralization within the company's operating units varied. In the mail order plants, the tight time controls needed to coordinate the filling and shipping of customer orders mandated a fairly high degree of centralized control. In contrast, less centralization was necessary in the retail stores where the nature of the work performed required less interdepartmental coordination. Even among stores, however, there was a certain amount of variation in organization and degree of decentralization. These differences were themselves a direct consequence of General Wood's philosophy of decentralized management. He held his managers accountable for sales and profit results, but insisted that they have wide discretion in the way they achieved those results. As a result, some stores were organized in a taller, more hierarchical fashion than other stores of comparable size offering similar lines of merchandise.

A study of a group of medium-size stores following the brief recession of 1949 found that the heads of selling departments in stores with the "flatter" (i.e., less hierarchical) structures tended to be more competent than their counterparts in the "taller," (more hierarchical) structures. This appeared to be a direct consequence of the fact that managers with broad spans of control were spread very thin and the amount of surveillance and support they could give to the thirty-odd individual department heads reporting to them was limited. These managers were under a "structural necessity," as it were, to develop strong organizations at the department head level because the key to successful store performance lay in the competence of the men and women staffing such positions. The only way they could build satisfactory hardware businesses, for example, was to find or develop good hardware merchants who did not need close day-to-day supervision.

Managers of stores with the "taller," more hierarchical structures, on the other hand, had sharply reduced their spans of control by introducing an intervening level of supervision between themselves and their department heads, and it was primarily to persons at this intermediate level that they looked for results. These sub-executives, having fewer people reporting to them, were able to provide closer and more detailed supervision and the store manager was under significantly less pressure to build strength at the department head level.

Not only were managers in structures with broad spans of control under strong compulsion to recruit superior personnel for these positions but those personnel, once in place, were exposed to a rich learning and development experience. To function effectively in that structure, department heads had to learn to accept and handle greater autonomy than their counterparts in other stores who worked under closer supervision. They had to make more decisions on their own and take greater responsibility for their units' performance because the structure within which they were working did not permit them to turn frequently to higher authority for direction.

Most emphatically, managers of these stores did not delegate blindly. By and large, they had good people judgment. They could select subordinates with development potential, follow their progress closely, and sense when individuals were ready to assume more responsibility. They were able to bring people along as fast as they were ready, but not so fast as to exceed their growing capacities. Because these managers were not burdened by the details of many departments, they were able to give help to those who needed it and stay as close to them as necessary until they were ready to stand on their own feet.

Not everyone found these stores comfortable places to work. People had to take more responsibility than some want to assume. There was support, but not nearly as much as in stores with more structure on which to lean. Those who could not adapt were likely to be weeded out fairly quickly, voluntarily or otherwise. But for men and women willing and able to accept responsibility, these stores and their managers offered challenging opportunities for personal growth and achievement.

Another intriguing finding of the study was that managers of stores with different structures tended to differ in their attitudes toward the people who worked for them. These differences were not black-and-white but shades of gray. Managers of stores with "flatter" structures tended to have more confidence in their subordinates and take more pride in them than did their counterparts, who felt it necessary to introduce an intervening level of management to provide closer supervision. Having selected good people, trained them well, and placed more reliance on them, they expected them to do well and by and large they did. Managers of stores with "taller" structures, in contrast, tended to have less confidence in people and felt they needed closer control.

The implications of these attitudinal tendencies were clear: *Given the exceptional degree of free reign permitted by Wood's philosophy of decentralized management, managers tended to organize their stores in ways that would enable them to relate most comfortably to the men and women in their employ.* Those who tended to have less trust in people opted for organizations that provided closer supervision and control; those who trusted people more preferred structures that allowed greater freedom and called for higher levels of initiative on the part of subordinates in performing their jobs. There is much to be said for organizing to build on human strength rather than to compensate for human weakness.

An illustration on a larger scale of the organizational consequences of attitudes toward subordinates is seen in the contrast between Sears, Roebuck and Montgomery Ward during the contemporaneous General Wood and Sewell Avery regimes. The Avery organization was as highly centralized as Wood's was decentralized. Avery ran his company with a dictatorial hand, while Wood permitted and expected his subordinates to exercise large measures of independent judgment. Wood often expressed his confidence in the men and women of Sears. Judging by the frequency of news accounts of the firing of Ward executives, Avery apparently had little confidence even in his own top people. The Sears organization was characterized by high levels of morale and esprit de corps, while Ward's was noted for internal friction and conflict.

In economic terms, Sears adapted far more successfully than Ward's to the changes and opportunities of the postwar world.

Publication

Only small portions of Sears' research in employee relations and organization structure were ever published. Unlike studies conducted under university auspices that typically have publication in view, studies conducted independently by Sears or in collaboration with SRI were basically done for administrative purposes, that is, to provide officers and executives with information and recommendations helpful in the discharge of their managerial responsibilities. Most reports, in fact, were simply interoffice memoranda. When a study had served the purpose for which it was made it was filed away and attention was turned to other more immediately pressing matters.

Sponsored work with the Committee on Human Relations was "scholarly," while that with SRI was essentially "consulting"; work done independently by Sears staff, of course, was straightforward "managerial" work. Fortunately, some of the more important of the SRI and Sears work found its way into David Moore's doctoral dissertation where they have a degree of permanence they would not otherwise have had. The second edition of Gardner's *Human Relations in Industry*, written in collaboration with Moore, drew heavily on his Sears experience but could hardly be regarded as an account of the Sears research. Neither could my own book, *Big Business and Free Men*, published years later, be so regarded although it incorporated many of the insights gained from work done in the 1940s and early 1950s.

Some of my writing during this period is on the public record because some of my speeches at business meetings and lectures before university and professional groups found their way into print. Several papers presented before conferences of the American Management Association were reproduced as parts of AMA proceedings, and thus received some recognition in both business and academic circles. In 1950 I presented a paper on management decentralization before the annual meeting of the Academy of Management, and over the years I lectured frequently before university groups—Columbia, MIT, Chicago, Minnesota, and UCLA among others. A number of management scholars took interest in what we were doing, notably Peter Drucker, Rensis Likert, Douglas McGregor, Eliot Chapple, Frederick Harbison, John Mee, Harold Koontz, and, from overseas, Elliott Jacques of Great Britain's Tavistock Institute. Prior to 1957 when the Academy of Management established its Journal, the American Management Association offered the principal means by which new thinking on management theory and practice gained circulation.

Such writing as I was able to do was essentially extracurricular, done in my spare time on evenings and week-ends. All of it except for my book was "occasional," prepared for specific events such as appearances before business groups and professional societies. Some of these were published by the sponsoring organizations and thereby gained a measure of circulation, but not until I retired in 1978 was it ever possible for me to devote more than sporadic time to putting my thoughts on paper.

VARIETIES OF PRACTICE

Following what I now look back upon as the halcyon days of working with university people and SRI, I moved through a variety of organizational and managerial experiences, beginning with a two-year leave of absence, 1953-55, from Sears to serve as Assistant Secretary of Commerce in the new Eisenhower administration.

Department of Commerce

As Assistant Secretary for Administration during the first two years of the Eisenhower presidency, I was responsible for dealing with the organizational trauma that accompanied change in the political leadership of government. In any organization, a change at the top always produces stress and strain, and this is doubly true when the change involves policies as well as persons. The 1952 election brought to Washington the first Republican administration in twenty years, after a campaign in which the successful candidate and his supporters pledged far-reaching changes in governmental policy. There was understandable apprehension among many civil servants, especially those at senior levels, as to what the change in party might mean for their careers, and equally understandable unease among incoming presidential appointees as to the loyalty and support they could expect from organizations built under years of opposition-party leadership.

One of the difficulties of the incoming appointees to the Department of Commerce and other major agencies was the fact they did not know the key people whose work it was their task to direct and oversee. In Commerce, I dealt with this problem by undertaking, with professional aid, a detailed, objective evaluation of the senior personnel of the entire department. By and large, I found them to be well-qualified for their jobs and anxious to serve the new administration. This step reassured both incoming officers and top civil servants, and the work of the department proceeded much more smoothly from that time forward.

A more dramatic move was my intervention to reverse the unwarranted dismissal of the director of the National Bureau of Standards, who had crossed swords with the new Assistant Secretary for Domestic Affairs to whom he reported. The dismissal attracted wide public attention and outraged protest from the scientific community. My independent investigation demonstrated the injustice of the action to the Secretary's satisfaction, and reinstatement of the director went a long way toward establishing confidence in the fairness and integrity of the new departmental administration.

Far less dramatic but no less important was my refusal to approve, for what I considered good reasons, the department security officer's recommendation to cancel the security clearance of one of the professionals of the Bureau of International Trade. This was during the McCarthy period and my action was severely criticized in certain quarters, but Secretary Weeks supported my position. This episode was not widely known outside the department, but was greeted with relief by members of the professional staff who had reason to be concerned for the security of their jobs and reputations during the McCarthy years.

At my initiative a number of steps were taken to simplify and streamline the work of the department. These were conducted in cooperation with the staffs directly concerned, and strongly supported by them. For the most part, I found government workers at least as interested in doing their jobs well as their counterparts in private industry, and in some ways more so. Efforts to eliminate elements in working situations that impeded output or undermined quality were warmly welcomed.

While a fair amount of cost reduction was achieved in this manner, the budgetary goals of the new administration could not be realized without significant personnel cutbacks. Because of civil service requirements, RIF (reduction in force) procedures are cumbersome and often arbitrary and unfair in concrete situations. To preserve as much justice as possible while assuring strict compliance with civil service requirements, I retained the executive director of the National Civil Service League as a consultant to my personnel staff and a personal adviser to me, with the result that the painful RIF process was accomplished without serious impairment of departmental efficiency or morale.

In at least partial consequence of these and other actions—all warmly supported by Secretary Weeks—the Department of Commerce was widely credited with making the smoothest transition of all the executive departments to the change in administration.

Return to Sears

My tour of duty in Washington ended early in 1955, when I was called back to Sears to become vice president for public relations. The public relations philosophy developed under General Wood and continued by his immediate successors differed sharply from that of most corporations. On the principle that public attitudes, like employee attitudes, are based on the kinds of experience people have with the company rather than on claims the company makes for itself, Sears sought to shape its corporate policies and behavior to meet public expectations and thereby earn the support needed to accomplish the company's business goals. In this respect, the aims of the public and the employee relations functions were closely parallel, and I found myself quite comfortable in my new responsibilities.

I had five productive and satisfying years in this position, but unfortunately for my purposes a new chief executive who took office in 1960 had very different ideas about the role of public relations. After a year of increasingly stressful disagreement, I left to seek more satisfying work elsewhere. The parting was without rancor, and in the thirty years since I have maintained cordial relations with successive generations of Sears management.

Management Consulting

In 1961, I became a partner of Cresap, McCormick and Paget. in charge of the firm's central region headquartered in Chicago. Although Cresap at that time was one of the country's preeminent international consulting firms, its central region had fallen on evil days for a variety of reasons, and it was my task to restore it to profitable operation. Turning an ailing organization around is not easy. It takes time and involves painful decisions, and some of those I had to make caused me sleepless nights. In due course, my efforts were successful and well before the time I left the firm ten years later the region's practice had been restored to vigorous health.

One of the things I learned in my consulting work is that organizations are fragile. They can and do change, but too-drastic or too-rapid change can severely impair their ability to function. At the same time, companies *must* change if they are to survive. There are natural mechanisms in organizational processes that are resistant to change and therefore, within limits, have survival value. The danger is that these mechanisms, if not kept in check, will operate so effectively in slowing or preventing needed change as themselves to endanger the organization's long-term survival. Ironically, nothing in business is more dangerous than success. Success is always built on conditions and circumstances that change, and unless timely adaptations are made the enterprise may not survive.

One of my consulting engagements developed into a long-term relationship with Control Data Corporation and its remarkable chairman, William C. Norris. My first assignment, in 1968, was a review of his top management organization, and this was followed in succeeding years by a series of tasks that gave me close familiarity with virtually every phase of the business except the purely technical. In due course I was invited to join the board of the company's wholly-owned subsidiary, Commercial Credit Company, and not long after that the board of the parent company as well. In these capacities, I worked closely with Norris and came to know him well; I was and remain one of his great admirers. I also had the unique opportunity of seeing from a responsible inside position the sad train of events that carried a major corporation from a period of high prosperity into a time of crisis that brought it breath-takingly close to bankruptcy, and in the process required drastic changes in management and business strategy. My years of association with Norris and Control Data (which went far beyond my time with Cresap) were rich with learning.

I thoroughly enjoyed my work at Cresap, but pressures of my managerial and professional responsibilities left precious little time for the writing I had been wanting for so long to do. Accordingly, in the spring of 1972, I took an early retirement with the intention of moving to a home my wife and I had built in Florida and devoting my time to organizing and getting down on paper the ideas that had been accumulating in my mind for years. I had not finished cleaning out my desk, however, when I received an invitation to join the faculty of newly established Sangamon State University in Springfield, Illinois as professor of public affairs and management. Because teaching was something I had wanted to do for a long time, I accepted.

Public Higher Education in Illinois

Actually, I had been closely involved with public higher education in Illinois for some years, not as a teacher but in connection with public policy and the organization of higher education in the state. In 1966 I chaired a citizens committee on governing structure as part of the master planning process mandated by the legislature for the state's system of public higher education. Our committee had the knotty problem of dealing with entrenched vested interests and sharp community and institutional rivalries, but after hearings and conferences that extended over the better part of a year our committee recommended a "system of systems" under which senior institutions would be grouped into four "systems," each with its own governing board and comprised of two or more administratively autonomous institutions. This innovative structure was incorporated into appropriate legislation and has successfully served the governance needs of Illinois public higher education for a quarter of a century.

Largely in consequence of this experience, I was appointed by Governor Otto Kerner to the State Board of Higher Education. Based on projected increases in enrollment, the board proposed and the 1969 session of the legislature approved the establishment of two new senior universities, but left to the board the questions of institutional location, mission, and governance. The chairman of the board appointed me to head a committee to address these sensitive issues.

Two of the three issues were settled quickly. As to location, our committee recommended that one school be sited in the southern part of the Chicago metropolitan region and the other in Springfield, the state capital. As to mission, we determined that both should be upper-division schools to serve as capstones to the community college system. The Chicago area school would serve the special needs of urban life, and the Springfield school would build on its location in the capital of the state to become a "public affairs" university.

The governance issue turned out to be a stormy one. The University of Illinois made a determined effort to incorporate the Springfield school, because of its capital-city location, into the U of I system. The issue was settled effectively, if not amicably, by our decision to assign the school to the Board of Regents for governance, a position endorsed by the Board of Higher Education and the governor and duly ratified by the legislature. The Chicago area school was assigned, without dissent, to the Board of Governors of State Colleges and Universities.

Sangamon State University

The Springfield school, christened Sangamon State University, opened its doors in 1970. I joined the faculty in July of 1972, and soon thereafter was asked to head a committee planning a new undergraduate management program to be ready by the fall of 1973. I had been thinking about management education for a long time, and this was a unique opportunity to try out ideas that had been growing in my mind. There was no curriculum in place, no vested faculty interests to work around—for that matter, no faculty. In effect, our committee had an empty blackboard on which to work, and we proceeded with gusto.

The program we developed was "generic," designed to help prepare students for careers in either the public or private sector. The program viewed management in its general sense as applying to the administration and direction of the affairs of business, governmental, and other forms of organizations and designed on the premise that management is in fact a *general* study, that there is more commonality than difference between different kinds of organizations, and that the curriculum should focus on those concepts and principles that are more generic and less specific in character.

These were deeply held convictions of mine growing out of my experience with many kinds of organizations. I was confident that studying the application of common principles to a variety of organizational environments would contribute to better comprehension of those principles and help students better understand the differences between organizations and how to adapt to them. These aims would be achieved not by offering separate coursework in the public and private sectors but by integrating the subject matter of the program into a *single core course of study* comprising half of each of the students' two years at Sangamon.

The design and delivery of such a program presented formidable problems. Few suitable textbooks were available, and because the program differed so sharply from traditional programs, faculty was hard to recruit. In practice, many compromises had to be made, but the basic concept of *generic* program prevailed—at least during the years I remained at Sangamon State.

The Kellogg School, Northwestern University

I spent six happy years at Sangamon, but reached the state's mandatory retirement age of 68 in 1978. At this point, good fortune again intervened and I was offered a special postretirement appointment as professor of management in what has since been renamed the J.L. Kellogg Graduate School of Management of Northwestern University. I was also named "Senior Austin Fellow," faculty adviser to the school's current Austin Scholars, thus bringing me full circle to the Austin Scholarship I myself had held a half century earlier.

My duties at Kellogg are light but my appointment provides me the facilities of a great university, the most important of which are membership in a community of brilliant scholars and access to a magnificent library. My time is largely my own, spent chiefly in research and writing.

In 1964, well before I became a teacher myself, I was elected Fellow of the Academy of Management, the professional society of collegiate teachers of management. The Fellows Group is an autonomous unit within the Academy created to recognize members who have made significant contributions to the science and practice of management. In 1987, I was elected to a three-year term as Dean of Fellows, an office in which I took great pride. I am also a Fellow of the International Academy of Management. Membership in these two societies brings me into professional contact with a select national and international community of scholars, with some of whom I have formed warm and rewarding personal friendships.

"Side" Activities

Throughout the business and academic stages of my career, I have been engaged in a number of "side activities" that brought me into contact with the managerial problems of a still wider variety of institutions. Some of the more important of these will be noted briefly.

In addition to my NRA and Department of Commerce experience, I learned at first hand something of the work of other governmental agencies, at both state and national levels. During the Korean War, I served as an industry member of a panel of the Wage Stabilization Board dealing with retail compensation problems, and in 1959 I was appointed by Governor William Stratton as a member of the Chicago Medical District Commission.

President Kennedy in 1961, incensed at the indignities he had suffered raising money for his successful election campaign, appointed me as a Republican member of a tri-partite commission to devise means for bringing the disorderly process of political finance under a measure of public control; this was the first major effort of its kind in this country. The President was pleased with our unanimous report but was assassinated before he was able to do anything about it. His successor, Lyndon Johnson, had no interest in reforming existing systems of political fund-raising, and while no legislation came directly from the efforts of our commission some of our more important recommendations were picked up later and enacted into law. There was, however, one significant direct result: When our work as a commission was completed we reconstituted ourselves into the Citizens Research Foundation (CRF), a private organization that became and still is the recognized authority on the financial aspects of American politics. I continued as a director of CRF for about twenty years.

Over time, I gained a fair amount of experience with political organizations and their management. I had been brought up in a family firmly committed to the Democratic Party, and in the 1930s had myself been an ardent New Dealer. By the mid-1940s, however, my views had begun to change. I had lost none of my concern for the grave economic and social problems that President Roosevelt had sought to address, but from personal experience in the National Recovery Administration and close observation of the course of subsequent history I had grown increasingly skeptical of the merits of centralized direction of economic affairs and of the capabilities of government to manage the delivery of vital human services. This skepticism was reinforced by my experience at Sears, which deepened my conviction of the superiority of decentralization in the management of large organizations. I did not like what I saw as the extreme conservatism of certain elements of the Republican Party, but as time went on I felt more and more comfortable with the thinking of mainstream Republicans. By the time of the 1952 presidential campaign, I was ready to change parties and to do so aggressively.

Because I greatly admired General Eisenhower, I proposed to organize a "Democrats for Eisenhower" movement. Following the nominating convention, however, I was counseled by Republican leaders in whom I had confidence to join my efforts with the Citizens for Eisenhower-Nixon forces. This I did, and as co-chairman of that organization for Illinois played an active role in the ensuing campaign. General Wood had been a leader of the pro-Taft forces and was bitter over Taft's defeat for the nomination, and while he was rather quizzical over my enthusiastic support for Eisenhower our differing political views did not affect our working relationship. (Incidentally, my activities in the 1952 campaign had nothing to do with my subsequent appointment as Assistant Secretary of Commerce. When I was offered that position by Sinclair Weeks, the new Secretary of Commerce, I learned to my chagrin that he had no knowledge of the hard work I had done to help elect

President Eisenhower. He was offering me the job because of the good things he had heard about my "organizational savvy" from friends on the faculty of the Harvard School of Business where he was a member of the Board of Visitors.)

In 1958 I became president of the United Republican Fund, at that time the principal fund-raising arm of the party in Illinois, and a year later a member of the National Republican Finance Committee. Deeply distressed by the outcome of the 1960 election and the calamitous weaknesses I had seen in the party's organization, in 1961 I founded and headed for its first year the Republican Citizens League of Illinois to aid in recruiting and training volunteer workers for the regular Republican organization.

Perhaps because of my Democratic origins, I was never an ideological Republican and was able to deal with Democratic leaders willing to meet me half-way on a basis of mutual courtesy and respect. I got along very well, for example, with Chicago's Mayor Richard Daley. I used to think that every time he needed an identifiably Republican figure for a public service job he would call on me. Three times he asked me to chair a "Non-Partisan Committee for National Political Conventions" to spearhead the city's efforts to bring the presidential nominating conventions of one or both parties to Chicago. This was a two-fold task: selling the merits of Chicago to the national committees of the parties, and raising, chiefly from corporate sources likely to benefit from the event, the increasingly large sums required to underwrite convention costs. We were successful in securing the 1960 Republican and the 1968 Democratic conventions, but fortunate in losing both in 1972; by that time, the cost of hosting national conventions had reached a point where they had lost much of their attractiveness to all but a very few cities in the country.

During these years, I was active in efforts to promote racial justice. As a member of the labor relations committee of the Chicago Association of Commerce and Industry, I played a part in securing that organizations's support for the passage of fair employment practices legislation in Illinois, a previously unheard-of position for a chamber of commerce to take, and a key factor in the passage of that legislation in 1959. (I will never forget the dismay of the chamber's lobbyist in Springfield who found he had to promote a stand that for years he had aggressively opposed.) For some years, I was a director of the Chicago Urban League and its chief fund-raiser. Under the leadership of its executive director, Edwin C. ("Bill") Berry, the League played a significant role in helping ameliorate some of the underlying causes of unrest in what the League aptly called "the most segregated city in America."

Other positions I held included director, for twenty years, of the Chicago Theological Seminary, and president for five of Greater Chicago Churchmen, lay arm of the Church Federation of Chicago. In 1958 I chaired the Winnetka Citizens Committee on Teacher Salaries in my home village. Our report attracted national attention for its condemnation of the penurious prevailing levels of teacher compensation and its innovative proposals for remediation.

These incremental activities—political, civic, educational, and otherwise—absorbed considerable amounts of time and energy but were personally gratifying and I hope served useful purposes. From these I learned a great deal about how different kinds of organizations work and about human behavior in a wide variety of institutional environments. In this respect, they were valuable supplements to my occupational career.

RETROSPECT AND PROSPECT

Looking back over the years, I see that I have always lived with tension between the desire to be actively involved in current affairs and the temptation to pursue a more leisurely and contemplative life. Until recently, the desire for involvement has prevailed. I find deep satisfaction in now being able to indulge the contemplative quest that has always held such attraction. I find special satisfaction in the fact that my years of activity have given me a rich store of experience on which to reflect, and my situation at the Kellogg School provides an ideal setting for that purpose.

The first significant fruit of this season of reflection was *Shaping an American Institution: Robert E. Wood and Sears, Roebuck*. I had the exceptional good fortune to work with Wood over half his time as the company's chief executive, in a position that gave me a unique opportunity to observe his management practices and to draw from them inferences that I think are of some significance to management theory. The most important of these, to my mind, are related to Wood's largely successful efforts to tap the creative resources of the people who comprised the giant Sears organization. His approach derived not so much from any carefully thought-out set of principles as from an inherent understanding of how to rally and direct the combined drives of large numbers of people to accomplish common purposes.

The second significant product was *William C. Norris: Portrait of a Maverick*. Like the Wood/Sears book, this is a study of a man and the company he built, written from the standpoint of long-term, first-hand knowledge. Unlike the earlier book, this deals in only passing fashion with management per se and concentrates instead on Norris's unconventional ideas about the role of business in modern society—certainly a subject important to management. Wood was one of the first American businessmen to enunciate (and practice) a philosophy of corporate social responsibility, but Norris with his efforts to convert social needs into business opportunities carried that philosophy a long step forward.

In very different ways, Wood and Norris were fascinating people with whom to work, and in my books I have tried to capture both their quality as individuals and their significance in the annals of enterprise. In both cases, I have sought to formulate systematically the essence of their business philosophies. Wood was much more interested in action than in explaining it; Norris has written and spoken at length, but for the most part has reached only a limited—and often hostile—business audience. In these two books, and in numerous papers I have written over the years, I have tried to interpret two original and challenging thinkers for the wider audience they both deserve.

I have two new projects now in process and another on the back burner, plus a number of papers of more limited scope. One of my current projects is gathering together and judiciously pruning some of what I consider the most important papers I have written over the years; I think that, collectively, there are some things here of more than passing value. The second immediate project is my memoirs. I have lived through more than eighty percent of the twentieth century, and have participated in or been a close observer of many of the important events of those turbulent years. I want to expand on my NRA and Commerce experiences, my years in politics, and what I sought to do at Sangamon State. I am writing my memoirs first for my own pleasure and second for my family. If some publisher is interested, I shall be glad to make the manuscript available.

The last major project on my agenda at this time is a systematic statement of my thinking on management and the role of business in society. I still have a lot of "practice" to distill into "theory."

PUBLICATIONS

1948

Discovering and evaluating employee attitudes. *Personnel* (November).

1949

Psychology of labor-management relations. Industrial Relations Research Association, *Proceedings.*

Democratic principles in business management. *Advanced Management* (March).

1950

Factors influencing employee morale. *Harvard Business Review, xxvii* (January).

Organizational structure and employee morale. *American Sociological Review, 15*(April).

Attitude surveys as a tool of management. American Management Association, *General Management Series No. 145.*

1951

Planned executive development: The experience of Sears, Roebuck and Co. American Management Association, *Personnel Series No. 137.*

1952

Some aspects of organizational structure in relation to pressures on company decision-making. Industrial Relations Research Association, *Proceedings.*

1953

Toward an improved career service. *Personnel Administration* (September).

1955

Education for business leadership. Graduate School of Business, University of Chicago, *Journal of Business* (January).

The federal service: Its problems and its future. *Congressional Record* (February 16), pp. A973-A978.

1956

Developing patterns of management. American Management Association, *General Management Series No. 182.*

1957

Research in industrial human relations. New York: Harper & Brothers.

Management's approach to human relations. In J.C. Worthy et al. (Eds.), *Research in industrial human relations.* New York, Harper & Brothers.

Planning for corporate aid to education. American Management Association, *General Management Series No. 186.*

1958

Religion and its role in the world of business. Chicago Theological Seminary, *Register* (March).

1959

Big business and free men. New York: Harper & Brothers.

1960

Political fund-raising today. In J.M. Cannon (Ed.), *Politics USA.* Garden City, NY: Doubleday.

Review and evaluation. Introduction to L.J. Shapiro, *Company giving.* Chicago: Survey Press.

1962

Financing presidential campaigns. Report of President's Commission on Campaign Costs.

1963

The Church and the businessman. *The Christian Century* (October 9).

1965

Changing concepts of the personnel function. In *Management and its people: The evolution of a relationship.* American Management Association.

1966

Governing structure. Report of Committee N, Illinois Board of Higher Education.

1967

Report of the Special Committee on New Senior Institutions. Illinois Board of Higher Education.

1971

Governing structure. Report of [Second] Committee N, Illinois Board of Higher Education.

1972

Management succession. In J.J. Famularo (Ed.), *Handbook of Modern Personnel Administration.* New York: McGraw-Hill.

Proposal for a bachelor's degree in management. Report to Board of Regents, Sangamon State University.

1975

The beginnings of the management program. Sangamon State University.

1977

Campaign money. *Illinois Issues* (November).

1979

The Austin scholarships: A history. Evanston, IL: J.L. Kellogg Graduate School of Management.

Behavioral dimensions of span of management theory. In M. Zimet & R.C. Greenwood (Eds.), *The evolving science of management.* New York: Amacom.

Preparation for careers, not jobs. *Community College Frontiers* (Summer).

1980

Sears, Roebuck: General Wood's retail strategy. Business History Conference, *Proceedings* (March).

1981

An entrepreneurial approach to social problem-solving. *Business and Economic History, Series 2* (Vol. 12).

1983

Introduction. In W.C. Norris, *New frontiers for business leadership.* Minneapolis, MN: Dorn Books.

1984

Shaping an American institution: Robert E. Wood and Sears, Roebuck. Urbana/Chicago: University of Illinois Press.

Managing the social markets business. In H. Brooks, L. Liebman, & C. Schelling (Eds.), *Public-private partnership: New opportunities for meeting social needs. Cambridge, MA: Ballinger.*

1985

Robert E. Wood: Merchandiser to middle America. In R. L. Naught (Ed.), *Giants in management.* Washington, DC: National Academy of Public Administration.

Risk-taking, innovation: A board function? *The Corporate Board* (March-April).

Evolution of marketing strategy at Sears, Roebuck. Michigan State University, Second Workshop on Historical Research in Marketing, *Proceedings* (June).

The General and his children. *Directors and Boards* (Winter).

1986

Human relations research at Sears, Roebuck in the 1940s: A memoir. In D.A. Wren (Ed.), *Papers dedicated to the development of modern management*. Ada, OH: Academy of Management.

1987

William C. Norris: Portrait of a maverick. Cambridge, MA: Ballinger.

Profile of William C. Norris. Society for Technology Transfer, Roundtable on Science and Technology, Purdue University, *Proceedings* (April).

1988

The Austin scholarships: A History (2nd ed.). Evanston, IL: J.L. Kellogg Graduate School of Management.

NOTES

1. "The F.C. Austin Scholarship Foundation Announcement of Scholarships," undated [1930], Northwestern University Archives.

2. For a more complete description of the Austin Scholarship program, see J.C. Worthy. 1987. *The Austin Scholarship Program: A History* (2nd ed.). Evanston, IL: J. L. Kellogg Graduate School of Management.

3. For a fascinating account of Whiting Williams and his work, see D.A. Wren. 1987. *White Collar Hobo*. Ames, IA: Iowa State University Press.

4. R.E. Wood to officers and retail policy committee, October 27, 1938 (Sears Archives).

5. J.D. Houser. 1938. *What People Want From Business*. New York: McGraw-Hill Book Company.

6. For a more complete account of this committee and its work, see D.G. Moore. 1986. The Committee on Human Relations in Industry at the University of Chicago, 1943-1948. In D.A. Wren, *Papers Dedicated to the Development of Modern Management* (pp. 45-56). Academy of Management.

7. For an overall summary of the Yankee City studies, see W.L. Warner & P.S. Lunt. 1941. *The Social Life of a Modern Community*. New Haven, CT: Yale University Press.

8. A. Davis, B.B. Gardner, & M.R. Gardner. 1941. *Deep South*. Chicago: University of Chicago Press.

9. J.C. Worthy. 1950. Factors Influencing Employee Morale. *Harvard Business Review, XXVIII*, 61-73.

10. Moore left Sears in 1950 to pursue graduate studies at the University of Chicago, where he completed his doctorate in 1954. He joined the faculty of Michigan State University in 1956 to introduce the study of behavioral sciences into the business administration curriculum. Warner joined him there three years later as MSU's first University Professor.

11. W.F. Whyte. 1948. *Street Corner Society: Social Structure in an Italian Slum*. Chicago: The University of Chicago Press.

12. W.F. Whyte. 1948. *Human Relations in the Restaurant Industry*. New York: McGraw-Hill.

13. J.C. Worthy. 1950. Organization Structure and Employee Morale. *American Sociological Review, 15*, 169-179.

14. For a more complete description and analysis of social factors at work in the Sears setting, see D.G. Moore. 1954. *Managerial Strategies in Organizational Dynamics in Sears Retailing*. Unpublished Ph.D. dissertation, Department of Sociology, University of Chicago.

15. For a more detailed account of this study, see J.C. Worthy. 1986. Human Relations Research at Sears, Roebuck in the 1940s: A Memoir. In D.A. Wren, *Papers Dedicated to the Develoment of Modern Management*. Academy of Management.

16. Cf. p. 53 in J.C. Worthy. 1984. *Shaping an American Institution: Robert E. Wood and Sears, Roebuck*. Urbana and Chicago: The University of Illinois Press.

17. D.G. Moore, *Managerial Strategies*.

18. B.B. Gardner & D.G. Moore. 1950/1955. *Human Relations in Industry*. Chicago: Richard D. Irwin.

19. J.C. Worthy. 1959. *Big Business and Free Men*. New York: Harper & Brothers.

JAi

Advances in Strategic Management

Edited by **Paul Shrivastava,** *Department of Management, Bucknell University,* **Anne Huff,** *College of Business and Commerce, University of Illinois* and **Jane Dutton,** *Graduate School of Business Administration, The University of Michigan*

Volume 9, 1993, 404 pp. $73.25
ISBN 1-55938-647-9

CONTENTS: Introduction, *Paul Shrivastava, Anne Huff, and Jane Dutton.* **PART I. GLOBAL CHANGE AND GLOBAL CHALLENGES. Globalization and Strategy Content Research: Critical Reflections and New Directions,** *Richard A. Brahm.* **Commentary,** *Jean-Francois Hennart.* **The Internationalization of Service Firms,** *Susan Segal-Horn.* **Commentary,** *Robert M. Grant.* **Sustainable Strategy in a Greening World: Intergrating the Natural Environment into Strategic Management,** *Gary M. Throop, Mark Starik and Gordon P. Rands.* **Commentary,** *Stuart L. Hart.* **The Challenge of Global Change for Strategic Management: Opportunities for Charting a New Course,** *David L. Cooperrider and Diana Bilimoria.* **Commentary,** *Jean Pasquero.* **PART II. MEETING THE CHALLENGE: STRATEGIC CHANGE AND ORGANIZATIONAL FORMS. Envisioning Strategic Change,** *Charles J. Frombrun.* **Commentary,** *John H. Grant.* **Strategies, Organizational Learning, and Careers: The Fallout From Restructuring,** *R.M. Jalland and H.P. Gunz.* **Commentary,** *William D. Guth.* **Determinants of Information Technology Investments: Effects of Top Management Compensation and Stock Ownership,** *Lawrence Loh and N. Venkatraman.* **Commentary,** *Anne Sigismund Huff.* **Strategic Flexibility, Firm Organization, and Managerial Work in Dynamic Markets: A Strategic-Options Perspective,** *Ronald Sanchez.* **Commentary,** *Christopher A. Bartlett.* **PART III. COLLECTIVE RESPONSIVES TO A CHANGING WORLD. A Sino-Hungarian-U.S. Perspective on Joint Venture Success,** *Inga S. Baird, Marjorie A. Lyles, and J.B. Orris.* **Commentary,** *Livia Markoczy.* **An Investigation of Natural and Organizational Culture Influences in Recent European Mergers,** *Philippe Very, Roland Calore, and Michael Lubatkin.* **Commentary,** *David M. Schweiger.* **On Collective Strategy in the Public Policy Domain,** *Michael Russo.* **Commentary,** *Alfred A. Marcus.* **Development Bridging Organizations and Strategic Management for Social Change,** *L. David Brown.* **Commentary,** *Pradip N. Khandwalla.*

Volumes 1-8 (1983-1992) $73.25 each